D1349990

THE WILES LECTURES GIVEN AT
THE QUEEN'S UNIVERSITY OF BELFAST

SUCCEEDING JOHN BULL

America in Britain's Place
1900–1975

SUCCEEDING JOHN BULL

America in Britain's Place
1900–1975

A study of the Anglo-American relationship
and world politics in the context of
British and American foreign-policy-making
in the twentieth century

D. CAMERON WATT

Stevenson Professor of International History in the
University of London

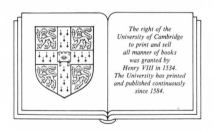

The right of the
University of Cambridge
to print and sell
all manner of books
was granted by
Henry VIII in 1534.
The University has printed
and published continuously
since 1584.

CAMBRIDGE UNIVERSITY PRESS

Cambridge
London   New York   New Rochelle
Melbourne   Sydney

Published by the Press Syndicate of the University of Cambridge
The Pitt Building, Trumpington Street, Cambridge CB2 1RP
32 East 57th Street, New York, NY 10022, USA
296 Beaconsfield Parade, Middle Park, Melbourne 3206, Australia

First published 1984

Printed in Great Britain at the University Press, Cambridge

Library of Congress catalogue card Number: 83-7813

British Library cataloguing in publication data
Watt, Donald Cameron
Succeeding John Bull. – (The Wiles lectures given
at the Queen's University of Belfast)
1. United States – Foreign relations – 20th century
I. Title   II. Series
327.73   E744
ISBN 0 521 25022 6

FOR FELICIA

Contents

Preface

This book, it should be clear, is not a history of Anglo-American relations since 1900. It is not even a straightforward history of how the United States came to take the place Britain occupied for most of the nineteenth century, that of the primary world and oceanic power confronting a grouping of largely land-based continental powers. It is rather a study of how this process was perceived and understood (or misconceived and misunderstood) by those whose decisions and activities in the conduct of British or American relations with the external world comprise the historical reality of British or American 'foreign policy' in this century. It is a study of the rôle perceptions of Britain played in the decisions and actions of those who were responsible for formulating and executing American 'foreign policy' and of the rôle perceptions of America played in the parallel activities of the foreign-policy-makers in Britain. It is not a particularly happy story; indeed it has tragic elements in it – no doubt to balance the more hilariously absurd and ironic elements that equally tend to occur occasionally. It is a story of a relationship which from time to time went deeper than that of mere friends or allies even though its 'special' character usually disappointed those who tried to build on it. It is a relationship too that has changed with the new generations, the new entrants who, every decade or so, arrive at positions of responsibility and decision in sufficient numbers to alter the balance, the emphasis and the flavour of activity on each side of the Atlantic. This book propounds a hypothesis; to prove or disprove it will require a great deal more work than has been done so far.

Acknowledgments

This book could not have been written without the stimulus comprised in the invitation to give the 1981 Wiles Lectures in History at Queen's University, Belfast: I owe a deep debt of gratitude to Professor Lewis Warren for extending to me the invitation to give these lectures and to Mrs Janet Boyd without whose generosity in establishing the Wiles Trust the invitation would not have been possible. I should also like to express my thanks to Professor A. E. Campbell of Birmingham University, to Dr John Thompson of Cambridge, Dr Callum Macdonald of Warwick, and Dr Peter Blair of Queen's University, Belfast, who led the discussion on each of the four lectures on which this book is based and from whose comments I have greatly benefited. I am also very grateful to Dr Robert Boyce, Dr David Reynolds, Dr Brian McKercher, Dr Ritchie Ovendale, Professor Roger Louis, Dr Tony McCulloch and Dr Peter Boyle, all of whom helped me with material, and early sight of their own work in the field over the last two years. I have been greatly helped by the staff of the British Library of Politics and Economic Science, of the Senate House Library of the University of London, of the Institute of Historical Research of the University of London and of the Royal Institute of International Affairs. My own research in the State and Navy Department archives, and into numerous private papers in the United States and in the Canadian National Archives conducted in the years 1960–1, was made possible by a fellowship from the Rockefeller Foundation. I learnt a great deal about American foreign policy under the Kennedy administration while attending the weekly 'round-table' sessions on current American foreign policy conducted by the late Professor Arnold Wolfers at the Washington Center for Foreign Policy Research in the months October 1960 to June 1961, when I was allowed to sit in on the deliberations of such eminent figures as Charles Burton Marshall, Reinhold Niebuhr, Robert Tucker, Ernest Le Feber, Robert Good, the Hon. Christian Herter, Roger Hilsman, and many others. Finally I have benefited greatly from reading and reflecting on the work done by my own students, at both the M.A. and Ph.D. level in the Department of International History at the London School of Economics, especially Miss Caroline Anstey, Mr John Nelscn, Dr James Compton and Mr Sean Greenwood.

1

Introduction

The nature of international history; the foreign-policy-making groups in Britain and the United States; the concept of historical generations; particular problems in the contemporary historiography of Anglo-American relations in the twentieth century

The nature of 'international history'

The status of 'diplomatic history' today is not what it should be, or what it used to be. It enjoys a bad press both in Britain and in the United States.[1] It is supposedly devoid of intellectual content, a refuge only for painstaking plodders, 'dry-as-dusts', unable to see the wood for the trees. In France and elsewhere it comes under the general ban laid on all examples of *l'histoire événementielle*. Even in Britain, despite its metamorphosis over the last twenty-five years into 'international history' (the history of 'international relations'), it is dismissed as élitist by social historians, largely ignored by economic historians, and lies almost totally outside the ken of oral historians, psychohistorians and the various attempts now being made to adapt mathematical and statistical techniques to the study of historical data. It is equally a matter of contempt to many students of the new branch of the study of political 'international relations'. To them it is devoid of intellectual content; its practitioners are men who are afraid of any conceptual approach to the subject, persons only concerned with the study of minutiae.[2]

[1] See, for example, the introduction to Alexander de Conde (ed.), *Encyclopaedia of American Foreign Policy. Studies of the Principal Movements and Ideas*, New York, 1978, vol. I. p. xii. For a recent, if somewhat distrait, discussion of the issues involved see Walter LaFeber, '"Ah, if we had studied it more carefully"; The Fortunes of American Diplomatic History', *Prologue*, 11, 1979.

[2] I remember particularly the contempt and ridicule which David Singer, the well-known advocate of a theoretical approach to the study of international relations, chose to heap upon the special subject, 'Anglo-German Naval Relations, 1933–1939' in the international history degree programme at the London School of

1

In view of this persistent hostility, and in view of the theme of these essays, it is worth while beginning with an exposition of the concept of 'international history' and a defence of the concept against its detractors. Historically speaking, the study of international history originated in the study of the relations between states; in particular, of the relations between the major European states in the nineteenth century and of the culmination of these relations in the First World War. The controversy over the origins of that catastrophe could not be confined to the history or the archives of any nation. The great historians who took part in that controversy had, however, already learnt their craft in the study of the aftermath of the Napoleonic wars, of the Eastern Question, or of the wars of Italian and German unification. They were often nationalistically partisan in their approach; but rarely if ever did they ignore the legal, intellectual, social and political penumbrae of their subject matter.

Their preoccupation with the concept of the nation state, however, proved inadequate in itself to sustain the weight they wished to put upon it. Their successors, particularly since the Second World War, have come to look behind these formal constitutional–legal structures to the realities which underlay them, the sociopolitical groups which exercise power within individual states and maintain linkages with each other and with their supposed political rivals, both within their boundaries and across them. Once historians began to concentrate on the so-called decision-makers and their political alternatives, their attention was increasingly drawn to the exploration not only of what divided them from their presumed opponents but of what they shared in common. And as

Economics, not caring that its supervisor and originator was among his audience. David Singer has since earned a magisterial rebuke from Professor A.E. Campbell for his comments on Donald S. Birn, 'Open Diplomacy at the Washington Conference of 1921–1922. The British and French Experience', *Comparative Studies in Society and History*, 12, 1970. Singer's comments, 'Popular Diplomacy and Policy Effectiveness. A note on the Mechanisms and Consequences', *Comp. Stud. Soc. Hist.*, are condemned for irrelevance to Professor Birn's article and for lack of any evidence to substantiate them. 'While in form a comment on Professor Birn's [article] [Singer's comments] made little reference to it ... Rather it was a restatement of what some students of public opinion believe that the effect of public opinion on the conduct of foreign policy has been. There are few areas in which large and unsupported generalisations are more freely advanced. Neither in Professor Birn's paper nor in the history of modern international relations is there evidence to support them.' A.E. Campbell, 'Open Diplomacy (Comment on Birn and Singer)', *Comp. Stud. Soc. Hist.*, 14, 1972.

soon as this problem was looked at within a national context, it became obvious that there were concepts and interests shared across national boundaries as well as within them.

Oppositional groups maintained links with those in power, and with those in opposition in other countries. The weaker they felt themselves to be within their own political system, the more tempting the linkages with their equivalents abroad. Literary and cultural historians emphasised the transnational links and relationships. And the historian of the great sociopolitical movements found it impossible to remain within the confines of a single nation.[3] Inter-war internationalism, of both the conservative and the revolutionary kinds, reinforced this approach, as did the growing study of international law at the customary as well as the formal level. The historian could hardly ignore the realities of international, multinational or transnational institutions whether political like the League of Nations, or economic, from the international flow of capital, trade, exploitation and investment through the private multinational companies to its attempted control and direction through the Bank of International Settlements, the International Monetary Fund or the League of Nations Economic Committee.

The distinguishing mark of the international historian, however (reflecting the origins of the subject in the study of the origins of wars), has been a bias towards the study of international crises, and towards the rôle and responsibility of individual decision-makers in those crises. The study of international history is traditionalist in this sense only, that it marries the traditional concern of the historian with history as the record of the actions of individuals and of the moral justifications advanced for those actions with the search for causal and consequential relationships and linkages between events and actions over time. The international historian today is concerned to understand why, at given moments in time, identifiable individuals in positions of power, authority or influence chose, recommended or advocated one course of action rather than another.

To understand this, he or she must look both for the external factors which limited the range of choices presented to the individuals and for the internal factors personal to each individual

---

[3] See, for example, James Joll, *The Second International*, London, 1955; or F.S. Lyons, *Internationalism in Europe, 1815–1914*, Leiden, 1963.

which indicated the choice actually made rather than any alternative choices which suggest themselves to posterity. In the search for understanding, the historian is led outwardly to look for those factors by which the individuals under study identified the groups to which they felt they belonged and to which they gave their loyalties, factors which can be political, ideological, sociopolitical and socioeconomic; and inwardly to those factors of psychological make-up, education and experience which condition the individual's perceptions. Since the historian is usually concerned not with a single individual but with the interplay between a limited but identifiable group of individuals, the approach employed must be multibiographical or prosopographical.

The historian of international relations, concentrating, as he or she must, on the activities of small and structured groups of individuals involved in the making of policy within and for the various political units, has always found it essential to base his or her study on the examination of a multiplicity of archives, both public and, where possible, private. And in working on these archives the historian's attention is very soon drawn to the different ways in which the individuals (both as individuals, and as members of the various structured groups of policy-makers which provide the reality behind the shorthand words, 'London', 'Washington', the 'Quai d'Orsay', the 'Narkomindel', 'the City', 'Wall Street', the 'Joint Chiefs of Staff', 'Britain', 'Japan', 'America' used for purposes of historical narrative) actually thought of, interpreted the actions of, in a word *perceived* those with whom they dealt as members of policy-making groups of other nations and interests than their own. The international historian deals, in fact, with perceptions as well as decisions; with how such perceptions arise, how accurate they are in the light of what can be historically ascertained, and where and how and why they were distorted. The international historian deals with misperceptions as much as perceptions, misconceptions as well as concepts, misinformation, mistiming and mistake, as much as with intelligence, deception, decision and execution.

To those whom the study of international history attracts, other forms of history today often seem to depersonalise history and thus to abandon historical reality; some even appear to be inspired by a psychological need for pseudo-scientific certainty. These practitioners appear afraid of ethical judgment, anchored in one or more of the many forms of predestinational doctrine by which from time immemorial humanity has sought to evade consciousness of its own responsibility. Above all they seem to ignore the temporal, the evidential and the *événementiel* nature of their own everyday experience, and to judge the actors in the history they examine by different standards from those by which they judge themselves. The historian of international relations, in fact, neither can, nor wishes to ignore reality; that history, in short, happens over time, in succession, in the experience and memories not of statistically or conceptually identifiable abstractions, but of identifiable individual persons.

The relations of the historian with the social scientist who chooses to base his study on the same order of historical phenomena have been equally controversial in the past. But the historian should have nothing *per se* against the study by social scientists in abstract or conceptual form of aspects of those events; indeed he can profit enormously from such study, provided that it leads to the development of a workable language, easily recognisable in the realities of the historian's study, with which the nature, behaviour and observable actions and interactions of individuals and groups of individuals can be classified and analysed. Where he must object, however, is where each sub-discipline within the social sciences seeks to become more and more autonomous, evolving theories of causation which are entirely coherent within the terms of that sub-discipline alone. Such coherence is rarely observable in reality; and the very coherence of their models of causation may become a barrier rather than an illumination to the understanding of that reality.

The theme of these essays is to be the replacement of Britain by the United States as the major universal power on the periphery of the central Eurasian land mass (the 'heartland' of Sir Halford Mackinder) in the first seventy to seventy-five years of the twentieth century. Following the definition of international history already given, it is proposed to concentrate on the experience of this process and how it was perceived and conceived by those in each country who were responsible for the conduct of the political relations of the two states with each other and with the other states who were not part of their political systems. The concept of 'politics' and 'political' is here related to the making of policy; and that policy is interpreted as including policy in the field of economic and financial affairs as well as the narrowly political and the military.

The foreign-policy-making groups in Britain and the United States

The analysis proposes to focus on the 'decision-makers' in each country, following the method first used by the author some twenty or more years ago.[4] It is proposed to define and identify these decision-makers in two ways, normatively and ostensively. That is to say, those formally responsible for the conduct of foreign policy in each country will first be identified according to the legal and constitutional doctrine of each country. Historical evidence will then be examined to show which individuals and groups within the formal structure of responsibilities actually played major rôles in formulating and executing the foreign policy of each of the two countries. Most previous analyses of the British group of decision-makers have agreed that over time the membership of this group has been continuous and socially coherent to such a degree that it could be considered not merely as a numerical grouping but to some extent at least as a self-contained sociopolitical group or system of groups. Popular belief has it that the American system, with its change of the political direction of the career bureaucracies with each presidential election, is much less coherent and consistent over time than its British counterpart. That there are considerable differences between the British and American systems of making and conducting foreign policy is hardly deniable. But an examination of the historical evidence must show that, in the period under discussion, these differences lie in other directions than in the presence or absence of continuous membership of the foreign-policy-making groups in each country.

By far the most important difference between the British and the American systems results from the difference between the presidential and the cabinet system of government.[5] The American

---

[4] In a paper given to the European Association of American Studies in October 1960, published in 'America and the British Foreign Policy Making Elite 1895–1956' in *Review of Politics*, 1960. This analysis formed the basis of the first two chapters in D.C. Watt, *Personalities and Policies, Studies in the Formulation of British Foreign Policy in the Twentieth Century*, London and South Bend, Indiana, 1965.

[5] For an elaboration of this theme see Chapter 9 below.

system, originating as it does in the eighteenth century with its discussions of benevolent despotism, produced an ideal solution to the problems which exercised the political theorists of that era; a democratically elected monarch, embodying in himself the sovereign power of the electorate, limited in terms of office, limited by a written constitution the interpretation of which lies with the judiciary, and dependent in certain prescribed forms on the approval of a separate legislature which has complete budgetary control, must approve his appointments and ratify treaties. In the tradition of eighteenth-century absolutism, the ministers of the elected monarch, who is called the President of the United States, are his servants, his advisers and the executants of his decisions. He can, and frequently does, ignore them, override them or bypass them. Their authority is derived from him and from him alone. They are not elected, only approved. If they enjoyed political 'clout' before their appointment, it diminishes from the moment of their appointment.

In keeping with this the President can evolve or reject any system of cooperation or coordination between his various advisers that he chooses. He can employ a cabinet system or he can reject it. As a result, the lines of advice and communication within his administration run vertically rather than laterally. The American system is constantly open to discontinuities of thought and action within and between the various formal bureaucratic parts of the government and the personal advisory services of which the President avails himself. American bureaucratic politics resemble those of absolutist systems such as that of Imperial Germany in that the commonest form of conflict is over the demarcation of areas of responsibility and competence. In 1927 the US Navy evolved or was allowed to evolve (as it was prevented from doing in 1921 and 1929) a position on naval disarmament which was so rigid as to make international agreement impossible and conflict inevitable.[6] In 1930/31 the General Board of the US Navy campaigned in Congress against the ratification of the

[6] For evidence on this point see Chapter 3 below. See also W. Bickel, *Die anglo-amerikanische Beziehungen 1927–1930 im Licht der Flottenfrage*, Zurich Ph.D., 1970: David Carlton, 'Great Britain and the Coolidge Disarmament Conference of 1927', *Political Science Quarterly*, 83, 1968: Stephen W. Roskill, *British Naval Policy Between the Wars*, vol. I, *The Period of Anglo-American Antagonism*, London, 1962.

London Naval Treaty.[7] By contrast, in October 1944 the British Foreign Secretary objected in the plainest possible terms to a strategic appreciation by the Chiefs of Staff which considered the eventuality of post-war conflict with the USSR. It was withdrawn after a personal confrontation.[8] The British system had evolved machinery for reconciling military and political considerations and responsibilities in 1902 with the establishment of the Committee of Imperial Defence. It did not always function. But it existed. It was not until 1939 that the State–War–Navy Coordinating Committee was established in the United States. Its functioning even then depended on the use the President chose to make of it: as was to be equally true of its post-war successor, the National Security Council.

The American foreign-policy-making groups must be defined in the following terms. The President is advised by the Secretary of State, his ambassadors and ministers, whether political or career appointments, and by the personnel of the State Department and the Foreign Service. To these must be added the other cabinet officers whose work impinges on foreign policy, that is, the Secretaries of the Treasury, Commerce, War and Navy Departments, their political appointments and career public servants and senior military and naval officers. In Congress the chairman and members of the Committees for Foreign Relations, for the Army and the Navy, and for Commerce are the most important, with the Senate Committees outranking those of the House. To these must be added the officers of the Federal Reserve Banks after 1914. The 'attentive publics'[9] are more difficult to define; but apart from members of Congress an important rôle in leading and forming the opinions of these publics was played by the US press, especially in the inter-war years and after, by their long-standing representatives abroad as foreign correspondents and by the syndicated political columnists.

In this practice the element of continuity of membership is much

[7] See US Senate, 71st Congress, Second Session, Senate Committee on Foreign Relations, *Hearings on the Treaty for the Limitation of Naval Armaments*, Washington, 1930: Raymond G. O'Connor, *Perilous Equilibrium. The United States and the London Naval Conference of 1930*, Lawrence, Kansas, 1962, pp. 112–17.

[8] Julian Lewis, 'British Military Planning for Post-War Strategic Defence, 1942–1947', Oxford D.Phil., 1981.

[9] As defined in J.N. Rosenau, *Public Opinion and Foreign Policy*, New York, 1961, 'opinion holders who are inclined to participate [in the foreign-policy-making process] but lack the access or opportunity to do so'.

stronger than American political mythology allows for.[10] In the first place, although by comparison with his British equivalent, the American career public official is outweighed by the political appointees, this is far from true of the military advisers to the President. The Chief of Staff to the Army and the Chief of Naval Operations, the General Board of the Navy and the General Staffs of both Services play a continuous and coherent rôle throughout much of the history of American foreign policy in this century. In the second place, and despite the various reforms of the State Department and the Foreign Service, the East Coast Ivy League provenance of the senior officials in the State Department, at least until the 1930s, is very striking indeed. Harvard graduates lead the field, with Yale, Amherst and Princeton prominent among the also-rans. In birth and upbringing the majority stem from the states of New England and the Old South, with a group from the industrial Middle West coming a very poor third. A very similar pattern shows itself when the political appointees of successive Presidents to State Department posts are examined. To this must be added the oligarchy of inherited wealth with the dynastic orientation towards public service so strikingly made their own by such *nouveaux riches* as the Kennedys. The established families of the Gilded Age, the bold bad industrial 'robber barons' of the later nineteenth century, left heirs as devoted to public service as their progenitors were to private banditry.

This element of continuity is enhanced when the swings of American politics between 1900 and 1975 are considered. The first twelve years are Republican, the next eight Democratic, the next twelve again Republican, the next twenty Democratic. Thereafter the see-saw continues with an octennial swing. But in the first half of the century each party remained long enough in power to attract its permanent camp-following of foreign affairs experts. And after 1920 the Council of Foreign Relations in New York was to give them a permanent forum for the discussion and analysis of current foreign policy problems. From 1950 onwards university schools of international studies and research institutions such as those run by the Rand Corporation, the Brookings Institute in Washington, the

[10] E. Digby Baltzell, *The Protestant Establishment, Aristocracy and Caste in America*, London, 1966. See also Morton Keller, *Affairs of State. Public Life in Late Nineteenth Century America*, Cambridge, Mass., 1977.

Johns Hopkins Washington Center of Foreign Policy Research
were to provide similar places of retirement and return.

The American élites were, however, never quite so sure of their
position as their British equivalents. The personnel of the State
Department found it difficult to enjoy (save on a personal basis)
the same cosy relationship of distant contempt towards their political overlords as was apt to tempt their colleagues in the Foreign
Office. Few Presidents, or for that matter Secretaries of State,
bothered to cultivate the kind of relationship which, for example,
Eyre Crowe enjoyed with Austen Chamberlain or Harvey with
Anthony Eden. No American career ambassador (or for that
matter political appointee either) dared to take a President to task
as, for example, Clark Kerr did Churchill on his visit to Moscow
in August 1942.[11] And where Congress was concerned it is difficult
to imagine any MP, even the late Richard Crossman, informing
a Foreign Secretary that his information on world affairs was
better than that of the Foreign Office, as Borah did Hull in
Roosevelt's presence in July 1939.[12] (He was wrong.) The parallels
between the British foreign-policy-making élites and their
American equivalents are in real terms much closer than political
myth allows. But the manner in which each perceived his own
position, and the degree by which the legitimacy of his position
and his views was accepted by others, differed enormously.
Colonel House's position was acceptable to all so long as he held
the President's support. No one would have dreamed of rebuking
him in the way that Balfour was to rebuke Philip Kerr at Paris.[13]
But when Wilson broke with him he became a political nonentity,
a fact it took the British some time to realise. Not that the position
of the Foreign Office and the professional diplomatist was ever as
strong as its defenders would have us believe.[14] But at its weakest

---

[11] On which see Inverchapel Papers, FO 800/300; Graham Ross, 'Operation
Bracelet: Churchill in Moscow, 1942' in D. Dilks (ed.), *Retreat from Power.
Studies in British Foreign Policy of the Twentieth Century*, vol. II, *After 1939*,
London, 1981.

[12] See Cordell Hull, *The Memoirs of Cordell Hull*, London, 1948, pp. 649–51;
Robert James Maddox, *William E. Borah and American Foreign Policy*, Baton
Rouge 1969, pp. 239–41.

[13] See Blanche Dugdale, *Arthur James Balfour*, London, 1939, vol.II, p. 200.

[14] See Alan Sharp, 'The Foreign Office in Eclipse, 1919–1922', *History*, 61, 1976;
Roberta Warman, 'The Erosion of Foreign Office Influence in the Making of
Foreign Policy, 1916–1918', *Historical Journal*, 15, 1972.

it was nearly as strong as the position of the State Department at its strongest.

It is when one turns to the influence of the industrial and financial élites in both countries that very great differences appear. Throughout this century the British financial élites, concentrated in the Treasury, the Bank of England, the great merchant banks and the major investment centres, have been able to exercise a rôle in the formation of British policy which has completely outweighed that of their industrialist equivalents.[15] Among the industrialists only the heads of the major British multinationals, in oil and in shipping, have exercised any substantial influence on foreign policy formulation. Others, ICI, Dunlop, Unilever for example, have had at best marginal influence. Only when the financial authorities became convinced of the comparative advantage of economic nationalism in the 1930s could industry exact any pressure for tariffs. Even then it had the chimera of 'free trade' to contend with. Since 1945 the balance has fluctuated with the balance of British trade and payments and with the course of European and Japanese competition.

One final difference must be noticed, which stems as much from the difference in geographical scale between the United States and the British system of foreign-policy-making. Both countries exhibit very considerable differences in regional attitudes to the current issues of foreign policy. Just as the non-industrial American Middle West was isolationist in 1940, while the main support for intervention lay east of the Alleghenies, so South East England was far more in favour of appeasement in 1938 than the industrial North: but the one was represented in Congress and the Senate; the other was much less apparent. The British government have their troubles with the regions (with the Lancashire cotton constituencies for example). But party discipline or party divisions make them much more manageable.

So as to cover the full scope of the seventy-five years in seven brief chapters, it is proposed to divide the period into six sections, each roughly corresponding with a political generation in the United States. The first covers the Republican and Democratic expansionists of the first two decades of the century, the period of physical and moral imperialism when the United States moved abruptly from

---

[15] This argument is based on the forthcoming work by Robert Boyce, *The Collapse of Economic Internationalism in Britain, 1924–1932.*

continentalism to the attempt to impose a *pax americana* on a warring world. The second, from 1919 to 1934, is a period of limited American and industrial intervention in Europe, one in which Britain was to try to recover the position of financial leadership, lost in 1914, only to abandon the attempt in the face of a revived American isolationism. The third period opens with the United States in almost total isolation from Europe, and Britain attempting to maintain European peace without American participation, an attempt which broke down so catastrophically as to convince the American leadership at the opening of the fourth period, which runs from 1940 to 1947, that America, for her own self-protection, could not but intervene, an intervention which led to war, victory, and for a brief two years the consideration of a second withdrawal. This fourth period ends with the Truman doctrine, the Marshall Plan, the conclusion of the North Atlantic Treaty. The fifth and sixth periods, from 1947–9 to the early 1970s, with 1963 as the dividing line, cover two generations, both of which perceived America as *the* dominant world power.

Each period it should be noted ends with an American catastrophe, as much moral as material. The first ends with the rejection of the Treaty of Versailles, the second with the great slump, the collapse of the London Economic Conference, the devaluation of the dollar, the American withdrawal from cooperation in negotiations on European security and the passage of the new American neutrality legislation. The third ends with the collapse and fall of France, and with it the collapse of American hopes that Britain and France, the last *European* democracies, could contain Hitler. The fourth, like the third, ends with what seems to be not an American but a British and European catastrophe, the winter of 1946–7 and the failure of sterling convertibility in 1947. But that year marked the defeat of American hopes of a European settlement based on British strength, necessitating American intervention in the Eastern Mediterranean, the Marshall Plan and the formal opening of the Cold War. The fifth period ends with the humiliation of the collapse of the 1960 summit and the death of Kennedy. The last ends with the defeat in Vietnam, the collapse of the South Vietnamese state, leading to SALT I, the Berlin agreement of 1971, the Helsinki agreement of 1975, détente in Europe – not itself a catastrophe but marking, with Britain's entry into Europe, the end of the Anglo-American political relationship as it had hitherto existed.

Each of the periods lasts between twelve and twenty years. During each period there are changes within the élites in each country. New groups enter into the policy-making process as, for example, the US military in 1940, the scientific élites in both countries in 1941 and afterwards. In each period the problem of analysis is made more difficult by the existence of ideologies and groups of influential persons who are transnational rather than national in their goals or in the entities with which they identify themselves, Pan-Anglo-Saxonism, Mid-Atlanticism, the union of the Anglophones (English-speaking peoples).

The concept of historical generations

In proposing to apply the concept of an historical generation to this analysis it is proposed to follow the recent discussion of the concept by Robert Wohl.[16] In a work which is basically a contribution to literary and cultural history Wohl draws mainly on four different schools of analysis: the French literary;[17] 'a collective state of mind incarcerated in a human group that lasts a certain period of time' – Karl Mannheim;[18] the Spanish historical élitist, Ortega y Gasset;[19] and the Finnish political scientist, Marvin Rinntala.[20] (It should be noted that with the exception of the last of these four, the concept is one that took hold of the imagination of European scholars essentially in the decades before and after the war of 1914–18;[21] and that the concept was born in the recognition that very rapid social and technological change could produce a very considerable difference of outlook between one age group and another, not in the traditional

---

[16] Robert Wohl, *The Generation of 1914*, London, 1980.

[17] François Mentré, *Les Générations sociales*, Paris, 1920.

[18] Karl Mannheim, 'The problem of generations' in Paul Kecskemeti (ed.), *Essays on the Sociology of Knowledge*, London, 1952.

[19] *The Modern Theme*, London, 1933; *Man and Crisis*, London, 1933.

[20] Marvin Rinntala, 'A Generation in Politics. A Definition', *Review of Politics*, 25, 1963; 'Political Generations', *International Encyclopaedia of the Social Sciences*, New York 1968. For a critical view of generational theories see also Alan B. Spitzer, 'The Historical Problem of Generations', *American Historical Review*, 78, 1973.

[21] Ortega y Gasset's first book was published in Spanish in 1922; Mannheim's essay in German in 1926.

generational age span of thirty years but in as little as ten or fifteen years.)[22]

Sociologists and literary historians exploring the concept of 'the generation' have tended to concentrate to excess on the concept of generational conflict. With this the historian of Anglo-American relations need concern himself little before the 1960s. What can concern him is, first, the recognition that the phenomenon of generational differences is most obvious at the élite level; secondly, that what makes an historical 'generation' is a series of experiences held in common (*Erfahrenszusammenhang*), which does not necessarily mean that there cannot be within such a group a marked dichotomy of reactions to that experience: that generational views unfold themselves over time (chronological entelechies) in reaction to constant factors; that a distinction can be drawn between political 'generations', actual generational complexes and generational unities. 'A "generation" is in fact a sociohistorical location that has to be understood in the relationship between (objective) social fact and the consciousness of social fact.'[23] Moreover, at any moment in time there is likely to be a dominant generation, an up-and-coming generation, and one just beginning, 'each living in its own version of the present'.[24] A 'generation' finally is not a rigidly defined chronological entity, 'an army of contemporaries marching its way across a territory of time ... What is essential to the formation of a generational consciousness is some common form of reference which provides a sense of rupture with the past and that will later distinguish the members of that generation from those that follow them in time.'[25]

To this the historian must add an elucidation. The political generation is not marked by the dates of birth of its members but by the dates at which they can be said to demonstrate political awareness by serious identifiable actions which embody a common

---

[22] Wohl distinguishes three separate literary generations among those French writers who experienced the war of 1914–18: those whose views were formed *before* 1914; those who were recruited to the front line straight from school; and those who were recruited too late to experience the fighting or the death they expected in it. For a rather similar point about this last generation in Europe see D.C. Watt, *Too Serious a Business, European Armed Forces and the Coming of the Second World War*, London, 1974, pp. 27–9.

[23] Wohl, p. 81

[24] Wohl, pp. 149–50.

[25] Wohl, p. 210.

element. Political generations pass through common learning experiences in the periods both before and after their entry into action, 'learning zones' as I have called them here, to which they will make appeal in justifying or advocating courses of action. They may not agree on the 'lessons' they derive from this common past. Indeed, an 'historical generation' may contain both an 'administration' in power and an 'opposition' seeking to replace or supplant it.

To apply the concept to the historical material under study (and this is essentially an exercise in the recognition and identification of subjectively observed historical data) one first has to make certain adjustments on both the American and the British sides. On the American side the first is to recognise that to define someone or some set of ideas as 'American' is, at centre, as much a *prescriptive* as a *descriptive* statement. The qualifications to such paraphrases are many: for example, the term 'hyphenated-American', implying an American of divided loyalties in matters of foreign relations, was not, until very recently, applied to Americans of English descent.[26] Differences in the external mood of a country the size of the United States need to be correlated with regional as well as national history. Hostility to British naval strength in the 1920s among senior American naval officers correlates directly with regional origin, those from the South being unaffected by the Anglophile sentiments of the New Yorker, William Sims, or his junior from Maine, Admiral Pratt.[27] In the South the populist hostility to British financial power of the 1880s overlaid all the traditional Anglophilia of the Southern plutocracy from whose ranks the naval officer rarely came anyway. There is equally an almost total absence from any part of the US foreign-policy-making élite groups of any identifiable West Coast element, save in Congress. Sociopolitical factors (social origins, non-élite educations) are only of importance where some sections of business and technological imperialism are involved.[28] One final factor, not without importance in view of the changes which came

---

[26] Franklin D. Roosevelt, however, is not normally classified as a Dutch American.

[27] On Admiral William Sims, Commander of American naval forces in European waters, 1917–19, see Elting E. Morison, *Admiral William Sims and the Modern American Navy*, Boston, 1962; on Admiral William Veazie Pratt, Chief of Naval Operations, 1929–33, see Gerald E. Wheeler, *Admiral William Veazie Pratt*, Washington, 1974.

[28] On the oil technologists see John de Novo, 'The Movement for an Aggressive American Oil Policy Abroad, 1918–1920', *Am. Hist. Rev.*, 61, 1956.

over the American foreign-policy-making groups after 1945, is that of the first generation European immigrants (Kissinger, Brzezinski, etc.).

On the British side three major qualifications have to be made to the usual assumptions of the social cohesion and unity of the British foreign-policy-making élite. The first lies in the very different career paths followed throughout the nineteenth and first half of the twentieth centuries by the professional soldier and the professional diplomat. The one lay in military service overseas as part of the system of imperial garrisons, and almost certainly, under the Carden system of linked battalions, involved service in India. The other involved the acquisition of a working knowledge of the French and German languages as a condition of entry into the diplomatic service, an acquisition which almost invariably involved periods of a year or more *en pension* in France and Germany. The soldier's path to promotion lay through action in India or in colonial wars in Africa or the Middle East. The diplomatist's path lay through service in the major European capitals. (Those sections of the service which dealt with Latin America, the Islamic world or the Far East tended to become self-contained sub-sections within the diplomatic service.) Only in Egypt, especially after the nominal declaration of Egyptian independence in 1922, did diplomatists who served in the High Commission in Cairo and soldiers who served with the British occupation forces, or in the early years of occupation on secondment to the Egyptian army, have any possibility of common experience. The external relations of the Indian Empire were handled not by the diplomatic service but by the Indian political service operating from Delhi. The professional naval officer, paying duty visits to European ports, or operating in one of the various squadrons scattered across the seas, was more likely to meet the diplomatist on common ground than was the soldier. He was, however, equally unlikely to penetrate far into Europe, although it is possible to identify a mildly Franco-phile element among the senior naval officers of the inter-war years.

This dichotomy in training and connection is paralleled by the development among the British foreign-policy-making élites of three differing schools of thought: neo-imperialism, which sought British strength in a united empire and avoided commitments to Europe; those for whom the European balance of power came first and the Far East was a distraction; and a third group, mainly outside the diplomatic and military sections of the élite, who looked towards the United States for support.

These differences in outlook are important in themselves. But they affect not only the conscious biases of those who hold them. They play a major part in creating what have been called the 'mental maps'[29] by which policy-makers reduce the geography they have experienced to manageable proportions; like Mercator's projection, these mental maps distort reality and alter scale. It is essential, however, to understand that for most American policy-makers before 1939 Europe lay not only geographically but also conceptually beyond Britain; and that Britain bulked so large for many of them that they could not see past it to what it was its policy-makers feared.

These orientations by profession require qualification from 1900 onwards in the increasing pull exercised on the loyalties and imaginations of members of the élite, dissatisfied with, or losing confidence in, British institutions, by external political models, be they in the form of the model of Imperial Germany which so fascinated Fabian social imperialists around the turn of the century,[30] or the Fascist or Soviet models of the inter-war years.[31] In the late 1940s and 1950s the North Atlantic mythos made a similar appeal to the loyalties and canons of self-identification to which individuals felt themselves answerable.

The third qualification that needs making is that there was an element of immigration into the British élites as significant as, though smaller than, that already noted in the United States. In the first place it came from ambitious native-born English speakers from the white Empire and Commonwealth.[32] To this must be added the second generation of the European Jewish immigration into Britain

---

[29] Alan K. Henrikson 'The Geographical "Mental Maps" of American Foreign Policy-Makers', *Int. Pol. Sc. Rev.*, 1, 1980.

[30] See Bernard Semmel, *Imperialism and Social Reform, English Social–Imperial Thought, 1895–1914*, London, 1960. See also H.C.G. Matthew, *The Liberal Imperialists: The Ideas and Politics of a Post-Gladstonian Elite*, Oxford, 1973; G.R. Searle, *The Quest for National Efficiency: A Study in British Politics and in British Political Thought, 1899–1914*, Berkeley, 1971.

[31] David Caute, *The Fellow Travellers: A Postscript to the Enlightenment*, London, 1973.

[32] Two examples from the British Foreign Service recruited before 1914 must suffice: Sir Maurice Peterson, British Ambassador in Moscow 1946–8 (from Canada); Rex and Allen Leeper (from Australia).

in the period before 1914 and the immigrant European scientists of the 1930s, the refugees from Nazism, who increase in importance as the nuclear physicists come to play their part in the formulation of British policy.

To understand the interactions between the various sections of the British élite and the American élite groups, attention must be paid to the sources of information each had available about the other. Before his entry into the élite, the individual candidate-entrant's information would come mainly from his education, from his familiarity with the literary images of the other country, from the popular stereotypes and from individual members of the opposite élite groups encountered on visits to the other's country – the Yank in Oxford, the 'Limey' in the States. Such contacts were not always conducive to international amity.[33] These popular images would be reinforced or modified by the reportage in the organs of the press to which the individual members of the élite had access. The rôle of the American correspondent in Britain, or the British correspondent in America, is of considerable importance.[34] The press on both sides of the Atlantic often did more to reinforce the biases already existing in public opinion. 'Press wars' were not uncommon.[35]

To this one has to add the machinery of official reportage on each country. There exists at present no study of the American Embassy in London later than the 1920s, and studies of American ambass-adors so far only cover the cases of Walter Hines Page (1914–18) and Joseph Kennedy (1938–40).[36] Publications of British dispatches from Washington are now appearing.[37] By far the most important guide to American opinion available to British policy-makers, however, was provided not by the Embassy in Washington but in the form of a weekly review of the American regional press by the

---

[33] *Confer* the future President Herbert Hoover's dislike for the British aristocracy, conceived during his period in Britain before 1914.

[34] Little or no study has as yet been devoted to this topic.

[35] For evidence on press wars in the 1920s, see Chapter 3 below.

[36] Ross Gregory, *Walter Hines Page. Ambassador to the Court of St James*, Lexington, 1970: Michael R. Beschloss, *Kennedy and Roosevelt: the Uneasy Alliance*, New York, 1981.

[37] Thomas S. Hachey (ed.), *Confidential Dispatches: Analyses of America by the British Ambassador 1939–1945*, Evanston, Illinois 1974; H.G. Nicholas (ed.), *Washington Dispatches 1941–1945. Weekly Political Reports from the British Embassy*, London, 1981.

so-called British Library of Information (BLI) in New York.[38] Its cessation in the late 1950s as part of the late Mr Selwyn Lloyd's attempts to cut Foreign Office expenditure is a striking example of the follies into which such exercises can lead the unwary.

Official reportage must also include political intelligence, a subject on which we as yet know little. The rôle of Sir William Wiseman as head of British intelligence in the United States in 1917–18 is well known.[39] Various ill-judged efforts have been made to depict Sir William Stephenson, who occupied a somewhat similar position during the Second World War, in a similar light.[40] The image of US military and naval power provided by British intelligence has so far only been covered in histories of Anglo-American relations before 1914.[41] American military intelligence on Britain during the 1920s appears from the recently published documents[42] to have relied entirely on the press. American naval intelligence played a singularly distorting rôle in the early 1920s, with its insistence that Lloyd George had offered the Japanese capital ships sufficient to swing the balance of power in the Pacific against the United States, a report which, though a total canard, became part of accepted US Navy doctrine.

For much of the period under study each government approached the influencing of opinion on the other country with considerable caution. During the period of American neutrality in each of the two world wars the influencing of American opinion was of prime importance to the British government. The full picture of British activities is still far from totally clear. In the 1914–18 war it began very early in the form of ostensibly private letters to selected American opinion-leaders.[43] In the 1940–1 period, the BLI in New

---

[38] For its reportage in the 1920s see Brian McKercher's forthcoming book, *Attitudes and Diplomacy. The Second Baldwin Government and the United States 1924–1929*.

[39] See W.B. Fowler, *British-American Relations 1917–1918. The Role of Sir William Wiseman*, Princeton, 1969; Sir Arthur Willert, *The Road to Safety: A Study in Anglo-American Relations*, New York, 1958.

[40] W. Stevenson, *A Man Called Intrepid*, London, 1976.

[41] See K. Bourne, *Britain and the Balance of Power in North America, 1815–1908*, London, 1967, pp. 326–38.

[42] USA Department of War, General Staff, *United States Military Intelligence 1917–1927*, introduced by Richard D. Challener, New York and London 1978, 30 vols.

[43] CAB 37/130 No. 35, December 1914, Wellington House Interim Report: J.D. Squires, *British Propaganda at Home and in the United States, 1914–1917*,

York retained a very low profile under orders from Lord Lothian, the Ambassador.[44] But this did not prevent John Wheeler-Bennett from quietly arming those who preached American entry into the war with argument and information.[45]

In peacetime there were hundreds of channels of contact, from the plutocratic oligarchic level of the Pilgrim Society, through the middle-class English Speaking Union, through the Rotary Club network, through the links between the Royal Institute of International Affairs and the Council of Foreign Relations and, most of all, through the universities. From this there was to develop one variety of the hybrid British American: not the descendant of intermarriage with actual dual citizenship, such as 'Chips' Channon, Lady Astor, Ronald Tree, or their like, important though they are; but the convinced believer in the community of Anglo-American interests. A high proportion of the war hawks of 1940–1 fall into this category, as do the British supporters of the American intervention in Vietnam in the 1960s.

Problems peculiar to the study of the contemporary history of Anglo-American relations

It is the activities of some of the historians in this group which have done most to bedevil the proper study of Anglo-American relations in contemporary times. The contemporary historian in this sense does not only lack perspective or distance from the events he studies. Far more than his colleagues who study the less recent past, he encounters at every turn pseudo-historians, seeking to establish a version of the recent past which will reinforce the political arguments of the present, 'politics projected back into the past' in the definition of a Soviet historian. Historical events, however, like entropy, develop from the past to the present. In the second place, he finds himself confronted in the field of Anglo-American relations with a vast American historical industry, the history of American 'foreign policy'. In its most honest form, and the one closest to

Cambridge, Mass., 1935, pp. 80–2; Lucy Masterman, *C.F. Masterman. A Biography*. London, 1939, p. 277; Nicholas Reeves, 'British Film Propaganda during the First World War', London Ph.D., 1981.

[44] Ronald Tree, *When the Moon was High, Memoirs of War and Peace, 1897–1942*, London, 1975, pp. 95–126.

[45] Mark L. Chadwin, *The Warhawks*, New York, 1970.

historical reality, this is the study of what contemporary Americans thought to be the ideas and ideals which American relations with the external world were supposed to embody, an exercise in the history of subjective opinions and perceptions which, willy-nilly, leads the practitioner in the large majority of cases to assume that those perceptions and opinions corresponded with external reality.

In the third place, however, the historians of Anglo-American relations, especially in Britain, find themselves confronted with the work of a convinced and dedicated group of 'Anglo-American' historians for whom the differences and conflicts which existed in those relationships are barriers to the proper understanding, as they conceive it, of the unique nature of those relationships, and which are therefore to be ignored where possible, and minimised where not.[46] (In some cases, notably the work of Professor Max Beloff, the dominance of this school has provoked an equal and opposite reaction.)[47]

The contemporary historian has to create in himself the illusion of distance from his subject that the lapse of time will present to those who come after him to study the same period. He has to watch for his own conscious biases and learn to distrust most of the evidence which seems to confirm them. He has to ignore those who confuse conscious and unconscious biases and argue as if the latter are only exhibited by contemporary historians. And he has to ignore those defeatist historical *littérateurs* who argue that only a sense of partisanship can infuse life into the writing of contemporary history and who equate the historian's ideal of objective historical writing with dullness and the avoidance of controversy.

He has to watch too the particular traps which beset the study of international history within the scope of a single language (and a

---

[46] Some examples of this approach on the British side are to be found in H.C. Allen, *Great Britain and the United States. A History of Anglo-American Relations, 1783–1952*, London, 1954; H.G. Nicholas, *Britain and the United States*, London, 1954; on the American side one might instance Bradford Perkins, *The Great Rapprochement*, London, 1969; Seth W. Tillman, *Anglo-American Relations at the Paris Peace Conference of 1919*, Princeton, 1962; M.T. Hogan, *Informal Entente: The Private Structure of Anglo-American Economic Diplomacy 1918–1928*, Columbia, Missouri, 1977: Gerald E. Wheeler, *Prelude to Pearl Harbor: the U.S. Navy and the Far East, 1921–1931*, Columbia, Missouri, 1963; Gerald E. Wheeler, 'Isolated Japan: Anglo-American Diplomatic Cooperation, 1927–1936', *Pac. Hist. Rev.*, 30, 1961.

[47] See Max Beloff, 'The Myth of the Special Relationship' in Martin Gilbert (ed.), *A Century of Conflict. Essays in Honour of A.J.P. Taylor*, London, 1966.

double culture). Not only is American evidence alone notoriously
faulty, especially in the case of President Franklin D. Roosevelt.
Very often, the complexities of American bureaucratic rivalry in
the advocacy of particular policies or courses of action can only be
followed in the British record of what was said by the American
participant in the conversation. Yet to the British, it was these
records which made up American foreign policy as they encountered it, not the internal *obiter dicta* of an off-duty President or the
rhetoric of his Secretary of State, to which American historians
have on occasion paid so much attention.

The historian has also to recognise that Anglo-American relationships were never entirely bilateral, at least on the British side,
though they were conceived of as such by American policy-makers
until the 1930s, if not beyond. In actuality, they were part of
multilateral problems of trade, payments, strategy, the balance of
power, the maintenance of Britain's position at a time when its
commitments were already outrunning its resources. And even
where British and American policy-makers seem to have reached a
common perception or common conclusions, they reached that
point by separate ways from separate perceptions (or misperceptions) of part or all of external reality.

The historian has also to cope with very considerable gaps and
confusions in the state of contemporary research. Some examples
have already been given. Two more obvious gaps are the antecedents of the attitudes and doctrines with which the American
military entered into the discussion of coalition strategy with the
British Chiefs of Staff in 1941, and the political influence of British
industry, especially the multinationals, on British foreign policy. In
the absence of any detailed study I have argued that this influence
was weak by comparison with that of British finance. Such study as
has been made of British industrial interests in, for example,
Central Europe in the inter-war years,[48] has shown it to have very
little influence on British policy, even where comparative 'giants'
such as Unilever or ICI are involved. One enormous source of
confusion lies in the present tendency to read back into the 1940s
the conviction of British weakness *vis-à-vis* the super powers to
which world opinion has now accustomed itself, a step which

---

[48] See, for example, Alice Teichova, *An Economic Background to Munich. International Business and Czechoslovakia, 1919–1938*, Cambridge, 1974.

ignores both the real calculus of power and the perceptions of the time.[49]

It follows from this introduction that the survey of relations between Britain and the United States which makes up this book is necessarily as much synthetic as the outcome of original research; and that it will inevitably suffer from *lacunae*. It is presented here, imperfect as it is, in the hope that it will stimulate debate and lead to further research. For, although the story of how America came to occupy 'Britain's place' is in the end a tragic one, a story of failures and missed opportunities, of misguided attitudes and misunderstandings, from which both nations have suffered, it is also a story of considerable achievement, and covers two world wars in which, even though the victors were far from behaving with the magnanimity, chivalry and goodwill Winston Churchill once enjoined upon them, those whom they defeated fought to advance tyrannies whose defeat was right and just and whose victory would have dismantled what little in the way of human progress the last two hundred years have achieved.

[49] William T. Fox, the creator of the term 'super power', in 1944 classified Britain unquestioningly as one of the three super powers. For F.D. Roosevelt, Britain was to be one of the four great powers who were to share and divide the governance of the post-war world.

2

1900–1919

From Theodore Roosevelt to the rejection of the Treaty of
Versailles; continentalism and the failure of moral imperialism

The first period to be analysed is that which saw the first entry of the
United States on to the stage of world politics and its first great
withdrawal. This period opens at the end of the Spanish–American
war and with the Diamond Jubilee of Queen Victoria and ends with
the failure of the United States Senate to ratify the Treaty of
Versailles and with the emergence of Britain, crippled and
impoverished, into the dubious light of victory over the Central
Powers. In terms of the formal relations between Britain and the
United States, the period divides itself into four main sections: the
Anglo-American settlement of the major issues of conflict between
the two countries between 1898 and 1905;[1] the abortive Anglo-
American arbitration treaty and conflicts over dollar diplomacy;
American neutrality during the great European war; and finally the
two years of co-belligerency.

Politics in the United States in this period were dominated by the
rise of the Progressive movement, which, although divided in its
loyalties between the Republican party, the Democrats and, in 1912,
Theodore Roosevelt's breakaway Progressive party, imparted one
and the same impetus to all three, an impetus the manifestations of
which vary from party to party only with the entrenched strength of
business, machine and states rights conservatives. In international
affairs, by far the greatest number of the leading progressives were
imperialist and expansionist in their attitudes during the first decade

---

[1] Admirably dealt with by the two Campbells, one American, one British: Charles S.
Campbell Jr, *Anglo-American Understanding, 1898–1903*, Baltimore, 1957; A.E.
Campbell, *Great Britain and the United States, 1895–1903*, Glasgow, 1960.

of the twentieth century, even such 'irreconcilables', in 1919 terms, as William Borah and Robert La Follette.[2] Old style isolationism remained firmly established in the conservative majority of the Republican party in Congress, in the party machines made anxious by ideological forces, and in the new entrants into politics they brought with them. In addition it encompassed the left of American politics in the Socialist party, with its 1 million votes in the 1912 election, and among the 'Wobblies', the International Workers of the World (IWW). After 1914, progressives were to become increasingly divided between the moral imperialists, whose cause Wilson made his own, in time to win the 1916 election, and the more pragmatic Republicans whose opposition was to deprive the Treaty of Versailles of its two-thirds majority in the Senate.

In generational terms, the group responsible for the Anglo-American *rapprochement*, with the single exception of Theodore Roosevelt himself, belonged to the Republican ascendancy established during the Gilded Age. Of the two Secretaries of State and the two ambassadors to the Court of St James most deeply involved in this process, John Hay, Joseph Choate and Whitelaw Reid came of age during the Civil War. Elihu Root, McKinley's Secretary for War, Roosevelt's close friend and Hay's successor at the State Department, came of age during reconstruction, but in the North. Root and Choate were leaders of the American legal profession during the Gilded Age; Hay, Lincoln's private secretary and biographer, had served both as diplomatist and as Assistant Secretary of State, before appointment by McKinley to the London Embassy in

[2] See William E. Leuchtenberg, 'Progressivism and Imperialism: The Progressive Movement and American Foreign Policy, 1898–1916', *MVHR*, 39, 1952–3: Professor Leuchtenberg's thesis, predictably, has aroused a good deal of criticism. See Walter Trallner, 'Progressivism and World War I: A Reappraisal', *Mid-America*, 44, 1962; Howard Allen, 'Republican Reformers and Foreign Policy, 1913–1917', *Mid-America*, 44, 1962; Warren Sutton, 'Progressive Republican Senators and the Submarine Crisis, 1915–1916', *Mid-America*, 47, 1965; Padraic C. Kennedy, 'La Follette's Foreign Policy: From Imperialism to Anti-Imperialism', *Wisconsin Magazine of History*, 46, 1963; Barton J. Bernstein and Franklin A. Leib, 'Progressive Republican Senators and American Imperialism, 1898–1916: A Reappraisal', *Mid-America*, 50, 1968. Their argument is essentially that 'progressive senators' (on whom they concentrate) supported Roosevelt's foreign policy as part of the whole reformist programme, and that from Taft's administration onwards there is no constant pattern in progressive attitudes to the major foreign policy issues. The reader is left with the feeling that if Professor Leuchtenberg's definition of 'progressivism' had been a little too all-embracing, the definition of 'imperialism' by his critics is equally open to such objection.

1897. Reid moved to New York to buy and edit the *Tribune* before serving Benjamin Harrison as Minister in Paris. Apart from their Republicanism, the main element they shared in the era of social Darwinism was the achievement of success and wealth through talent.

Theodore Roosevelt, who took over the leadership of this group on McKinley's death and was to dominate Progressive Republicanism until its débâcle in 1916, belonged by birth to quite a different generation, that of Wilson, Bryan, Josephus Daniels, Charles Evans Hughes, Frank Kellogg, Philander C. Knox, Robert Lansing, Walter Hines Page, even of Senator Borah; yet in political terms he is clearly their senior, having forced his way into national politics under Harrison, and been pitchforked into the Presidency by the unholy combination of Boss Platt, who secured his nomination to the Vice-Presidency, and McKinley's assassin. Roosevelt is remarkable also for the fact that long before he emerged so suddenly into prominence he had developed and cultivated deep emotional and intellectual friendships with a group of Englishmen who, though not of any great political significance in terms of British politics, shared his views of the world.[3] They included Cecil Spring-Rice, Arthur Lee, later Lord Lee of Fareham, St Loe Strachey of *The Spectator* and Lord Bryce.[4] They shared an historicism which regarded Germany as the nearest threat to Anglo-Saxon hegemony, Russia as the more serious long-term threat and beyond that, the 'yellow peril' of Asia with which Tzarist pan-Asiatic propaganda from time to time strove to identify itself. They thought that Anglo-Saxon hegemony, which they believed was in the process of coming into being, represented the highest form of civilisation. They followed Admiral Mahon in regarding that hegemony as being based on sea power, but they did not regard its triumph as by any means assured. Indeed they imbibed from Van Wyck Brooks a deep pessimism as to the prospect of the

---

[3] David H. Burton, 'Theodore Roosevelt and his English Correspondents: The Intellectual Roots of the Anglo-American Alliance', *Mid-America*, 53, 1971; see also J.A.S. Grenville and G.B. Young (eds.), *Politics, Strategy and Diplomacy: Studies in Foreign Policy, 1873–1917*, New Haven, 1966, Chapter 8, 'The Expansionists: The Education of Henry Cabot Lodge'.

[4] Edmund Ions, *James Bryce and American Democracy, 1870–1922*, London, 1968. See also Peter Neary, 'The Embassy of James Bryce in the United States, 1907–1913', London Ph.D. Thesis, 1967.

higher civilisation maintaining itself in face of the challenges from the lower civilisations.

On the British side, the years between 1900 and 1919 were to foreshadow the history of the remainder of the century as Britain plunged from the position of banker to America's expansion to total dependence on American financial support in 1916–17. British attitudes to America were to lag far behind these developments, the experience of which was to have a traumatic impact on the foreign-policy-makers of the inter-war years and afterwards. In 1897, as Professor A. E. Campbell has pointed out, élite British opinion did not recognise the United States as a country conforming to the same standards as those of the major European powers. United States government was regarded as ignorant of the conventions of civilised diplomatic intercourse. The Washington Embassy was recognised to require quite a different type of emissary from that required by Paris, Berlin, Rome or St Petersburg.[5]

In 1900 the pressing needs of Britain's increasing military isolation seemed to argue convincingly for the settlement of the existing areas of conflict.[6] The cold realism of Lord Salisbury and his diplomatic advisers[7] was to be swamped entirely by a flush of irrationality, perhaps best described as the search for a 'possible United States'. This search, it should be emphasised, was far more concentrated in the world of British literature and politics than in the British diplomatic service, where the unfortunate Sir Mortimer Durand was to find his lack of physical fitness a handicap for which his India-generated pan-Anglo-Saxonism could not compensate, and where Spring-Rice was to be isolated from his colleagues in

[5] See, for example, Lord Hardinge of Penshurst's account of his refusal to accept appointment to Washington and proposal of Lord Bryce as ambassador, *The Old Diplomacy*, London, 1947, p. 132.

[6] The arguments of the 'realists' are admirably set out in Bourne, *Britain and the Balance of Power in North America*, pp. 313–401. As always, the military and naval strategists were to swing uneasily between realism and fantasy. For an example of the latter see the summary of the war plan W 14 of 1906–7 for a war against a United States–German alliance, produced for instructional purposes, in Bourne, pp. 399–401.

[7] Lord Balfour, a later convert to Atlanticism, wrote to Henry White in 1900, 'harmonious cooperation between the two great Anglo-Saxon states' would be difficult to obtain since 'large numbers of the most loyal citizens of America are not of British descent or, if of British descent, came from that part of Ireland which has never loved England', Balfour to Henry White, 12 December 1900, Balfour Papers, Add. MS-49742 (fo. 68).

London by the strength of his Americophilia.[8] The search for a 'possible America' sprang from the reformist social imperialism which took hold of British political thought and expression from 1895 onwards.[9] This mood, and the milieu from which it sprang, was far from optimistic. Its drive lay towards increasing the efficient operations of the British machinery of state by the introduction of scientific methods and organisation. It was heavily influenced by primitive theories of social genetics, couched in Darwinian terms. Its advocates were well aware, both intuitively and by active observation, of the challenges to Britain's position embodied in German, Russian and American industrial growth. British investors, the three hundred thousand or so whose wealth and willingness to risk their capital for capital gains made London the centre of the developing world's risk capital, were far from ignorant or without contacts with the rising mercantile and industrial–technological élites of the United States.[10] Intermarriage, visits to the United States, which were to be incorporated increasingly in the *Wanderjahre* of the more adventurous of their offspring, and the increasing counterflow of English Americans seeking out their 'roots', all combined to enhance awareness of the United States.[11]

In the beleaguered state in which Britain found itself during the South African war, the necessity of ending the isolation of the nineteenth century led British statesmen successively to seek out a German alliance, achieve one with Japan and bury the colonial hatchet with France. The *rapprochement* with the United States could easily be fitted into this category of diplomatic action. The

---

[8] On which see, for example, Sherrill P. Wells, 'The Influence of Sir Cecil Spring-Rice and Sir Edward Grey on the Shaping of Anglo-American Relations, 1913–1916', London Ph.D., 1978. See also the comments on his views as 'by nature an alarmist', Lord Curzon, 17 September 1916, Hardinge Papers, vol. 25, p. 28: 'our experience is that it is not much use asking him questions'. Lord Robert Cecil, 25 December 1916, Cecil Papers, FO 800/198, cited in Stephen Hartley, 'The Irish Question as a Problem in British Foreign Policy, 1914–1918', London Ph.D., 1980, pp. 94ff.

[9] See Bernard Semmel, *Imperialism and Social Reform: English Social–Imperial Thought, 1895–1914*, London, 1960; see also Elie Halévy, *Imperialism and the Rise of Labour*, vol. V, London, 1949. See also the sources cited in Chapter 1, footnote 30, above.

[10] Herbert Feis, *Europe the World's Banker, 1870–1914*, New York, 1961 (reprint edition).

[11] On this see the evidence in Bradford Perkins, *The Great Rapprochement. England and the United States 1895–1914*, London 1969.

absence of any language barrier and the growth of the white settler colonies of Australia, Canada and New Zealand towards Dominion status promoted Americans in Britain into a different status from that of visiting Europeans, that of colonial aspirants to the status of Englishmen, a categorisation which alternately angered and amused those Americans who experienced it. It should be noted that, despite its apparent solidity, British society was far from static in 1900. Upward mobility, both by talent from the professional classes and by the acquisition of wealth from developments in newspaper ownership, distribution and industrial innovation, was producing would-be entrants into the ruling élites from among those who were previously unacceptable by reason of their birth, their education or their membership of minority groups. The flood of would-be entrants, whether Jewish, Scots, Welsh or Armenian in origin, whether members of Lord Milner's *Kindergarten*, the more raffish social set which made up the Edwardian Court, or the earnest reformers of the Fabian Society, made it easy for Canadians, Australians, South Africans and Americans to come in with them; and where the Tory establishment tried to close ranks, the Liberals were the beneficiaries. Even the Tory party would discard the scion of the Salisburys for a Scots Canadian shipping magnate as its leader before 1914 brought the 'Golden Age', of which Mr Harold Macmillan has written, to an end. British society remained socially wide open, just as British opinion, in rejecting both Field Marshal Lord Roberts's call for universal conscription and Joseph Chamberlain's campaign for imperial protection, was to continue Britain's internationalist position for another two and a half decades. In the meantime, the United States was a useful partner to Britain in the increasing establishment of international standards of behaviour and institutions, whether in Theodore Roosevelt's interventions in the first Moroccan crisis and the termination of the Russo-Japanese war, or in the movement towards international arbitration and the Second Hague Conference.[12] The performance of the Taft government was more of a disappointment.[13] British opinion looked for a victory by Theodore Roosevelt in the 1912 election. Instead, it was

[12] For the most recent study see Jost Dülffler, *Regeln gegen den Krieg. Die Haager Konferenzen 1899 und 1907 in der internationalen Beziehungen*, Berlin, 1981.

[13] The best study of Anglo-American relations in this period is in Edmund Ions, *James Bryce*. Hopes of a victory by Theodore Roosevelt in 1912 appear to have influenced the appointment of his friend Spring-Rice to the Washington Embassy.

confronted by Wilson and conflict over Mexico of a kind that exacerbated the incoming régime's suspicions of British motives.[14]

The outbreak of the First World War was to put a considerable strain on the relationship between the two countries. Until 1916, Wilson's admiration for, and confidence in, Sir Edward Grey, and his belief in the essential community of the Democratic and Liberal approaches to world politics, did much to limit these strains. Wilson's action in repealing the discriminatory clauses of the 1912 Panama Canal Act earned him the reputation in Britain of being a 'gentleman'. By early 1916 he was to enjoy a much less flattering reputation. British 'grey' propaganda, clandestinely organised and directed at upwards of 15,000 carefully selected élite leaders,[15] had done much to build on the biases of East Coast 'Anglo' opinion, much of which was more Republican or Rooseveltian than Wilsonian in its political orientation; this did nothing, however, to ease Wilson's own increasing resentment of British blockade and black list practices. He saw his rôle as that of mediator,[16] a concept which for him increasingly included virtual dictation of the final terms of peace. His preliminary efforts in this direction were bitterly resented.[17]

The year 1916 was to prove particularly traumatic. The failure at Gallipoli and the 'blood-letting' on the Somme were to set in motion developments which, by December 1916, had brought to authority

[14] See P.R. Calvert, 'Great Britain and the New World, 1905–1914', in F.H. Hinsley (ed.), *British Foreign Policy under Sir Edward Grey*; Cambridge, 1977; see also P.R. Calvert, *The Mexican Revolution, 1910–1914: The Diplomacy of Anglo-American Conflict*, Cambridge, 1968.

[15] J.D. Squires, *British Propaganda at Home and in the United States, 1914–1917*, Cambridge, Mass., 1935; Lucy Masterman, *C.F. Masterman. A Biography*, London, 1939, p. 277; CAB 37/130, No. 35, December 1914, Wellington House Second Report. See also M.L. Sanders, 'Wellington House and British Propaganda during the First World War', *Hist. J.*, 18, 1975; Philip M. Taylor, 'The Foreign Office and British Propaganda during the First World War', *Hist. J.*, 23, 1980; Nicholas Reeves, 'British Film Propaganda during the First World War', London Ph.D. Thesis, 1981.

[16] C.M. Mason, 'Anglo-American Relations: Mediation and Permanent Peace', in Hinsley (ed.) *Grey*; Ernest R. May, *World War and American Isolation, 1914–1917*, Cambridge, Mass., 1959.

[17] For some examples see D.C. Watt, *Personalities and Policies*, pp. 31–4; for other comments, e.g. by Eyre Crowe, 5 October 1916, see Hartley, 'The Irish Question', p. 129; for comments by Sir Arthur Nicolson, see Wells, p. 29; Walter Long, Lansdowne, Cecil and Selborne in Cabinet, 23 June 1916, CAB 37/150/15, Hartley, pp. 191–5.

in Britain a coalition of the *jusqu'au-boutistes* headed by Lloyd George. This coalition was an uneasy but uncompromising mixture of British populism, the new business tycoons (the Geddes brothers, Northcliffe, etc.) and Tory nationalism.[18] Colonel House's most ambitious effort at mediation had failed, leaving both Wilson and the British Cabinet feeling cheated. As part of the preparedness campaign, designed to provide the President with the military and naval 'clout' to ensure his domination over any eventual peace treaty, the US Navy had embarked on a programme of capital ship construction, deliberately designed to overhaul British naval primacy by 1925.[19] Still worse, the British suppression of the Easter 1916 Rising in Dublin had alienated substantial parts of hitherto pro-Allied opinion,[20] leading even Theodore Roosevelt to comment on the contrast between the summary treatment of the Irish leaders and that of Carson and Campbell, the Ulster leaders who had been preaching armed revolt in 1914 (supported by German arms) and were now in the Cabinet.[21] The bulk of the Cabinet, led by the old High Tories, had reacted so fiercely against both Wilson and those who felt some account should be taken of American opinion as to make any real movement very difficult.[22] Even members of the American department of the Foreign Office were suffused with impatience and hostility towards the United States. The American Ambassador in London, Walter Hines Page, and Sir Cecil Spring-Rice in Washington, had lost most of their credibility with their home governments. Wilson's image of Liberal Britain had gone entirely, replaced by a caricature of business, political bossism and selfish, arrogant, overbearing, navalist imperialism.[23] The British

---

[18] On which, Robert J. Scully, *The Origins of the Lloyd George Coalition: The Politics of Social Imperialism, 1900–1918*, Princeton, 1975, is of great interest despite its excessively Marxist overtones.

[19] Warner R. Schilling, 'Admirals and Foreign Policy, 1913–1919', Yale Ph.D., 1953; David Trask, *Captains and Cabinets: Anglo-American Naval Relations, 1917–1918*, Columbia, Missouri, 1972. I was unable to consult Jeffrey J. Safford, *Wilsonian Maritime Diplomacy, 1913–1921*, New Brunswick, 1978.

[20] See the evidence cited in Hartley, 'The Irish Question', pp. 94ff.: Alan J. Ward, *Ireland and Anglo-American Relations, 1899–1921*, London, 1969, p. 118.

[21] Roosevelt to Arthur Lee, 17 June 1916, Elting E. Morison (ed.), *The Letters of Theodore Roosevelt*, vol. VIII, Cambridge, Mass., 1951, p. 1054.

[22] Hartley, 'The Irish Question', pp. 191ff.

[23] To do Wilson justice, it should be said that he refused to exploit the Irish question in his 1916 election campaign, choosing, so Spring-Rice reported, to campaign against 'hyphenated Americanism' of all kinds. See Spring-Rice to FO, 16 June, FO

image of America as a quasi-Dominion, linked to Britain by a common culture and purpose, was equally shattered.

To those members of the Cabinet and their advisers who were not inclined to let nationalist sentiment rule their heads, the most alarming feature of the Anglo-American relationship in 1916, however, was the revelation of British and Allied dependence for war finance on the United States, and on the Wilson government for access to that finance. The Wilson administration was very well aware of that dependence and clearly determined to use it. Indeed, only German folly in opening unrestricted submarine warfare prevented British bankruptcy.[24]

American entry into the war only emphasised this dependence. By July 1917, Wilson could write: 'England and France have not the same view with regard to peace that we have by any means. When the war is over we can force them to our way of thinking, because by that time they will, among other things, be financially in our hands.'[25] This power was to be applied with as much force as Wilson's own conviction would allow. When America entered the war, it became essential to Wilson's plans for an imposed settlement that America's allies were not defeated but only weakened by Germany.[26] His determination was matched for their own purposes by the Secretary of the Navy and his Chief of Naval Operations and by the military and financial élites in America. Throughout the disastrous year of 1917 the American administration did little in naval or shipping terms to save the desperate position of the Allies.[27] Instead, US shipping moved to dominate the carrying trade with Latin America. The American army once in France was withheld from action to aid its British and French partners during the great

371/2294, and 20 October 1916, FO 371/2796. Observing the results of the 1916 election, the Foreign Office tended therefore to underestimate the ability of Irish Americans to cause trouble.

[24] See John Milton Cooper, 'The Command of Gold Reversed: American Loans to Britain, 1915–1917', *J.Am. Hist.*, 60, 1973; Kathleen Burk, 'The Diplomacy of Finance: British Financial Missions to the United States, 1914–1918', *Hist. J.*, 22, 1979; Roberta A. Dayer, 'Strange Bedfellows: J.P. Morgan and Co., Whitehall, and the Wilson Administration During World War I', *Business History*, 18, 1976.

[25] Wilson to House, 21 July 1917, House Papers, Box 121.

[26] Kathleen Burk, 'Great Britain in the United States, 1917–1918; The Turning-Point', *Int. Hist. Rev.*, 1, 1979.

[27] This theme is explored in detail in Edward B. Parsons, *Wilsonian Diplomacy: Allied–American Rivalries in War and Peace*, St Louis, Missouri, 1978.

German offensive of 1918, despite desperate appeals from Balfour, House, Herbert Hoover, Admiral Sims and others.

President Wilson, however, suffered from three grave handicaps. In the first place, he could not keep his policy hidden from British observers nor prevent the Cabinet taking what precautions it could against its consequences for Britain's post-war position.[28] Secondly, his policy depended also upon timing. His position of dominance over the Allies would not really be secured until 1919, when American troops would be over in Europe in force. The German collapse in October 1918, and his own over-eager response to their shrewd attempt to exploit the divisions between himself and the Allies, by appealing for an armistice on the basis of his Fourteen Points, destroyed this timetable entirely. It had in any case been disrupted by the deliberate refusal of the British to provide shipping adequate for the proposed movement of American troops to France in August–October 1918.[29] In the third place, Wilson's command over the American electorate was precarious and over Congress still more so. Since he had ideas and concepts but no working programme, individual advisers but no coordinated organisation, his ability to force his views on either the British or French government, which had both ideas and concepts and a working programme, was much more in doubt than he believed.

The American electorate, and even the most active of their would-be political leaders, were equally unready for the sudden reversal in the power relationships between Britain and the United States in the years 1915–17. Much of the sympathy won by British propaganda for British aspirations sprang from a conscious recognition of the parallels between the British and American positions. Both the British and Americans had feared the massive growth of German naval power and territorial ambitions.[30] Both were habituated to the idea of isolation from Europe. The possibilities of

[28] For the British government's action to prevent British oil, mining and chemical investments passing into American hands see CAB 23/5, 14 September, 8 October 1917; Parsons, *Wilsonian Diplomacy*, p. 81, footnote 54. For the effects on Wilson of the de Bunsen mission to Latin America, see Parsons, *Wilsonian Diplomacy*, pp. 138, 149; Balfour Papers, 49699.

[29] Edward B. Parsons, 'Why the British Reduced the Flow of American Troops to Europe in August–October 1918', *Canadian J. Hist.*, 12, 1977–8.

[30] For the rôle of the German threat in American planning for war *before* 1914, see Richard D. Challener, *Admirals, Generals and American Foreign Policy, 1898–1914*, Princeton, 1973; J.A.S. Grenville, 'Diplomacy and War Plans in the

competitive militarism had been much reduced by the increased emphasis on continental defence that each power felt obliged to develop from 1905 onwards, America on the North American continent and the Caribbean, Britain on the North Sea and the Mediterranean. Of course, British power and the world position Britain enjoyed was the yardstick by which American imperialists measured and constructed America's goals, a 'Navy Second to None',[31] and the dollar taking the place of the pound.[32] British trade and British investments blocked and threatened American business; moreover, in Britain commerce and finance went hand in hand with government, or so it was believed. And in 1917–18, it seemed that Britain controlled the vital raw materials on which industrial expansion depended, and which, it was feared, were being exhausted in America, especially oil and rubber.[33] Britain controlled the world's largest merchant marine. Britain controlled the world's cables.[34]

American reactions, especially those of President Wilson and his administration, to the war and to the collapse of Germany were themselves of European origin. Wilson might be bitterly angered by the way Lloyd George upstaged his Fourteen Points in his address to British Trade Unionists of 5 January 1918.[35] But the ideas ventilated by Lloyd George were those of British intellectual radicalism, the programme of the Union of Democratic Control fed to Colonel House via William Buckler of the US Embassy in London,[36] just as the ideas of progressive imperialism and social reform had been drawn to a considerable degree from Fabianism on the one side, and

United States, 1890–1917', *Transactions of the Royal Historical Society*, 5th Series, 1961.

[31] As argued by Warner Schilling, 'Admirals and Foreign Policy'.

[32] Cooper, 'The Command of Gold Reversed'.

[33] See John de Novo, 'The Movement for an Aggressive Oil Policy Abroad'.

[34] This subject still lacks a proper study. But see, Parsons, *Wilsonian Diplomacy*, pp. 110, 168–9, 193.

[35] David R. Woodward, 'The Origins and Intent of David Lloyd George's January 5, 1918 War Aims Speech', *The Historian*, 34, 1971–2. Unlike Wilson's Fourteen Points Speech, the Lloyd George speech was intended to be more than an exercise in the higher rhetoric of war aims, being aimed at Austro-Hungarian ears as much as at his trades union audience.

[36] See Lawrence W. Martin, *Peace Without Victory. Woodrow Wilson and the British Liberals*, Yale University Press, New Haven, Conn. 1958. The Buckler papers are with the House Collection at Yale.

British aristocratic social reform on the other, and had developed in reaction to the doctrines of British nineteenth-century liberal econ-omists.[37] The new element Wilson brought to their doctrines, which he demonstrably shared with progressive imperialists over the Mexican issue, was his determination to use American power to the limit to make over his co-belligerents, his dependants, the world itself, in America's image.[38] In this he outran the limited imperialism of the Republican progressives, if not the ideas of Theodore Roosevelt himself. Wilson discovered, in negotiation with his part-ners in co-belligerency, that the strength of America's position could be used to thwart his co-belligerents but not to force America's aims upon them; he could not command that strength anyway, and the attempt to command it and to encash it would provoke a revulsion against his policies not merely among the élites, but also among the mass electorates, the 'peoples' of his co-belligerents. The disaster which overtook his plans for world peace, his treaty and his adminis-tration was one which was inherent in the progressive moral imperialism he embodied and voiced, and in the authoritarian rôle of the American presidency itself. At Paris he found himself part of a cabinet, not a presidential system of government.[39] He was to prove appallingly ineffective in such a rôle. But his own style of govern-ment left him without a substitute to take his place. Lansing advised, kept an office (and a diary) and expressed his powerlessness in bitter little caricatures. House fixed things, and people, but could act only as Wilson's *éminence grise*. Wilson was a monarch – without a chancellor.

One need only contrast the apprehension with which in Novem-ber 1918 Lloyd George discussed Wilson's impending arrival in Europe with the relaxed confidence he was to display in the Imperial War Cabinet after meeting him in London to see how quickly the

[37] See Arthur Mann, 'British Social Thought and American Reformers of the Progressive Era', *MVHR*, 41, 1954–5.
[38] See the admirable survey by Samuel P. Wells, 'New Perspectives on Wilsonian Diplomacy: The Secular Evangelism of American Political Economy', *Perspectives in American History*, 6, 1974.
[39] See Lord Hankey, *The Supreme Control at the Paris Peace Conference*, London, 1963: In 1917–18, cabinet-based governments were in the majority in the vic-torious coalition. In 1943–5, they were not, a point of some significance in the comparison of Britain's relations 'at the summit' with the United States in the concluding phases of the two world wars.

mercurial Welshman had taken his measure.[40] With Balfour and Lord Robert Cecil to out-philosophise or out-moralise him, with Hankey to control the agenda and keep the minutes, with America's military representatives on the Armistice Commissions, inadequately instructed and subordinate to Foch and Beatty,[41] Wilson would have been doomed to failure even with a united Congress and electorate behind him. As it was the Allied military and naval élites remained unswayed by his ideals. Keynes delivered a massive assault on his economic and financial ignorance and the destruction they had wrought upon Europe's economy. Britain, driven off gold in March 1919,[42] merely bounced back into more efficient competition with American trade.[43] And the idealists, who thought they heard in Wilson's rhetoric the new ordering of international society for which they had hoped, sank into despair.[44]

The disaster which overtook Wilson's moral imperialism had its roots in the generational make-up of the American foreign-policy-making élite of the time. It is noticeable how experience of American power and the comparisons drawn by those mentors of the American business and financial élites who took part in the first expansion of American economic entry into Europe before 1914, between American efficiency and the comparative 'openness' of American society with what they chose to regard as the caste-ridden structure of British society, seems to develop *pari passu* with the

[40] For Lloyd George's apprehensions see Lloyd George to Lord Riddell, 10 October 1918, *Lord Riddell's War Diary*, London, 1933; Minutes of the Imperial War Cabinet, 11 October 1918, Sir Robert Borden Papers, MG 26, H 4(a) vol. 395; Bridgeman Journal, entry of 7 November 1918; Frank Cobb to Colonel House, 16 November 1918, Colonel House Papers, Drawer 4, Folder I; Imperial War Cabinet, Shotham's Notes of Meeting of 28 November 1918, Sir George Foster Papers, Folder 79. For Lloyd George's attitude to the meeting with President Wilson, see Imperial War Cabinet, Minutes of Meetings of 30, 31 December 1918, Sir George Foster Papers, Folder 79.

[41] Admiral Fremantle to Admiral Beatty 27 October 1918, Admiral Fremantle Papers, FRE/310, MS.56/041: Allied Naval Council, Sixth Meeting, 28 October to 4 November 1918, *Report* No. 26 of 5 December 1918: Mermaix (Gabriel Terrail), *Fragments d'Histoire, 1914–1919*, vol. V, *Les Négociations secrètes et les Quatre Armistices*, Paris, 1931; Allied Naval Council, Annual Report, Appendix documents Nos. 246 and 249.

[42] Burk, 'Great Britain in the United States', pp. 197ff.

[43] No adequate study of this episode as yet exists. On the issues in Latin America see Joseph S. Tulchin, *The Aftermath of War. World War I and United States Policy Towards Latin America*, New York, 1971, pp. 30–4.

[44] For an excellent contemporary reflection of this see the extracts from Harold Nicolson's diary printed in his *Peace-Making 1919*, London, 1934.

increasingly uninhibited development of moral evangelist imperialism in the United States from 1905 onwards.[45] These standard-bearers of American expansionism were inevitably from a younger generation than that which had brought about the Anglo-American détente of the years 1898–1905. Parrini has shown how the American banking community was divided between those bankers whose interests lay basically in the financing of commerce on British lines (e.g. Morgan's) and those who were much more interested in industrial involvement (Vanderlip and the Rockefeller-backed National City Bank).[46] But both sections looked towards the capture or 'Americanisation' of the world-wide British banking system and the replacement as its centre of London by New York.

The activities of the US bankers, their background and the development of their determination to take over the position of financial dominance previously enjoyed by London has still not been adequately studied. This determination in fact has a great degree of ambivalence, both as regards the nature of the Anglo-American relationship, and as regards the best manner in which that takeover should be effected, whether by 'takeover' in the financial and market sense, that is by operations akin to the merger or capture of rival interests from within, or whether by challenge from without. The purely financial interests, of which J.P. Morgan was the most significant, by far preferred the former kind of operation, the more so once they had successfully bid for the position of agents for the British government in the United States.[47] The alternative policy was favoured by the Rockefeller interests led by Frank Vanderlip of the National City Bank, an unsuccessful rival bidder for the position of agent for the Allied governments, who was instrumental in founding and directing from behind the scenes the American International Corporation and in attracting to its vice-presidency that embodiment of Rooseveltian imperialism in financial and business terms, Willard Straight, himself a former associate of J.P. Morgan & Co., an apostle of the doctrine of American

---

[45] See the sources cited in Leuchtenberg, 'Progressivism and Imperialism', and in Samuel P. Wells, 'British Strategic Withdrawal' and 'New Perspectives'.
[46] Carl Parrini, *Heir to Empire. United States Economic Diplomacy, 1916–1923*, Pittsburgh, 1969.
[47] See Dayer, 'Strange Bedfellows'.

business expansion abroad since his activities as Consul-General in Manchuria, in the years 1906–8.[48]

The major thrust of the hostility on which Wilson's health and his policies foundered was, however, the contrast between his aspirations and the changes in American government which would be required to bring them about. Whatever he or Josephus Daniels, his Secretary to the Navy, might say about the US naval construction programme of November 1918, it would demand a level of government expenditure, control and taxation entirely irreconcilable with the organisation of American political and financial society. His proposed commitments to the League threatened Congressional limitations on federal foreign-policy-making powers. They were difficult to reconcile with the previous American legal treaties (though perhaps less difficult than they seemed). Wilson was confronted by conservative internationalist 'reservationists' and radical–populist isolationist 'irreconcilables'.[49] The real issue, however, lay not between participation and the irreconcilables, of whom there were reckoned to be only nineteen senators, six from the Middle West, five from the Far West, six from the eastern seaboard and two from the South. It lay between those who wished to participate in world politics with a free hand, and those who were committed to the restraints of an international organisation.

The British government, desperately anxious for American entry into the League, despite the divisions within the Cabinet and the bureaucracy over its obligations, might have been able to accommodate the former,[50] although the proposals for such an accommodation strained to the limit the divisions between High Tory imperialists, conservative realists and Lloyd George's more progressive and Atlanticist supporters.[51] But the President's crippled

---

[48] Harry N. Scheiber, 'World War I as Entrepreneurial Opportunity: Willard Straight and the American International Corporation', *Political Science Quarterly*, 84, 1969.

[49] See W.G. Carleton, 'Isolationism and the Middle West', *MVHR*, 32, 1946.

[50] See George W. Egerton, 'Britain and the "Great Betrayal"': Anglo-American Relations and the Struggle for the Ratification of the Treaty of Versailles, 1919–1920', *Hist.J.*, 21, 1978; Leon E. Boothe, 'A Fettered Envoy: Lord Grey's Mission to the United States, 1919–1920', *Review of Politics*, 33, 1971.

[51] The rôle of the British Atlanticists deserves more development than I have been able to give it here. It was mainly confined, however, to spelling out the implications of Wilson's actions and doctrines, so that they were properly understood. Their American opposites received no attention whatever from Wilson.

intransigence, and his second wife's antipathies towards Sir Edward Grey and Colonel House, ruled the idea out of court. Wilson, the patrician conservative who relied on the masses to implement his politics against the 'special interests', proved less sensitive to the realities of popular opinion than the plebeian Lloyd George, misled, . it may well be, by his failure to appreciate the precariousness of his own electoral victories in 1912 and 1916. His doctrines, imported from his European equivalents, the high bourgeois intellectual reformists of the Union of Democratic Control (UDC) and their European equivalents, lacked native American roots and had little to do with either American experience or American political traditions, unlike the expansionist continentalism of Theodore Roosevelt's progressivism, or the economic expansion of the Republican régimes which were to follow him.

3

1919–1934

From the rejection of Versailles to the triumph of populist
isolationism; limited intervention and the attempt to recover
British pre-eminence

The effect of the virtual paralysis of the Wilson administration in the
last year and a half of its life was to accentuate the ever-present
fissiparous forces in American foreign-policy-making. Each
department of the US government, State, Navy, War, Commerce,
and Treasury, developed its own foreign policies; so did the oil
lobby, the New York banking confraternity, and American
exporters abroad, especially those exporting to Latin America. The
Republican victory in the 1920 presidential election was to impose
on this maelstrom of activity an element of control, exercised not so
much by the President as by the three most powerful members of his
Cabinet, Charles Evans Hughes, the Secretary of State, Andrew
Mellon at the Treasury and Herbert Hoover at Commerce. They
cannot be said to have exercised this control by mutual agreement; it
was rather that they had arrived at a common consensus as to who
should exercise leadership in public matters. Over a large and
important area of US foreign relations they felt leadership should lie
with private business and finance.[1] They were determined to see that
that leadership should be so exercised, by using their personal and
private influence and pressure to see that it was. Industry repaid
them by insisting on State Department action in the name of the
'Open Door', where foreign governments, especially that of Britain,
were felt to be exercising political power to stand in the way of

[1] This argument follows Michael Hogan, *Informal Entente: The Private Structure of
Cooperation in Anglo-American Economic Diplomacy, 1918–1928*, Columbia,
Missouri, 1977. See also Ellis W. Hawley, 'Herbert Hoover, the Commerce
Secretariat and the Vision of an "Associative State" ', *J. Am. Hist.*, 61, 1974.

business. American companies were not, however, averse to the slamming shut of that door, provided that they were safely inside.[2] Although there was frequent friction between Commerce and State over who should act, there was little disagreement on 'how'; though the State Department was far from sharing, or indeed understanding, Hoover's vision of what had been called the 'Associative State'.[3] The Republican leadership was not 'isolationist',[4] nor, in important respects, did it appear so to the British government.[5] The leadership was, however, determined to stay clear of the coercive proposals under consideration by the European powers under the disguise of the League of Nations.

In generational terms, three age-groups can be distinguished among those who controlled American foreign policy in the 1920s. The first group, born between the mid-1840s and mid-1860s, were in the main contemporaries of Theodore Roosevelt, who did not, however, share in his early rise to leadership.[6] The second group, born in the period 1865–75, included President Coolidge, and most of the American bankers who were to play so large a part in the diplomacy of the 1920s.[7] The third group consisted of scions of the east coast high bourgeoisie who had entered the United States Foreign Service in the era of American imperialism and who were now, by the Rogers Act of 1924, to take the lead in turning that Service into a proper professional organisation.[8] The Democratic victory of 1912, and the comparative lack of interest of the American business and financial communities in foreign affairs *before* that date, were to bring these three different age-groups

---

[2] See the evidence in Hogan, *Informal Entente*; Benjamin Shwadran, *The Middle East, Oil and the Great Powers*, London, 1947; Michael B. Stoff, *Oil, War and American Security*, New Haven, 1980.

[3] Hawley, 'Herbert Hoover'.

[4] William Appleman Williams, 'The Legend of Isolationism in the 1920s', *Science and Society*, 1954; D.C. Watt, 'U.S. Isolationism in the 1920s. Is it a Useful Concept?', *Bulletin of the British Association of American Studies*, New Series, no. 6, 1962.

[5] See the evidence cited in Watt, 'Isolationism'; Brian McKercher, 'The British Foreign-Policy-Making Elite', London Ph.D., 1979.

[6] Kellogg, Henry Cabot Lodge, Andrew Mellon, Myron T. Herrick, Charles Dawes, Alanson Houghton, Charles Evans Hughes, Henry Stimson.

[7] Thomas Lamont, Benjamin Strong, Russell T. Leffingwell, Dwight Morrow.

[8] Led by Wilbur Carr of Coolidge's generation, they included William Castle, Joseph Grew, Hugh Gibson, Nelson Trusler Johnson, Hugh Wilson. See also Waldo H. Heinrichs Jr, *American Ambassador. Joseph C. Grew and the Development of the United States Diplomatic Tradition*, Boston, 1966.

together into a single political generation, which only began to come to maturity in 1916 when America's leaders suddenly became conscious of American power in the world. They did not, on the whole, follow President Wilson into the cul-de-sac into which his determination to use that power, not merely to give America the leading part on the stage of world politics, but to make her playwright, producer, director and theatre owner as well, was to take him. They thus preserved some of the pragmatism which had so distinguished Theodore Roosevelt senior.

President Wilson's fate taught America's leaders that neither Congress nor the American electorate understood or would support permanent institutionalised American involvement in world politics. They were to learn from the years 1920–1, however, that involvement, as such, could not be avoided; but that it could only be justified to American opinion in terms of American initiatives. Their first lesson came from the disastrous impact on the American economy of the failure of Europe's economy to revive after the end of the war.[9] The second lesson came from the rapid mobilisation of the 'Mugwump' element in American life to overwhelm the big naval programme with which the Harding administration came to Congress in March 1921.[10] The United States National Council for the Limitation of Armaments, formed in October 1921 in the aftermath of the 'Mugwump' victory, embraced the battle-scarred veterans of the National League of Women Voters, the Federal Council of Churches of Christ, the American Federation of Labor, the National Grange; the Church Peace Union and the Federation of American Farm Bureaux. Before such a formidable alliance of organised labour, the Bible Belt and American Womanhood, Congress quailed and the Navy, in its impotence, deduced British subversion.[11] It was only by way of very neat footwork and a modicum of deceit that Secretary of State Hughes got his summons to a disarmament conference at Washington on the record a day ahead of Lloyd

---

[9] See Melvyn G. Leffler, 'Political Isolationism, Economic Expansionism or Diplomatic Realism: American Policy towards Western Europe, 1921–1933', *Perspectives in American History*, 8, 1974, p.421; Melvyn G. Leffler, *The Elusive Quest: America's Pursuit of European Stability and French Security*, Chapel Hill, 1979.

[10] Adelphia Jan Bowen Jr, 'The Disarmament Movement, 1918–1935', Columbia University Ph.D., 1956.

[11] See Rear Admiral Knox, USN, preface to Samuel Eliot Morison, *A History of U.S. Naval Operations in World War II*, vol. I, Boston, 1947, pp. xlii–xliv.

George's proposed invocation of a conference on the Far East, thus ensuring that Congress would accept it.[12] Even then, Hughes had to set his face steadfastly against British proposals for a preliminary conference, leaving the disgruntled British with the feeling that they had been outmanoeuvred by Hughes's lack of confidence in his ambassador in London.[13] The need for such footwork, incidentally, was caused by Hughes's too efficient use of Canadian influence at the Dominions Conference in June 1921, to thwart British plans to renew the Anglo-Japanese alliance. Hughes had enlisted that influence by a variety of both open and clandestine contacts with the Canadian government,[14] some at least undertaken on Canadian initiative.

The expansion of the concerns of American diplomacy to cover oil, rubber, cables, the cinematograph, radio, finance (war debts, reparations, loans, central bank cooperation in the management of international credit organisations), shipping and naval disarmament followed on naturally from the experience of American mobilisation for total war and the reluctant involvement of the United States in the inter-Allied wartime planning and control agencies. But the conviction that these were to be the important problems of the future sprang naturally from the economic approach to international politics imbibed from virtually all American literature on the subject, from Mahon and Sumner onwards. With this widening of activity, and the ideological preference of the Republican leadership for private rather than public action, discussion of the membership of the élites has to be widened to include oil men, bankers, industrialists and admirals. Hoover's use of the Commerce Department, as an instrument to provoke initiatives by the corporate organisations of industry, was not as successful as he could have hoped.[15] But the bankers, urged on by the conviction that European political and financial stability was essential to American prosperity, moved

[12] See the historical summary by Dr Beeritz, 'Calling the Washington Conference', Charles Evans Hughes Papers; for evidence as to the need for footwork see W.T. Steed, *Through Thirty Years, 1892–1922*, London, 1924, vol. II, pp. 362–4.

[13] Colonel House Diary, entry of 29 July 1921.

[14] See Charles Crane to Hughes, 2 April 1921, *USNA*, RG59, SD 741.9411/80: Henry Stimson Diary, entry of 6 July 1932; Michael G. Fry, *Illusions of Security: North Atlantic Diplomacy, 1918–1922*, Toronto, 1972, esp. pp. 92–102, has the fullest account of these contacts.

[15] Hawley, 'Herbert Hoover'; Joseph Brandes, *Herbert Hoover and Economic Diplomacy: Department of Commerce Policy 1918–1928*, Pittsburgh, 1962.

steadily into European politics.[16] Congress, however, while prepared to applaud American initiatives which might upstage the
League of Nations' pretensions, was not willing to consider any
commitments, even to bridge the possibility of conflict between a
League of Nations' intention to check a would-be aggressor and
American neutral rights. The wiser members of the élite were
certainly ahead of Congress on this from 1930 onwards,[17] but they
were not prepared to bargain on the point with the unquenchable
French thirst for more security.

Relations with Britain were dominated by the central position
Britain occupied in American maps of the world. In Europe
American policy-makers might deal directly *with*, or, as in 1923–4,
upon France.[18] Indeed the British had occasion to be very worried by
signs of an American–French *rapprochement* in matters of finance
and disarmament in the years 1927–8, when Anglo-American
tension was greatest.[19] But in the rest of the world, China, South East
Asia, Africa, the Middle East, Latin America, there was only one
nation that mattered, whether to Congress or to the élites: that was
Britain. And towards Britain, even the most Anglophile members of
the élites were ambivalent, an ambivalence exemplified by Elihu
Root's backing for the Five Power naval proposals at Washington,
on the grounds that they made British action impossible without
American support.[20] This ambivalence, especially on financial
matters, was to stir up considerable resentment in the Tory party
leadership:[21] and after the breakdown in Anglo-American relations
at the Geneva Three Power Naval Conference in 1927, and the
unforgivable offence given by the Anglo-French compromise proposals the following year,[22] Republican élite opinion wrote off the

16 Paul P. Abrahams, 'American Bankers and the Economic Tactics of Peace, 1919', *J. Am. Hist.*, 1969.
17 See Kellogg to Lothian, 15 May 1930, Lothian Papers: Stimson Diary, entry of 17 October 1931.
18 See Stephen A. Schuler, *The End of French Predominance in Europe. The Financial Crisis of 1924 and the Adoption of the Dawes Plan*, Chapel Hill, 1976.
19 Frank C. Costigliola, 'Anglo-American Financial Rivalry in the 1920s', *J. Econ. Hist.*, 37, 1977; McKercher, 'British Foreign-Policy-Making Elite'.
20 Chandler P. Anderson Diary, entry of 26 November 1921.
21 Even in Churchill.
22 There is considerable, but not entirely satisfactory, literature on these episodes. See Wolf Heinrich Bickel, *Die anglo-amerikanische Beziehungen 1927–1930 im Licht der Flottenfrage*, Zurich, 1970; David Carlton, 'Great Britain and the Cool-idge Disarmament Conference of 1927', *Pol. Sci. Q.*, 83, 1968; David Carlton,

Tory party as fundamentally inimical to American interests and promoted the Socialist, Ramsay MacDonald, to the rôle of most trusted Englishman, a rôle which was to reconcile America to the National Government of 1931 and defuse even the renewed crisis over naval disarmament in the summer and autumn of 1934.

The new élites were the product of the 1900s: they saw nothing un-American in economic expansion or the establishment of economic dominance. They were also the children of the organisational revolution of the 1900s. They understood bureaucracy: they took to large-scale economic management as the modern, technocratic American way. Attempts to categorise them as the political expression of oligopolist capitalism are largely pointless exercises in labelling. As believers in American expansion they tended to move from industry to government and back again. As many worked for salaries as for profits. They represented a new class, that of the managers of large-scale enterprises; and as such they provided America with an impetus that made its industry the marvel of Europe.

Seven British governments held office between 1920 and 1933, the Lloyd George coalition, the Conservatives twice, Labour in a minority twice and two 'National' governments. Beneath them the apparatus of government remained undisturbed, the only novelty being the formal incorporation into the foreign-policy-making process of the military advisers, the Chiefs of Staff, in a subcommittee of the Committee of Imperial Defence, charged with evolving a common approach to strategic problems when asked to advise the CID or the Cabinet. This charge, until 1933, they manifestly failed to answer, the Chief of Air Staff maintaining a point of view on the future singularly different from that of his colleagues.

The Permanent Under Secretary of the Treasury from 1919 until 1938, Sir Warren Fisher, did much to improve the efficiency of the civil service as a source of advice to the Cabinet. The Secretary to the Cabinet from 1916 until 1938, and to the CID, Sir Maurice Hankey, did his best to ensure that the machinery of government and decision-making functioned on a basis of clear records and full

'The Anglo-French Compromise over Arms Limitation, 1928', *J. British Studies*, 8, 1969; Stephen W. Roskill, *British Naval Policy Between the Wars*, vol.I: *The Period of Anglo-American Antagonism*, London, 1962; McKercher, 'The British Foreign-Policy-Making Elite'.

information within the system. This did not exclude ferocious divisions of opinion within the defence and foreign-policy-making sides of the machinery; it did, however, secure their resolution where that was possible.

Even excluding the novelty of the two Labour governments, the shape of British politics and the nature of the political section of the foreign-policy-making élite changed markedly over the period. The government Lloyd George presided over presented an uneasy marriage between the progressive industrialists Lloyd George had brought into politics during the war, together with the more enterprising of the old Liberal party leadership, on the one hand, and, on the other hand, the Conservative party as it had begun to change during the 1900s, with the decline of the landed interest and the rise of second and third generation industrialists in the party such as Baldwin (iron and steel) and Bridgeman (coal). The break-up of the coalition in 1922 was followed by the reunion of the Tory leadership (Austen Chamberlain, Birkenhead) with those who had replaced them, under Baldwin's leadership, between 1924 and 1929. The second Labour government broke up in 1931 under the stresses of the financial crisis, yielding to a National government which reintegrated some veterans of the Asquith Liberals (Simon, for example) with the principal leadership of the Labour party under MacDonald, excluding the more imperialist-minded Conservatives (Churchill and Amery, for example) on the right, and driving the Labour party back into a second and equally uneasy period of exile and internal conflict.

Apart from the brief period when the *fin de siècle* radicalism of the Union of Democratic Control tried to capture the Labour leadership's approach to foreign policy, the views of the foreign-policy-making élite exhibit a remarkable consistency throughout the period even in their internal divisions. Whatever the age of the individuals concerned (and so far as the political and bureaucratic element is concerned, the average time at which the leading figures can be said to have entered into political awareness was well before the turn of the century), it was the more recent past rather than their early political education which played the dominant part in shaping their attitudes to external policy. They laboured under the revelation of Britain's dependence on the financial and industrial potential of the United States experienced in the years 1915–18 and of Britain's vulnerability to the outburst of economic nationalism in America experienced in the last two years of Wilson's presidency.

Reflection on the military experience of the war, on the commitments entered into before 1914 to a continental strategy and on the single-minded resistance of the Army leadership during the war to any operations which might direct attention away from the Western Front, led to a prolonged and bitter post-war debate on the respective merits of a continental and a maritime strategy,[23] which by ignoring the political context in which the commitment to a continental strategy had been arrived at swung heavily in favour of the traditionalists. Advocates of air power complicated the entire debate by arguing that the technological proclivities of air warfare were such that conventional warfare was a thing of the past.[24] Defence depended in their view entirely on strategic deterrence through air power. The narrow margin by which Britain had evaded defeat by the German submarine blockade reinforced the determination of those more strategically minded members of the élites not to brook any interference with or challenge to British sea power or its freedom of operation in time of war from a political enemy. The euphoria of victory in 1918, that same euphoria and jingoistic ultra-patriotism which produced the 1918–22 Parliament, expressed itself in 1918–20 in a burst of economic nationalism which matched and imitated its American equivalent, especially in the rhetoric with which its spokesmen hailed the extension of British power over the resources of oil[25] and rubber on which the technology of the future was felt to depend.

Beneath the surface of British politics the business management and individual leadership which had risen to power under Lloyd George was, however, to suffer severe defeat, its individuals being either driven back into opposition (as was Lord Beaverbrook, for example) or retiring into industry, again where their success was not matched by corresponding political influence (Geddes brothers into

---

[23] On which see Michael Howard, *The Continental Commitment*, London, 1971.

[24] H. Montgomery Hyde, *British Air Policy Between the Wars, 1918–1939*, London, 1976; George H. Quester, *Deterrence Before Hiroshima*, New York, 1966; Sir Charles Webster and Noble Frankland, *The Strategic Bombing Offensive Against Germany*, vols. I, IV, London, 1961.

[25] See the evidence cited in John de Novo, 'The Movement for an Aggressive American Oil Policy Abroad, 1918–1920', *Am. Hist. Rev.*, 61, 1956.

Dunlop rubber, Murray of Elibank into railways, McKenna into industrial banking, Mond into chemicals).

The bureaucratic element in the policy-making élite under the political leadership of Balfour and, for a time, of that maverick from Round Table days, Leo Amery, worked hard to contain and divert the nascent nationalism of the white settler element in the Empire into a common support of British policy through the machinery of the CID; efforts to make of the imperial conferences a formal instrument for maintaining a common imperial foreign policy were, however, frustrated. The Commonwealth came to function both as a financial entity and as a permanent alliance, as a voting bloc within the League of Nations on most issues, and as a limitation and a distraction in debates over British foreign policy.[26]

The development of interdepartmental cooperation under Fisher and Hankey (under whom the CID had ramified by the mid-1930s into more than one hundred interdepartmental committees charged with maintaining, improving and monitoring the nation's war-making capacities) considerably weakened the Foreign Office by establishing the Treasury, the Board of Trade and the Service Ministries firmly in the new fields of financial, commercial and strategic foreign policy. It was not until the aftermath of the naval crisis with the United States in 1927–8 that the Foreign Office established an expertise in matters of disarmament.[27] The Foreign Office did not acquire an Economic Section until 1934 and it remained puny in power by comparison with the Treasury and the Board of Trade.

The main drive of British foreign policy went inevitably into an attempt to restore the position of supremacy which Britain had

[26] Norman Hillmer, 'The Foreign Office, the Dominions and the Diplomatic Unity of the Empire', in D. Dilks (ed.), *Retreat from Power. Studies in British Foreign Policy of the Twentieth Century*, London, 1981; Norman Hillmer, 'The Anglo-Dominions Alliance, 1919–1939', in *15ᵉ Congrès International des Sciences Historiques, Rapports*, vol. III, Bucharest, 1980; Nicholas Mansergh, *Survey of British Commonwealth Affairs: Problems of External Policy, 1931–1939*, Oxford, 1952; D.C. Watt, *Personalities and Policies*, pp. 139–58; see also Hans E. Bärtschli, *Die Entwicklung vom imperialistischen Reichsgedankes zur modernen Idee des Commonwealths im Lebenswerk Lord Balfour*, Berne, 1957, esp. pp. 125–31, 136–8; H. Duncan Hall, 'The British Commonwealth of Nations in War and Peace', in William Y. Elliot and H.D. Hall (eds.), *The British Commonwealth at War*, New York, 1943; R.F. Holland, *Britain and the Commonwealth Alliance, 1918–1939*, London, 1981.

[27] The expert, significantly, was R.L. Craigie, of the American Department.

enjoyed outside Europe in 1914, especially in the fields of finance and trade. Under the dominant leadership of Montagu Norman at the Bank of England internationalism triumphed over the demands, both of traditional heavy industry and of the newer innovative industries, for some kind of protection against American competition.[28] Norman's quest which involved cooperation with American bankers to secure the economic recovery of Europe, but no more, depressed industrial growth and revival and exacerbated social conditions in Britain, without ever generating the strength to dispense with American cooperation. Indeed in 1927–8 Norman found himself confronted with the same incipient alliance between Paris and New York which frightened the Cabinet in the disarmament field and provided the basis for the Kellogg pact. In every sphere Britain's drive for recovery was confronted with the problem of the United States in one form or another.

British élites tended, therefore, to divide into four parties. There were the old-style nationalists, contemptuous of the United States and unable to reconcile themselves to the American intrusion into Britain's traditional fields of interest in Europe, in the Near and Middle East or elsewhere (Bonar Law, Curzon, Joynson-Hicks, Eyre Crowe, Austen Chamberlain and the Army and Air Ministry leaderships). Second was a numerically very limited but strategically important group of mid-Atlanticist Americophiles (Lord Balfour, Theodore Roosevelt's close friend, Lee of Fareham, at the Admiralty in 1921–2, Lloyd George's secretaries, John Grigg and Philip Kerr (later Lord Lothian), and, intermittently, Winston Churchill). There were those, overlapping with the Americophiles, who saw the hope of re-establishing British power exclusively in the transformation of the Empire, neo-imperialists of whom Hankey was perhaps the most strategically placed, Samuel Hoare during his days at the Air Ministry promoting air links throughout the Empire, and Amery. Finally, there was a larger, more amorphous group, best described as being 'in search of a possible America', that is an America which would fit that image of the power with which cooperation was most possible and most fitting. Which of the many possible Americas they chose depended on their own political orientation. A few (Ramsay MacDonald, Lord Robert Cecil, Lloyd George, even Churchill in some of

---

[28] This paragraph is based on the forthcoming work of Dr Robert Boyce. See also Costigliola, 'Anglo-American Financial Rivalry'.

his many moods and changes) looked towards cooperation with the Wilsonian 'Mugwump' America. More looked for the Anglophilia of a Theodore Roosevelt (Admiral Beatty in 1921–2, for example). Neo-imperialists occasionally looked for Americans who seemed willing to accept Dominion status.

From 1920 onwards, however, a growing conviction can be found among those in search of a 'possible America' that the United States in reality was hostile, inimical and above all 'foreign'.[29] The new generations of Americans were 'growing apart' from Britain.[30] This conviction developed at different speeds in differing sections of the élites. It did not really catch hold of the Admiralty until 1927 or about the same time as the Treasury and the Bank of England were beginning to acknowledge the hostility to the ambitions of the Bank of England of even seemingly the most Anglophile of New York bankers.[31] The limitations on their freedom of action including the increasing strength of the Dominions, Canada and South Africa particularly, where geographical or racialist factors made for a pro-American orientation of their foreign policy, enhanced the bitterness of the reaction. Anxiety and even talk of possible war[32] (especially among the élites of the older Armed Services[33] and among European observers, including Adolf Hitler)[34] flared up on two occasions, in 1920–1 and again in 1927–9. The first focused on conflicts of interest in Latin America, the Near and Middle East and the Far East and was largely settled by the Washington treaties of 1922. The second was largely ended by the joint initiatives of the Hoover and MacDonald governments (a major rôle being played by the return to national power of Henry Stimson as Secretary of State) and by the careful education of informed public opinion on both sides of the Atlantic by the mid-Atlanticists who had established

---

29 'Hitherto, it seems to me, we have been inclined to deal with the United States from a wrong angle. We have treated them too much as blood relations, not sufficiently as a foreign country.' Foreign Office memorandum, November 1927, cited in McKercher, 'The British Foreign-Policy-Making Elite'.
30 Vansittart, then head of the American Department, commented in 1927 on the decline of the 'Anglo-Saxon element in the total population of the United States'.
31 Costigliola, 'Anglo-American Financial Rivalry'.
32 'War is not unthinkable between the two countries', Craigie memorandum, 12 November 1927, FO 317/12812.
33 See, for example, Sir Esmé Howard to Austen Chamberlain, 1 September 1927, Austen Chamberlain Papers, AC 27.
34 See *Hitler's Secret Book*, London, 1961, p. 756.

themselves in the Council of Foreign Relations in New York and the Royal Institute of International Affairs in London, organisations which had been founded by the professional experts attached to the British and American delegations to the Paris Peace Conference of 1919.[35] The latter is noted for the first appearance of the university and research institution-based academic 'clerisy' which is perhaps still the strongest and most pertinent of all links between the two Anglophone cultures, at least at the élite level.

The flow of events in the period 1920–34 divides essentially into six sub-divisions, two periods of conflict (1919–23 and 1926–9), two of cooperation (1924–6 and 1929–31) and two sub-periods in the disastrous breakdown of American power which followed the 1929 crash.

The period of Anglo-American relations which followed the collapse of President Wilson's efforts to secure the ratification of the Treaty of Versailles was one in which the nationalists on each side very largely made the running. Whether over Ireland, the Middle East, in trade rivalry in South America, or over war debts, the Anglophobes in the United States and the imperial isolationists in Britain directed policy and dominated the press. The American bankers, the group most interested in European stability in the United States, were defeated in their initial attempts to use the war debts reparation issue as an entry point for American influence by the electoral terror of the US Treasury when faced with the necessity of recognising the relationship between the two.[36] The British government were able to defeat for a time American manoeuvres to dispossess Royal Dutch Shell of its dominance over the Venezuelan oil industry[37] and there was to be a long and bitter exchange of unpleasantnesses over the position Britain occupied *vis-à-vis* Iraqi and Iranian oil reserves.[38] There was equal unpleasantness over the control of the international

---

[35] For evidence see the correspondence between Philip Kerr, Lionel Curtis, Robert Buell, of the American Foreign Policy Association, Whitney Shephardson, Sir Robert Borden, Mr Bourdillon, Charles P. Howland of the Council for Foreign Relations, Walter Lippman, Sir Maurice Hankey, Professor Charles Webster 1927–9 in Lothian Papers, 'General Correspondence' and in special file, 'R.I.I.A. Anglo-American Relations'.

[36] Abrahams, 'American Bankers'.

[37] Stephen G. Rabe, 'Anglo-American Rivalry for Venezuelan Oil, 1919–1920', *Mid-America*, 57, 1976; see also Tulchin, *The Aftermath of War*.

[38] Hogan, *Informal Entente*, pp. 159–85.

cable network.[39] By far the most serious issues, however, were the threat posed to British naval supremacy by the two great US naval construction programmes of 1916 and 1918,[40] and the sword of Damocles hanging over all Britain's hopes of recovering the position of financial strength which London had enjoyed in 1914, the issue of Britain's war debts to the United States.[41]

British hopes of Lord Grey's mission as special envoy to the United States in 1918 were totally disappointed,[42] as were efforts to use Colonel House and the Morgan connections as mediators. A formal request for the cancellation of war debts was turned down by Wilson's Secretary of the Treasury in terms which angered the Cabinet. The accession to power of the Republicans was even more alarming, Sir Auckland Geddes reporting that the new administration was intent on supremacy and looked 'for the opportunity to treat us as a vassal state so long as the debt remains unpaid'.[43] On the naval issue and the Anglo-Japanese alliance, to which American nationalists and the American naval establishment took such strong exception,[44] for the sake of keeping Canada in the Empire the British government allowed themselves to be outmanoeuvred by an American administration which knew it had no hope of obtaining Congressional approval for completion of the existing naval construction programme.[45] Lloyd George's hopes of rebuilding British

[39] Tulchin, *The Aftermath of War*, pp. 205–33; this subject still lacks an adequate examination from the British side. But see Hogan, *Informal Entente*, pp. 105–28.

[40] Roskill, *British Naval Policy Between the Wars*, vol. I, pp. 90–1; Seth P. Tillman, *Anglo-American Relations at the Paris Peace Conference*, Princeton, 1961; J. Kenneth Macdonald, 'British Naval Policy and the Pacific and Far East. From Paris to Washington, 1919–1922', Oxford D.Phil., 1975.

[41] See, *inter aliis*, Melvyn G. Leffler, 'The Origins of Republican War Debt Policy, 1921–1923: A Case Study in the Applicability of the Open Door Concept', *J. Am. Hist.*, 59, 1972; Roberta Allbert Dayer, 'The British War Debts to the United States and the Anglo-Japanese Alliance, 1920–1923', *Pac. Hist. Rev.*, 45, 1976; Benjamin D. Rhodes, 'Herbert Hoover and the War Debts, 1919–1933', *Prologue*, 6, 1974.

[42] George W. Egerton, 'Britain and the "Great Betrayal": Anglo-American Relations and the Struggle for United States Ratification of the Treaty of Versailles, 1919–1920', *Hist. J.*, 21, 1978: Leon E. Boothe, 'A Fettered Envoy. Lord Grey's Mission to the United States, 1919–1920', *Rev. Pol.*, 33, 1971.

[43] Cited in Dayer, 'British War Debts'.

[44] US Navy war planners continued to plan for a Pacific war as if the Anglo-Japanese alliance were still a reality for ten years or more *after* its abrogation.

[45] The exclusion of the General Board of the US Navy from the later stages of the formulation of the naval disarmament proposals presented at Washington (of senior US naval officers only Admiral Coontz, the CNO, and Admiral Pratt were

predominance by integrating the 'economic' fragments of Europe into a 'commercial and financial community led by London',[46] on a basis not of gold but of a gold-exchange standard, were defeated when the Geneva Conference collapsed in April 1922; the American banking community's spokesman, Benjamin Strong, refused to participate in such a scheme, Poincaré replaced Briand and Weimar Germany made its own separate deal with Soviet Russia. The collapse of the Lloyd George government in October 1922 temporarily removed from power the extreme British nationalists, Churchill, Birkenhead, Austen Chamberlain, and Lloyd George himself, and cleared the way for the final British surrender, the very onerous settlement of Britain's war debts negotiated by Baldwin in January 1923.[47]

This 'surrender' represented on the American side the victory of an alliance between the New York banking community and the economic expansionists who followed Hoover's line of thought,[48] over the State Department, Treasury isolationists and the strategic nationalists ensconced in the General Board of the US Navy. On the British side it represented a victory of the anti-European isolationist wing of the Conservative party, allied with the leadership of the mercantile–financial community led by Montagu Norman of the Bank of England. For them the decision to abandon gold in March 1919 had always been a temporary expedient,[49] and the return to gold was an essential step in the recovery of London's pre-1914 financial pre-eminence.

The debts' settlement was followed, after the brief interruption of the first Labour government, by the reunification into the Conservative party's ranks of that part of the Coalition leadership which could be said to have Conservative attachments. Austen Chamberlain became Foreign Secretary, Churchill became Chancellor of the

involved) led the General Board within ten years or so to maintain that they were of British not American provenance. See General Board memorandum 488–2 of October 1932 in Admiral Hilary P. Jones Papers, Naval Historical Foundation, Box 259.

[46] Costigliola, 'Anglo-American Financial Rivalry'.
[47] Dayer, 'British War Debts'.
[48] Costigliola, 'Anglo-American Financial Rivalry'.
[49] *The Report of the Committee on Currency and Foreign Exchange after the War*, 15 December 1919, had recommended the return to the Gold Standard as soon as possible, a recommendation endorsed by the Chancellor of the Exchequer, Austen Chamberlain.

Exchequer and Birkenhead was Secretary of State for India. The first Labour government, however, was marked by three significant events. The first was the re-establishment of cordial relations with the American government.[50] The second was the wholehearted support of the British bankers in their cooperation with their American opposite numbers in the drafting and pressing through of the report of the Dawes Committee of Experts.[51] It is noticeable in this context that the British Treasury were far less enthusiastic about the bankers' cooperation than was MacDonald or Montagu Norman. The third event was MacDonald's rejection of the Draft Treaty of Mutual Guarantee, which sought to strengthen the peace-keeping aspects of the League of Nations, on advice from the military,[52] only to return to a similar version of the same proposals in the so-called Geneva Protocol. It was this document, when the incoming Baldwin government sought American reactions, which Charles Evans Hughes described in curiously hysterical terms as a 'New Holy Alliance'.[53] This rejection only served to confirm the Cabinet in a view to which they were inclined by instinct, by the advice of the Chiefs of Staff and by their increasing concern about Dominion isolationism,[54] after the failure of their efforts to secure machinery for the evolution of a common agreed foreign policy for the Empire.

The second Baldwin government were nevertheless to begin by doing their best to cultivate good relations with the United States, and to end in an almost total breakdown of Anglo-American relations, accompanied by back-stage anxieties about the probability of an Anglo-American war. Such a breakdown was always inherent in the mixture of attitudes to America displayed by the Cabinet and the professional foreign-policy-making élite. The Cabinet itself was a mixture of imperial isolationists, a few

---

[50] Coolidge to Kellogg, 15 February 1924, Coolidge Papers, Box 203.

[51] Schuler, *End of French Predominance. Financial Crisis 1924, passim*. The Dawes plan was largely drafted by Sir Josiah Stamp.

[52] For the Admiralty's objections see CP 311(23), 3 July 1923.

[53] David H. Burks, 'The United States and the Geneva Protocol of 1924: a "New Holy Alliance" ', *Am. Hist. Rev.*, 66, 1959. For a British record of the same conversation see Esmé Howard to Austen Chamberlain, 9 January 1925, Austen Chamberlain Papers, AC 25.

[54] The British evidence decisively rebuts the view of David S. Cheever and H. Field Havilland Jr, *Organising for Peace*, Boston, 1954, p. 126, that the American view was the major factor in the British decision to abandon neutrality.

Atlanticists (notably Viscount Cecil and Lord Eustace Percy) and Europe-facing traditionalists for whom America might be an ally or an associate in the difficult job of pacifying Europe if the American government were prepared to conform to their expectations. The difficulty for this group (the majority in the Cabinet) was the American reluctance so to perform and Coolidge's inability to control the various sections of the American élite, most notably the General Board of the Navy.

For all three sections of the British élite, America presented severe problems.[55] The imperial isolationists reacted bitterly to the American naval challenge, or put more accurately, to their colleagues' determination to take it seriously. Nor had they forgiven the Republican government for their war debts policy. The Atlanticists found, to their dismay, that Congress was congenitally responsive to the Anglophobes, as was the US press; Cecil, being a Wilsonian in his approach, found Kellogg difficult to deal with. Those whose first preoccupation was the security and stability in Europe needed the United States for any advance on the disarmament front, and had to find some way of circumventing the possible hostility of the United States in the event of the League Council instituting sanctions against a state in breach of the Covenant. All of this took place against a background of the latent but easily aroused resentment felt by the British public against the United States.[56]

The Baldwin government had, however, or so they thought, established a reliable working arrangement with President Coolidge, on whose honesty and goodwill the British Ambassador in Washington reported most fulsomely,[57] and had learnt from the successful

---

[55] For the following analysis see McKercher, 'British Foreign-Policy-Making Elite'.

[56] For Foreign Office views on this point see the minutes by Robert Craigie, 12 October 1925, FO 371/10646, and Hirst, 20 October 1926. The Foreign Office was supplied with weekly analyses of American press opinion by the British Library of Information in New York. According to Vansittart, the 'sub-editor of one of the cheaper [British news]papers' told him, 'he could at any time double his circulation by open hostility to America'. Minute 7 November 1927, FO 317/12041.

[57] Howard to Chamberlain, 6 November 1925, Austen Chamberlain Papers, AC 53. The Foreign Office had a much lower opinion of Kellogg, and of his successor, Alanson Houghton. On Kellogg see Austen Chamberlain to Howard, 28 January 1925 – 'a somewhat tired man who had lost his grip and decision and ... very much dependent on the advice of his staff', Austen Chamberlain Papers, AC 50; on Houghton, see Robert Cecil to Austen Chamberlain, 22 April 1925, 'when he comes here he will be nearly as tiresome as Harvey'. Ambassador Lord d'Abernon

negotiations on American war claims against Britain that, provided matters were kept low-key and at the professional level, quite unpublicised diplomacy could well bring about agreement.[58] The Baldwin government had equal success in smoothing the way for American participation in the Preparatory Commission to the Disarmament Conference. The return to the Gold Standard was not so happy an experience. Despite Norman's determination to bring it about, the manner in which it occurred (involving a victory by the Bank of England and the merchant banks over the joint stock banks, the clearing banks with their connections with industry, the Federation of British Industry and the National Farmers' Union) would have been disruptive in itself. But more alarming for the future was the evidence that, had Britain not returned to gold, South Africa, Australia and Canada would have done so anyway, linking themselves irretrievably with the dollar.

The breakdown in 1927–9 came as a result of three separate sets of developments. On the industrial level French and German economic cooperation against the increasingly ominous intervention of American bankers and industrialists in Europe, and the failure of British interests to negotiate their entry into this cooperation, strengthened demands for an imperial industrial bloc, which in three areas, rubber, cotton and cinematographs, led to strong American reaction not against Europe but against British activities. Norman found that to maintain the Gold Standard made him more rather than less dependent on American support, especially after the collapse and restabilisation of the franc in 1926–7 had led to direct Franco-American cooperation and the bypassing of the League of Nations Economic Committee which Norman had chosen as the instrument by which, under London's control, American money could be used to stabilise Europe. Instead the Bank of England was confronted with a Bank of International Settlements under American dominance with French support.[59] And in the field of

reported Houghton to be 'one of those Americans who believes or affects to believe that the English Government is in deep design [*sic*] and disregard of conventional morality, something between Machiavelli and Mephistopheles', adding, however, that 'this conviction has not prevented him from cooperating broadly with British Policy during his Embassy in Berlin'. Austen Chamberlain Papers, AC 52.

58 McKercher, 'The British Foreign-Policy-Making Elite'.
59 Costigliola, 'Anglo-American Financial Rivalry'; Leffler, 'Political Isolationism'; Leffler, *The Elusive Quest: European Stability*; Frank C. Costigliola, 'The Other

disarmament, the breakdown of the Geneva Conference in 1927 led to the publication of Anglo-American differences in a manner which destroyed the political confidence each government had in the other's trustworthiness.[60] The breach was rubbed in by little details such as the American conclusion of an Arbitration Treaty with the nominally independent but British occupied Kingdom of Egypt, and the opening of direct, though not necessarily official, diplomatic contacts between Washington and Ottawa,[61] and Canberra.[62]

Of all these developments, however, the naval breakdown was the worst. On the American side it can be traced to the abandonment by Coolidge and Kellogg of that strict control of the US Navy leadership which had made the Washington agreements possible and which, when reactivated by Stimson in 1929, was to pave the way for the London Naval Treaty of 1930.[63] On the British side the drafting of the British scheme was left to an Admiralty which had successfully defied the Treasury in 1925 over the cruiser construction programme. As a result Admiral Hilary P. Jones, the principal American Naval delegate and a convinced pan-Anglo-Saxonist in his earlier years, came to believe that Admiral Beatty had deliberately deceived him as to the chances of an agreement.[64] And the Admiralty, the

Side of Isolationism: The Establishment of the First World Bank', *J. Am. Hist.*, 59, 1972.

[60] See, for example, the minute of 28 October 1925 by Sir Cecil Hirst: 'The debts and similar claims on the part of the United States have already made the average Englishman think the Americans are dirty swine', FO 371/10646; and of Thompson, 29 October 1928: 'Mr Hoover is nothing less than a cold aggressive nationalist – an efficient calculating machine who will push commercial and maritime competition with this country to the utmost', FO 371/12812.

[61] See Willingdon to Baldwin, 9 August 1927; Willingdon to George V, 13 February 1928, both in PREM 1/65; Willingdon to Baldwin, 6 November 1977, Baldwin Papers, vol. 96. See also P.G. Wrigley, *Canada and the Transition to Commonwealth. British–Canadian Relations, 1917–1936*, Cambridge, 1977; P. Kaswak, 'American Foreign Policy Officials and Canada, 1927–1941: A Look Through Bureaucratic Glasses', *International J.*, 32, 1977.

[62] See Craigie to Australian High Commissioner in London, 18 February, 6 March 1919, FO 371/13519; M. Ruth Megaw, 'Undiplomatic Channels: Australian Representatives in the United States, 1918–1939', *Hist. Studies* (Melbourne), 15, no. 60, 1973.

[63] According to the secretary of the American delegation to the Geneva Naval Conference, its chairman, Hugh Gibson, had to spend 'a great deal more of his time convincing his friends, than his enemies'. Hugh R. Wilson to Castle, 16 December 1927, Hugh Wilson Papers.

[64] Kellogg to Coolidge, 10 August 1927, SD 500.A 15al/573c, FRUS *1927*, vol. I, pp. 157–9.

majority of the Cabinet, and much of the British press came to the conclusion that taking any notice of American views in international affairs was an exercise in unreality which a beleaguered and struggling Britain simply could not afford.[65] The conflict was greatly exacerbated the following year by the negotiation, in alarm at the possibility of an American–French *rapprochement*, of a set of Anglo-French proposals which would have restricted construction of those kinds of warship favoured by the US Navy (of which they possessed in 1927 not a single example) while allowing unlimited construction of the types of warship Britain favoured.[66]

The 1927 Conference unleashed the most bitter press war, fanned by the presence on the British delegation of an official of the Foreign Office press department (an 'ungentlemanly act' bitterly resented by the American side)[67] and by the action for the Americans of a Mr William Shearer[68] who, two years later, sued various US armament firms for the non-payment of a $50,000 fee for his work in the break-up of the Conference. The Geneva correspondent of the *New York Times*, Wythe Williams, was later reported to have been reminded by his editor that he was reporting a disarmament con-

[65] This view was expressed very strongly by Admiral Lord Beatty, the retiring First Sea Lord, Beatty to Keyes, 6 [August 1927] *Keyes Papers*, ed. Paul G. Halpern, vol. II, *1919–1938*, London, 1981; by Bridgeman, First Lord of the Admiralty, Bridgeman Journal, and in *J. Royal Inst. Int. Affairs*, V, 1928; and by Winston Churchill, who wrote to Bridgeman on 22 December 1926: 'I am no longer prepared to take dictation from the US and if they attempt to bully us by threatening a large programme I hope I shall be able to range myself with you and Beatty...obviously the President does not want to build, only to bluff and bluster.' Martin Gilbert (ed.), *Churchill, Companion Volume*, 3, London, 1979, pp. 899–901.

[66] On the 1928 naval compromise see Carlton, 'The Anglo-French Compromise'; Roskill, *Naval Policy*, vol. I, pp. 498–516; McKercher, 'The British Foreign-Policy-Making Elite'.

[67] Gibson to Castle, 30 September 1928, RG 59, SD 500.A15 Franco-British. Gibson T.19 to State Dept, 21 June 1927, SD 500.A15A1/303, also copy with Kellogg's minute in Coolidge Papers, file 20.

[68] On Shearer's activities at Geneva see US Naval Historical Foundation, Admiral Schofield Diary, entries of 1, 8, 20 July 1927. *The Times*, 5 July 1927, carried a report on his activities which when picked up by the London Correspondent of the *New York Times* led Kellogg to address an enquiry to Hugh Gibson, *FRUS 1927*, vol. I, pp. 960–97. Gibson replied that he knew of 'no one answering the description', *FRUS 1927*, vol. I, p. 106, a statement which was almost certainly a lie.

ference not a battlefield.[69] In the aftermath of the Conference the Foreign Office succeeded in persuading the Cabinet to undertake the most serious review of the issue of belligerent rights, in reaction to misleading information from the United States that this was the real issue.[70] The discussion greatly divided the Cabinet and the foreign-policy-making establishment, leading to bitter charges of appeasement[71] and snide comments about Foreign Office officials being unable to face their American wives across the breakfast table.[72] The unfortunate Craigie was the subject of the most ferocious attacks from, among others, Winston Churchill.[73] As for the admirals, Admiral Sir Roger Keyes looked forward with hope to commanding the British fleet in battle against the US Navy should it attempt to interfere with Britain's blockade of an aggressor.[74] Admiral Pound felt that Commander Locker-Lampson (RN retired, MP and the Parliamentary Under Secretary in the Foreign Office) had 'cold feet' and 'should be hung as a traitor'.[75]

[69] On Wythe Williams see his own account, *Dusk of Europe*, London, 1937, pp. 250–5; see also Howard to Austen Chamberlain, 23 June 1927, Austen Chamberlain Papers, AC 57; Chamberlain memorandum of talk with US Ambassador, 8 July 1928, Austen Chamberlain Papers, AC 50; Kellogg to Geneva, 11 July 1927, *FRUS 1927*, vol. I, p. 93; Bowen, 'The Disarmament Movement'.

[70] The information came in part from Colonel House and reflected his wartime concerns, and in part from General Preston Brown, US Army, commanding the Boston military district. Howard to Tyrrell, in Austen Chamberlain Papers.

[71] Hankey to Tom Jones, October 1928 in T. Jones, *A Whitehall Diary*, II, pp. 147–9.

[72] Bridgeman Journal, entry July 1929. Both Craigie and Vansittart were married to American wives as was Lindsay, then Permanent Under Secretary. Lady Craigie, as she was to become, was a formidable advocate of British sea power. Her occasional *rencontres* with American admirals on the subject are legendary.

[73] *DBFP*, Ia, vol. V, pp. 857–75, memorandum of 12 November 1928. Churchill's own views were set out very trenchantly in his memorandum to the Cabinet of 20 July 1927: 'No doubt it is quite right in the interests of peace to go on talking about war with the United States being "unthinkable". Everyone knows this is not true. However foolish and disastrous such a war would be, it is, in fact, the only basis upon which the naval discussions at Geneva are proceeding. We do not wish to put ourselves in the power of the United States. We cannot tell what they might do if, at some future date, they were in a position to give us orders about our policy, say, in India or Egypt, or Canada or any other great matter behind which their electioneering forces were marshalled ... I would neither trust America to command, nor England to submit.' Gilbert, *Churchill, Companion Volume*, 5.

[74] Keyes to Churchill, 20 January 1928, Paul G. Halpern (ed.), *Keyes Papers*, vol. II, *1919–1938*, London, 1981.

[75] Pound to Keyes, pp. 237–9, 19 December, 1927, *Keyes Papers*, vol. II, pp. 234–6. See also Pound to Keyes, 24 January 1928, pp. 239–41. Diary of Admiral Sir Barry Domville, entries for 18 October, 15 November 1927. Sir Maurice Hankey

In all this turmoil the Kellogg pact passed on the British side of the
Atlantic as a total irrelevancy, on which the United States government would have to be humoured, once the initial alarm at what
seemed still more evidence of American preference for France as
against Britain as her major point of contact with Europe had
passed. The major problem was still that of American power and
what the Foreign Office and Austen Chamberlain felt to be the total
lack of any single policy in the driving seat.[76] Baldwin was said to
have come to loathe the Americans so much that he could not bear
meeting them.[77]

In 1929 both governments changed. Hoover abandoned the
Department of Commerce for the Presidency and appointed Henry
Stimson, a notorious and determined advocate of Anglo-American
cooperation, as his Secretary of State. Two months later the Baldwin
government, defeated in the British general election, made way for
the second Labour government. Despite a formidable warning from
Baldwin to his successor – 'The American money power is trying to
get hold of the natural resources of the Empire. They are working
like beavers'[78] – MacDonald was to make the restoration of good
Anglo-American relations his first priority. Stimson, whose views on
the American Navy Department were scathing,[79] shared this view.[80]
He very quickly took steps to see that 'the deciding power was in the
hands of civilians rather than naval experts'.[81] He was much aided in
this by the succession as Chief of Naval Operations of Admiral
William Veazie Pratt, USN,[82] a disciple of Sims, a dedicated Anglophile and a man who had decided that any international agreement

cast similar aspersions on *The Times*, Hankey Diary, entry 12–18 November
1928.

[76] 'Has anyone in the State Department or Administration thought out American
interests or American policy? Have they any machinery for thinking out such
questions? I fear the answer to both questions is "No".' Chamberlain to Howard,
14 January 1929, Austen Chamberlain Papers, AC 57.

[77] Neville Chamberlain Papers, note of December 1927.

[78] Tom Jones, *A Whitehall Diary*, II, entry of 8 March 1928.

[79] See H. Stimson and W. McGeorge Bundy, *On Active Service in Peace and War*,
London, 1948, p. 506. It 'frequently seemed to retire from the realm of logic into a
dim religious world where Neptune was God, Mahon his prophet and the United
States Navy the one true Church'.

[80] Stimson and Bundy, *On Active Service*, p. 164.

[81] Stimson to Howard, 9 May 1929: SD 500. A15A3/1: see also *FRUS 1929*, vol. I,
pp. 112–13.

[82] Wheeler, *Prelude to Pearl Harbor*, passim.

was better than none as it would, so he believed, oblige Congress to find funds actually to construct the ships, the construction of which was approved by ratification of an international agreement. Pratt brought forward younger naval officers who were far from accepting established Navy dogma on the size and gun calibre of US naval vessels.[83] Stimson consulted the admirals of the General Board one by one so as to avoid a collective statement of their views. And when the London Naval Treaty once signed was bitterly challenged by the General Board in Congress, both men made sure that the congressional committees were presented with the bewilderingly wide range of the various schools of thought that the doctrinal practices of the General Board had suppressed. The General Board conceded and as a power in US naval policy never recovered.[84] MacDonald on his side overbore the unhappy successors of Beatty as First Sea Lord, Admirals Field and Madden, who, like Pratt, salved their consciences by reflecting that the abandonment of paper claims might just possibly result in the Royal Navy getting real ships. Most importantly he succeeded in his famous visit to America in October 1929 not only in establishing relations of cordiality with Hoover and Stimson, but also in extracting from the US Navy an admission that the obsolete British naval bases in the West Indies represented no real threat to American security.[85] The way was clear for Anglo-American cooperation first on the conclusion of the London Naval Treaty and then in the preliminaries for the World Disarmament Conference. For MacDonald France rather than America was the threat to peace and British security.

In this he was undoubtedly mistaken. A far more serious threat to the whole fragile fabric of Anglo-American cooperation had virtually coincided with his visit to Washington. The Wall Street crash was to destroy American power for a decade. Its effect was particularly damaging to the commercial–mercantile financial community of New York whose financial penetration of Europe and Britain had at least provided grounds on which Britain and the United States could cooperate. The Smoot–Hawley tariff in itself represented a victory for the economic nationalism of small-scale,

---

[83] Wheeler, *Prelude to Pearl Harbor* pp. 300–20.
[84] Jay Pierrepont Moffat Diary, entry of 14 July 1931.
[85] See D.C. Watt, 'American Strategic Interests and Anxieties in the West Indies, 1912–1940', *J. Royal United Services Institute*, 108, 1963.

localised business as against the growing power of the multinationals.[86] The central power of the New York Federal Bank which
Benjamin Strong had wielded with such dexterity was challenged by
its much less internationalist fellow bankers. The American
economy had depended on the constant injection of new capital and
on constant expansion of production and markets. The destruction
of mobile capital in the crash and its long drawn out aftermath
brought economic activity in the United States down to catastrophic
levels. Unemployment multiplied.

The consequences were to spread throughout Europe. Without
the annual flood of dollar investments, what investment money
remained in Europe ran for cover to Paris. The gold holdings of the
Bank of Paris rose to mountainous heights. Those of the Bank of
England, where Norman laboured mightily to keep the ideal of
central bank cooperation in being, did not. The Bank of England's
reserves went to bolster those of Austria and Germany. And when
the Vienna Credit-Anstalt bank failed, followed by the Dresdener
Bank in Germany, the resulting pressure on the Bank of England was
too great. Collapse was temporarily staved off with American and
French money, made available on terms which broke the Labour
government and led to the establishment of the National government under MacDonald. Six weeks later the same National
government, economic internationalism defeated and broken, abandoned the Gold Standard for a managed exchange. This was to be
followed by the negotiation of a system of imperial protection and of
countervailing duties to protect British industry against foreign
'dumping'.

The financial crisis had seen Hoover's last effort to maintain
financial internationalism and with it the stability of Europe. In the
words of the Washington Embassy's annual report for 1931,[87] the
Hoover moratorium 'delayed too long and then harshly and without
due forethought sprung upon an unprepared though mainly
appreciative world. It failed of its immediate and full effect and its
author, deceived, disappointed and ever fearful of Congress, re-
adjusted his attitude and his conventions to the isolationism that is
better suited to both his temperament and his politics.' Hoover's

[86] On the opposition to the 1930 tariff see Joan Hoff Wilson, *American Business*, pp.
      94–6. His concern for small business led President Hoover to support the tariff.
[87] FO 371/15874.

return to isolationism was marked for the British by the equivocal rôle he played in the Manchurian–Shanghai crisis of 1931–2[88] and by the manner in which his insistence on reverting to public diplomacy aimed at domestic opinion 'torpedoed' the World Disarmament Conference in the summer of 1932.[89] The course of the Manchurian–Shanghai crisis not only revealed the fundamental distrust with which the new leaders at the Foreign Office[90] had come to regard the United States as a potential ally after the 1927–9 crisis, despite the part the Foreign Office had played in negotiating the subsequent *rapprochement*,[91] but also created a great gulf of misunderstanding arising out of what Stimson saw as the British failure to back his non-recognition note of 7 January 1932.[92] Underlying this misunderstanding, however, it is apparent, there lay the deeper resentment of a generation for whom America's rôle in the First World War and during the prolonged pressure on the British government throughout the 1920s to assume automatic obligations in support of the League (not to mention the war debts and naval disarmament issues) had left a deep and abiding hostility towards the United States. The view that the United States' government habitually mistook high-sounding rhetoric for action, and that to follow American sentiments would imply for Britain the hazards of counteraction by those against whom the sentiments were expressed, without any hope of America translating sentiment into reality, took hold of the Cabinet, the Foreign Office, the Treasury and the Chiefs of Staff.[93]

[88] See Christopher Thorne, *The Limits of Foreign Policy. The West, the League and the Far Eastern Crisis of 1931–1933*, London, 1972.

[89] On the Hoover message of 22 June 1932 to the Disarmament Conference see Stimson Diary, entries of 24, 25 May, 3, 18, 19, 21 and 23 June 1932; Norman Davis Papers, Box 20, records of 19 and 21 June 1932.

[90] Sir Robert Vansittart, head of the American Department of the Foreign Office, 1927–8, succeeded Sir Ronald Lindsay as Permanent Under Secretary in the Foreign Office in 1929 on Lindsay's apointment to the Washington Embassy in 1930.

[91] See, for example, Vansittart's memorandum of May 1931, 'The Foreign Policy of the Empire', Vansittart Papers; and of January 1932, CP4/22, CAB 27/476 cited in Thorne, *Limits*, p. 123.

[92] R.A. Hecht, 'Great Britain and the Stimson Note of 7 January 1932', *Pac. Hist. Rev.*, 38, 1969; Thorne, *Limits*, pp. 247–8, footnotes 1 and 6; Sir John Pratt, *War and Politics in China*, London, 1943, pp. 225–8; R.N. Current, 'The Stimson Doctrine and the Hoover Doctrine', *Am. Hist. Rev.*, 59, 1953–4; Thorne, 'The Shanghai Crisis of 1932: The Bases of British Policy', *Am. Hist. Rev.*, 75, 1970.

[93] This was the occasion for Baldwin's famous remark, 'You will get nothing out of Washington but words: long words, but only words', Thorne, *Limits*, p. 247.

On top of this débâcle and despite the continuing close co-operation of Stimson and his new assistant, Norman Davis, with MacDonald and the British negotiators at the World Disarmament Conference, the differing reactions of Britain and the United States to the economic crisis were destroying the social basis of their cooperation. For America there seemed no end to the downhill slide of the economy.[94] For the British Cabinet, the defeat of the economic internationalists and the management of sterling by the Exchequer, were leading inevitably towards partial economic recovery, tariffs and imperial economic nationalism. Just as inevitably, given the collapse of constitutional government in Germany, the European powers, with Britain at their head, were led to revive the war debts and reparations issue. Indeed it was the news of the cancellation of reparations at Lausanne which drove Hoover into overriding Stimson's opposition and dispatching his 'message' to the Disarmament Conference with the aim of showing that armaments expenditure, not war debts, was the cause of the European slump.[95] Any hope of American action on the debts issue in the political climate in the election year of 1932 was completely unrealistic. But with the delivery of the Hoover message, with its revival in an acute form both of the practice of appealing to the American electorate rather than the foreign partner and of the naval issue in Anglo-American relations, there was nothing to do but adjourn the conference. And with its adjournment the United States lost its one remaining source of power over European politics.

The electoral victory of the Democrats, and the long 'lame-duck' session of Congress and defeated President which followed, despite all Stimson's vain efforts to educate the incoming President in the realities of international politics,[96] saw the new incumbent fall decisively under the influence of those who argued that America did not really require the international economy and that America's

[94] On 7 February 1932, Stimson confided to his diary that the United States was 'in an emergency like war', Stimson Diary, entry of 7 February 1932.

[95] Stimson Diary, note of 19 June 1932: Record of transatlantic telephone conversation between Hoover, Stimson, Gibson and Norman Davis, 19 June 1932, Norman Davis Papers, Box 20. The American refusal to attend the Lausanne Conference stymied British attempts to divert the meeting from the simple issue of the 'connection between reparations and war-debts'. See T. McCulloch, 'Anglo-American Economic Diplomacy and the European Crisis, 1933–1939', Oxford D.Phil., 1978.

[96] These may be followed in detail in the Stimson Diaries.

economic recovery could not wait on that of world trade.[97] In 1892 and 1896 the Populists had called for the separation of America's economy from that of the rest of the world by the abandonment of the Gold Standard for bimetallism. In the intervening period American agriculture had become one of the few sectors of the American economy that was fundamentally dependent on world trade and the level of world prices for primary products. Radical economic isolationism had, however, persisted, and the crude economic doctrines of Populism became the refined economic nationalism of the Chicago economists. When Roosevelt took over, the American banking system was undergoing a devastating series of failures and unemployment stood at an all-time high. Yet the American gold reserves in Fort Knox were astronomical and the American trade balance with the rest of the world was extremely positive. The first New Deal fed the unemployed, found them jobs, put a halt to the worst excesses of the cut, burn and run school of American agriculture. But the economic isolationism it practised destroyed much of American agricultural productive capacity, without in any way strengthening or reviving the American economy or rebuilding its capital investment. When the American economy took off again, as it did from 1940 onwards, it was under the stimulus of war and a substantial amount of the capital investment which fuelled that take-off was provided by British war orders (a Marshall plan in reverse almost).

The period in which economic nationalism dominated Franklin Roosevelt's views was a limited one – two to three years at most. His incoming Secretary of State, Cordell Hull, believed so firmly in the classic doctrines of international trade as the alternative to war that he was to write in his memoirs that had the Anglo-American trade agreement of 1938 been signed four years earlier there would have been no Second World War.[98] But the recovery of economic internationalism in America was to come too late. The crucial period was the summer of 1933 and the World Economic Conference.

The Foreign Office had been the more inclined to welcome Roosevelt's nomination as their view of Hoover became more

[97] See Elliot A. Rosen, 'Intranationalism v. Internationalism: The Interregnum Struggle for the Sanctity of the New Deal', *Pol Sci Q.*, 81, 1966.

[98] Cordell Hull, *Memoirs*, vol. I, London, 1948, p. 530; see also Arthur W. Schatz, 'The Anglo-American Trade Agreements and Cordell Hull's Search for Peace, 1936–1938,' *J. Am. Hist.*, 57, 1970.

critical,[99] and as the war debts issue appeared increasingly as the central obstacle to Britain's financial recovery. The decision to meet the December 1932 payment had already divided the Cabinet between the Treasury and the President of the Board of Trade.[100] Sir Ronald Lindsay wooed the President-elect, seeking an early meeting between him and Ramsay MacDonald. Even Roosevelt's inaugural, with its clear warning that his administration would put American economic recovery before that of the European–American economy which had emerged in the 1920s, was welcomed. But the debts issue was irretrievably bound up in American thinking, with images of the money and banking élites on whose machinations the Wall Street crash and the slump were blamed. It was Cordell Hull who sought to enlist MacDonald's prestige to influence American opinion;[101] Congress in the meantime was blocking Norman Davis's appointment as Roosevelt's representative at the Disarmament Conference because of his long-standing connections with the house of J.P. Morgan. The British records show that the Cabinet strategy at this time pinned everything on avoiding an Anglo-American crisis. A British default over the war debt payments was narrowly avoided in June by the device of Roosevelt declaring that a token payment of $10 million would not be regarded as a default, a demonstration, if one were needed, that Roosevelt and Hull did not wish gratuitously to bring about a breach; but the breach was to be unavoidable. British policy was to aim for a stabilisation of currency values and commodity prices, and a reduction of tariffs, with a resumption of international lending as soon as possible thereafter. Roosevelt had no control over Congress; his advisers in Washington were divided; and no one in the new administration really understood the degree to which the British proposals represented the last stand of economic internationalism in Britain.

Roosevelt's decision to devalue the dollar, his repudiation of the

---

99 On Hoover's famous 'Grass will grow in the streets' (if Roosevelt is elected) speech, delivered at Madison Square Gardens, New York, on 31 October 1932, immediately before the election, the young Frank Roberts minuted, 'This is Mr Hoover's last and most devastatingly inept appearance in the role of the Fat Boy.' FO 371/15875, 17 November 1932, cited in McCulloch 'Anglo-American Diplomacy'.

100 Lord Runciman, President of the Board of Trade, commented, 'Instinct told them to pay and reason not', CAB 23/73 63[32], 28 November 1932.

101 Lindsay to Foreign Office, telegrams 175 and 176 of 24 March 1933, FO 371/16669, cited McCulloch, 'Anglo-American Diplomacy'.

agreement on stabilisation concluded during the London Economic Conference between the financial members of the American delegation, Neville Chamberlain, and Bonnet for the French, and the gratuitous insult contained in his message of 2 July 1933, dispatched from the deck of the USS *Annapolis*, in consultation with Louis Howe and Henry Morgenthau, made the break inevitable. The British assumption was that they were dealing with a bunch of ignorant and opportunist amateurs, for whose failures Britain and Europe would provide the obvious scapegoat.[102] Roosevelt, it was felt, was turning away towards Latin America where an American trade drive to capture British markets was expected.[103] The subsequent negotiations on British war debts were unhappy,[104] the resignations of Dean Acheson and Oliver Sprague were taken as ominous evidence of the victory of the Anglophobes, William Bullitt and Louis Howe, in Roosevelt's entourage.[105] The Gold Reserve Act of January 1934, which set up an American equivalent to the British Exchange Equalisation Fund, was expected to lead to a 'gigantic struggle' between the two funds, and the Johnson Act, which forbade the raising of any loans in America by governments adjudged in default on their existing loans, was the final insult.[106] The way was open for the British default, despite Foreign Office warning. 'Whether you take the politician, the economist or the banker', wrote Sir Frederick Leith-Ross, the Cabinet's chief financial adviser, in May 1934 to Sir Ronald Lindsay,[107] 'I believe the overwhelming majority would now either welcome a complete suspension of payments or regard it as inevitable ... [the change in opinion is] most marked in the City where American monetary experiments are resented'. British default accompanied by the brusquest of notes drafted by the Treasury, whose 'heavy hand' the Foreign Office deplored,[108] followed inevitably, despite Roosevelt's efforts to devise some kind of

---

[102] Lindsay to Foreign Office, 27 July 1933, FO 371/16600; Vansittart memorandum to MacDonald, MacDonald Papers, PRO 30/69/1/3214.

[103] Minutes by MacDonald, Roberts and Craigie, 2–3 August 1933, FO 371/16618.

[104] McCulloch, 'Anglo-American Diplomacy'.

[105] Lindsay to Foreign Office, telegram 621 of 15 November 1933; Lindsay to Craigie, 22 November 1933, FO 371/16600.

[106] Davis to F.D. Roosevelt, 6 November 1934.

[107] T.188/75, 7 May 1934, cited in McCulloch, 'Anglo-American Diplomacy'.

[108] CAB 23/79, 22(34)2 of 30 May 1934; Wellesley minute, 3 July 1934, FO 371/17587.

cosmetic disguise for the act.[109] 'The Cabinet had momentarily decided that Americans might find themselves confronted with a situation in which [British] goodwill towards themselves might be of great importance',[110] a lapse into the higher lunacy of surprising proportions.

The Cabinet was influenced in this view by the looming signs of trouble in the Far East where the Japanese intention of denouncing the Washington and London naval treaties was becoming more and more apparent as the final date for such denunciation approached. The Japanese army in Manchuria was steadily spreading its influence throughout the five provinces of northern China. There was talk of a rearmament programme of staggering proportions. The need to renew the Naval Arms Limitation system of the 1920s was clear. On this one ground, and this alone, the necessity of Anglo-American cooperation might possibly overcome the injured pride, the mutual suspicions and the feelings of personal betrayal which the events of 1933 had written so deeply into the attitudes of the new foreign-policy-making élites on both sides of the Atlantic.

[109] Lindsay to Foreign Office, telegram 158 of 18 May 1934, FO 371/17586.
[110] Simon to Lindsay, telegram 113 of 30 April 1934, FO 371/17586, McCulloch, 'Anglo-American Diplomacy'. This telegram was the joint work of Vansittart and Sir Frederick Leith-Ross, and approved before dispatch by Neville Chamberlain, Simon, Baldwin and MacDonald.

4

1934–1940

From the deficiency requirements programme to the Churchill coalition; the failure of Britain's 'Little Europe' policy

The thirteen years between 1934 and 1947 are usually taken to comprehend at least four separate historical periods, pre-war, European war, world war and cold war. To treat them as a single unity or to divide them into less than four periods seems at first sight profoundly unhistorical. By the microhistorical standards applied to the writing of twentieth-century historical monographies this is no doubt true. But from the point of view of the participants these thirteen years were a unity of experience. And from the point of view of this study this feeling of unity is confirmed by the very considerable degree of continuity observable in the membership of the policy-making élites. The only real change observable occurred not in 1939, 1941 or 1945, but in the summer of 1940 when the membership of the élites was enormously widened. This was a result of the defeat of France and the successful demonstration of Britain's ability and determination to continue the war which led to an enormous increase, in both Britain and America, in the scope and number of the various groups active in various aspects of that 'total foreign policy' which is the political concomitant of total war.

In Britain, the entry of the Labour and Liberal opposition into coalition with the Conservatives, at whose head Winston Churchill had replaced Neville Chamberlain, was of importance principally in securing that Churchill's electoral defeat in 1945 involved no very major breach in the conduct and outlook of British foreign policy. The political changes in 1940 were much more important in British domestic politics than they were in Britain's relations with America or Europe. The machinery of the Chiefs of Staff, the Treasury and the Foreign Office continued unchanged. The removal from office between 1938 and 1940 of Sir Maurice Hankey, Sir Warren Fisher and Sir Horace Wilson among senior civil servants; of Admiral Lord Chatfield, Generals Gort and Ironside at the Chiefs of Staff level; of Leslie Hore-Belisha, Sir Samuel Hoare and (in so far as like Sir Samuel Hoare he was exiled to an embassy, albeit in Washington) Lord Halifax is much more significant; as is, on the diplomatic plane, the disappearance from active policy-making between 1938 and 1941 of Lord Perth, Sir Robert Vansittart, Sir Nevile Henderson, Sir Robert Craigie, Sir William Seeds, Sir Ronald Lindsay and Lord Perth's successor in Rome, Sir Percy Loraine. But Churchill's reorganisation of the machinery of government and of Anglo-American relations was to draw into the ranks of those who advised on policy whole platoons of new administrators, dealing with trade, purchases, financial relations, scientific relations and so on, as well as academic economists, university historians and even philosophers (the future Sir Isaiah Berlin).

On the American side the field is dominated by President Roosevelt until his death in April 1945. Some of his Cabinet continued to serve under Truman until the gulf between his adjustment to the new perils presented by West European weakness and Soviet counter-pressure led to a parting of the ways between the new President and the survivors of Roosevelt's New Deal Cabinets of the pre-war era, Harold Ickes, Henry Morgenthau and Henry Wallace, for example. Some American revisionist historians have made much of the abandonment of the impetus of the New Deal under the pressures of approaching war and the inflow into Washington of the so-called 'economic royalists'; obsessed by the notion that the 'cold war' of the 1950s and the 1960s was a bilateral Soviet–American confrontation between populist–revolutionary socialism and monopoly imperialist capitalism, they have spread abroad a version of the events of the years 1944–7 in which Britain does not figure at all and the Soviet leadership is a totally un-self-motivated conception, the dynamic for whose actions is provided entirely by reaction to American policy.

Such 'cultural imperialism' (that is, as practised by revisionist historians rather than that practised by President Truman and his advisers) tells us much about the perceptions of some of the most influential schools of American historiography, though little to their credit. But as an account of the course of United States policy between the death of President Roosevelt and the decisive turn of American policy against Europe and the Soviet Union involved in the events of 1946–7, it is more than a little misleading. Indeed, from the point of view of Anglo-American relations the significant new entrants into the foreign-policy-making process in 1940 are the military, the scientists and the New Deal domestic bureaucracy quite as much as the mercantile–financial–industrialist elements identified as 'economic royalists'. Indeed the dominant ideology in matters economic and financial with which Britain had to cope in the years 1945–7 was the same as in the 1930s: the economic liberalism, the hostility to trade blocs, tariff groupings and the sterling area of Cordell Hull, Henry Morgenthau, the US State Department and the Treasury. The most significant figure with whom British policy-makers in this field had to reckon, America's answer to Lord Keynes, was an alleged Soviet informant, Harry Dexter White.

In analysing the generational element in the élites on both sides of the Atlantic in this period the division into four main groups is clearer and more apparent than in any of the preceding periods here analysed, and remarkably parallel in each country. The first and most senior consists of those who held high office *before 1919*: Chamberlain, Churchill, Simon, Beaverbrook, Franklin Roosevelt, Josephus Daniels, Bernard Baruch are examples. The second group consists of those whose experience of the same period was acquired as staff officers or advisers ('aides' as the term is used by the composers of American press headlines), during the 1914–19 period, especially at the Paris Peace Conference: Bullitt, Joseph Grew, Breckenridge Long, Norman Davis, General Marshall, Admiral King are cases in point on the American side; Keynes, Hankey, Vansittart, Perth, Ronald Lindsay, Lothian, Hoare perhaps, on the British side. The third group consists of those whose experience was begun in the 1920s: Sumner Welles, Hull, Byrnes, Stettinius, Henry Wallace, J. Pierrepont Moffat, Joseph Kennedy, Joseph Davies on the American side; Halifax, Eden, Attlee, Bevin, Cadogan, Craigie, Jock Balfour, Clark Kerr on the British. The final group, too numerous to mention, are those whose real point of entry into the policy-making groups occurs in or after 1939–40.

The parallels in age and date of entry into political activity of the two national sets of élite members can, however, be extremely misleading. Not only are the American and British participants in events experienced in common – common 'learning zones' of experience so to speak – inclined to derive different conclusions from their perceptions and memories of those experiences. The significant 'learning zones', that is the periods of time, the experience of which seems to have struck those who passed through them as most significant, differ markedly in the American and British versions of events. For the Americans the most significant periods are the years 1919–20, with the collapse of Wilsonianism, of naval imperialism and the American withdrawal from Europe; the 1920s, with the rise of anti-imperialist historiography of the nineteenth century and of revisionist writings on the origins of the 1914–18 war[1] and on the circumstances of the American entry into that war; and the years 1931–4, remembered chiefly for the slump, the disasters which overtook American agriculture, the failure of the economy to revive under the New Deal, the need for economic nationalism and the failure of collective security in the Far East (allegedly as a result of Britain's failure to follow America's lead).

On the British side the years 1918–21 were seen as those in which traditional British diplomatic methods and goals were abandoned under American pressure (including the alliance with Japan) only for Britain to be left trying to work an American-inspired system from which America had pusillanimously withdrawn. The 1914–18 war was remembered as one in which Britain had abandoned its traditional maritime 'peripheral' strategy for one which at devastating cost to British youth concentrated on the Western Front and a brainless war of attrition. The late 1920s were remembered for the Anglo-American crisis and the vain sacrifices which had been made to end this crisis. The years 1931–2 were striking mainly for the experiences of American uselessness as an associate in attempting to manage the crisis in the Far East, in world trade and across the international exchange, a period crowned in 1933 by Roosevelt's characteristically American preference for domestic recovery and politics over international cooperation. Imperial economic internationalism and the managed pound had led to a degree of British economic and financial recovery which compared very favourably with that of America.

[1] On which see Warren I. Cohen, *The American Revisionists: Lessons of Intervention in World War I*, Chicago, 1967.

From these experiences American opinion had concluded that Britain as a partner in American purposes was unreliable, immoral, corrupt and invariably ended with the lion's share (in both the proverbial and the symbolic sense). America did not need Europe or Britain and was best off tending to domestic recovery. The effects of such attitudes in reinforcing similar tendencies in Britain were either ignored or regarded as typical evidence of British immorality. The recovery of American economic strength, it was felt, might make possible a revival of America's moral rôle in the world, it being taken as axiomatic that wars were economic in origin. Ruling opinion in Britain, by contrast, tended to conclude that America was fundamentally unreliable. Sacrifices to earn American good approval were a pointless concession to amiable post-prandial rhetoric. Britain should know that British interests lay in the white Dominions, in India, in China, in the Middle East, in the Eastern Mediterranean and in Scandinavia. These interests should be developed, and protected where they were already established.

The effects of these differing perceptions of the 'lessons of the past' were to break up the policy-making élites in each country into separate factions and interests, often, though not always, at odds with each other, or to reinforce their divisions where the system of government had already established them. In the United States insistence on the primacy of domestic recovery meant that foreign policy remained almost entirely the province of the State Department and the US Navy. In domestic issues the New Deal saw an enormous expanse in the Federal bureaucracy. But this bureaucracy was hardly involved at all directly in matters of foreign policy before the critical years of 1939–40.[2] This development greatly enhanced the rôle of the professionals of the State Department and the US Foreign Service in policy-making on regional matters. Figures such as Wallace Murray in Near Eastern affairs,[3] Stanley Hornbeck[4] and

---

[2] See the perceptive remarks of Randall Bennett Woods, *The Roosevelt Foreign Policy Establishment and the 'Good Neighbors'. The United States and Argentina, 1941–1945*, Lawrence, Kansas, 1979, p. 11.

[3] See Bruce R. Kuniholm, *The Origins of the Cold War in the Near East*, Princeton, NJ, 1980, pp. 186–7.

[4] On Stanley Hornbeck, see Richard Dean Burns and Edward M. Bennett, *Diplomats in Crisis: United States–Chinese–Japanese Relations, 1919–1941*, Santa Barbara, Cal. and Oxford, 1974, pp. 91–117.

Joseph Grew[5] in Far Eastern affairs and J. Pierrepont Moffat in European affairs[6] played a rôle out of all proportion to the limited rôle of the 'striped-pants cookie-pushers' in policy-making in American political mythology. Of the other departments of the US government the Treasury emerged in 1935–6 as a major element only because of the ideological and internationalist convictions of Henry Morgenthau, Roosevelt's Jewish Secretary of the Treasury,[7] whose convictions and strong concern with European events owed a good deal to the experience and teaching of his father, the US Ambassador to Turkey, 1913–16. The high command of the US Navy was also intimately concerned in matters of foreign policy as the threat from Japan grew more imminent. Three successive Chiefs of Naval Operations, Admiral William Standley,[8] Admiral William D. Leahy,[9] and Admiral Harold 'Betty' Stark,[10] played increasingly central rôles in developing Roosevelt's strategic perceptions before the appointment of Admiral Ernest King[11] marked the return of the Anglophobe nationalism of the 1920s to the high command of the US Navy. Standley and Leahy can be described as the earliest converts among the American policy-making élites to the doctrine of strategic realism and the necessity of Anglo-American cooperation.

Roosevelt's new Secretary of State, Cordell Hull, by contrast, was obsessed with his concept of reciprocal trade negotiations as the key to peace.[12] For him this was his yardstick – in relations with Britain

---

5   On Joseph Grew see Waldo H. Heinrichs, *American Ambassador Joseph C. Grew and the Development of the US Diplomatic Tradition*, Boston, 1966; Burns and Bennett, *Diplomats*, pp. 65–90.

6   There is, as yet, no respectable study of Moffat. But see Nancy Harrison Hooper (ed.), *The Moffat Papers: Selections from the Diplomatic Journal of Jay Pierrepont Moffat, 1919–1943*, Cambridge, Mass., 1956.

7   John Morton Blum, *From the Morgenthau Diaries*, vols. I–III, Boston, 1961–7.

8   On Admiral Standley, see William H. Standley, *Admiral Ambassador to Russia*, 1955, and Meredith William Berg, 'Admiral William H. Standley and the Second London Naval Treaty, 1934–1936,' *The Historian*, 33, 1970–1; Admiral of the Fleet Lord Chatfield, *It Might Happen Again*, London, 1947, pp. 69–70.

9   On Leahy, see his memoirs, *I was There*, London, 1950.

10   Admiral Stark as yet lacks a biographer. I was unable to consult the unpublished work of R.G. Albion, 'Makers of Naval Policy, 1798–1967', Harvard University Microfilm.

11   Admiral E.J. King, USN and W. Whitehall, *Fleet Admiral King*, London, 1953; Thomas B. Buell, *Master of Sea-Power. A Biography of Fleet-Admiral Ernest J. King*, Boston, 1981.

12   Cordell Hull, *Memoirs*, 2 vols., London, 1948; Julius Pratt, *Cordell Hull*, 2 vols. New York 1964; Richard N. Kottman, *Reciprocity and the North Atlantic Triangle, 1932–1938*, Ithaca, New York, 1968; Arthur W. Schatz, 'The Anglo-

particularly. Otherwise he was terrified of congressional isolationism and mortified by Roosevelt's obvious preference for Sumner Welles.

Among the generation below Cordell Hull one can isolate Sumner Welles as a man whose prior experience in inter-American affairs had completely unfitted him for dealing with balanced power relationships. The remainder, while sharing common experience in thwarted Wilsonianism, seem to divide into advocates of three alternative policies; isolationism pure and simple, intervention in Europe or hemispheric solidarity, this last being that policy preferred by the majority.

On the British side the overwhelming fact after 1933 was the disparity between Britain's commitments and the various threats to its interests in different parts of the world on the one hand, and the inadequacy of its financial, industrial and military resources to meet these threats, on the other.[13] This fact dominated all discussion of British policy within government, driving it inevitably into debate over which threatening power could be 'appeased' most easily and at least cost to British interests. Such considerations not only dominated major problems, such as those posed by the conjunction of Japanese expansionism in the Far East, Italian ambitions in the Mediterranean and the German threat to Central Europe, but also exerted a decisive influence over regional issues such as those involved in the Arab revolt in Palestine or in the Turkish claims for the remilitarisation of the Dardanelles. The main divisions were factional rather than interdepartmental, imperial isolationists such as Hankey and successive First Sea Lords arguing that the threat

American Trade Agreement and Cordell Hull's Search for Peace, 1935–1938', *J. Am. Hist*, 57, 1970; William R. Allen, 'Cordell Hull and the Defence of the Trade Agreements Programme, 1934–1940', in Alexander De Conde (ed.), *Isolation and Security*, Durham, NC, 1957; Detlef Junker, *Der unteilbare Weltmarkt: Das ökonomische Interesse in dem Aussenpolitik der USA, 1933–1941*, Stuttgart, 1975.

[13] There is now an enormous literature on the intragovernmental debate over British foreign policy in the 1930s towards the would-be aggressor states which supersedes the older emotional, guilt-ridden and politically inspired literature of the period before the 1960s and the opening of the British archives. Some of it is reviewed in D.C. Watt, 'Appeasement. The Rise of a Revisionist School?', *Pol. Q.*, 1965; D.C. Watt, 'The Historiography of Appeasement', in Alan Sked and Chris Cook (eds.), *Crisis and Controversy. Essays in Honour of A.J.P. Taylor*, London, 1976. See also Esmonde Robertson (ed.), *The Origins of the Second World War*, London, 1971, especially his introduction.

from Japan made it essential to settle with Italy, if not (and in this they had the whole-hearted support of much of the MacDonald and Baldwin Cabinets) avoiding any new commitments to France or Belgium against Germany.

Contemplating a possible war with Nazi Germany, whom the Defence Requirements Committee of 1934 identified as the most serious long-term threat to Britain, arguing that Japan was unlikely to proceed to threaten vital British interests in the Far East unless it could be sure that Britain was distracted by the possibility of conflict in Europe, members of the élite were particularly sensitive to the consequences of the Johnson Act of 1934 and the American neutrality legislation of 1935–6 on British ability to enlist American financial and industrial resources to its aid in a future war with Germany as it had done in the 1914–18 war.[14] Given that Britain could be expected to face an all-out attack, particularly in the air, from Germany in the initial stages of a war, it was taken as axiomatic that Britain would need time to bring its own economic strength to bear once that attack had been survived. Financial strength became as important as military. Finance was the 'fourth arm' after the three armed services.[15] If Britain were to stay within its strength then it would need to tailor the kind of war it wished to fight to the limit of that strength; hence arose the doctrine of the war of 'limited liability'. From 1936 to 1939 the hand of the Treasury lay heavy on the formulation of British strategy and struggled to control the direction of British foreign policy too. Its heads were as little enamoured of the United States as they were of Germany, towards which the Permanent Under Secretary, Sir Warren Fisher, manifested feelings that can only be described as racialist.

To members of the British-policy-making élites the Roosevelt administration presented itself as an ally either as an incomprehensible and irrelevant impossibility or a barely tolerable but unavoidable potentiality. Sir Ronald Lindsay set the tone in 1934, reporting on Roosevelt's obsession with domestic issues.[16]

[14] 'We only just scraped through the last war with Germany with every assistance we could get from the USA. The deduction is plain ... In any crisis of life and death – the present is not one – this might well mean our "death".' Minute by Sir Robert Vansittart, 8 January 1936, FO 371/19825.

[15] George Peden, *British Rearmament and the Treasury, 1932–1939*, Edinburgh, 1979.

[16] British Embassy, Washington, Annual Report, 1934, FO 371/18761.

In all major claims of policy, the devaluation of the dollar, the experimentation of the New Deal, the silver policy, no regard has been paid to foreign interests ... Nevertheless the real grievance of the world against America is not that she has been selfish, for that might be forgiven by governments that are themselves not entirely altruistic; and not even that she has supplied insults in the place of collaboration for to that we are all accustomed; but that the measures which she has adopted should have produced such very modest results to her own benefit; for the comparative failure of the New Deal induces danger and uncertainty everywhere, and retards or imperils the success that others may hope for or achieve.

Roosevelt's own methods of government were everything that tidy-minded, single-purposed British bureaucrats abhorred. In the first place he encouraged bureaucratic and individual competitiveness, without realising the power that it put into the hands of his servants to thwart his own initiatives. Whatever he meant by the Chicago Quarantine Speech of 6 October 1937, he can hardly have realised that British enquiries as to its meaning would be fobbed off by Sumner Welles (with whose ideas of an armistice day message it was clearly irreconcilable),[17] else his comment to Lord Murray of Elibank, 'I did hope for a little more selfish spirit in your Foreign Office'[18] would be unforgivable. His relations with his political allies, at best guarded, at worst of utter hostility, made it the more difficult for foreign governments to know which manifestations of his latest ideas should be taken seriously. His preference for special envoys and confidants exposed them to intrigue and isolation; as, for example, when the unfortunate Norman Davis was frozen out of his special relationship with the President by an unholy alliance between Hull and Sumner Welles after his attempt to exploit Roosevelt's momentary interest in Anglo-American cooperation at the end of the Brussels Conference in November 1937.[19] The millionaire Joseph Davies was intended to act in a similar manner in US relations with

---

[17] Sumner Welles told the British chargé d'affaires: ' "Quarantine" was a remote and vague objective ... emphasis should rather be placed on the President's other remark "that America was actively engaged in the search for peace".' FO 371/21544.

[18] Roosevelt to Murray, 7 October 1937, Murray of Elibank Papers, Folio 8809, p. 45.

[19] Cordell Hull, *Memoirs*, vol. I, pp. 554–5; Hooper, *Moffat*, p. 184; *Foreign Relations of the United States, 1937*, IV, pp. 52–4, 175–7, 180–1, 183–5, 187, 193, 197, 200.

Germany,[20] as Norman Davis with Britain. Roosevelt's friendship with Mackenzie King had no doubt a good deal to do with his own hopes of detaching Canada from the Empire. But King seems rather to have acted as yet another channel by which disguised isolationist ideas could be fed to the President. King was a thorough-going isolationist himself for reasons of Canadian domestic politics. Not until Hopkins emerged on the scene in 1940 was Roosevelt properly served and in a position to carry out his own foreign policy.[21]

Roosevelt's methods of government were the more difficult to cope with in that, while keeping the thread of foreign policy firmly in his own hands, he neither cultivated a court (as had Theodore Roosevelt) nor made himself particularly accessible to foreign ambassadors. Sir Ronald Lindsay rarely got to see Roosevelt and never knew which of the latter's many minions it would be best to cultivate. The appointment of Philip Kerr, Lord Lothian, as Lindsay's successor improved matters considerably. But the real argument in favour of Lord Halifax's embassy (apart from Churchill's desire to remove all would-be heads of a compromise peace government as far as possible from London)[22] was that the President could hardly make himself inaccessible to a former British Viceroy and Foreign Secretary. Nor, at least until 1940, did Roosevelt have anything approaching an adequate intelligence service, or, indeed, make intelligent use of what he had.[23] Indeed the information he relied on came from the most peculiar and tainted of sources. His figures on German aircraft production in 1938 (which exaggerated the actual production figures by a factor of ten) he got from Colonel

---

20 On Joseph Davies's original appointment see Callum A. Macdonald, *The United States, Britain and Appeasement*, London, 1981, p. 9: see also Joseph E. Davies, *Mission to Moscow*, New York, 1941; George F. Kennan, *Memoirs, 1925–1950*, London, 1967, pp. 82–4: Richard H. Ullman, 'The Davies Mission and United States–Soviet Relations, 1937–1941', *World Politics*, 9, 1957; on Davies's wartime rôle in Soviet–American relations, see Elizabeth Kimball Maclean, 'Joseph E. Davies and Soviet–American Relations, 1941–1943', *Diplomatic History*, 3, 1979.

21 On Hopkins see particularly David Reynolds, *The Creation of the Anglo-American Alliance, 1937–1941. A Study in Competitive Cooperation*, London, 1981, pp. 179–81.

22 Sir Samuel Hoare's appointment to the Madrid Embassy in 1940 was inspired by much the same reasoning or suspicion.

23 A fact which makes his momentarily correct comments to Baron Rothschild in February 1939 a singular piece of historical irony, *And so to America*, London, 1941, pp. 258–9.

Lindbergh and William Bullitt.[24] His information about secret Nazi plans to subvert Latin America seems to have been drawn from the over-heated imaginations of some South American socialist journalists. He cancelled a trip west for a sensational return to Washington apparently on the basis of a report in Claud Cockburn's *The Week*, the same source he relied on for much of his belief about the rôle of the Cliveden set in manipulating British politics and the American Ambassador.[25]

His internationalism, couched as it often was in his later years in appropriately Wilsonian terms, has to be reconciled with his hostility towards European colonialism. His views of this appear to have been the most curious mixture of historical anachronisms (as witness his attempt to urge the experience of the Founding Fathers on those concerned with the possible transfer of power in India)[26] and his acceptance of the standard colonialist theory that some races were not ready for self-government.[27] He was, in fact, a moral imperialist on a super-Wilsonian scale, determined not only to make as much of the world over into the American image as was possible, but also prepared to contemplate the large-scale, and presumably enforced, movements of population of an immensity which makes Hitler's and Stalin's efforts in this direction seem quite small scale.[28]

His methods of evolving a policy decision have been stigmatised as procrastination modified by indiscretion. But perhaps the most severe criticisms that can be levelled at him concern his inability to

---

[24] On this episode see Orville Bullitt, *For the President, Personal and Secret*, Boston, 1972, pp. 292–300, 302–3; Colonel Charles A. Lindbergh, *The Wartime Journals of Charles A. Lindbergh*, New York 1970, entries of 9 September, 30 September, 1 October, 2 October; Murray of Elibank to Halifax, 22 October 1939, Elibank Papers, Folio 8809. John McVickar Haight Jr, *American Aid to France 1938–1940*, New York, 1970.

[25] On the accuracy of *The Week*'s reporting in 1939, see D.C. Watt, '*The Week* That Was', *Encounter*, 38, May 1972.

[26] See for example *FRUS 1942*, vol. I, pp. 715–17, Roosevelt to Chiang Kai-shek, 12 August 1942; Nicholas Mansergh (ed.), *Constitutional Relations Between Britain and India: The Transfer of Power 1942–1947*, vol. I, no. 508, Sir Girja Shankar Bajpai, Indian agent-general in Washington to Viceroy, 2 April 1942, reporting on a conversation with the President; *FRUS 1942*, vol. I, pp. 615–16, Roosevelt to Churchill, 10 March 1942; *FRUS 1942*, Roosevelt to Churchill, 11 April 1942, pp. 633–4.

[27] Witness his comments to Molotov on the Indo-Chinese, made in June 1942, *FRUS 1942*, vol. II, pp. 581–3.

[28] On Project 'M' see Henry M. Field, *M Project for FDR: Studies in Migration and Settlement*, Ann Arbor, 1962.

handle Congress (as witness the disaster of the attempt to repeal the neutrality legislation in the spring and summer of 1939) and his uncanny gift for picking the worst possible man for a diplomatic appointment.[29] His early appointments left much to be desired but can be excused on the familiar grounds than an incoming President does not pick his own staff; they have usually picked him. But his wartime appointments, Standley in Moscow, the nice but inefficient Winant in London, the unspeakable Patrick Hurley in Chungking (not forgetting the two equally unhappy military appointments in China of Stillwell and Wedemeyer), the dispatch of the Phillips mission to India in 1943, or the signalling of the Argentine's final abandonment of neutrality in April 1945 by the dispatch of the bullying braggart, Spruille Braden, as ambassador,[30] vary between mistakes and the creation of major disaster areas in American foreign policy.

In his attitude to Britain, Franklin Roosevelt epitomises that ambivalence which is characteristic of much of his country. As an oligarch of Dutch descent he could avoid the more sentimental and genealogically influenced Anglophilia of much of his class. As a politician he recognised the necessity of a strong Britain. Britain was America's shield against Europe, a shield he was prepared to go very far to see strengthened and burnished. Yet he was unable to reconcile his conviction that America needed British power with a recognition that the continuation of that power depended on Britain successfully solving the problems posed by the evolution of the Commonwealth and Empire towards self-government. The anti-colonialism which, if his admirers (and children)[31] were to be believed, went much deeper than conventional Independence Day rhetoric, was impossible to reconcile with the maintenance of Britain's status as a world power. His views were an extraordinary compound of prejudice and ignorance, strengthened by his conviction that all arguments in

---

[29] In November 1933 Lindsay had reported of Roosevelt that 'he was a bad judge of advisors and he tended more and more to treat criticism as disloyalty', 29 November 1933, CAB 23/77 66(33)1 Appendix. Cited in McCulloch, 'Anglo-American Diplomacy'.

[30] His appointment of Professor William Dodd, to the surprise of the Professor and everybody else, as Ambassador to Berlin in 1933 cannot exactly be claimed as among his more successful experiments.

[31] Elliott Roosevelt, *As He Saw It*, New York 1946, *passim*; Foster Rhea Dulles, 'The Anti-Colonial Policies of Franklin D. Roosevelt', *Pol. Sci. Q.*, 70, 1955.

favour of the continuance of colonial rule were initiated by the self-interest of those who advanced them.

Towards the successive governments of Britain his attitudes were determined by an equally ambivalent mixture of prejudice and ignorance. Having handled the British default, with what was by his standards a considerable degree of tact and understanding, he appears to have concluded in May 1934 that the British did not want to cooperate with America, and that he would have to wait for a change of government.[32] The change from MacDonald to Baldwin and the replacement of Simon by Hoare and Eden at the Foreign Office in June 1935 seemed just what he wanted. Hoare's involvement in the Hoare–Laval pact was an enormous shock. But his replacement in turn by Eden restored the balance. But the Baldwin government duly gave way to the Chamberlain government and Roosevelt allowed himself to become convinced that the Chamberlain policy of appeasement represented the victory in London of the 'economic royalists' against whom he was campaigning in America.[33] Chamberlain was, he believed, attempting to engineer an Anglo-German money and trade deal, the effect of which would be to exclude American trade from Europe, Africa and Latin America.

Roosevelt was no more able than any of his American contemporaries to understand the perceptions of Britain's economic and financial weakness which obsessed the Cabinet and the Treasury throughout the 1930s. Instead he was dominated by the notion of Britain's wealth and opulence. In 1938 he believed British disposable assets in the United States to stand at some $7,000 million.[34] In

---

[32] Or so he told Stimson, Stimson Diary, entry of 17 May 1934; see also Phillips Diary, 14 August 1934, also McCulloch, 'Anglo-American Diplomacy'.

[33] Roosevelt to Cudahy, 16 April 1938, *FDR Personal Letters*, II, p. 232; St Quentin to Bonnet, 11 March 1938, *Documents Diplomatiques Françaises*, IIe série, t. VIII, p. 729; Blum, *From the Morgenthau Diaries*, II, p. 123. See Bingham to Roosevelt, Chamberlain 'lives and breathes only in the atmosphere of the money-changers of the city', Edgar Nixon (ed.), *Roosevelt and Foreign Affairs 1933–36*, vol. III, pp. 484–8; also Roosevelt to Morgenthau, 'As long as Neville Chamberlain is there we must recognise that fundamentally he thoroughly dislikes America' (1936) cited in Blum, *From the Morgenthau Diaries*, vol. I, p. 141; Bowers to Roosevelt 24 August 1938, Roosevelt Papers, PSF 6A, Diplomatic Correspondence; in 1940, Harold Ickes, Roosevelt's Secretary of the Interior called Chamberlain 'the evil genius not only of Great Britain but also of western civilisation', Ickes, *Secret Diary*, vol. III, entry of 4 May 1940.

[34] Harold Ickes, *Secret Diary*, vol. II, entries of 17 and 23 September 1938; the US Department of Commerce and the Federal Reserve Banks put the figure at less than one-third of that amount.

January 1939 he rebuked Lord Lothian for his talk of British weakness.[35] In the winter of 1940–1, even while concentrating on the Lend-Lease Bill which alone made it possible for Britain to continue fighting, he persisted in his belief that Britain had plenty of cash in hand to cover its existing orders.[36] Even in August 1944 Roosevelt could write to Morgenthau: 'This is very interesting. I had no idea England was broke.'[37] In 1939, however, he felt the main problem Britain faced was one of loss of nerve rather than material weakness *vis-à-vis* Germany. Interestingly the historians have still been unable to agree how far his view was correct. It is, however, one which fits in with his belief not only that war springs from economic motivations but that the outbreak can be deterred in the same way.

From the middle of 1935 he began to be worried by the possibility that a new European war might threaten the recovery of America and all that he was trying to do through the New Deal. From 1936 to 1938 he toyed with various ideas of the economic reordering of the world by the summoning of an international conference and followed closely the discussions of the League of Nations on access to raw materials and on transforming itself into a purely economic association.[38] As the threat of Japanese action against China matured so his mind turned towards the idea of the kind of economic pressure which might be used to restrain Japanese expansionism. That the Quarantine speech was intended in this sense as a *ballon d'essai* of a typically Rooseveltian kind[39] seems to be born out by his revival of the scheme in his conversation with Sir Ronald Lindsay in December 1937 at the time of the USS *Panay* crisis with Japan.[40] He returned to the same

---

[35] Ickes, *Secret Diary*, vol. II, entry of 29 January 1939.

[36] See Warren F. Kimball, 'Beggar my Neighbour: America and the British Interim Finance Crisis, 1940–1941', *J. Econ. Hist.*, 29, 1969.

[37] Blum, *From the Morgenthau Diaries*, vol. I, p. 308.

[38] See Francis L. Loewenheim, 'An Illusion that Shaped History. New Light on the History and Historiography of American Peace Efforts before Munich', in Daniel R. Beaver (ed.), *Some Pathways in American History*, Detroit, 1969; Macdonald, *The United States, passim.*

[39] As argued by John McVickar Haight Jr, 'Franklin D. Roosevelt and a Naval Quarantine of Japan', *Pac. Hist. Rev.*, 40, 1971; John McVickar Haight Jr, 'Roosevelt and the Aftermath of the Quarantine Speech', *Rev. Pol.*, 24, 1962; for an earlier, contrary, view see Dorothy Borg, 'Notes on Roosevelt's "Quarantine" Speech', *Pol. Sci. Q.*, 52, 1957.

[40] Lawrence W. Pratt, 'The Anglo-American Naval Conversations on the Far East in January 1938', *International Affairs*, 47, 1971.

theme in his address to a far from enthusiastic Congress of January 1939 when he spoke of methods of opposing aggression other than by war.[41] It was to form the main element in his policy towards Japan from the summer of 1939 onwards.

In all of this Roosevelt's views and prejudices were echoed by the bulk of his admirers. By 1939 he was inclined to listen much more to those who argued, as did Morgenthau and Ickes, that Naziism constituted an ideological movement which threatened democracy; it was not only the 'Cliveden set' nonsense of the Popular Frontists in Europe, whose sentiments were so markedly shared by the majority of the American foreign correspondents in Europe, to which he was so responsive.[42] It is difficult to see him agreeing with Moffat's proposed policy of doing everything to avoid a line up of the democracies against dictatorship.[43] It is in fact in his ability to rise above his own generational, social, political and nationalist prejudices and react to the real issues that this maddening yet admirable figure differs so strikingly from those who served him, the Berles, Sumner Welleses and Moffats, the petty-minded self-styled 'realists' of the State Department.[44]

It cannot be said that anyone among the British policy-makers could earn a similar accolade before Churchill's return to power in September 1939. Eden, despite his later self-glorification, cannot. The remainder of the Baldwin and Chamberlain Cabinets were driven by necessity as they perceived it rather than by any vision. The official and private records of the time are stuffed with the most vivid expressions of their dislike and resentment of the Roosevelt administration. The President was an 'amateur',[45] with no settled convic-

---

[41] *Public Papers 1939*, p. 3. From the recording of this speech preserved in the BBC sound archives, it is clear that the applause which greeted this section of his speech was much thinner than that which greeted the major part of his remarks.

[42] See Roger W. Buckley, 'The American Press Corps' view of Nazi Germany. Memoirs of Selected Correspondents', London M.A. Dissertation, 1965.

[43] Moffat Papers, pp. 182–3, entry of 13 November 1937: 'my personal preoccupation is to ... discourage any formation of a common front of the democratic powers'.

[44] Reynolds, *Anglo-American Alliance*, p. 68.

[45] Sir Ronald Lindsay to Foreign Office, 27 July 1933, FO 371/16600. 'Mr Roosevelt is, in these matters, an almost complete amateur and an opportunist, in a country where both types tend to predominate. He is constantly out of his depth, as journalists whom he entertains at his intimate bi-weekly talks at the White House frequently testify.' Cited in McCulloch, 'Anglo-American Diplomacy'.

tions,[46] who 'ran away' when the time came for action,[47] his policy 'shamelessly immoral',[48] and 'stark, staring madness'.[49] Even Sir Ronald Lindsay, who had backed Roosevelt's candidature in 1932 and was to do the same in 1936 could refer to him as 'totally unreliable'.[50] He was 'prone to act impulsively and without proper perspective'.[51] After his re-election, however, Vansittart discerned signs that 'something might be made out of Mr Franklin D. Roosevelt II who may not be the same man as Mr Franklin D. Roosevelt I'.[52] He was, in any case, ahead of his people and much abler than his advisers, few if any of whom awoke any sentiments of warmth or enthusiasm in British assessments. The British government were, in fact, remarkably well informed about the various currents of opinion both in administration circles and in the country. They paid much attention to key Senators such as Borah.[53] Where the government were at a loss was in understanding Roosevelt's methods of government or in knowing what weight to give to the various influences and currents of opinion around him. They were slow to perceive the importance of Henry Morgenthau who was to encounter head-on the most obstructive of Treasury reactions to his various initiatives.[54] Lindsay's exclusion from the Roosevelt Court, allegedly the product of his own connections and the impeccably right-wing Republican origins of the second Lady Lindsay (a Colgate Hoyt of New York),[55] was disastrous here.

The experience of 1933–4, alluded to in the previous chapter, also

[46] Leith-Ross report, 29 November 1933, CAB 23/77, 66(33)1. These and subsequent citations are from McCulloch, 'Anglo-American Diplomacy'.
[47] Note of 4 June 1933, T.188/74, Leith-Ross Papers.
[48] Warren Fisher minute, 15 September 1933, T.188/74, Leith-Ross Papers.
[49] Leith-Ross to Fisher, 27 October 1933, T.188/74, Leith-Ross Papers.
[50] Gore-Booth minute, 4 October 1934, FO 371/17581.
[51] Craigie minute, 13 November 1936, FO 371/19827.
[52] Vansittart minute, 11 November 1936, FO 371/19836.
[53] James W. Weinberger, 'The Attitude of the British Embassy, Washington, D.C. and the Foreign Office towards Senator William E. Borah, 1935–1940', London M.A. Dissertation, 1979.
[54] Witness the reception by Sir John Simon of his telephoned communication during the crisis over the Japanese attack on the USS *Panay*, December 1938 in Blum, *From the Morgenthau Diaries*, vol. I, pp. 489–92.
[55] Hull, *Memoirs*, vol. I, p. 380; private information. Sir Ronald Lindsay's first wife, Martha Cameron (d. 1918), was the daughter of Senator J. Donald Cameron of Pennsylvania; his second, Elizabeth Sherman Hoyt, was the daughter of Colgate Hoyt, of New York, railway director, banker and Stock Exchange broker, said to be a Republican of the 'rock-ribbed' variety.

dominated much of the thinking of the Treasury as of its chancellors and ex-chancellors. Second only to the Treasury was the Board of Trade which bore the brunt of the American trade negotiations. Runciman was won over to the idea and to Anglo-American cooperation by his visit to the White House in January 1937,[56] only to be replaced by Oliver Stanley when Chamberlain became Prime Minister. It took another fifteen months of argument to bring an Anglo-American trade agreement to function. During the negotiations Hull was driven on at least one occasion to talk seriously of telling the British 'to go to hell', while America laid down some more battleships and withdrew into 'our own shell'.[57] In October 1938 Oliver Stanley spoke of 'the state of bitterness and exasperation which usually results from dealing with the United States government'.[58] The Treasury indeed pushed very hard for an agreement with Japan in 1934.[59] Sir Frederick Leith-Ross had hoped to bring about economic cooperation with Japan on his visit to the Far East in 1935–6.[60] Chamberlain returned to the idea again in the winter of 1936–7.[61] But there were two unbeatable obstacles. The old Anglophile nobility in the Japanese policy élite had no control over the army, least of all over the field officers in the Kwantung and north Chinese armies, and were being challenged even within their two strongholds, the Foreign Ministry and the Imperial Court. And neither in the Dominions nor with the political mass of British opinion was any action acceptable which might lead to a total break with the United States.[62]

The truth was that if Britain were to find itself at war either in Europe or in the Far East there was no apparent way, short of a

---

[56] McCulloch, 'Anglo-American Diplomacy', has the best summary of this. See also Runciman to Baldwin, 8 February 1937, PREM 1/281.

[57] Hickerson to Moffat, 8 November 1937, Moffat Papers, Box 12.

[58] To the Cabinet: 11 October 1938, CAB 24/229.

[59] cf. D.C. Watt, *Personalities and Policies*, pp. 83–9; Ann Trotter, *Britain and East Asia 1933–1937*, Cambridge, 1975, pp. 88–131; Ann Trotter, 'Tentative Steps for an Anglo-Japanese Rapprochement in 1934', *Modern Asian Studies*, 8, 1974; see also Chamberlain to Sir John Simon, 1 September 1934, Simon Papers.

[60] V.H. Rothwell, 'The Mission of Sir Frederick Leith-Ross to the Far East, 1935–1936', *Hist. J.*, 18, 1975.

[61] O.S. Ogbi, 'The Foreign Office and Yoshida's Bid for Rapprochement with Britain in 1936–1937', *Hist. J.*, 21, 1978; O.S. Ogbi, 'British Imperial Defence and Foreign Policy in Asia and the Pacific and the Impact of Anglo-Japanese Relations', University of Birmingham Ph.D., 1975, esp. Chapter 11.

[62] Watt, *Personalities and Policies*.

collapse on the enemy's domestic front,[63] that Britain could conceivably win without American aid. This, in itself, was bad enough. What was worse was that if Britain were to have any chance of preventing war by deterring a potential aggressor then it had to have at the best the appearance of American support. The strength of isolationism in the country was taken as axiomatic. To that axiom had to be added the reality of the American neutrality legislation. The Cabinet felt itself confronted with an impossible dilemma. It could wait while the process of 'education' into a sense of the real world plodded its slow way forward under Roosevelt's leadership (Eden's solution). Or it could decide to count on nothing from Washington and strive towards deterring the potential enemies without it. Hence the discussions of the 'Gold Medal Army' and the 'war of limited liability'. The difficulty here was the multiplicity of possible enemies. The difficulty with waiting for the US to move from first grade to eighth grade and beyond to college was that so slow a timetable might not impress Britain's potential enemies. In the end the increasing necessity of American aid to deter Japan and the parallel need of the appearance of American support to deter Hitler ruled overt continental isolationism out of court as a possible policy.

In the meantime there were the trade negotiations, where it took a long time for Hull's ability to bring about American tariff reductions to win credence. The first American victory over British obstructionism was in fact scored by Morgenthau in forcing the Anglo-American French Stabilisation Agreement of September 1936 on a reluctant and sceptical British Treasury,[64] even though he failed to get Chamberlain to agree to hold the pound at the $5 mark. In each case what brought the British government to enter negotiations and

---

[63] Reynolds argues persuasively that, throughout the winter of 1939–40, this was, in fact, Chamberlain's main hope; see also D.C. Watt, 'Les Alliés et la résistance allemande (1939–1944)', *Revue d'Histoire de la Deuxième Guerre Mondiale*, 36, 1959; Peter Ludlow, 'The Unwinding of Appeasement', in Lothar Kettenacker (ed.), *The 'Other Germany' in the Second World War: Emigration and Resistance in International Perspective*, Publications of the German Historical Institute, London, Stuttgart, 1977, pp. 9–48, and the documentary appendix, pp. 141–87, especially FO memorandum of 24 February 1941, 'Summary of Principal Peace Feelers, 1939–March 1941', FO 371/26542; Peter Ludlow, 'Papst Pius XII, die britische Regierung und die deutsche Opposition im Winter 1939/40', *Vierteljahresheft für Zeitgeschichte*, 20, 1974.

[64] McCulloch, 'Anglo-American Diplomacy', has the fullest account.

sign an agreement were the so-called 'imponderables', a deliberately esoteric disguise for the crude fact that Britain needed American goodwill. The trade negotiations took longer, and even their conclusion changed matters very little. American suspicions of British economic approaches to Germany in the period November 1936 to March 1939,[65] and the whole range of minor pin-pricking conflicts, over small islands in the Pacific,[66] commercial air routes, rubber, cotton, tin, oil, tobacco, etc., continued to poison the atmosphere.[67] Yet Britain needed the appearance of American support to deter Hitler. Once war was really joined Britain would need the reality. In British political strategy up to May 1940 America figured as the *dea ex machina*, the goddess who would descend from the machine and restore order and harmony in the last act. The Greeks, however, stood in awe of their goddesses, and Neville Chamberlain certainly hoped profoundly that America might never have to be invoked.[68]

America, however, failed to function properly as a deterrent in 1939. In the winter of 1938–9 matters seemed to be going swimmingly. Roosevelt's secret message to Chamberlain via Murray of Elibank[69] was accompanied by news of a major expansion of the US Army Air Force. Roosevelt's congressional address of 4 January 1939, his address to the Senate Military Affairs Committee on 31 January, his radio address from Key West on 18 February, were felt in both London[70] and Washington[71] to have had a marked effect on

---

[65] On which see Reynolds, *Anglo-American Alliance*, pp. 49–52; Hans Jürgen Schroeder, 'Die Vereinigte Staaten von Amerika und die britische Appeasement-Politik', paper presented to German Historical Institute, London, Conference on Appeasement, June 1980; C.A. Macdonald, 'U.S. Views of British Appeasement, 1937–1939', to be published; C.A. Macdonald, 'The United States, Appeasement and the Open Door', unpublished paper.

[66] See M. Ruth Megaw, 'The Scramble for the Pacific: Anglo-United States Rivalry in the Pacific in the 1930s', *Hist. Studies* (Melbourne), 15, 1973; Lowell T. Young, 'Franklin D. Roosevelt and America's Islets; Acquisition of Territory in the Caribbean and the Pacific', *The Historian*, 35, 1972–3.

[67] On these subjects in general see Ernest Gilman, 'Economic Aspects of Anglo-American relations in the Era of Roosevelt and Chamberlain, 1937–1940', London Ph.D., 1976.

[68] 'Heaven knows I don't want the Americans to fight for us. We should have to pay for that too dearly if they had a right to be in on the peace terms', Neville Chamberlain to Ida Chamberlain, 29 January 1940, Neville Chamberlain Papers, 18/1/1140.

[69] Elibank Papers.

[70] For Chamberlain's reactions see Reynolds, *Anglo-American Alliance*, pp. 47–8.

[71] For Roosevelt's views see Adolf E. Berle, *Navigating the Rapids*, p. 213.

Hitler. They had a good deal to do with lulling Chamberlain into that mistimed sense of euphoria to which the unfortunate Sir Samuel Hoare was to fall victim on the eve of the German march into Prague.[72] Thereafter, however, the magic failed. The really major disaster was Roosevelt's Good Friday message to Hitler,[73] an appalling piece of nonsense dreamed up in a hurry in response to a suggestion from the conservative anti-Nazi opposition in Germany.[74] Hitler was given the chance of making fun of the President in his speech of 28 April.[75] There followed the 'shambolic' failure of the Administration's attempt to repeal the 1937 neutrality legislation, in which Roosevelt demonstrated once again his inability to manage Congress. Comments in Britain were predictably bitter.[76] Thereafter Hitler, reinforced by evidence from his military attaché in Washington, General Boetticher, on the isolationism of the American military,[77] wrote America off as a serious political factor in his calculations.[78] Not until the summer of 1940, when he faced the prospect that if he conquered Britain, the United States as the residual legatee of the British Empire would be the major beneficiary, did he concern himself with Roosevelt again. The American refusal to do anything to aid the British in resolving the crisis with Japan they blundered into over Tientsin in July 1939 only confirmed

[72] *FRUS 1939*, vol. I, pp. 14–17, Kennedy to Hull, 17 February 1939. See also *The History of the Times*, vol. IV, part 2, pp. 959–60.

[73] Gunter Moltmann, 'Franklin D. Roosevelt's Friedensappel von 14 April 1939', *Jahrbuch für Amerikastudien*, 1964, pp. 91–109.

[74] Reynolds, *Anglo-American Alliance*, p. 48.

[75] For the text see Max Domarus (ed), *Hitler, Reden und Proklamationen 1932–1945*, Munich, 1965, vol. II, pp. 1166–79.

[76] Reynolds, pp. 57–8. Neville Chamberlain wrote of Congress, 'their behaviour over the neutrality legislation is enough to make one weep, but I have not been disappointed for I never expected any better behaviour from these pig-headed and self-righteous nobodies', Chamberlain to John Buchan, 7 July 1939, Buchan Papers.

[77] On the views and reportage of General Boetticher, see James V. Compton, *The Swastika and the Eagle. Hitler, the United States and the Origins of the Second World War*, London, 1968, pp. 105–26, 'General von Boetticher's America'.

[78] As witness his failure to refer to the United States in his speeches to his military commanders of 23 May, 22 August and 23 November 1939; these speeches were put in evidence in the Nuremberg Trial Proceedings as documents L-79, 798-PS and 789-PS. They may easily be consulted in English translation in *Trials of War Criminals before the Nürnberg Military Tribunals*, vol. X, 'The High Command Case', Washington, 1951, pp. 671–8, 698–702, 823–30. He is said to have concluded that Roosevelt was solely concerned with re-election, *Documents on German Foreign Policy, 1918–1945*, vol. VI, no. 296, Hewel Memorandum.

him in his views. There was therefore little point in Roosevelt's various manoeuvres over the winter of 1939–40 to bring about a negotiated peace, or, put perhaps more accurately, to secure that if there were to be negotiations towards this end he would be involved.[79]

British hopes of a breakdown on Germany's domestic front were as doomed to failure as Chamberlain's previous hopes of a European settlement without American (or Soviet) participation. The German conservative opposition to Hitler lacked both leadership and resolution. Its rout in November 1939[80] spelt the end of Chamberlain's hopes even though contacts between the British government and various intermediaries[81] were to last until the eve of the German invasion of Norway in April 1940 and of France and the Low Countries in May 1940. But even before Britain's armies withdrew from the continent, leaving behind everything but their honour, and Britain girded itself to face Hitler and Mussolini alone, the revolt in the Tory party against Chamberlain had replaced him with Churchill; Little Europeanism in Britain died with this change. Churchill was an unashamed Atlanticist; and his hopes of Britain's survival and ultimate victory were pinned firmly on the United States.

[79] Stanley E. Hilton, 'The Welles Mission to Europe, February–March 1940; Illusion or Realism?', *J.Am.Hist.*, 58, 1971; Reynolds, *Anglo-American Alliance*, pp. 80–3.

[80] See Comité d'Histoire de la 2e Guerre Mondiale, *Français et Britanniques dans la drôle de Guerre, Actes du Colloque franco-britannique tenu à Paris du 8 au 12 décembre 1975*, Paris 1979.

[81] See the sources cited in footnote 63 above.

5

1940–1947

From Lend-Lease to the Truman doctrine; America's return to
Europe, its second withdrawal and return

The advent of Winston Churchill to power was to change the
direction of British policy completely. But, despite the special
pleading advanced by Roosevelt's hagiographers,[1] the actual relationship between the two men was much more tentative at first than
Churchill alleged,[2] and was never treated on Roosevelt's side with all
the warmth that Churchill did his utmost to infuse into it. Churchill
was pre-eminently a patriot whose somewhat romanticised image of
Britain included its Empire, the white Dominions and the Navy, and
did not, in the long run, exclude non-white membership; though, in
the short run, many of his attitudes were distinctly racialist.
Throughout his career he had fluctuated between the vision of a
permanent association of the principal English-speaking nations and
ignored reactions to American economic and imperialist nationalism. Since his exclusion from office after 1929, he had visited
America and enhanced the range of his American friendships and
contacts. His romanticism was, however, merely the palette from
which he painted. He had always a very firm grasp indeed of the
realities of politics, power and *potentiel de guerre*. He was only too
well aware both of the strains of Anglophobia and exclusivist

[1] Joseph Lash, *Roosevelt and Churchill, 1939–1941. The Partnership that Saved the West*, New York, 1976.
[2] In his *War Memoirs*. For a more realistic view, James R. Leutze, 'The Secret of the Churchill–Roosevelt Correspondence, 1939–1940', *J. Contemp. Hist.*, 10, 1975; see also Warren F. Kimball, 'Churchill and Roosevelt: The Personal Equation', *Prologue*, 6, 1974; Warren F. Kimball, '"Gabble": Churchill and Roosevelt Talk' and Martin Gilbert, 'Churchill and Roosevelt, the Background of the Relationship and its Testing Times', papers presented to the Conference of the British and United States Committee for the History of the Second World War, London, July 1980.

American nationalism in American politics and of the relative size and scale of Britain's and America's industrial strength and mobilisable forces. In Roosevelt he saw a fundamentally heroic figure, dominating American politics, capable of rising in vision above the nuts and bolts, the close and detailed bargaining of everyday politics and the minutiae of past grievances. He laid himself out to court and flatter Roosevelt from the beginning. In general he was not disappointed in Roosevelt, at least not until the winter of 1944–5. In insisting on the primacy of his vision of Anglo-American cooperation he could be both ruthless and unscrupulous. It turned him against General de Gaulle.[3] It led him to ruin the career of Sir Robert Craigie – as I shall show later. It led him to withhold from the Cabinet Roosevelt's increasingly tiresome and irrelevant messages on India.[4] It led him to set at nought a Cabinet decision that he should protest against Roosevelt's Indo-Chinese policy.[5] His memoirs were similarly slanted. And yet in the end his hopes were disappointed – though his necessities were not.

With the collapse of France in the summer of 1940, the whole of Roosevelt's preceding policy, of building up Britain and France as a bulwark against German expansion in Europe, collapsed with it, and Roosevelt was suddenly confronted with the possibility of a Europe united by Hitler in hostility against the United States, allied with Japan and able to mop up most of Latin America. Hemispheric isolationism took on an entirely different view. His reactions were slow; but, by the time of the Japanese attack on Pearl Harbour eighteen months later, the number of groups participating in the various aspects of the foreign-policy-making process had grown enormously.

First, and in some ways the most important for Britain's relations with America, were the US Army General Staff. Here we enter into an area into which few other than military historians

[3] Elizabeth Barker, *Churchill and Eden at War*, London, 1978, pp. 82–3, 85, 93, 96–7, 99, 102–3, 108, 117.
[4] See Clauson to Laithwaite, 20 April 1942, in Nicholas Mansergh (ed.), *Constitutional Relations between Britain and India: The Transfer of Power, 1942–1947*, vol. I, no. 656. For Roosevelt's messages see *FRUS 1942*, vol. I, pp. 615–16, 633–4.
[5] See Chapter 10 below. In 1943 he minuted to Mr Attlee: 'Nothing is easier than to find grounds of disagreement with the President and few things would be more unhelpful.' PREM 3 181/2, 23 July 1943, cited Barker, p. 87.

have penetrated.[6] Like its sister service, the US Navy, the Army had been forced to develop its own foreign policy in the inter-war years.[7] This policy could be described as one of hemispheric isolationism. The US Army had no Mahon-style doctrines to lead it to embrace either overseas expansion or pan-Anglo-Saxonism. Its soldiers had only a limited experience of modern war, their involvement in the 1914–18 war ending before it had really got into its stride. Their overseas experience, even at the senior level, tended to have been acquired in the Philippines, America's mini-India, in the 1900s and 1920s.

On the other hand, the Army leadership, especially George C. Marshall, the Chief of Staff in 1940, had learnt the hard way how to manage Congress.[8] The apparatus of the separate congressional committee had given to its leaders direct access to congressional opinion in a way impossible in Britain. The Army had learnt to be more sensitive to congressional than to administration opinions. Congress voted the budget, and Congress in its turn had come to trust the US Army. Marshall gave Roosevelt a degree of congressional control he had not always enjoyed before.

The US Army leadership approached the problems of the Second World War in a very different state of mind from their British colleagues. Very little has been written on the development of military strategy or thought in the US Army between the wars.[9] The strategy advocated by the Joint Chiefs of Staff after the American entry into the war, however, betrays no sign of the rethinking of traditional doctrine current in Britain. Direct cross-channel attack, objection to diversionary attacks as wasteful of American force, and the notorious but questionable distinction[10] drawn between political and military objectives, are the highest form of sophistication in the

---

[6] Studies of the development of American military strategic thought between the wars are largely lacking.

[7] Fred Greene, 'The Military View of American National Policy, 1904–1940', *Am. Hist. Rev.*, 66, 1960–1.

[8] See Forrest C. Pogue, *George C. Marshall*, vol. I, The Education of a General, *1880–1939*, New York, 1966.

[9] The defence of the Philippines against attack by superior Japanese forces appears to have been their major preoccupation; Greene 'The Military View'; Louis Morton, 'Germany First: The Basic Concept of Allied Strategy in World War II', in Kent Greenfield (ed.), *Command Decisions*, Washington, DC, 1960.

[10] See Mark A. Stoler, *The Politics of the Second Front: American Military Planning and Diplomacy in Coalition Warfare, 1941–1943*, Westport, Conn., 1977.

field of strategic ideas detectable in the thinking of the US military leadership. 'Concentration of forces' was the doctrine. Allies were an alien concept in their military thinking.

Unlike the US Navy, which had at least an Anglophile element in the high command, the US Army had none (or none that has emerged so far). Such study of the First World War as had been carried out left the US military with no respect for British generalship. It had been palpably unable to win in 1914–18;[11] and its military record in 1939–41 was not such as to inspire respect.[12] The senior military officers tended to be of Middle Western origin or from the Old South, though not from its old, comparatively Anglophile, families. After their fear of Bolshevism, distrust of Britain is the major factor discernible in their recorded reactions to the initial approaches made by Britain in 1940, and to their contacts with British strategic thinking at the Argentia Conference in August 1941.[13] Nor were they immune to the image of German military professionalism. General Wedemeyer, from Omaha, of mixed German–Irish parentage, Marshall's leading strategic planner, spent two years at the German War College. His father-in-law, General Embrick, whom Marshall recalled from retirement to act as his senior strategic adviser, a Pennsylvanian of Scottish–German pioneer descent, was equally hostile.[14] General Boetticher, the main source for Hitler's belief in American isolationism, did not invent his reports. They were based on his good contacts with members of the American High Command.[15] These men had had little or no hand in the decision to put defeat of Germany first in November 1940. Plan Dog was drafted by Admiral Stark, who put maintenance of the European and Far Eastern balances of power and prevention of the disruption of the British Empire as the definition of America's goals.[16] In the summer

[11] Forrest Pogue, *George C. Marshall*, vol. II, *Ordeal and Hope*, New York, 1966, p. 133.
[12] Victories over the Turks in Palestine in 1918 and over the Italians in Libya in 1940–1 clearly did not count, being won against 'lesser breeds'. The British victory of 8 August, 1918, Ludendorff's 'blackest day' for the German Army, seems to have passed largely unnoticed by American military historians intent on the American experience at St Mihiel.
[13] Stoler, *Politics of the Second Front*, pp. 14–15; (General) Albert C. Wedemeyer, *Wedemeyer Reports*, New York, 1958, pp. 442–5.
[14] Pogue, *Marshall*, vol. II, pp. 133–4.
[15] Wedemeyer, pp. 10–11.
[16] For the reaction of the US military see Stoler, *Politics of the Second Front*, pp. 7–8.

of 1940, conviction that Britain would be defeated, and fantasies about Nazi subversion in South America were their two most absolute conceptions.[17]

Their first major encounters with the British military left them appalled at the efficient and unified organisation underlying the presentation of Britain's strategic proposals, and galvanised life into their own machinery for strategic planning and the provision of strategic recommendations to the President. Their British colleagues were, however, equally ill-prepared to cope with them. No serious efforts had been made to keep up or improve on the contacts between the two armies made in 1917–18.

The British general staff were divided into pan-Anglo-Saxonists and imperial isolationists. They did, however, understand the importance of providing a coalition Chiefs of Staff for a coalition High Command. The British Joint Staff Mission to Washington became after Pearl Harbour an essential component in this relationship.[18] The dispatch of General Dill to Washington, after his breakdown in health made his replacement as Chief of Staff by Alanbrooke unavoidable, was a stroke of genius. Dill succeeded in establishing relations of confidence with Marshall which ended only with Dill's death.[19] It did not overcome such manifestations of continuing Anglophobia as the comment of the Joint War Planning Committee in May 1943 shows, 'Britain exploits the resources and peoples of other nations to ensure her position of dominance'.[20] The Dill–Marshall relationship and the brooding presence of Henry Stimson as Secretary for War contained this nativism.[21]

It was the diplomatic skill and genius of General Eisenhower which succeeded in establishing from the early planning of the North African invasion a degree of Anglo-American harmony, which for convenience sake can be called 'Shaefism', which was to become characteristic of Anglo-American military contacts *in Europe*. It matched the success of the Joint British Staff Mission (JBSM) in

[17] David C. Haglund, 'George C. Marshall and the Question of Military Aid to England, May–June 1940', *J. Contemp. Hist.*, 15, 1980.

[18] There is, as yet, no really adequate study of the British Joint Staff Mission to Washington.

[19] Wedemeyer, characteristically, regarded Dill's influence on Marshall as 'pernicious'. Wedemeyer, pp. 164–7, 187–8

[20] Stoler, *Politics of the Second Front*, pp. 82–8.

[21] Stimson and Bundy, *On Active Service in Peace and War*, pp. 142–3, 149, 158–9, 168–74, 176–80.

Washington and was greatly to mislead and inhibit British thinking about relations with America for much of the post-war period.

Second to the importance of the Army is the entry into foreign-policy matters of the New Deal bureaucracy and its enormous inflation by the continuous interventions of new agencies and entry of new personalities. Four groups are of particular importance. The Secretary of the Interior, Harold Ickes, who was equally responsive to the anxieties of American large-scale industry and determined to enforce political statist leadership upon them,[22] gathered around himself a like-minded group of industrial managers. Other entrants from private industry, equally responsive to ideas of industrial imperialism overseas, included Hull's two successors as Secretary of State, Stettinius, who came in as the head of Lend-Lease, and Byrnes. With their entry into the positions of power the 1920s conflict between the large 'multinationals' and would-be 'multi-national' firms came to the fore again.[23]

The effect of America's entry into the war was to revive the hopes of the State Department's economic internationalists. Convinced that the outbreak of war had merely confirmed their beliefs, they seized on the chance of planning for the peace (as they had hoped for a time to use Britain's need of Lend-Lease) to work for the destruction of the British imperial economic bloc, to dismantle Ottawa and to break up the sterling area.[24] They were now joined by the economists of the Treasury, who, apart from a few Keynesians, largely shared the views of Hull and the State Department economists. The Treasury, however, outweighed the State Department considerably in the bureaucratic balance of power in Washington and, although Bretton Woods was a victory for American financial conservatism over Keynesianism it was Harry Dexter White's victory, and his brand of conservatism was far from that of New York bankers, though it was as much the product of

---

[22] See Michael B. Stoff, *Oil, War and American Security. The Search for a National Policy on Foreign Oil, 1941–1949*, New Haven, Conn., 1980.

[23] On the alleged imperialism of the US multinationals, see Frank Straker, 'The Multinational Corporation. The New Imperialism?', *Columbia Journal of World Business*, 5, 1980.

[24] See the discussion in Warren F. Kimball, 'Lend-lease and the Open Door: The Temptation of British Opulence, 1937–1942', *Pol. Sci. Q.*, 86, 1971. On similar discussions in the summer of 1944, see George C. Herring Jr, 'The United States and British Bankruptcy, 1944–45: Responsibilities Deferred', *Pol. Sci. Q.*, 81, 1971.

White's sense of American political realities as it was of his economic outlook.[25]

The politics to which Mr White was sensitive were of course American rather than international and specifically congressional. The sense of being the mainspring of the fight against Hitler is already clearly established at the time of the Lend-Lease debates, long before America's entry into the war. From 1942 onwards it was to manifest itself repeatedly in sentiments in which an American sense of moral superiority went hand in hand with the consciousness of American power. The Wilsonian vision of making over not only America's enemies but her allies is particularly obvious on issues of anti-colonialism.[26] The very real necessity of making Anglo-American agreements palatable to Congress became inevitably an indispensable ploy in American negotiations with Britain. Here President Roosevelt's past record of failure in managing Congress became an asset rather than a debit. His success in securing and maintaining a bipartisan consensus in Congress was enhanced by the conservatism of the 1942 Congress. His habit of recruiting new blood from the Senate (as with Truman in 1944) helped to avoid trouble between Congress and the Administration. It added, however, to the stuffiness and immobility of American thinking.

Another new element, in some senses crucial, was the entry into policy-making of the scientists and the scientific administrators. Here the interposition of the conviction of American power is even more striking than in Congress, for being the less expected. Over wide areas of scientific work, Anglo-American cooperation appears to have functioned admirably.[27] British scientists, and the equally important group of refugee scientists from Europe, were, with a few exceptions, internationalist in the sense of pre-1914 internationalism. They worked and published the results of their work

[25] Armand van Dormael, *Bretton Woods: Birth of a Monetary System*, London, 1978; Richard N. Gardner, *Sterling–Dollar Diplomacy. The Origins and Prospects of Our International Order*, 2nd edition, London, 1969; David Rees, *Harry Dexter White, A Study in Paradox*, New York, 1973.

[26] On this see D.C. Watt, 'American Anti-Colonialist Policies and the End of the European Colonial Empires, 1941–1962', in A.N.J. den Hollaender (ed.), *Contagious Conflict. The Impact of American Dissent on European Life*, Leiden, 1973. A revised version is included in this volume as Chapter 11.

[27] M. Gowing, 'Anglo-American Scientific Cooperation in the Second World War', paper presented to the Conference of the British and United States National Committee for the History of the Second World War, London, July 1980.

for the world. But with the atomic bomb matters were to be very different. On the British side, Lord Cherwell expressed distrust at the idea of putting Britain completely at the mercy of the Americans; and at a vital moment the American proposal for joint cooperation was not taken up. The reward for Britain was to find the imposition of military security on the free exchange of information from the American side as a result of a decision, in which Roosevelt and Stimson participated, to create an American monopoly of the bomb, and on the post-war commercial exploitation of atomic power. With very great effort Churchill succeeded in getting this reversed, but the subsequent history of the agreement was not altogether happy. 'The salad is heaped in a bowl permanently smeared with the garlic of suspicion', wrote Sir Ronald Campbell early in 1945.[28] Where the British participated it was as 'junior partners'. The Anglo-American partnership on the laboratory floor was friendly and fruitful. The difficulty lay in the nationalisms of the scientific administrators and the consciousness of American industrial and scientific capacity compared with Britain's 'six men on a hand-made bicycle'.

The limits of what the Anglophiles in America could do, and the difference between their version of Atlanticism and American nationalism, can be seen most clearly in the attempts to obtain America's entry into the war in 1940–1. Lord Lothian's embassy still awaits a proper study; but it was clearly an enormous success. Despite the attacks on his avoidance of propaganda[29] and the minimal scale of operations of the British Library of Information, once the real block in London had been removed, the liaison between the British Information Services (BIS) in New York and the 'war hawks', the Committee to defend America by Aiding the Allies, and the Century Club Group (stuffed as the latter was with the Council for Foreign Relations end of the foreign-policy community) was both covert and effective.[30] The BIS made effective use, where

[28] Cited in M. Gowing, *Britain and Atomic Energy, 1939–1945*, London, 1964, p. 235. British records and United States memoirs disagree as to the degree of warmth which existed in the relations between General Groves, the US military man in charge of the Manhattan project, and Professor Chadwick, head of the British scientific mission in Washington.

[29] Ronald Tree, *When the Moon was high: Memoirs of War and Peace, 1897–1942*, London, 1975.

[30] Mark Chadwin, *The Warhawks*, New York, 1970; William M. Tuttle Jr, 'Aid to the Allies Short of War Versus American Intervention, 1940', *J. Am. Hist.*, 56, 1969–70.

possible, of inter-war inter-university contacts, especially of pre-war British beneficiaries of Commonwealth Fund fellowships in America. These inter-university contacts were to surface with equal force between the historians of the Office of Strategic Services (OSS) research and analysis staff and those of the Foreign Office Research Department.[31]

The British government were in fact able at this point to call to their aid a factor which to a certain extent existed in their relations with Europe, but to nothing like the same extent, the degree to which British and American society had already begun to interpenetrate each other, especially at the level of the imagination and the image their respective societies had formed of the other. Not only were there links between the two university systems and the research communities built around them: there were all kinds of other links, between Rotary societies, interlocking business and financial relationships, and connections at the level of the development of managerial philosophy, and contacts at the level of radical and progressive ideas. Studies of Labour's attitudes to the New Deal are, so far, in their infancy and concentrate on the initial years of the New Deal rather than the later 1930s.[32] But as British Labour became more and more concerned with war against Germany, its pragmatic right wing and the unions developed links with American unionism, and came more and more to think of America, with all its faults, as the land where the battle against Fascism was still unsettled, and as the only natural ally for British democracy.

The impact of America on Britain and vice versa was relatively unhampered by knowledge or direct experience. Britain in the Blitz, under Churchill, became in the hands of American reportage the heroic struggle so many historians are now determined to question. America offered sanctuary for British children,[33] collected bundles for Britain and devoured Hollywood's *Mrs Miniver* as though it was

---

[31] D.C. Watt, 'Every War Must End: War-Time Planning for Post-War Security in Britain and America in the Wars of 1914–1918 and 1939–1945. The Roles of Professional Historians', *Transactions of the Royal Historical Society*, Fifth Series, 28, 1978.

[32] Barbara Malament, 'British Labour and Roosevelt's New Deal: The Response of the Left and the Unions', *J. British Studies*, 17, 1978; Richard Pear, 'The Impact of the New Deal on British Economic and Political Ideas', *Bulletin of the British Association of American Studies*, New Series, No. 4, 1962.

[33] For one account of this see Philip Bailey, *America Lost and Found*, London, 1981.

gospel. American 'volunteers' enlisted in the British Army and Air Force.

The impact of America on Britain was rather more complicated. For the movie-going population the Hollywood image of America, even in the hands of the heavily realistic school of directors, was of a land of Cockayne. To that, before the American entry into the war, was added the Churchillian image of Roosevelt, himself only a voice, but a voice second only to Churchill, heard through oceanic waves of static, the voice of an authentic democratic leader. The arrival of the GIs was a rather different experience.[34] In one sense it confronted the British people with the reality of American wealth and power. The GIs attracted camp-followers, male and female, disrupted the ordered tenure of the British countryside, awoke sexual and material jealousy. Black soldiers presented a peculiarly difficult problem.[35] All in all, however, the popular image and approval of America acted as a limiting factor on such anti-Americanism as ruled among the élites. Attempts to mobilise the image of America as a classless society by the 'populist' opposition in Britain, that unholy alliance of Beaverbrook, the surviving popular front ideologists (Tom Wintringham, for example), the 'people's war' advocates, *Picture Post*, and the Commonwealth party, had very little immediate effect (though their influence on the adolescents of the 1940s, who today make up the Social Democratic Party, is another matter).

Many of the images each élite had cherished of the other failed to survive the friendships and relationships which sprang up along all the fissures opened by interpenetration. The sheer multiplicity of openings which the plurality, both of American society as a whole and of the élites in particular, offered, became a weapon, perhaps the most potent weapon in the continuum of Anglo-American negotiations which underlay the pre-1942 association and the post-1942 alliance. Many Americans did not notice it though it was very noticeable to the US joint military planners and Joint Chiefs of Staff, and particularly resented in the one theatre of war where separation rather than interpenetration was the rule, in the Pacific war. In its preliminaries the British government had anchored themselves so

---

[34] Norman Longmate, *The GIs: The Americans in Britain, 1942–1945*, London, 1975.

[35] See Christopher Thorne, *Allies of a Kind*, London, 1978, p. 143; for a more detailed account, Christopher Thorne, 'Britain and the Black GIs', *New Community*, 3, 1974.

firmly to the American strategy that the alternative strategy of postponing a confrontation until victory in Europe was achieved, urged by Sir Robert Craigie from Tokyo, was never given a hearing. Instead, at the critical moment, pressure was exerted on Washington not to accept the Japanese compromise.[36] Pearl Harbour was duly attacked, Sir Robert Craigie suppressed; Churchill's comments on his final dispatch indicated deep satisfaction, even though the price of America's entry into the war was some very bad moments for his government and the eventual loss of the empire east of Suez.[37]

Interpenetration was a good tool for the British at the tactical level. It is, however, arguable that at the strategic level it deceived the British more than the Americans, since it did little to curb the determination of those at the top to make it clear where the crown rested. The weakness in the American position, however, lay in the same plurality which made interpenetration possible. Only the President could make one of it. Roosevelt preferred not to, save where congressional support was necessary. His negotiations, his visions of post-war America and of a post-war security system, remained his own private property, much of which left no mark either in the American archives or on his successors. Roosevelt was sure that he could control British policy in the post-war era. The Quebec agreements on nuclear sharing were only the final hook with which he hoped to secure British good behaviour after the war's end.

Roosevelt's Achilles' heel lay in his fear of a 1919-style resurgence of isolationism in the United States. He was therefore determined not to be enlisted to fight British causes in Europe: this determination was shared by his military.[38] Security in Europe, stability in France:[39] these were British, not American, problems. Above all, he was determined not to be drawn into the Anglo-Soviet conflict. Over

---

[36] Richard J. Grace, 'Whitehall and the Ghost of Appeasement, November 1941: *Diplomatic History*, 3, 1979.

[37] On Sir Robert Craigie's final report of 4 February 1943 and its suppression by Churchill see FO 371/35957, F7900/7301/G42 [Japan 75] F821/821/G, F 5062/G, F5766/G with minutes by Ashley Clarke 21 September 1943. Churchill to Eden 19 September 1943.

[38] As witness its opposition to a Mediterranean strategy in 1942–4 and to a final offensive towards Berlin and Prague in April 1945.

[39] As witness his attitude to the division of Germany into separate zones of occupation. See William Franklin, 'Zonal Boundaries and Access to Berlin', *World Politics*, 16, 1963–4; see also Tony Sharp, *The Wartime Alliance and the Zonal Division of Germany*, Oxford, 1975, pp. 42–4, 46–9, 61–3, 64–7, 82–9, 90–1.

the Soviet Union he had no hooks. Stalin would therefore have to be courted, wooed, constantly chatted up. Poland was, of course, a problem but principally because of the Polish vote in the 1944 elections. His vision of a world dominated by the Big Four, with America leading, could be destroyed by Soviet suspicion, intransigence, refusal to cooperate. In the meantime, why should not Britain cooperate with America on America's terms, on oil,[40] on commercial airlines,[41] over the Argentine?[42] To this the British really had no reply. 'Do you want me to beg, like Fala?' asked Churchill bitterly at Quebec in October 1944.[43]

The issues aroused by the American conflict with Britain over the Argentine[44] formed a particular case of Anglo-American conflict, which embodied in its strongest form the American conviction that they were engaged in an ideological war against Fascism anywhere and everywhere, and the British desire not to complicate the existing pattern of conflict by forcing into the enemy camp a country on whose exports Britain was so dependent. American anti-Fascism was reinforced by the long-standing incompatibility between Argentinian evocations of pan-Hispanic pan-Americanism against America's pan-Americanism. British pragmatism was reinforced by the memories of the long history of American challenges to British economic investment in the Argentine. To complete the circle, American hostility to the Argentinian government involved the fear that Britain and 'the City' wished to maintain this régime as part of a planned post-war alternative of closed economic blocs against the economic internationalist system desired by Hull, the State Department and the Treasury.[45] British realism involved a calculation of Britain's weakness *vis-à-vis* both the United States and Argentinian nationalism. Braden's failure in turn epitomises the real

---

[40] Stoff, *Oil, War and American Security.*
[41] This subject still lacks a real examination. But see Robert Bothwell and J.L. Granatstein, 'Canada and the War-time Negotiations over Civil Aviation: the Functional Principle in Operation', *International History Review*, 2, 1980.
[42] Callum A. Macdonald, 'The Politics of Intervention: The United States and the Argentine, 1941–1946', *J. Latin American Studies*, 12, 1980.
[43] Cited from the Morgenthau Presidential Diary, p. 1512, memorandum of 15 September 1944 by David Rees, *Harry Dexter White: A Study in Paradox*, London and New York, 1973, p. 273.
[44] Macdonald, 'Politics of Intervention'; Sir David Kelly, *The Ruling Few*, London, 1953; Woods, *The Roosevelt Foreign Policy Establishment.*
[45] Macdonald, 'Politics of Intervention'.

inability of the United States government to cash in on the predominance of which most members of the policy-making élites in America, especially the new wartime entrants, were so conscious.

For the British élite the United States represented a particularly difficult problem. Most were conscious of the change in the relationships between the two countries which the increasing disparity between the careless, disorganised and only partial mobilisation of American strength underlined and the ebbing British strength, despite the almost total mobilisation of British resources for national ends by the consensus totalitarianism of the wartime years; but few had so acute a sense of the timing of the change as did Churchill. Eden, by contrast, had a far sounder grasp of many of the diplomatic issues than his master, while displaying the same apparent blindness to the nature of power which was to ruin his career at Suez. Within the civil service, the Foreign Office and the Chiefs of Staff mechanism, pan-Anglo-Saxonism, internationalism, continental isolationism and imperial isolationism, with strong anti-American overtones, can all be found. What struck contemporary Americans, especially those already predisposed towards suspicion of Britain, and is equally striking today,[46] was the degree of consensus across the whole political coalition on matters of external policy, especially on the central issues of imperial and Commonwealth development.

There was only one possible method of dealing with the dilemmas posed by the disparity in British and American power and by the differences between American goals and British interests, possible that is to the generations which made up the Churchill coalition, given their education, tradition and common learning zones. Anglo-American conflict was culturally unthinkable and strategically impossible. Reordering of the remnants of what was generally agreed to have been the thoroughly unsatisfactory system of international relationships between the wars was either impossible or potentially disastrous without American participation. There remained only patient, *ad hoc*, issue by issue discussion, negotiation and consultation in which all the remaining prestige and authority on which Britain could call could be brought to bear on the American élites, mass propaganda, the technique employed by

[46] See the passages in William Roger Louis, *Imperialism at Bay: The United States and the Decolonisation of the British Empire, 1941–1945*, Oxford, 1977, pp. 11–16.

Lloyd George at Versailles, being generally agreed to be self-defeating. There was, however, one difference from Versailles. This time Britain did not enjoy the aid of Dominions' statesmen in the same way as in 1919. They were too busy evolving policies designed to exercise their own independence. On occasion Dominions' independence could be effective, as with the Australian rôle at San Francisco; but it could no longer be orchestrated. Bit by bit, as with Lord Haley, Hilton Poynton and Kenneth Robinson of the Colonial Office on trusteeship, Sir Charles Webster and Gladwyn Jebb and others at Dumbarton Oaks, Keynes, Duncan Robertson, Lionel Robbins and Redvers Opie at Bretton Woods, Sir John Dill and Admiral Sir Henry Moore (the only British admiral who could cope with Admiral King) on the Joint Staff Mission, Sir William Strang on the European Advisory Commission, the British succeeded in gaining what Acheson perceptively described[47] as 'a chance to talk the matter over with us before the thing crystallised ... to go over it with us, pointing out their views and to be allowed to come in on the formulation at the start'. There can be little doubt that a similarity of education and élite status and the parallelisms in their respective approaches to internationalist issues greatly aided this process. It depended, however, on a willingness to cooperate on the American side.

This willingness was not apparent where the British leadership was confronted by Soviet expansion into Eastern Europe. Indeed, the difference between the British and American attitudes to the Soviet Union dated back to Teheran and before and grew *pari passu* with British consciousness of Britain's increasing weakness *vis-à-vis* the strength of America's forces on the ground and in the air. Churchill, already conscious of the growing disparity between British and American power, found himself neglected by Roosevelt at Teheran even when he was not in an actual dissenting minority. Equally, he was denied the prior discussions with Roosevelt that he wanted before Yalta as he had been before Teheran. To American policy-makers, from Roosevelt downwards, the biggest danger was an Anglo-Soviet confrontation in which Britain would demand American support.[48] Contrary to what revisionist historians in the

[47] Cited in Blum, *From the Morgenthau Diaries*, vol. III, p. 233.
[48] Elizabeth Kimball Maclean, 'Joseph E. Davies'; *FRUS Quebec*, p. 190 cited Thorne, *Allies of a Kind*, p. 381.

United States now maintain, both Roosevelt and the State Department were prepared to accept Soviet predominance in Poland and south-eastern Europe, provided only that that predominance was not exercised to establish single party states and to exclude America entirely.[49] They were not prepared to be manipulated into a conflict with Russia to suit Britain's imperial ends.[50] Churchill argued against this determination and these illusions in vain. He was prepared to be ruthlessly realistic over Poland but it was essentially a matter of honour for him; for Roosevelt it was only a matter of the Polish-American vote in the 1944 elections.

Churchill's famous percentages agreement with Stalin of October 1944 was thus monitored and regarded as acceptable by the State Department,[51] even though for form's sake the usual protest against spheres of influence was registered. It represented a postponement of the Anglo-Soviet confrontation the State Department dreaded. To Churchill, it was the best that could be salvaged. It must be said that the dominant view within the Foreign Office, led by Eden, was to find evidence of Soviet goodwill and to suppress all views that threatened this, even to the point where there was a head-on collision between Eden and the Chiefs of Staff on their provision of strategic advice for post-war planning which included mention of the Soviet Union as a possible enemy.[52]

The changes of 1945, the brief period of the Churchill caretaker government, followed by the victory of the Labour party in the July 1945 General Election in Britain, and the death of Roosevelt

---

[49] Eduard Mark, 'American Policy towards Eastern Europe and the Origins of the Cold War, 1941–1946: An Alternative Explanation', *J. Am. Hist.*, 68, 1981.

[50] Thorne, *Allies of a Kind*, p. 499, citing Hopkins in May 1945; Forrestal Diaries, entries of 16 March, 20 May 1945.

[51] Mark, 'American Policy', citing minutes of the State Department Policy Committee, preserved in the papers of Harley Notter. This would seem greatly to modify the picture of State Department uncertainty as to the details of the Churchill–Stalin agreement hitherto accepted by American diplomatic historians: cf. Albert Resis, 'The Churchill–Stalin "Percentages" Agreement on the Balkans, Moscow, October 1944', *Am. Hist. R.*, 83, 1978; see also Hugh de Santis, *The Diplomacy of Silence. The American Foreign Service, the Soviet Union and the Cold War, 1933–1947*, Chicago, 1980, p. 125.

[52] On which see Llewellyn Woodward, *British Foreign Policy in the Second World War*, London, vol. V, pp. 203–10; see also Julian Lewis's work, cited in Chapter 1, footnote 8 (Oxford D. Phil, 1981).

and the succession of Truman to the Presidency,[53] despite the
arguments of individual revisionists, are significant more for the
changes of styles at the top of the decision-making structure than for
any basic changes in outlook, image or approach among the élite as a
whole. The main change on the British side was the substitution of a
pentarchy, Attlee, Bevin, Cripps, Morrison and Dalton, under
Attlee's remarkable chairmanship, for the unease and discontinuities of Churchill's relationship with Eden and his Cabinet.
Attlee and Bevin had both played a leading part in the deliberations
of the Post-Hostilities Planning Committee during the coalition.

In the American case the significant changes came later, with the
retirement of Stimson and the freezing out of the progressive New
Deal elements in Roosevelt's Cabinet, Ickes, Morgenthau, Henry
Wallace and their supporters, or earlier (as alleged by some revisionists), with the substitution of Stettinius for Hull. American historians
looking backwards have made much of the failure of the proposed
American loan to Russia,[54] the abrupt cancellation of Lend-Lease,[55]
and Truman's rough treatment of Molotov before the San Francisco
Conference.

They are, however, falling into the traps which beset all historians
looking for antecedents: those involved in separating incidents from
their immediate historical context. Much more significant,
especially in view of British anxieties *vis-à-vis* the relentless advance
of Soviet troops into Central Europe, the coup in Roumania which
followed the euphoric friendship of Yalta (and had clearly been
planned while the Big Three were still meeting), was Truman's echo
of Roosevelt's suspicions that Britain was trying to drag America
into its conflict with the Soviet Union. Truman rejected Churchill's
pleas for pre-emptive military moves against Berlin and Prague and
snubbed Churchill's initial advances which were delivered personally to the new President by Joseph Davies and underlined by
Hopkins's last visit to Moscow.

[53] Lord Halifax, the British Ambassador, was not impressed by Truman, calling him
an 'honest and diligent mediocrity ... a bungling, if well-meaning, amateur',
animadverting to the 'Missouri County court-house calibre of his personal entourage', FO 371/57606, cited in Peter G. Boyle, 'The British Foreign Office View of
Soviet–American Relations 1945–46', *Diplomatic History*, 3, 1979.

[54] Thomas G. Paterson, 'The Abortive American Loan to Russia and the Origins of
the Cold War, 1943–1946', *J. Am. Hist.*, 56, 1969–70.

[55] George C. Herring Jr, 'Lend-Lease to Russia and the Origins of the Cold War,
1944–45', *J. Am. Hist.*, 56, 1969–70.

It is not surprising in the light of this to find significant elements in the Foreign Office beginning to turn back towards a Europeanist policy. The British delegation to San Francisco went with instructions to back the French rather than the American position over Indo-China.[56] It was in May 1945 that a group of the ablest and most energetic of the Foreign Office planners began to revive interest in the creation of a West European bloc.[57] Somewhere about the same time the Foreign Office's Northern Department began discreetly to shed its leading Russophiles. The Foreign Office's change of view matched that of the incoming Foreign Secretary, Ernest Bevin, whose initial advocacy of a British participation in a West European bloc to match the strategies of the United States dates back to his visit to America in 1925 as part of a capitalist–Labour mission, led by Sir Henry Steele-Maitland, to study American mass production methods.[58] The circumstances of May 1945 seemed more than adequate to revive the conviction that he had then formed.[59] The new Foreign Secretary was to set his planners at work on a West European bloc within a month of his return from Potsdam.[60]

The realities of American foreign policy which confronted the new government were, in all truth, forbidding: the cancellation of Lend-Lease;[61] the disappointment of Keynes's hopes of a free American

[56] See Chapter 10, below, for citations from the text of the instructions to the British delegation to the San Francisco Conference.

[57] For the development of the idea of a West European security 'bloc' in the Foreign Office, especially among those concerned with forward planning, see FO memorandum July 1945, cited in Victor Rothwell, *Britain and the Cold War, 1941–1947*, London, 1982, pp. 406–13 and 523. See also Turner to Troutbeck, 15 May 1945 together with the minutes of Con O'Neil and Ward of 30 May and 4 June on it, FO 371/C2432/22/G, and the minutes of a meeting of 25 July 1945 between Harvey, Ronald, Hall-Patch and Jebb from the Foreign Office, Wilfred Eady of the Treasury and Percy Lieschning of the Board of Trade, FO 371/UE 2534/813/53 cited in Sean Greenwood, 'The Origins of the Treaty of Dunkirk; Anglo-French Relations, 1944–47,' London Ph.D., 1982.

[58] In 1927, he had introduced a motion into the Trades Union Congress calling on the General Council to promote the creation of a European public opinion in favour of Europe becoming an economic entity. See Alan Bullock, *The Life and Times of Ernest Bevin*, vol. I, London 1960, pp. 286–8. Both Bevin and Attlee had spoken in favour of a bloc of West European nations under British leadership in 1944, see CAB 87/66 of 27 April, CAB 66/53 of 26 July 1944.

[59] For the meetings between Bevin, Cripps, Dalton, Hall-Patch, Eady and Lieschning of 10 August and 17 August see FO 371/UE3683/53 and UE3689/3683/G.

[60] Hoyer-Millar memorandum, 'Anglo-French relations and a western group', 6 August 1945, FO 371/49069 Z 9639/13/G.

[61] Blum, *From the Morgenthau Diaries*, vol. III, pp. 447–8.

grant-in-aid for British reconstruction and the substitution of an onerous loan;[62] the breakdown of collaboration on atomic development;[63] the confinement of the military channel of communication via the Joint Staff Mission in Washington to discussions on the exchange of honours;[64] the revival of Anglophobia by the Republican party in its early preparations for the 1946 mid-term and 1948 elections, especially noticeable in the hearings on the Anglo-American loan. The Foreign Office was sufficiently worried to create an Interdepartmental Committee on American opinion and the British Empire 'as a sort of general staff for the projection of the British Empire'.[65] Bevin and Attlee were convinced believers in Anglo-American friendship, hoping to prevent American withdrawal from Europe, hoping to convince the American government of the seriousness of the Soviet 'threat', seen not as a military but as a political and subversive threat to Western European stability, and particularly anxious to involve the United States into acceptance of, and support for, what the Joint Planning Staff recommended should be a 'British Monroe Doctrine' for the Middle East.[66] Bevin's Palestine policy and the British negotiation of private agreements on Middle Eastern oil, to replace the 1944 and 1945 Agreements which fell foul of the Senate,[67] were equally part of the same policy. And when Bevin realised in December 1946 that United States support for Britain's Palestine policy could not be relied on, he immediately turned his mind to the withdrawal from the Palestine mandate.

The State Department, as it happened, was far from united on the question of how far it was prepared to go in recognising the primacy of British interests in the Middle East. By instinct, Loy Henderson and Wallace Murray of the Office of Near Eastern and African Affairs were dedicated to the idea that America had some particular mission to the Arab world, a mission springing from America's innocence of the crime of colonialism. America, in their view, had a deep interest in the movement for Arab unity and in Arab efforts to

[62] Gardner, *Sterling–Dollar Diplomacy*, pp. 184–7.
[63] M. Gowing, *Independence and Deterrence; Britain and Atomic Energy, 1945–1952*, London, 1974, vol. I, pp. 92–123.
[64] Private information.
[65] Clark Kerr Papers, FO 800/300, folios 232–7.
[66] CAB 128/3, CP(45)7 of 11 September 1945; Bevin Memorandum, 17 September 1945.
[67] Stoff, *Oil, War and American Security*, pp. 184–95.

'extricate themselves from the commitments they were freed to make before the beginning of the Second World War to various great powers giving those powers special positions and privileges which detract from the full independence of those countries'.[68] The belief that the Arab nationalist movement looked to America 'to support them in their efforts' to prevent Britain and France from attempting yet again 'to consolidate their pre-war spheres of influence', and that American diplomatists in the area were looked to for 'honest, politically disinterested information and good counsel' was urged on President Truman, as it had been on President Roosevelt by the US ministers to Egypt, Saudi Arabia, Syria and the Lebanon.[69] To this they added the gratuitous advice that there need be no conflict with Soviet policy in the area since Soviet policy paralleled that of the United States, advice which Truman himself echoed. Henderson's greatest fear was that the United States would withdraw into isolation after the Second World War, as she had in 1919, standing 'idly by while the western victors ... divided the Near East into spheres of influence to suit themselves',[70] and he was instrumental in obtaining a specific assurance from Truman that this would not happen again.

This sentimental anti-colonialism, had it been the only policy urged on Truman by the State Department, would have gone a long way to confirm the anxieties and suspicions of the United States which inspired the Colonial Office and the old Middle Eastern hands of the Foreign Office. The European and Soviet experts in the State Department,[71] the OSS[72] and the Chiefs of Staff,[73] however, urged the President to avoid anything likely to damage American interests in the Middle East, which, in their view, were bound up with the strength of the British position. Despite this advice, however,

[68] *FRUS 1945*, vol. VIII, pp. 10–11, Henderson to Brigadier Vaughan, 10 November 1945.
[69] *FRUS 1945*, vol. VIII, pp. 11–18, Henderson memorandum, 'Replies of the President', 13 November 1945.
[70] Henderson to Vaughan, 10 November 1945.
[71] Grew memorandum, April 1945, Bohlen Papers: Kennan memorandum, 24 February 1948, *FRUS 1948*, vol. V, pp. 655–9.
[72] See JCOS, Leahy record, Folder 88, OSS Research and Analysis memorandum, 2 April 1945; *FRUS 1944*, vol. V. pp. 485–6; *FRUS 1945*, vol. VIII, pp. 2–3, 727–30.
[73] *FRUS 1946*, vol. VII, pp. 631–3; Leahy to Byrnes, 13 March 1946, JCOS Leahy Papers, folder 110.

Truman, desperate to preserve the Democratic coalition which had been the basis of Roosevelt's continuous electoral success, followed the Zionist line supplied to him by David K. Niles of his staff, by Gentile Zionists (and Anglophobes) such as Senator Robert Wagner and Representative Emmanuel Celler, and by the young Clifford Clark, his contact with the Democratic party organisation in New York. Britain carried the main burden of supporting Turkish and Greek resistance to Soviet pressure, which, with the increasing costs of supporting the British zone in Germany,[74] led to a steady haemorrhage of the American and Canadian dollar loans. In the meantime, the British Embassy in Washington observed a steady increase in the 'realism' and 'maturity' of American attitudes towards the Soviet Union.[75] Contrary to the version of developments advanced by many revisionists, the Washington Embassy saw this as arising not from changes in view among the policy-makers, but from American 'grass-roots' opinion, 'a remarkable example of the democratic process at work, because the driving power has come not from the top but below. Events and public opinion have forced the obviously uncertain and reluctant administration into affording for the world at least some measure of the leadership which the US ought to be providing', so the Counsellor in the Washington Embassy, Donelly, reported in March 1946.[76]

The way was therefore open for the issue of the Truman doctrine, for the 'Fifteen Weeks' and the Marshall Plan. Here we begin to approach the frontier of contemporary historiography, where revisionists, traditionalists and synthesisers in America quarrel over responsibility for the Cold War and capitalist imperialism, while British historians recite the myths of Dalton's and Bevin's seminal rôle in translating American rhetoric into concrete proposals and orchestrate the European reaction. Recent research emphasises the convergence of American and British diplomatic and military advice[77] and calls attention to the rôle of the British Embassy in

[74] D.C. Watt, 'Hauptprobleme der britischen Deutschlandpolitik, 1945–1949', in Claus Scharf and Hans-Jurgen Schröeder (eds.), *Die Deutschlandpolitik Grossbritanniens und die britische Zone, 1945–1949*, Wiesbaden, 1979.

[75] Boyle, 'British Foreign Office View of Soviet–American Relations'.

[76] FO 371/57606, cited in Boyle, 'British Foreign Office View of Soviet–American Relations'.

[77] Scott Jackson, 'Prologue to the Marshall Plan: the Origins of the American Commitment to a European Recovery Program', *J. Am. Hist.*, 65, 1978–9.

Moscow in the evolution of Kennan's long telegram,[78] and of policy on the economic recovery of Western Germany.[79] But the effects of this convergence and its translation into a reformulation of the old mid-Atlanticist stance, but with ideological overtones from wartime cooperation against Nazism, belong to the last parts of this study.

[78] See Roberts to Warner of 2 March 1946, FO 371/56840, N3369/971/8. For Roberts's action equivalent to and parallel with Kennan's 'long telegram' see FO 371/5673, N4065/97/38, telegram 181 of 14 March 1946, N4156/97/38, telegram 189 of 17 March 1946, N4157/97/38 telegram 190 of 18 March 1946.

[79] John Gimbel, *The Origins of the Marshall Plan*, Stanford, 1976.

6

1947–1963

From the Marshall Plan to the end of the 'New Frontier'; the dominance of the United States and Britain's decline assisted

The thirty years which followed the announcement of the Truman doctrine in March 1947 form a much longer period without major war than any of the periods hitherto covered in this study. The period presents a rather unusual picture when the generational divisions are compared with what are watershed years in the decline of British power and Anglo-American relations, the years of disaster 1963–4. In the space of one short twelve-month period, President Kennedy was assassinated and his team broken and divided by the adjustment to the succession. The advance of the multilateral force proposals destroyed the chances of American-led détente in Europe just at the time when its most obdurate opponent in Europe, Dr Adenauer, had finally been driven into retirement by the progressive elements in his party. Instead, President Johnson plunged his country blindly onwards into a policy of intervention in South East Asia and a conflict that America could not wage without destroying the culture, such as it was, to whose aid it had come, and could not win. In Britain the death of Hugh Gaitskell, followed by the enforced retirement of Harold Macmillan, saw the break-up of the Conservative party with the progressive loss of its outward-looking reformist wing and the advent to power of a Labour party already so bitterly divided that the new Premier, Harold Wilson, felt obliged to exercise a policy of party management most reminiscent of the policy of Count Taafe in the twilight of the Habsburg Empire, since it worked on the principle of keeping all factions in a state of balanced dissatisfaction.

At first sight British politics also seem to exhibit the phenomenon of a generational division in 1963–4 to correspond with the loss of the Anglo-American relationship which is so marked a feature of the years after Harold Wilson's ascent to the premiership, a loss which is far from being the responsibility of the British side of the partnership. American political life on the other hand seems to divide not at 1964, but rather at 1960, with an election contested between two 40-year-old candidates who had both served only as junior officers in the Second World War, and junior officers, moreover, in the Pacific, the theatre of war America had largely monopolised, rather than in the combined headquarters of the European or Mediterranean theatres. A second division seems at first sight to come with President Nixon's election in 1968 and his appointment of a Republican administration one half of which was composed of his Californian and other cronies and the other half of mavericks from the American policy establishment.

A closer view of the developments in America, however, shows that the general pattern is distorted by the 1960 election. On the Democratic side the distorting factor is the bold, not to say piratical, capture of a party machinery that had stagnated since the Roosevelt era by a personal machine based on money, academic know-how and political skills of a kind only Bostonian, New York or Chicago Irish politics could foster. On the Republican side the distorting factor lay in the choice in 1952 of a presidential candidate without political experience at any but the highest levels and the consequent failure of the Republican party either to resolve its internal conflicts or to produce adequate political machinery to consolidate the victory their all-conquering but non-political candidate had won for them. The electoral victories of the Democrats in 1960 and the Republicans in 1968 were achieved by the narrowest of margins in American history. Yet the consequences for American foreign policy were enormous. The first introduced into the American foreign-policy-making process a new university-based élite whose average age precluded experience of anything but American omnipotence, or so it seemed. The second brought to the control of American foreign relations for a crucial period a first generation immigrant from Europe, whose personal experience was deeply rooted in the processes of that civil war, which had destroyed European order and planted the super-powers in Europe's centre in the years 1939–45, a man whose approach to the methods of conduct and the concepts of foreign-policy-making in the United States was profoundly out of character and keeping with the American political process.

On the British side one can see a sub-division in the first period, with the Conservative victory in the 1969 election and the Labour victories in the two elections of 1974, representing a loss of confidence in the British political process which may have much to do with the very radical decline in British self-confidence and morale in the years 1967–75, years in which the British electorate began belatedly to realise the true degree of Britain's world strength and found itself faced with the onset of double-digit inflation. Indeed it can be argued that the loss of confidence went much further than the realities of the decline in Britain's position or the actual rate of achievement in the field of foreign relations of either the Conservative or the Labour governments of the period actually warranted.

The crucial 'learning periods' on the British side appear to lie in the years 1946–51, 1956–8 and, in the second period to be dealt with in Chapter 7, in the years 1967–70. These are the years in which Britain committed itself firmly to the Atlantic Alliance without being able to achieve the freedom within it that had partly motivated the commitment, achieved a partial economic recovery from the exhaustion of the war years, only to see the stakes for the maintenance of that economic strength raised beyond the limits of its pockets by the demands of the Cold War, while bringing about a degree of social reform and redistribution of wealth that went a considerable way to conceal the decline that was to follow by the rise in the general level of income and social welfare consequent upon that reform.

On the American side the significant learning zones for the first generation appear to be the years 1942–5 and 1949–52, years in which American strength was at its greatest and most active, without in any way requiring the measures of social mobilisation which other less fortunate powers normally feel obliged to employ to maintain their international position when under challenge. For a later generation the significant learning zone came towards the end of the period under study in the years 1967–70, years whose effects are still being worked out in American politics today by an administration elected in much the same mood as that which distinguished the Wahabi movement in late eighteenth-century Arabia, the Mahdist risings in the Sudan from which General Gordon died, the Boxer risings in late nineteenth-century China, the Maji-Maji risings in

German Tanganyika, or the Mau-Mau in Kenya, movements to which the central doctrine inspiring the insurrectionists in each case was that their native culture had been defeated by the alien because of its failure to keep to the purity of the ancient traditional ways, outbreaks to which the word 'atavistic' is normally applied.

Despite the changes in the British position in the years 1945–60, the British foreign-policy-making élites retained a very considerable degree of cohesiveness at least until the late 1960s, though signs of a loss of confidence can be seen in the repeated efforts to redefine Britain's rôle by governmental enquiry from the Plowden report of the early 1960s onwards.[1] The various alternative policies which occupied the political parliamentary parts of the élite in debate in the first half of the century were, however, dropping one by one out of the realm of rational discussion. The option of imperial isolation which had so beguiled the right in the inter-war years ceased to be a tenable concept as the Commonwealth itself increased in number with the achievement of Dominion status by India, Pakistan and Ceylon in 1947, and the pre-war concept of the Commonwealth as a community united by organs of common defence proved impossible to maintain. The option of neutralism as it manifested itself in 1947 on the left of British politics in the improbable disguise of support for British membership of a European bloc, a Third Force opposed equally to American or Soviet ties,[2] was defeated both by developments in Europe and by the Labour leadership. Some of its advocates were expelled from the party. Others, faced by the Soviet challenge to the British (and Allied) position in Berlin in 1948, took, for a year or so, a position of such total opposition to the Soviet Union that the views of some of the subsequent leaders of the Labour left in the 1950s seem today almost unbelievably belligerent.[3] The left's subsequent embrace of a new style of imperial isolationism, in its hankering after the neutralist or non-aligned position, occupied in 1955 by the nations attending the Bandung Conference, was never a realistic

[1] Cmnd 2276(1964). *Miscellaneous No. 5. Report of the Committee on Representative Services Overseas.*

[2] See Walter Lipgens, *Die Anfänge der europäischen Einigungspolitik, 1945–1950: Erster Teil; 1945–1947*, Stuttgart, 1977, pp. 551–3, 563–7.

[3] M.A. Fitzsimons, *The Foreign Policy of the British Labour Government, 1945–1951*, Notre Dame, 1953; Henry Pelling, *America and the British Left, from Bright to Bevan*, London, 1956; Eugene Meehan, *The British Left Wing and Foreign Policy*, New Brunswick, N.J., 1960; Leon D. Epstein, *Britain. Uneasy Ally*, London, 1954; M.A. Fitzsimons, 'British Labour in Search of a Socialist Foreign

alternative, although it took considerable hold of Labour party activists during the years in which the Campaign for Nuclear Disarmament was at its strongest, from 1959 to 1961.[4] These were, however, also the years in which the Labour party suffered its third consecutive electoral defeat.

Within the Labour leadership Bevin himself, as already noted,[5] was a dedicated advocate of the creation of a West European bloc, even showing himself sympathetic from time to time to ideas of a European customs union.[6] But the patterns of British trade (in which the Argentine was, for the time being, more important to the British economy than Western Europe) gave weight to the opposition of the Treasury and the Board of Trade to anything likely to cramp any further the very limited field of operation open to an economy still very largely under siege and still more dominated by the psychology of the besieged. Throughout the Labour government and administration, political and professional opinion remained remarkably united on the necessity of trying to regain British freedom of action *vis-à-vis* the United States, whether in the fields of nuclear energy and armaments, in the field of overseas finance, trade and investment, or in the special areas of British interest in the Middle East, South East Asia and Africa. Freedom of action or independence did not, however, mean isolation from the United States. Political and military cooperation with America was deemed essential in view of the Soviet military predominance in Central Europe and what were taken to be the clear signs of Soviet intentions of employing that predominance in one form or another. But alliance and cooperation did not mean the easy acceptance of American predominance but rather a return to the position of 1942, of equal votes within the Alliance. And as American policy shifted towards the support of the

Policy', *Review of Politics*, 12, 1950; Leon D. Epstein, 'The British Labour Left and US Foreign Policy', *American Political Science Review*, 14, 1957.
[4] On the Campaign for Nuclear Disarmament see Christopher P. Driver, *The Disarmers: A Study in Protest*, London, 1964; see also A.J.R. Groom, *British Thinking about Nuclear Weapons*, London, 1974.
[5] See p. 106 above.
[6] See, for example, the memorandum of Mr Bevin's conversations with M. Ramadier of 22 September 1947, FO 371/67673, Z 846/25/17 and of 26 September 1947, FO 371/67673, Z 8652/25/17/G and the Foreign Office memorandum of 8 October 1947 of the meeting between representatives of the Commonwealth Relations Office, Treasury, Board of Trade, Colonial Office, Bank of England and Ministry of Fuel with the Foreign Office, FO 371/67673, Z 9053/25/17.

movement towards West European integration to the point
whereby, at least for the years 1949–51, the control of the movement appeared to have passed out of London's hands, so British élite
opinion on both sides of the political divide and within the professional policy-making élite turned, disastrously as it was to prove,
against any closer degree of European integration. The happiest
period for British policy on European integration was to be 1952–5,
years in which British control of the Organisation for European
Economic Cooperation, which the Marshall Plan had created, made
for considerable progress in the removal of barriers to the movement
of goods and manpower over the whole of that part of Europe which
was not under Soviet control, while enabling Britain to block
proposals for closer economic integration in the form of common
markets for agricultural produce, customs unions and the like.[7]

The drive for independence within the Anglo-American and
Anglo-European relationships, however, was to suffer total defeat in
the years 1953–6, the years of the last incarnation of Britain's
wartime leadership, Churchill and Eden. The lesson drawn by Eden's
successor was again one remarkably similar to that drawn in 1944:
that only by interpenetration and by taking advantage of the plural-
ism of the American policy élites could British interests be preserved.
This was essentially the policy of Macmillan. It broke down with
President Kennedy's assassination for two reasons, one organisational, the other attitudinal. Put crudely, interpenetration can only
work when the will to listen to British representations is significantly
present in large sections of the American policy élites. Even then it is
ineffective if the President and his immediate entourage choose to
insulate themselves from the various policy-oriented bureaucracies
in their own countries as first Lyndon Johnson and then Nixon and
Kissinger (the latter both with and after Nixon) chose to.

The events of the years 1947–9 were to confront Britain with the
prospect of isolation as the third and weakest of the three world
powers in a position where British interests were directly vulnerable
to Soviet pressure and where American aid seemed essential – more
essential in fact to Britain than the continuance of British power was
to the United States. This development was bad enough in itself: but
the consequent polarisation of conflict in the Far East, in South East
Asia, in Latin America and in Africa spelt disaster to the hopes of

[7] On this period see D.C. Watt, 'Grossbritannien und Europa, 1951–1959; die Jahre
Konservative Regierung', *Vierteljahresheft für Zeitgeschichte*, 26, 1980.

re-establishing British power through the development of the Commonwealth. The manner in which India achieved its independence
was a gift which carried with it permanent strategic embarrassment
vis-à-vis Pakistan on both its land frontiers. Another new member of
the Commonwealth was bad enough, since it destroyed the defence
links with Britain which had been so significant an element in
Commonwealth cohesion in the inter-war years; British military
weakness compounded this to the point where the Pacific Dominions and Canada came to acknowledge the United States rather than
Britain as their senior partner in security. Labour hopes of a 'new
Commonwealth', linked by aid and development to Britain, failed
with the failure of the Colonial Development Corporation.[8] There
remained the sterling area which could no longer mobilise the kind
of international capital which the new developing entrants into the
Commonwealth required. Indeed, the legacies of the war in the
Middle and Far East were enormous sterling debts (the sterling
balances) of which India (£400 million) and Egypt (£80 million)
were the largest debtholders.

Bevin's 'Europeanism' was an alternative to the Empire as a
back-up to British power. It was, however, completely different
from the kind of Europeanism which, both in America and in
Western Europe, was now taking hold of policy-makers' imaginations. The need for aid against the Soviet Union followed in part
from challenges by the Soviets to British-supported governments in
areas of traditional British sensitivity, Greece, Turkey, Iran. Much
more serious a threat, however, was that posed by the consequences
of the Soviet occupation of Eastern and Central Germany, and the
economic and security policies pursued by the Soviet authorities,
policies which took such little account of British interests in the
financial and economic recovery of Germany as to give rise eventually to the suspicion that the Soviet leadership willed the consequences of their actions and desired to see the break-up of the
economies of Western Europe.[9]

This challenge resulted in the permanent distortion of American
thinking, both at the popular and the political levels and throughout
much of the military and civil bureaucracies on the subject of
American military and economic aid to Europe, in that it seemed to

[8] D.J. Morgan, *The Official History of Colonial Development*, 5 vols., London,
1980.
[9] Private information.

imply that America, secure in the possession of nuclear weapons, could contemplate with equanimity, at least from the strategic point of view, a Soviet dominion over Western Europe. It followed therefore that American aid to Europe, whether military or economic, was an act of magnanimity, demanding recognition if not reward, and that conflicts over the manner in which the aid was given, or suggestions that under the circumstances it was as burdensome as it was of assistance, became politically impossible. Both American and British élites, anxious that these issues should not be openly explored, entered therefore on a conspiracy to misrepresent their relationship and to inhibit reform, the Americans because questioning would reveal the facts of hegemony, the British for very much the same reason. Strategically, however, as the Joint Chiefs of Staff had said from the beginning,[10] and were forced to reveal publicly during the Senate Hearings on General MacArthur's dismissal, America needed its European allies as much as if not more than they needed the United States, and magnanimity was not the issue at all.

Faced with the reality of the Soviet presence in Central Europe, with what appeared to American policy-makers as a drive for the expansion of Soviet power inherent in the ideology of the Soviet state, and with the very marked disparity between Soviet and American military strength consequent on the Soviet slowness in demobilisation, the American response was the evolution of the doctrine of containment. As originally formulated by George Kennan, 'the doctrine' was more political than military in context.[11] In its military form, however, it reinforced the necessity of Britain to America: as such it was some way from translation into actuality. In its place was already established the commitment to support Greece and Turkey, disguised as global commitment (the Truman doctrine), and the Marshall proposals, the first an immediate reaction to the impending financial collapse of Britain, the second the outcome of a world-wide survey of the need for further military and economic assistance by the State–War–Navy Coordinating Committee (SWNCC) undertaken in the aftermath of the Truman speech, a survey initiated under twin stimuli, the apparent imminence of a

10 See JCS 1769/1 of 29 April 1947, *FRUS 1947*, pp. 738–50.
11 George Kennan, *Memoirs 1925–1950*, London, 1968, pp. 354–67; see also C. Ben Wright, 'Mr "X" and Containment', *Slavic Review*, 35, 1976, and Mr Kennan's rejoinder, *Slavic Review*, 35, 1976, pp. 32–6.

British financial collapse and the equal need to take over from Britain, as already agreed, the financing of the German Bizone's economy. The survey was itself embarked upon in the light of the clear evidence that wartime American estimates of the scale of aid needed to put Western Europe's economy on its feet again had been wildly naïve in their failure to accept the possible existence of a long-term dollar gap, and a degree of consensus between business, professional economists and the administration's economic advisers that the American economy was heading for a short-term recession.[12] Although, by the time the SWNCC's report was prepared, inflation rather than recession seemed the danger, the administration decided to go ahead with the offer of a new aid programme. The response from the potential recipients in Europe would probably have been muted had not the British Foreign Secretary, Bevin, already established relationships of confidence with his French opposite number, Georges Bidault, and had not the British government, especially with the imminent (and disastrous) fulfilment of the convertibility clause of the 1945 Loan Agreement, been desperate for further American financial aid, not merely for Britain itself but for France, Germany and Italy.

It should be noted that the British government were a good deal less than happy with some aspects of the European Recovery Programme (ERP) which involved annual appropriations with concurrent investigations by the Appropriations Committee of the House of Representatives, to which accounts of their stewardship of ERP grants had to be given, and which bid fair to stifle the European Cooperation Administration with endless requests for statistical information. The European Recovery Programme involved the threat of interference in British internal affairs, interference with Britain's long-term trading and payments arrangements within the sterling area and the Empire and Commonwealth, and, most of all, pressure on Britain to integrate into a united Europe. Indeed, in June 1948, the Treasury were driven to examine the consequences of refusing Marshall Aid, only to decide that rejection would carry such severe economic consequences as to be virtually unthinkable.

British policy-makers were much less happy as it developed that the European Cooperation Administration's chief administrator, Paul Hoffmann, and his staff were devoted to the concept of

[12] See Scott Jackson, 'Prologue to the Marshall Plan', *J. Am. Hist.*, 65, 1978–9.

federalising the separate states of Europe into a United States of Europe on USA lines, an idea first floated by the Fulbright resolution in Congress in March 1948. Such proposals were in equal strength resented and condemned by British policy-makers. Most alarming were the arguments of those Americans who saw the American engagement in Europe essentially as a temporary measure and who backed European federation as a preparation for such withdrawal.

Their arguments carried little weight alongside the overwhelming importance in British thinking of securing an American military return to Europe as a means of containing Soviet expansion. Soviet action in Iran, Stalin's speech of May 1946, the second round of the Greek rebellion in 1946, Soviet pressure on Turkey, the Soviet rôle in encouraging illegal immigration into Palestine, and the clear evidence of Soviet preparations for takeover in Germany, led to the establishment of a Russia Committee to coordinate intelligence on Russia, in which two schools of thought, the historicist and the ideological, came to identical conclusions about the irreconcilability of Soviet aims and British interests.[13] To deter Stalin, the presence of US military forces in some strength and readiness was essential. The main fear, however, was that American opinion might swing as violently against Russia as it had hitherto praised her. The degree of Soviet opposition to the Marshall Plan, the formation of the Cominform and the prohibition of Polish and Czech participation in the OEEC swung all sections of Labour opinion into fear and suspicion of Soviet intentions. Soviet reactions to the drive to unify the Bizone and the evidence that the Soviets were developing German paramilitary 'barrack police' forces in their zone intensified that suspicion. And emphasis on Britain's rôle in European resistance to Soviet expansion seemed the only way of countering American attacks on Socialist mismanagement of the British economy.[14]

The hostility and suspicion shown by the British Labour leadership towards the Soviet Union had been a consistent element in their thinking on international matters since the Nazi–Soviet pact. The events of the autumn of 1947 brought together in Bevin's mind

---

[13] See D.C. Watt in the forthcoming book by G. Niedhart (ed.), *Der Western und die Sowjetunion seit 1917.*

[14] Bevin memorandum, 12 February 1947, FO 371/62420; Rendel minute of 14 February 1947, FO 371/61053; Inverchapel to Bevin, 4 June 1947, FO 371/61048; Balfour to Wright, July 1947, FO 371/61003; Inverchapel to Bevin, 27 August 1947, FO 371/61056.

his wartime hopes for a European 'community' and his fears of the Soviet Union. The outcome was his famous scheme for a European community advanced in January 1948.[15] The community was to form the European end of a link between a 'spiritual federation of the West' against the Soviet threat. The Brussels pact of March 1948 was only the first step in Bevin's grand plan. It broke down at two levels: the American preference for European union as opposed to alliances; and American ambiguity on the need for a North Atlantic Treaty of Alliance, and, once that had been accepted, on the degree of American commitment to it.

American opinion was in fact obsessed with the notion of playing John Adams to a European confederacy.[16] At first, there was a refusal to take the Soviet military threat seriously and to argue that economic recovery should come first. When the events of March and April 1948, the coup in Prague, the Soviet–Norwegian crisis, the rumours of Soviet action in Italy following a Communist success in the April elections, the signature of the Brussels treaty, and General Clay's warning telegram on Soviet intentions in Germany[17] led to a war scare and pressure for the adoption of universal military training in the United States, the line taken was that American participation in the Brussels Treaty would weaken the rôle of the Treaty Organisation as an instrument (the 'hard core') of development towards European unification. When the Washington exploratory talks were held in July 1948 following the Vandenburg resolution and the opening of the Berlin blockade, the line was that the promise of American aid for European defence would be a spur to European self-help. Even when two years of British pressure

---

[15] Lawrence Kaplan, 'Towards the Brussels Pact', *Prologue*, 12, 1980; see also *FRUS 1948*, vol, I, pp. 5–6, Inverchapel to Marshall, 13 January 1948, with enclosure 'Summary of Mr Bevin's Views on the Formation of a Western Union'.

[16] See the account from the American side of the negotiations to establish NATO in Alan K. Henrikson, 'The Creation of the North Atlantic Alliance, 1948–1952', *Naval War College Review*, 32, 1980; I am grateful also to Dr William D. Miscamble for letting me see his paper, 'The Origins of the North Atlantic Treaty: Policy Formulation in the Department of State', delivered to the biennial conference of the Australia and New Zealand American Studies Association, Sydney, Australia, August 1980; Timothy P. Ireland, *Creating the Entangling Alliance: The Origins of the North Atlantic Treaty Organization*, Westport, Conn., and London, 1981.

[17] For General Clay's telegram see Jean Edward Smith (ed.), *The Papers of General Lucius D. Clay, Germany 1945–1949*, vol. II, Bloomington, Indiana, 1974, pp. 568–9.

following the signature of the Treaty in April 1949 led to the appointment in December 1950 of Eisenhower as Supreme Allied Commander, Europe (SACEUR), and the long-delayed decision to reinforce the American ground forces in Europe, it was argued that the commitment should only be for a few years until European forces were built up – six to seven years was Eisenhower's estimate.[18]

Through all this the British Cabinet had two aims: first, to secure the commitment of American military forces to Europe – only in this way could Britain relax some of the strain of maintaining so rigorous and yet so widely stretched a resistance to Soviet military pressure and claw back some of the resources so committed and apply them instead to economic recovery; and, secondly, to obtain for Britain a special position as America's chief partner in the new alliance. In the attempt, most notably at the July 1948 talks, Britain so alienated the French as to contribute greatly to the destruction of the Bevin–Bidault axis, which had been so effective in 1947, without in any way convincing American decision-makers. The Pentagon, conscious of American military weakness, dragged its heels on any commitment to NATO, even resisting the idea of full membership of three of the five regional defence planning groups. The State Department, despite the cordiality of Acheson's relations with Bevin, turned more and more towards France. The Schuman plan marked the American decision that Britain must be coerced, or driven by neglect, willy-nilly into a clear relationship with Europe. For the Labour leadership the whole economic side of its foreign policy in 1948–9 was a long rearguard fight[19] against this American and Franco-Beneluxian obsession, over the structure of the OEEC, over the European Payments Union, and during the sterling devaluation crisis in the autumn of 1949. The American embrace of the Schuman plan heralded the American abandonment of efforts to break the sterling area and the Labour government directly. In its stead America would wait for a change of government in Britain,

[18] Ireland, *Creating the Entangling Alliance*, pp. 206–7. The statement as to Eisenhower's view that American troops would only need to stay in Europe '6–7' years rests on the oral evidence of Admiral Eccles USN to Professor Henrikson in *Creating the Entangling Alliance*, footnote 103.

[19] This paragraph is based on a paper presented by Mr Scott Newton of the University of Birmingham, 'The Schuman Plan in post-war British–American relations', to the Association of Contemporary Historians Conference, July 1981.

and in the meantime bypass Britain in favour of France, and, through France, West Germany.

British expectations of NATO were only beginning to be disappointed when the Korean war broke out. For Britain and for Anglo-American relations the war was in the long run a disaster, even though in the short run the diversion of American military forces into a major land war with China seemed to have been avoided after Attlee's trip to Washington in the winter of 1950, and the defeat of MacArthur, first, by Truman's dismissal, and second, in the subsequent Senate Hearings.

Anglo-American differences over China and Japan have figured in previous chapters: the end of the war in the Far East did nothing to change matters. Conscious of its own military and financial weakness, Britain had watched while American generals and diplomats fumbled at efforts to end the Chinese civil war, and MacArthur established an American military satrapy in Japan. Throughout 1947 and 1948, British efforts in the East had been absorbed in partitioning India and nursing the sub-continent through the post-partition birthpangs. For Britain the Cold War in the Far East began in 1948–9 with the Communist uprising in Malaya,[20] which governmental intelligence traced to a Communist gathering in India the previous year.[21] For Britain the Far East was exactly that – far away and Eastern, the end of a long line of communication which ran via Suez, India, the Malay Straits to Shanghai and Hong Kong.[22] To American eyes, China lay beyond Japan, at the other side of the Pacific, the Far West rather than the Far East.

Once the image of the Chinese Communists as populist peasant revolutionaries had faded and the Kuomintang collapsed, America's adjustment to a Communist victory was clearly going to be not only a long process but also one inextricably interwoven with US domestic policies.[23] Mao's victory resulted in the expulsion from the Asian

[20] See D.C. Watt, 'Britain and the Cold War in the Far East', in Yonosuke Nagai and Akira Iriye (eds.), *The Origins of the Cold War in the Far East*, Tokyo and Chicago, 1977.

[21] Anthony Short, *The Communist Insurrection in Malaya, 1948–1960*, London, 1975, pp. 45–9.

[22] See the revealing account of his visit as Permanent Under Secretary to the Foreign Office to the Far East in 1949 in Lord Strang, *At Home and Abroad*, London, 1956, pp. 249–50.

[23] For an interesting discussion of American perceptions of the Far East and their interaction with considerations of domestic politics see Thomas G. Paterson, 'If

mainland not only of the Kuomintang régime, but also of a hundred years of American missionary endeavour. The attack on South Korea came too quickly on its heels for American opinion to have adjusted to the facts. Britain, pursuing the Indian vision of a common Asian polity, hoping to salvage most of the enormous British investments in China, and following several years of advice from the Foreign Office's 'China-watchers' that the natural Chinese dislike of barbarians, and what was believed to be their ingrained national characteristic, love of trading, would outweigh Marxist–Leninist doctrine in the formation of the new régime's foreign policy, was ready to recognise the People's Republic in return for new negotiations on British trade and investment in China. Acheson was conscious of pressures and attractions in the same direction until the outbreak of the Korean war diverted his and the foreign policy establishment's attention to what they took to be a new Stalinist technique, that of aggression by proxy. Swept by the belief that the United Nations was facing a challenge analogous to the challenge to the League of Nations posed by the Manchurian crisis in the autumn of 1931, the Truman Cabinet bustled and hustled both itself and its allies into a military reply. But the rhetorical invocation of the 1930s was much more real to London than to Ohio or California, and what, seen from London, was a UN High Command, seen from Ohio or Houston or Los Angeles became an American war, to be fought as drastically and finished as quickly as possible, if necessary by using America's nuclear capacity.

When the State Department took advantage of the war to regularise America's use of Japan as the main element in the offshore containment of China and the Soviet Union, the Foreign Office, deprived of Bevin's authority and led in this matter mainly by the Minister of State, Kenneth Younger, fought the drafting of the Treaty all the way, but in vain. The Treaty was signed and Australia and New Zealand sought security in the ANZUS pact, not concerned with the exclusion of Britain whose claims to be a Far Eastern power had gone down in December 1941 with Admiral Tom Phillips RN on HMS *Prince of Wales* sunk in the South China Sea. Any hope of dividing China from the Soviet Union or pacifying

Europe, Why not China? The Containment Doctrine, 1947–1949', *Prologue*, 13, 1981.

the Far East disappeared as a thoroughly aroused China switched its interest from the Korean front to Indo-China.

The Korean war confronted the British defence authorities with a military problem in Europe of alarming proportions. In a desperate mood of pessimism they reported that Britain, if subjected to immediate attack in Europe, would last thirty days at the most before her defences were overrun.[24] The American reaction was even more serious. Having united with the French in turning down in August 1950 a modest Anglo-German request that West Germany should be allowed to raise small paramilitary police forces to match those of East Germany,[25] by mid-September America was calling for major West German rearmament. The British, arguing that the need for troops on the ground in Europe was far too urgent to open up issues like this, found themselves confronted with the Pleven plan for a European army.[26]

The issue of how German rearmament was to be reconciled, first with the deep-rooted prejudices and anxieties of the British and French electorates, and then with the central control of military decision-making so dear to American military hearts, was to take five years to settle. In the process the French political balance, already seriously disturbed by the demands of the war in Indo-China, and Britain's balance of trade were both irretrievably overloaded. British political life barely survived the bitter debate over German rearmament:[27] it did not survive in the same way the enormous rearmament programme the Labour government felt obliged to enter upon, nor the resignation of Bevan and Wilson, which was to provide the Labour left with a major leader throughout the 1950s. The magnitude of the British rearmament programme seriously strained Britain's productive and financial capacity. The resultant domestic inflation added to the inflation in world raw material prices, consequent upon the American stock-piling programme. The terms of trade turned disastrously against Britain and it took only a year after Churchill's victory in the November 1951

---

[24] Attlee Papers, Box 35.
[25] See Gerhard Wettig, *Entmilitarisierung und Wiederbewaffnung in Deutschland, 1943–1955*, Munich, 1957, p. 295.
[26] General Edward Fursdon, *The European Defence Community, A History*, London, 1980.
[27] See Manfred Michel, 'German Rearmament as a Factor in Anglo-German Relations, 1949–55', London Ph.D., 1963.

General Election before he had reverted to his rôle in the 1920s and was chairing a Cabinet concerned to bring about a very considerable reduction in the British rearmament effort.

At the same time, American anti-colonialism, deprived of its traditional targets in Asia by the establishment of Indian independence, the British withdrawal from Pakistan, and the Dutch withdrawal from Indonesia, and unable to challenge the French rôle in Indo-China because this was perceived not as a war of colonialist versus native freedom-loving insurrectionist, but as part of the containment of China, found a new focus of criticism, on Britain's rôle in the Middle East. Two major points arose, the first in the breakdown of the multinational consensus in the Middle East into overt conflict between the American companies associated with the Arab–American Oil Company (ARAMCO), and Anglo-Iranian Oil Company (AIOC) in its various ramifications around the Gulf. ARAMCO was, in fact, driven into this conflict by the old monarch, Abdul Aziz Ibn Saud, and his designated heir, King Saud Ibn Abdul Aziz, in their bid for Arab leadership in rivalry with the Hashemite dynasty on the thrones of Jordan and Iraq. The Anglo-American agreement of 1949 was barely a year old when Anglo-Iranian and the British political advisers scattered throughout the sheikhdoms of the Arabian coasts began to report on what seemed to be systematic efforts by Saudi emissaries and money to subvert the loyalties of the inhabitants of these sheikhdoms.[28] To this disagreement was added a second one as the Israeli–French axis kept the Americans supplied with anti-British propaganda materials, culled freely from the BBC's Arabic services, and the 'grey' station of Sharq al Adna, broadcasting from Cyprus.[29]

Those American companies which operated within the old Red

[28] See J.B. Kelly, *East Arabian Frontiers*, London, 1964; Donald Hawley, *The Trucial States*, London, 1970, pp. 188–91; J.B. Kelly, *Arabia, the Gulf and the West*, London 1980, pp. 60–74. On the US rôle in this see J.B. Kelly, *Arabia*, pp. 257–8.

[29] For an account of the 'grey' radio station *Sharq al Adna* (obviously based on Israeli and French sources) see Roy Alan, 'Arab Voices, British Accents and the Pitfalls of Propaganda', *The Reporter*, 19 September 1957; see also Richard Pearce, *Three Years in the Levant*, London, 1949; Hugh Thomas, *The Suez Affair*, London, 1967, p. 131. For material on the rôle of this radio station in 1956 see *The Times*, 15 May 1956, 12, 13, 17 July 1956; *Daily Telegraph*, 13 July 1956, 1 November 1956; *Le Monde*, 15 July 1956; *New York Times*, 4 October 1956; *Bourse Egyptienne*, 8 November, 18 December 1956; *Manchester Guardian*, 1 November 1956.

line area moved steadily inside the sterling system, in part at least to keep as much of their operations as possible outside the reach of American anti-trust legislation.[30] ARAMCO did not follow them, preferring to export and operate in dollars to markets in South East Asia, Japan and the west coast of America, and adopting, in its fear of Saudi expropriation, a profit-sharing arrangement which the sterling zone oil companies had to follow. Thus when the Iranian government of Dr Mossadegh nationalised Anglo-Iranian and tried to break its own way into the international oil market, past the legal blockade imposed by AIOC, various American 'major' oil companies appeared to be too openly temptable for good Anglo-American relations, either at the company or at the national level.[31] The resolution of the dispute on terms which excluded Anglo-Iranian (now renamed British Petroleum) was generous but not forgotten by the more emotional of imperial patriots.[32] Management of the Iranian resources was given to a consortium of the principal multinationals.[33] Oil earnings were by now so important a part of the British sterling account that their size was kept a state secret.

The return of Winston Churchill with Eden to power in November 1951 and Dwight D. Eisenhower's victory in the presidential elections of 1952 mark the period in which American hegemony was asserted in a manner which made it open for all to see. Churchill's efforts to re-establish the Anglo-American intimacy he felt the Labour government had thrown away, by visiting America soon after his election, were rebuffed both privately and openly. In private, it was made clear to him that Acheson and Truman did not wish to take part in a purely bilateral Anglo-American relationship[34] (which might have damaged their exceptionally close relationship with the French), and in public, where he was forced to confirm that supreme command of NATO naval forces on the Atlantic should go to an American admiral. He was to receive a similar rebuff from Eisenhower after the latter's election.[35] NATO became even more

[30] Mira Wilkins, *The Maturing of Multinational Enterprise: American Business Abroad from 1914 to 1970*, Cambridge, Mass., 1974, pp. 299–30, 315, 319–21.
[31] David Carlton, *Anthony Eden. A Biography*, London, 1981, pp. 306–7.
[32] e.g. John Biggs-Davidson, *The Uncertain Ally*, London, 1957.
[33] Wilkins, *Multinational Enterprise*, pp. 322–3.
[34] Dean Acheson, *Present at the Creation. My Years in the State Department*, London, 1969, pp. 307–8.
[35] Sir John Colville, in John Wheeler-Bennett (ed.), *Action This Day*, London, 1968, pp. 129–30.

obviously an instrument of American hegemony with the adoption by the Eisenhower administration of the 'New Look', a programme which envisaged the cutting back of American ground forces by half a million men.[36] NATO shrank to being a trip-wire manned by America's European allies and backed by Strategic Air Command and a mobile reserve in America. The reform of NATO's structure, even at the expense of a military programme, which was seen by everyone to be an exercise in military and political absurdity, had given NATO a SHAEF-style command structure in Supreme Head-quarters Allied Powers Europe (SHAPE) and a political secretariat headed by Lord Ismay.[37] But this structure, even under a succession of senior American commanders, could not ensure American commitment to Europe beyond a peradventure. Indeed SHAPE tended to develop a 'European policy' of its own. The idea of a separate European deterrent was to emerge this way, from the coming together in the autumn of 1960 of West Germany's Adenauer, Belgium's Paul Spaak and the current NATO Supreme Commander, General Vandenberg.[38] In NATO's ideology, the alliance represented a coming together of the states of the North Atlantic littoral which shared common ideals and a common dedication to democracy and the rule of law. In military terms it was no more an alliance of equals than the Confederacy of Delos of the fifth century BC had been.

This was perhaps least obvious over Germany. The second five years of the East–West struggle for Germany were fought out over the rules and procedures by which Germany should be united: but the issue was unreal.[39] Neither Britain and France on one side, nor the Soviet Union on the other, were prepared to envisage a Germany in terms other than its being firmly and securely anchored on their side of the 'Iron Curtain'. The 'control of Germany' issue outweighed the 'unity of Germany' issue. The way was easily open for a

[36] On the 'New Look' see Robert A. Divine, *Eisenhower and the Cold War*, Oxford, 1981, pp. 360–7.
[37] See Baron Ismay, *NATO: The First Five Years, 1949–1954*, London, 1955; Baron Ismay 'Report to the Ministerial Meeting of the North Atlantic Council at Bonn, May 1957', *NATO Letter*, 5, 1957.
[38] See the accent in G. Barraclough (ed.), *Survey of International Affairs, 1958–1960*, pp. 119, 123–4.
[39] D.C. Watt, *Britain Looks to Germany. British Opinion and Policy Towards Germany Since 1945*, London, 1965, chapters III and V.

tacit acceptance of the reality of the 'two Germanies' which, unfortunately for NATO ideology, it was to be discovered, necessitated a segregated, ghettoised East Germany, even where it was allowed to be reasonably prosperous.

It is the measure of Britain's continuing prestige as a great power that Eisenhower found it necessary to evade and stultify Churchill's last desperate bid in 1953–4 for a summit conference to catch and codify the moves towards a detente on the Soviet side which briefly followed Stalin's death,[40] before embarking on his own efforts in the same direction. But Eisenhower was very careful to evade Churchill's clutches, relying on the known opposition of Eden and the bulk of his Cabinet and Foreign Office to impede him, while employing Dulles as his invaluable weapon both to convince Congress of his bona fides and to filibuster the various Soviet initiatives into impotence. In his recent study of Eisenhower's rôle in the Cold War, Professor Divine has made it clear that Eisenhower always retained his authority over Dulles.[41] The latest evidence suggests that, contrary to the picture given in both Acheson's and Eden's memoirs, the relationship between Eden and Dulles was at first as harmonious as Eden's relations with Acheson were the reverse.[42] Eden had failed entirely to perceive the change in the power relationship between the United States and Britain as anything more than yet another factor to be woven into his foreign policy and overcome by his negotiating skill. Did not Britain after all have forces all over the globe? Did not Britain have the bomb?

It seems reasonable to accept that paramount among the motives for the British Labour government's decision to develop an independent atomic capacity was the determination to assert British independence from the United States once the Macmahon Act of 1946 had set at nought Churchillian hopes of common development.[43] The 1949 talks on the resumption of cooperation broke down when it became clear to the British that the principal American

---

[40] See D.C. Watt, 'Churchill und die kalte Krieg. Löste er ihn aus? Was unternehm er ihn zu be-enden?' (14th Annual Winston Churchill Memorial Lecture, Swiss Winston Churchill Memorial Foundation, Schaffhausen, May 1981), *Schweizer Monatsheft*, November 1981, *Sonderbeilage*.

[41] R. Divine, *Eisenhower and the Cold War*, Oxford, 1981, pp. 116–23.

[42] Carlton, *Eden*, London, 1981, pp. 300–2.

[43] Margaret Gowing, 'Britain, America and the Bomb', in David Dilks (ed.), *Retreat from Power. Studies in British Foreign Policy of the Twentieth Century*, London, 1981, vol. II, pp. 128–37.

goal was to obtain control over and reduce the British programme. Churchill in turn failed to overcome the by now deep-rooted American conviction that atomic energy should remain an American monopoly for both military and industrial purposes. The only effect of such agreements as were reached was to bar the way to any Anglo-French cooperation. Britain's first atomic test was outclassed within a month by the American explosion of their first thermo-nuclear device, an act which raised the whole matter on to a much more advanced and much more expensive level of competition.

The Indo-Chinese crisis and the subsequent Geneva Conference did little to enhance Anglo-American cooperation. In the British view American policy seemed to involve obtaining British support for a hazardously ill-defined policy of threats, possibly as a means of overcoming misgivings in Congress. Eden had already seen the point of partition for Indo-China. Indeed, the idea of creating a *cordon sanitaire* of independent states in South East Asia between the Chinese drive to reassert authority over the traditional outer limits of their empire and the vital position of Malaya and Singapore had begun to be developed in the Foreign Office almost as soon as it became clear that France was never going to re-establish its author-ity over the Annamese north of Indo-China. The idea of a South East Asian security pact on NATO lines was attractive in that it put Britain back into an area from which the ANZUS pact had expelled it: but not as a preliminary to ending the war. Eden, in fact, preferred something modelled on the lines of Locarno. Dulles felt betrayed even before the Geneva Conference met.[44] And Eden's magisterial warning:[45]

Americans may think the time is past when they need consider the feelings or difficulties of their allies. It is the conviction that this tendency becomes more pronounced every week that is creating mounting difficulties for anyone in this country who wants to maintain close Anglo-American relations. We, at least, have constantly to bear in mind all our Common-wealth partners, even if the United States does not like some of them...

did not improve matters. The final settlement of the crisis was a triumph for Eden, achieved with Soviet aid, both European members

---

[44] Carlton, *Eden*, pp. 342–3. See also Robert J. Randle, *Geneva 1954, The Settlement of the Indo-China War*, Princeton, NJ, 1972.
[45] Anthony Eden, Lord Avon, *Full Circle*, London, 1960, pp. 99–100.

of the opposing blocs uniting in fear of their Pacific partners dragging them into a third world war.

Eden's successful resolution of the incorporation of a rearmed West Germany into NATO, once the French Assembly, despite all Dulles's huffing and puffing, finally destroyed the European Defence Community, marked a further assertion of British independence. The resurrection of the Brussels Treaty and the creation of West European Union was difficult for America to oppose. It was noted in Washington that the United States was not a member of the new organisation.

For Dulles, however, Eden's move was a masterpiece and fully restored the friendliness between the two men. The accession of Eden to the premiership two months later was thus welcomed in Washington:[46] though Eden's views on the first Quemoy–Matsu crisis were characteristically ignored. The episode did nothing to reduce Eden's *folies de grandeur*. His relations with America were now to come to total shipwreck over the Middle East where, since the beginning of 1955, he was at odds with Dulles and Eisenhower; over the Baghdad Pact, which Dulles saw as an ill-advised attempt to turn the Northern Tier, of which he approved, into a British-backed challenge to both Egypt and Saudi Arabia; over the attempt to force Jordan into the pact in flat breach of an assurance given that no attempt would be made to expand the pact; over his backing of Nuri es Said in Iraq;[47] over his refusal to aid the Americans to split Saudi Arabia from Egypt by concessions over the Buraimi Oasis dispute; over Cyprus, where a head-on clash with the Cypriot Greeks and with Greece proper on the Enosis issue threatened NATO;[48] over the tactics to be followed against Colonel Nasser, whom Dulles felt should be 'cut down to size' for attempting to play the Russians off against America and for recognising 'Communist China' and, finally and most disastrously, over Suez.[49]

In all of this Eden gave the Eisenhower administration the impression that America was expected to support a British policy

[46] Carlton, *Eden*, p. 372.

[47] For an American diplomatist's view of Nuri es-Said see Waldemar J. Gallman, *Iraq Under General Nuri. My Recollections of Nuri es-Said*, Baltimore, 1964.

[48] See François Crozier, *Le Conflit de Chypre, 1946–1959*, Brussels, 1973.

[49] See D.C. Watt, 'The High Dam at Aswan and the Politics of Control', in W.N. Warren and N. Rubin (eds.), *Dams in Africa: An Inter-disciplinary Study of Man-made Lakes in Africa*, London, 1968.

which would inevitably lead to a head-on collision with Arab nationalism, which, both by natural inclination and on the urgings of the US oil companies, of Jefferson Caffery, the American Ambassador in Cairo and the local CIA network, the Eisenhower administration had convinced themselves was the wave of the future. British reliance on the Hashemites in Amman and Baghdad, on Turkey and on the tribal sheikhs of the Gulf struck American commentators as anachronistic. The backward and corrupt monarchy of Saudi Arabia, where the monarch, King Saud, was so incompetent and unrestrained that his own family removed him from power a year later, was, however, exempt from these strictures. Eden's turn towards Guy Mollet and France was already apparent in March 1956.[50] Yet, despite the obvious dissatisfaction with the United States that motivated him, Eden seems to have believed that America would be constrained to follow the British lead, first, by the strength of the Zionist vote which, since 1948, had been taken by élite British opinion to be a force no President could afford to buck in an election year, and, second, by the belief that nothing but inaction could be expected from Washington in the year of a Presidential election anyway.

Both clichés were based on misinformation and misunderstanding. The Zionist vote had not helped Adlai Stevenson in 1952, and would not help him in 1956. In any case, it was the Democratic not the Republican party which was vulnerable to the Zionist vote. The 1948 Presidential election in which Truman was threatened by Wallaceites on the left and by the breakaway of the Dixiecrats on the right was unique in American history. The idea that no action could be expected during a Presidental election year failed to distinguish between the position of an incumbent President seeking a second term and that of a lame duck President anxious not to damage his party's chosen candidate.

But if Eden failed to understand the United States, it is equally clear that neither Eisenhower nor Dulles ranked making allowances for Eden's domestic political difficulties as a major priority. Dulles's famous attack on colonialism at his press conference on 2 October 1956 was the breaking point. Eden found himself entangled in his own memories of the period of appeasement in the 1930s and in the national chauvinism of the Tory right wing. The Franco-Israeli

[50] Carlton, *Eden*, p. 403.

conspiracy was backed by what seems to have been an ill-judged belief that the ageing Wafdist politicians in Egypt represented a viable political alternative to Colonel Nasser. The resort to force, however, without any warning to Washington, broke American tolerance. Eisenhower and Dulles refused thereafter to deal with Eden. Winthrop Aldrich, the US Ambassador in London, dealt directly with other British Cabinet Ministers, bypassing the Foreign Office entirely.[51] The British invasion forces and the US Sixth Fleet exchanged pleasantries off the Egyptian coast. Eden, on his side, neglected the Washington Embassy which, possibly by design, was between ambassadors, and let it be known that he regarded the existing Tripartite Declaration as 'ancient history without current validity'.[52] Since the French had revealed the whole conspiracy to Ambassador Dillon, Eisenhower's fury, his encouragement of the run on the pound led by the Federal Reserve Bank of New York, and his obstruction of British drawing rights under the IMF, is understandable. His change within the space of a few hours from inviting Eden to come to Washington to calling the visit off is more difficult. His 'vitriolic reaction' thereafter against Eden, the humiliation of Selwyn Lloyd at the United Nations and the use of economic sanctions to enforce British withdrawal from Suez represented a ruthless use of American power against a friend and ally who had 'stepped out of line'.[53] The significant point is that, despite a Commons motion signed by over one hundred Conservative MPs censuring the United States, no de Gaulle emerged from among Eden's Cabinet. Instead, there emerged Harold Macmillan, now arguing that American aid was indispensable, however 'distasteful' the conditions under which it was offered.[54]

The Suez crisis marked, it is now clear, the turning point in Anglo-American relations. It was, however, to be nearly a decade before the degree to which Britain could be dispensed with by the United States became obvious to the man in the street. The reasons

[51] Winthrop Aldrich, 'The Suez Crisis: A Footnote to History', *Foreign Affairs*, 45, 1967: the Ministers concerned were Butler, Salisbury, and Macmillan. See also Carlton, *Eden*, pp. 456–7 citing Aldrich's oral evidence.

[52] Carlton, *Eden*, p. 444. The phrase was actually used by Sir Pierson Dixon, British Ambassador to the United States, to Henry Cabot Lodge, on the evening of 29 October 1956; but it is inconceivable, given Dixon's general view and evident distress at the time, that it was not used on instructions.

[53] Selwyn Lloyd, *Suez 1956*, London, 1978, pp. 212ff.

[54] Harold Macmillan, *Memoirs*, vol. III, *Riding the Storm*, London, 1971, p. 577.

for this are not purely personal, although the rôle of Macmillan in mending Britain's fences with Washington and ruthlessly exploiting all the assets which still remained from Britain's position in 1945 has a good deal to do with it. Britain was still the only external power solidly established in the Indian Ocean. Britain still guarded physically the oil of the Gulf. Britain was one of the powers occupying Berlin. Britain was a nuclear power soon to explode her own thermonuclear device. The Foreign Service could still produce a remarkable array of negotiating skills. Britain still had a very considerable fund of know-how, particularly in multilateral negotiations.[55] The sterling area still played a major rôle in world trade.

The biggest areas, however, in which Britain came to play once again the rôle of indispensable in American foreign policy was in relation to the emergence at the end of the decade of the new Paris–Bonn axis. The blame for this rests squarely on American shoulders. It was America's refusal to support the dying Fourth Republic over Algeria which led to the return of General de Gaulle to power in France. It was American and British equivocation over the Berlin issue, raised by the Khrushchev 'ultimatum' of November 1958, which made it possible for de Gaulle to exploit Dr Adenauer's fears that German aspirations might become the sacrificial lamb in an American–Soviet settlement. American Euro-ideologues helped to defeat Macmillan's alternative strategy in matters European of the European Free Trade Area.[56] From this it emerged that London was to play the partisan of America in the new unified Europe which Washington now expected to see come into existence.

There were other elements too. President Eisenhower's incursion into the politics of the Middle East with the Eisenhower doctrine was an unmitigated disaster.[57] Few of the régimes native to the area would have anything to do with it. The Lebanese régime, which did invoke it, provoked domestic civil war followed by American intervention in 1958 which was mismanaged and misconceived in its operation, and wound up by removing from power those who had called the United States to their aid. The difference between the

---

[55] These were particularly apparent in the current negotiations on disarmament: see Michael R. Wright, *Disarm and Verify*, London 1964. Sir Michael Wright was the leader of the British delegation in the later stages of the disarmament negotiations.
[56] On which see Watt, 'Grossbritannien und Europa, 1951–1959'.
[57] This is not the view of Divine, *Eisenhower and the Cold War*.

invasion of the Lebanon by forces armed with atomic cannon,[58] and the discreet use of small-scale mobility by which, simultaneously, British forces acted to prevent the revolution in Baghdad from spreading to Libya, Aden, Jordan and the Gulf, bore out most of what was being whispered about British skill and American brashness. The successful execution of the decolonisation of the East and West African colonies between 1956 and 1964, which involved the defeat of the Mau-Mau in Kenya and the speedy intervention in 1964 to contain military risings in all three East African territories[59] (though not in time to prevent a Marxist régime taking over in Zanzibar), enhanced Britain's reputation. The disaster of UDI still lay a year or two distant even though it was clear that the attempt to create a Central African Federation, like the similar attempt in the British West Indies, was a non-starter. Macmillan, Macleod and the 'Wind of Change', and the destruction of Lord Salisbury as the last of the imperialists, went down well in Washington.

Macmillan's greatest triumph lay not only in his re-establishing relations of cordiality with Eisenhower or reconstructing the Anglo-American nuclear cooperation which had been destroyed in 1946, but in finding a rhetorical fiction which, by flattering both sides, would reconcile both British and American élite opinion to the change in relationship. This fiction lay in the combination of the use of the term 'special relationship' with the invocation of the metaphor of Greece and Rome, one which satisfied British élitists' conviction of their own superiority of sophistication, subtlety and values over the United States and American consciousness of their present and future greatness, and of the power which underlay it. In an age when Arnold Toynbee's *Study of History* was an historical cult book and, of necessity in a severely abridged form, a best-seller on American campuses, such metaphors carried acceptance, if not conviction; the more so, as it was American and British actions which had for the time being eliminated the French or German alternatives. British and American delegations worked quietly and successfully together on the abortive disarmament negotiations. And when Eisenhower's summit policy was wrecked by the U-2 incident it was Macmillan

---

[58] For a candid and entertaining account of the American intervention in the Lebanon in July 1958 see Charles Thayer, *Diplomat*, London, 1960, pp. 54ff., esp. pp. 79–87.

[59] See D.C.Watt, 'British Intervention in East Africa: An Essay in Strategic Mobility', *Revue Militaire Générale*, 5 May 1966.

who bore the brunt of this and successfully diverted the Soviet attempt to exploit it at the autumn 1960 sessions of the United Nations General Assembly.[60]

The degree of Mr Macmillan's success should not, however, be overestimated. The formula of the 'special relationship' sprang readily to the mind of a man who had experienced the rôle of adviser to an American in supreme command, as had Macmillan in his period of attachment to General Eisenhower's headquarters in Algiers in 1943. But it ran counter to the increasing consciousness of American power, found so strongly entrenched in the middle and lower ranks of American command, and offended the Europeanist 'ideologues' who were so strongly entrenched among long-serving members of the State Department and the Treasury. It was, in fact, only a serious influence at two levels; among sections of the old East Coast, largely Democratic, foreign policy establishment entrenched in and around the Council for Foreign Relations; and among the younger generation from very similar backgrounds who had experienced Anglo-American cooperation in Europe in command, research or intelligence activities or joint planning and management activities on the economic side of the war. In both these areas the trend of American policy under Eisenhower had been watched with anxiety and distaste, as it had been among their analogues in Britain and Europe. Central to their position was the assumption of a common cause, a community of beliefs, a common purpose uniting America with Britain and with an idealised, Anglo-Saxonised (and definitely non-Gaullist) Western Europe in an 'Atlantic Community'.

It is characteristic of this group that their anxieties were to be voiced by a British journalist and *homme d'affaires*, the Hon. Alastair Buchan, fourth son of that most convinced of pan-Anglo-Saxonist Round Table British neo-imperialists, John Buchan, Lord Tweedsmuir, a foreign correspondent of the British press in Washington, first director of the London-based Institute of Strategic Studies, then in the process of gestation, writing in a magazine, *The Reporter*, widely believed to be the voice of the Americans for Democratic Action wing of the Democratic party.

Writing on the eve of the Presidential election on what

[60] See G. Barraclough (ed.), *Survey of International Affairs, 1958–1960*, Oxford, 1962, pp. 559–62.

'Europeans' wanted of the victor in the election, he said that it was to be treated consistently

rather than to be hailed as blood-brothers one moment and rabid imperialists the next ... After eight years of Eisenhower, Europeans care much less about his successor's views on colonisation or Formosa or disarmament and very much that there should be some rough correspondence between his words and the actions of his government; that his chief assistants do not say one thing in negotiations and another on Capitol Hill; ... that diplomatic negotiations should not be subject to continuous inter-agency disputes in Washington; that complex matters of inter-allied policy should not be the victims of chance *obiter dicta* at a casual press conference: above all that their own electorates should not have their nerves continuously rubbed raw by the dire predictions of Pentagon officials trying to justify their appropriations before Confessional Committees ...[61]

The passage could have been penned by any British diplomatist writing home from Washington from Sir Esmé Howard or Sir Ronald Lindsay onwards. What lent it power and significance, however, was, firstly, that it was penned for Americans to read and, secondly, that it was intended to be read in the context of joint American–European cooperation against the Soviet opponent, cooperation and *interdependence*. The dependence of Britain and its West European associates in NATO on American troops and the American deterrent against the Soviet Union was only acceptable if American officials recognised in their behaviour the existence of a concomitant dependence on the part of the United States on their European allies, a dependence which made them in some sense answerable not merely to their own local American constituencies, but also to the constituencies of their allies.

This dependence was inherent in the nature of the alliance. Just as failure to react to the anxieties and interest of differing constituencies in American politics would result in the loss of their support in Congress, if not in the American political process generally, so the failure to pay attention to, and weigh fairly, the anxieties and interests of the differing constituencies of opinion among their allies in Britain and Europe would lead to the alienation of those allies. This was a lesson which never sank very deeply into the conscious actions, let alone the sub-conscious processes, of the American élites in the hey-day of American power.

[61] Alastair Buchan, 'The Campaign seen from Europe', *The Reporter*, 23, no. 7, 27 October 1961.

The degree to which the Eisenhower administration, whatever the measure of success which Macmillan had scored in re-establishing good relations between himself and the President, had alienated élite opinion in Britain was to emerge very strongly in the first three months of 1961. The resentment of so long-standing an advocate of a close Anglo-American relationship as the retiring American Ambassador, John Hay Whitney, as expressed to the Pilgrim Society on the occasion of his 'farewell' dinner in January 1961, is itself symptomatic. On an occasion normally devoted to the conventional clasping of 'hands across the sea', he spoke of the 'caricature of the American attitude' over events in South East Asia, which 'apparently sprang so spontaneously to mind in a situation where admittedly there was scant access to the facts...', adding, 'I simply cannot believe that this is really what you think of us or of the President who has worked with such devotion for eight years in the cause of peace'.[62]

Whitney's resentment was provoked by the reportage of the British press and its echo in private conversation among the members of the British élites with whom he and his staff were in contact. There can be little doubt among anyone old enough to remember the climate of opinion in élite circles in Britain at that period that his protests reflected reality. It is also significant that their immediate occasion arose out of American policy in South East Asia, the one area (with the possible exception of the Middle East) in which British and American policies and perceptions over the previous thirty years had rarely if ever been in agreement, and had most often been in conflict.

It was therefore extremely fortunate both for Britain and for the Anglo-American relationship, that Macmillan was Prime Minister at the time of John F. Kennedy's election; it postponed further deterioration in the Anglo-American relationship for three years. It even offered a brief prospect of reconstruction. For the new President was to come to understand the need to appeal to constituencies outside that which, by so infinitesimal a margin, had elected him. This was the strongest reason why his sudden death was to come as so traumatic a shock to opinion outside America – a shock as great as, or even greater than, the death of Franklin Roosevelt on the eve of victory in April 1945.

[62] As reported in *The Times*, 12 January 1961.

None of this could have been easily foreseen in January 1961 on the eve of the new President's inauguration. The Kennedy administration swept a new generation into office.[63] It consisted in the first instance of three elements: elder statesmen and survivors from the State Department Policy Planning staff of the last Democratic era, 1949–52: Acheson, Dean Rusk, Kennan, Paul Nitze, for example; the usual political pay-offs, mainly from the reformist Americans for Democratic Action, and from minority groups represented in the old Roosevelt coalition; and, thirdly, a *mélange* of two elements drawn from the industrial management class of the 1950s, 'whizz-kids' with slide rules, and from the new university generation of political analysts from the new theoretical school of international politics.

The distinguishing mark of this new generation was their common experience, in fairly lowly ranks, of wartime service, even of Anglo-American cooperation; their belief in the applicability of formal intellectual analysis to problems of strategy, defence and foreign policy; their frequent erection of 'pragmatism' into an idealist dogma; their much greater knowledge and understanding of the realities of the Commonwealth and of British decolonisation policy than that displayed by any previous American administration; their much greater experience, from visits to European universities and visits from European scholars, of the differences between the American and British (or European) approaches to international politics. They had, however, no experience of anything but American strength. They believed as ardently as the Webbs and the British Fabians in the reformability of institutions, not excluding American institutions, by the processes of intellectual thought and logical application of the results.

As a group they shared a common anxiety over the course of the Cold War since 1958, and were highly critical of the Eisenhower foreign policy, which they believed had been principally the product of a lack of leadership from the top, the ideological obsessions of some of the President's advisers and consequent bureaucratic muddle and in-fighting.[64] Consciousness of their own inexperience

---

[63] On this see D.C. Watt (ed.), *Survey of International Affairs, 1961*, Oxford, 1965, pp. 5–9, 32–42.

[64] The effect of this was often vitiated by Kennedy's appointment of members of an older and more ignorant generation, as, for example, Chester Bowles or G. Mennen Williams. On Mennen Williams touring Africa in 1961 see Watt (ed.), *Survey, 1961*, p. 10, footnote 4. On Bowles see *Survey, 1961*, p. 11, footnote 1. For

and lack of knowledge exempted the operations of the CIA in the field of clandestine warfare from their criticisms. They contained, however, a high number of social science doctrinaires. One group believed devoutly in the possibility of 'modernising' emergent third world nations by careful social selection and indoctrination of the emergent élites. Others advanced theories of economic growth. Many had adopted the bargaining theories and applications of games theory to problems of international politics with which Thomas Schelling and the group responsible for founding the *Journal of Conflict Resolution* had sought to develop a theory of the interaction of state on state, with a doctrinaire fervour quite alien to that most urbane, original and open-minded of Harvard economists.

Their early approaches to the problem of the balance of nuclear power were entirely bipolar; indeed, the leading analyst of arms races maintained that a multilateral arms race was impossible.[65] Some were clearly so enamoured of their models (the forty-nine steps of 'escalation' for example)[66] as to resent the intrusion of a reality which destroyed the elegance and the intellectual beauty of their constructs. There was unfortunately no lack of bad historical analogy. The disappearance of a generation of old-style historians of European diplomacy left no legacy of historians capable of blowing the whistle when, for example, Robert Bowie devised a formula for nuclear power-sharing – the Multilateral Nuclear Force (MLF)[67] – designed to forestall a renewal in 1963 of a German demand for equality of rights in armaments similar to that which German nationalists had advocated, and Hitler claimed, in the early 1930s. The 'Euro-ideologues' were also present in force.[68]

The new President was, or believed himself to be, eminently capable of managing this variegated team. His own attitudes to Britain were potentially schizophrenic in a typically American style. As a young man on his father's Embassy staff in Britain, he had met and come to respect members of the young reformist Tory (and often

British reactions to Williams and Bowles see *Survey, 1961*, pp. 53–4. For a contemporary British foreign correspondent's impression of the Kennedy régime see Louis Heren, *Growing up on 'The Times'*, London, 1978, pp. 264–6.

[65] Professor Samuel Huntington. See D.C. Watt, 'The Possibility of a Multilateral Arms Race: A Note', *International Relations*, II, no. 6, 1962.

[66] Herman Kahn, *On Escalation. Metaphors and Scenarios*, London, 1965.

[67] On the MLF see George Ball, *The Discipline of Power. Essentials of a Modern World Structure*, London, 1968, pp. 205–11.

[68] Ball, *Discipline of Power*, pp. 100–6.

aristocratic) centre. He had on the other hand made the anti-colonialist campaign his own, at least between 1956 and 1959. From his analysis of British politics before 1939[69] he had derived a good deal of his philosophy, if one must term it that, of political leadership and innovation in the conduct of foreign relations. His appointment of Dean Rusk as Secretary of State was, however, a mistake. He looked for a source of innovatory ideas; he obtained a man of deep convictions, rather reserved and effective mainly as a manager of the office.

The Macmillan style of cabinet government was ideally suited to match the incoming administration.[70] Macmillan's style of government was 'presidential'. The past areas of Anglo-American friction had already been removed with the 'Wind of Change' speech, Macleod's spell at the Colonial Office and the South African withdrawal from the Commonwealth. Macmillan's decision to apply for entry into the European Community had already been taken in essence in the spring of 1960, under pressure from Eisenhower. The two heads of government, despite the great differences in age, established a rapport which went very deep. The appointment of David Ormsby-Gore, later Lord Harlech, as British Ambassador, gave Kennedy what Teddy Roosevelt had been denied with Cecil Spring-Rice, an ambassador who was an old and valued personal friend, the more significant since Kennedy was the first President since Roosevelt to cultivate an ambassadorial court. Unlike Roosevelt, however, he failed to establish similar relationships with the French or German Ambassadors.[71]

The social harmony at the top was matched by a similar degree of socialisation at the lower levels. Between the 'New Frontiersmen', drawn from the US universities, and the British unofficial foreign policy establishment there had grown up in the 1950s the same kind of transnational links which had been so significant in the late 1920s.

---

[69] John F. Kennedy, *Why Britain Slept*, London, 1940.

[70] See David Nunnerley, *President Kennedy and Britain*, London, 1972. Louis Heren does not mention this incident in his *Growing up on 'The Times'*, but depicts Rusk on his appointment as Secretary of State as a convinced Anglophile resigned to Britain's decline in status (p. 289). His disillusionment is all the more comprehensible.

[71] A fact which it is difficult to glean from their respective memoirs; Hervé Alphand, *L'Etonnement d'être*, Paris, 1978; Wilhelm G. Grewe, *Rückblenden, 1976–1951; Auszeichnungen eines Augenzeuges deutscher Aussenpolitik von Adenauer bis Schmidt*, Frankfurt, 1979.

The foundation of the Institute of Strategic Studies in London in 1959, with money from American and British foundations, institutionalised and drew in from Western Europe new members of this transnational Atlantic clerisy with similar contacts with the American university worlds. This was the more significant in that under the Permanent Under Secretaryship of Lord Caccia, who had seen the Harvard seminars on foreign policy at first hand, the barriers which had prevented the discussion of foreign policy issues between members of the Foreign Service and their unofficial opposites were, for a time, lowered. The Foreign Office even acquired its own policy-planning staff to which some of the ablest of the younger minds in the Office were attached.

The Kennedy administration's 'learning zone' in international relations lasted approximately from inauguration until the autumn of 1961. In that period it just averted disaster in Laos, made a laughing stock of itself over the Bay of Pigs, allowed Mennen Williams to involve the administration in a series of major rows in Africa, and lost control over the Congo, faced Khrushchev in Vienna only for the President to strike the Russian leader as a malleable wishy-washy tyro, and failed to react at all to the erection of the Berlin Wall.[72] Kennedy's mentor in much of this was Acheson, not at times notorious for the benevolence of his assessments of Britain.

The establishment of the relationship between Kennedy and Macmillan was in part aided by Kennedy's decision to dispense with Acheson. Thereafter the relationship flourished, proving itself particularly effective in the joint reactions to the Chinese invasion of India, in the Cuban missile crisis, and in the negotiation of the partial test-ban treaty in 1963.[73] British entry into Europe became the keystone of the 'Grand Design' with which Kennedy hoped to avoid major economic conflict between America and the enlarged

[72] Honoré M. Catudal, *Kennedy and the Berlin Wall Crisis. A Case Study in US Decision-Making*, Berlin, 1981. Watt (ed.), *Survey, 1961*, pp. 246–55; Grewe, *Rückblenden*, pp. 487–97.

[73] In deciding to settle for the partial test-ban treaty initialled in Moscow on 25 July 1963 by Mr Averell Harriman, Lord Hailsham and Mr Khrushchev, President Kennedy took a course urged on him with great force by Mr Macmillan to which both the majority of his own advisers on arms control negotiations and a powerful body of opinion in Congress were opposed. Harold Macmillan, *At the End of the Day*, London, 1973, pp. 456–85; Arthur Schlesinger Jr, *A Thousand Days. John F. Kennedy in the White House*, Boston, 1965, pp. 867–909; H.K. Jacobson and Eric Stein, *Diplomats, Scientists and Politicians*, Ann Arbor, Michigan, 1966, pp. 454–6; D.C. Watt (ed.), *Survey of International Affairs, 1963*, Oxford, 1972, pp. 12–22.

European Community. Where there were disasters, as over McNamara's attack on separate nuclear deterrents, or the cancellation of the Skybolt missile project to which the future of the British independent deterrent had become linked, they arose from Kennedy's less than total control over his administration. His efforts to save the day by the offer of Polaris missiles at Nassau in January 1963 provided the pretext for de Gaulle's veto of British entry and the consequent defeat of his 'Grand Design'. But in this Kennedy was the victim of his own Euro-ideologues, and of the extreme vulnerability of the British to rejection by de Gaulle, an experience they had already once undergone, in 1958, with his veto on negotiations between the Community and Britain on a free trade area.

How the relationship would have developed had not 1963 ended with the disappearance from the scene of both President and Prime Minister will long beguile 'counter-factual' historians. It is difficult, however, to believe that Kennedy would have wasted much time on the MLF once its consequences for the post-Cuban détente became apparent. Khrushchev's enforced resignation might have been avoided; while Dr Adenauer's disappearance from the German scene might have led to a joint American–German exploitation of the 'opening to the East' which was to appear as the Sino-Soviet schism in world Communism broke out into the open that very same summer. Above all, it is difficult to believe that Kennedy's political sensitivity would have trapped him as deep as his successor was to be trapped into conflict in Vietnam, a terrain so clearly unsuitable for the industrial kind of warfare which was the only war the US Army was equipped, psychologically and logistically, to wage. How Kennedy would have coped with Macmillan's Labour successors is less sure. For behind the façade of Premier and President, profoundly 'nativist' forces, hostile to and suspicious of when not actually contemptuous of each other's basic philosophies, were developing, counter-élites of the excluded, which historical accident was suddenly to promote to that participation in the highest levels of domestic political power which had hitherto always eluded them. Neither Harold Wilson nor President Johnson related to each other's natural constituencies. Wilson claimed kinship with Hubert Humphrey. Johnson and his propagandists appealed to the shades of Winston Churchill. Each had at his elbow less pragmatic and much less Atlanticist forces than either of them could comprehend.

1963–1975

From the succession of President Johnson to the signature of
the Helsinki agreement; Britain as a European power and the
destruction of the special relationship

The 'special relationship' really died with Kennedy, whose death
was preceded by the enforced resignation of Harold Macmillan
through ill-health. His successor, Sir Alec Douglas-Home, might
have been able to salvage something of the relationship had he had
longer in office. Indeed, his first visit to Washington in February
1964 seems to have gone extremely well, save for a controversy over
British plans to raise the bank rate from 4% to 5%. Sir Alec's
capacity for inspiring trust in those with whom he met went down
well in Washington, as did his abandonment of his hereditary title,
his directness of manner and the combination of apparent detachment from the grime and toil of everyday politics and acute political
instincts, which was his hallmark. The main doubt he left behind
him in the minds of an administration which was still virtually the
same as that over which President Kennedy had presided was in the
capacity of his Cabinet to manage the British economy, a doubt
which was the more worrying in that America's own balance of
payments was already less than entirely happy and the relations
between pound sterling and dollar were too close for easy disassoci-
ation or detachment.[1] The consequences of the disappearance from

[1] Henry Brandon, *In the Red: The Struggle for Sterling, 1964–1966*, London, 1966,
pp. 17–18; Sir Alec Douglas-Home, *The Way the Wind Blows*, London, 1976
characteristically does not mention the crisis at all; Lyndon Baines Johnson, *The
Vantage Point – Perspectives of the Presidency, 1963–1969*, London, 1972, deals,
en passant, with the original proposals to establish 'special drawing rights' through
the IMF, one of the results of the 1964 crisis, in an account of American reactions to
the devaluation of sterling in 1967, but sheds little light on the state of Anglo-
American relations in his account (pp. 315–19).

the scene of the 'two pillars' of the relationship were to be reaped in the full later in the autumn of 1964, with the coincidence of the general election in Britain and the presidential election in America. Each event was inclined to raise the utmost anxieties in the breasts of the public watchers from the other side of the Atlantic. The capture of the Republican party by the supporters of Senator Goldwater aroused a good deal of anxiety in Britain. For ten years or more Britain listened to their apparent views of the world, as relayed through the British press, as a potential site for a nuclear Armageddon: Britain was neither capable nor willing to put these views in their proper perspective in terms of the American political process. The death of Hugh Gaitskell and the defeat of George Brown in the subsequent election to the Labour party leadership by Harold Wilson, whom much of American opinion had been taught by American press reportage to regard as the leader of the neutralist, if not of the fellow-travelling, wing of the party, awoke equal anxieties in Washington.

As it happened the Labour party victory by a very narrow margin in the general election of October 1964 and President Johnson's obliteration of the Republican candidate in November were disastrous for Anglo-American relations in a rather different manner than had been expected. On President Johnson's side what was most disastrous for Britain was his intense suspicion and distrust of any relationship in which he did not have some very clear and exploitable hold over his associate. In domestic US politics, and still more in the administration, this meant that he not only demanded but enforced a loyalty and unity of purpose on the career as well as the political members of his administration. Washington, usually a Babel of competing advocates of opposing policies, 'leaky' as a sieve, pervious to penetration at all levels, became hushed, quiet, impenetrable. The Washington press corps protested bitterly;[2] but it was not only they who suffered. Anglo-American relations suffered with them. Johnson was so convinced of America's power and strength that he came to regard British ministers who visited Washington as mainly inspired by the desire to improve their position in domestic

---

[2] Much of this paragraph is based on personal impressions of Washington in visits made in 1965 and 1966. By an odd circumstance one of the very few journalists to have maintained the confidence and trust of the President and his entourage was a British journalist, Henry Brandon of the *Sunday Times*.

electoral politics.[3] And the record of the Wilson government in managing the British economy, overheated as it was by the attempt by the last Conservative Chancellor of the Exchequer to 'break through' to a higher growth rate by overspending, did little to disabuse him of his convictions. In the view of one very well placed observer,[4] Mr Wilson succeeded in re-establishing relations of personal confidence with President Johnson at the end of the crisis which overtook sterling in 1964–5 on a basis of the admiration of one political 'master-fixer' for another. But that same observer warned[5] that it was most unlikely that, should the Labour government fail to take command of the British economy, the United States either could or would mount the same kind of massive rescue operation that it did in the summer and autumn of 1965. His prophecy was largely to be confirmed by events.

One of the factors which militated against a second United States intervention was the degree to which President Johnson was to turn away from Europe after 1965. The Multilateral Nuclear Force, so dear to the heart of George Ball and the State Department's Euro-ideologists, was abandoned; as was the attempt to 'build bridges' in Eastern Europe urged on him by Professor Brzezinski, to take advantage of the Soviet Union's loss of control over its European state and party satellites in the era of 'polycentrism' and Sino-Soviet conflict. Instead, President Johnson was to immerse himself almost completely in the Vietnam conflict, only emerging, as in 1967, at the time of the Six Day War and the Glassborough 'summit', when a confrontation with the Soviet Union threatened *outside* South East Asia. America's European allies were left alone, Germany to pursue with considerable success, and somewhat to Washington's alarm, the *Ostpolitik* Johnson had abandoned.

Anglo-American relations in this period were conspicuous by their absence. In the main Britain was supported in Wilson's vain efforts to contain the effects of Rhodesia's unilateral declaration of independence.[6] American business interests in breaking the British

[3] H. Wilson, *The Labour Government, 1964–1970; A Personal Record*, London, 1971, p. 44.
[4] Brandon, *In the Red*, pp. 120–1.
[5] Brandon, *In the Red*, p. 123.
[6] Elaine Windrich, *Britain and the Politics of Rhodesian Independence*, London, 1978. This support, promised to Wilson on his visit to New York in December 1965, was particularly useful to Britain in its efforts to avoid UN intervention while

blockade of Rhodesia were checked. President Johnson remained content to let Britain lead in African affairs. And after his angry intervention had brought the Russian leader to Glassborough and Russian intervention in the Six Day Arab–Israeli War to an end, President Johnson was equally content to let Britain lead in Middle Eastern matters, letting Labour's Foreign Secretary take the lead in piloting Resolution 242 through the UN General Assembly, by which, for a time at least, the worst consequences of the Six Day War were contained.[7] But Harold Wilson's efforts to mediate in South East Asia, though covered by his conversation with Johnson in 1964, were deeply resented (and denounced in private with the coruscating obscenity for which the President was famous).

This was particularly true of the episode of the Commonwealth 'peace mission' of June 1965 and the special mission of Mr Harold Davies, MP, about as unsuitable an emissary as could have been found, to Hanoi. The episode of the 'Phase A–Phase B scheme', which George Brown took with him on his visit to Moscow in November 1966 and which was discussed during Mr Kosygin's visit to London in February 1967, was rather more serious, involving as it did the last-minute reversal of the American scheme with which the British mediators had been supplied, after it seemed that the Soviets were ready to accept it, and the immediate resumption of the bombing of North Vietnam which had been suspended while the negotiations were in progress. The British were left with a feeling that they had been used and deserted, either because of a failure of the American governmental machine to function or because the 'hawks' in Johnson's administration and the President himself had never intended the offer to come to anything.[8]

During this period President Johnson's warmest British contacts were with representative visitors from a small group of members of the unofficial British foreign policy élite, mainly experts either on Soviet communism or on Vietnamese language and culture.[9] Some of

---

trying to attract Security Council support for the economic blockade of Rhodesia, in April and November 1966, in May 1968 and in June 1969.

[7] George Brown, *In My Way*, London, 1971, pp. 226–7; Paul Gore-Booth, *With Great Truth and Respect*, London, 1974, pp. 369–70.

[8] Harold Wilson, *The Labour Government*, pp. 345ff; Chester L. Cooper, *The Last Crusade*, London, 1970, p. 342; Brown, *My Way*; p. 143; Gore-Booth, *Truth and Respect*, pp. 356–62; Johnson, *Vantage Point*, pp. 253–5.

[9] They included Dr Patrick Honey, then Reader in Vietnamese Studies in London University, and Robert Conquest, the 'Sovietologist', among others.

these were to give evidence to various official and unofficial investigations in Washington. The fact that the principal source of intelligence on Vietnam available to the British government came from the small British advisory mission in Saigon whose experts, while resolutely opposed to the policies of the North Vietnamese government and their Vietcong allies, found the American approach and the American conception of America's rôle in Vietnam totally unsuited to American ends, did very little to encourage candour in Anglo-American relations on the Vietnam issue. Since candour was not the most obvious quality in the whole system of internal communication within the American military establishment in Vietnam and between its heads and Washington, the British government laboured under a double disadvantage.

Most resented of all was the British failure to provide even token military support for the American military presence in Vietnam.[10] Mr Wilson, in fact, lost a good deal of political support from the left wing of his own party for his refusal openly to denounce American policy, though his statements on the bombing of North Vietnam were occasionally too equivocal to satisfy Washington.[11] Britain's main rôle *vis-à-vis* America in the years 1964–8 was as an echo-chamber and as a refuge for middle-class American youth in its loudly voiced dissent with the ethos and values which had plunged America into the chaos, danger and totally uncomprehended failure of the Vietnamese war – a situation which threatened to conscript American youth away from the new hedonism of rock-culture, soft drugs, 'dropping out', Woodstock and Haight-Ashbury.

In Britain the sight of American disorder was not without its effect on British youth. More serious, however, was the disappointment and disillusionment which accompanied the collapse of the Campaign for Nuclear Disarmament (CND) movement and expressed itself in the parallel and ironically much stronger popular youth culture of the 1960s in Britain. For nearly a decade British models, hair styles, music, accents and so on became dominant in America rather than vice versa. British youth found its own fashions and its own cult heroes, and American youth followed. 'Swinging London' played the rôle Old Vienna had played to Bismarck's Germany, the

---

[10] See Dean Rusk's remarks to Louis Heren of *The Times*, cited Nunnerley, *President Kennedy*, p. 227; see also Johnson, *Vantage Point*, p. 255.

[11] Gore-Booth, *Truth and Respect*, pp. 335–6, 345.

centre not of 'Wein, Weib und Gesang', but of 'pot, easy lays and rock', calm, stress-free, technologically backward, but a place of pilgrimage for a generation for whom unemployment and poverty were unimaginable and supposedly archaic concepts. What if Watts was burning and the pound steadily sinking. Flower power, peace and love would provide the answers.

At the political level, the appearance of Anglo-American harmony was maintained but the reality was more often reminiscent of a composition by Pierre Boulez.[12] Mr Wilson stuck to the 'East of Suez' position as long as he could, surviving both the 'confrontation' with Indonesia and the kind of American pressure which had so lately won Indonesia the reversion of Dutch New Guinea.[13] But the cost was such as to rule out any further enterprise on this scale. Britain's second attempt to enter the Community was vetoed by President de Gaulle. The British economy slid steadily downhill. The process of decolonisation became uglier, more bloody and more ignominious with the withdrawal from Aden.[14] And then all the years of American carping at Britain's imperialism and the survival of its ambitions long beyond its capability to realise them earned their just reward. In 1968 the Labour government announced the withdrawal of British forces from Malaysia, Singapore, the Indian Ocean and the Gulf.[15] The Senate, the administration, the oil companies, all were appalled. America was suffering the worst defeat in her history in Vietnam, her forces stretched to the limit, her budget desperately unbalanced. The British withdrawal was seen by many as a simple betrayal.[16]

[12] This is never explicitly mentioned in the memoirs of the day but emerges clearly from the absence of all but the most fleeting and perfunctory of references to American support in the British political memoirs and diaries.

[13] On which, see Chapter 11, below. The Anglo-Indonesian confrontation is dealt with briefly in David Owen, *The Politics of Defence*, London, 1972, pp. 94–7.

[14] See Humphrey Trevelyan, *The Middle East in Revolution*, London, 1970 for the personal account of the last British Governor of Aden. J.B. Kelly, *Arabia, the Gulf and the West*, London 1980, pp. 19–46.

[15] See D.C. Watt, 'The Decision to Withdraw from the Gulf. A Study in Political Irrelevance', *Political Quarterly*, 39, 1969; *Crossman Diaries*, entries of 4, 11, 15 January 1968; Kelly, *Arabia*, pp. 47–51; David Owen, *Politics of Defence*, pp. 97–108 presents the Labour party defence; Christopher Mayhew, *Britain's Role Tomorrow*, London, 1967, who resigned from the position of Minister for the Navy in 1967, the previous official defence of Britain's east of Suez rôle. See also Douglas-Home, *The Way the Wind Blows*, pp. 261–2.

[16] Kelly, *Arabia*, hints at this; but the author of this book experienced many of the US feelings here described at an Anglo-American conference, held at Ditchley Park

The presidential election of 1968 was a final disaster for any hopes the Wilson government may have entertained of restoring Anglo-American relations to the state they had enjoyed before President Kennedy's assassination. Hoping for a Democratic victory, Wilson had already sought American approval for the appointment as Ambassador in Washington of John Freeman, the former editor of the *New Statesman*, currently British High Commissioner in Delhi, an old friend and admirer of the defeated Democratic candidate, Hubert Humphrey. The election of Richard Nixon, who in his previous 'incarnation' as Eisenhower's Vice-President and defeated candidate in the 1960 presidential election had been the subject of a series of vitriolic personal attacks in the *New Statesman*, threatened a repetition of the Spring-Rice–Woodrow Wilson imbroglio. In his memoirs, Nixon makes much of Wilson's reaction, during his visit to Europe in May 1969, to his declaration that Freeman's rôle at the *New Statesman* was forgiven and forgotten.[17] But to forgive is one thing; to practise the kind of intimacy which Harlech had enjoyed with the Kennedy entourage was another. In any case, Nixon's consciousness of his own obscurity of origin made it difficult for him to enjoy real intimacy with anyone outside his private court of Californian nobodies and self-made men, whose conversation and activities were so devastatingly recorded for posterity on the Watergate tapes.

The Nixon election was a disaster for Anglo-American relations at more than the purely personal level. President Johnson, who suffered from the same consciousness as his successor of being an outsider where the east coast foreign policy establishment was concerned,[18] had developed so great a control of his administration as largely to drive from it those who retained links with the Kennedys or opposed his obsession with the Vietnam war. Those who remained, like Dean Rusk or the Rostow brothers, either discredited themselves totally with those who would not collaborate, or developed a sense of political survival which largely removed them from the interchange of ideas with their fellows outside the administration which had been a normal feature of

near Oxford, contemporaneously with the breaking of the news of the British withdrawal, from the US Senators and Congressmen present at the conference.
17 Richard M. Nixon, *Memoirs*, New York, 1978, pp. 370–1.
18 Doris Kearns, *Lyndon Johnson and the American Dream*, London, 1976, esp. pp. 41–2, 122, 313.

American foreign-policy-making in the past. Had Humphrey been elected these wounds and silences might have repaired themselves. But Nixon's election perpetuated the alienation of the traditional American foreign policy establishment from the practice of influence and authority they had enjoyed before Johnson. Nixon was far from surrounding himself with second-raters as had so often been expected. But the men he picked were the mavericks of the establishment, none more so than Henry Kissinger, who was to dominate, though by no means monopolise, American foreign-policy-making until 1976.

The old WASP (White Anglo-Saxon Protestant) foreign policy establishment itself was no longer what it had been. During the 1960s it was not only deeply and bitterly divided by the Vietnam war. It was being progressively infiltrated and subsumed by new entrants. Indeed, by the early 1970s observers of this phenomenon had abandoned talk of the 'establishment' and were instead talking of the 'foreign policy community'. And while the early path-breakers in this process were themselves of much the same élite as that of the 'establishment', as, for example, McGeorge Bundy, who had collaborated with Henry Stimson in writing the latter's memoirs, the other new entrants were of very different origins.

The phenomenon was acutely described by Leslie Gelb in 1976:[19]

The foreign policy community does not operate as a club of the like-minded, or conspiracy or a government board. It acts more like an aristocracy of professionals. Its members sometimes actually make the decisions, usually define what is to be debated and invariably manage the resulting policies.

The élite of the community comprises some 300 professors, businessmen, lawyers, Congressional aides, foundation executives, think tank experts and even some journalists ...

It is difficult to compare the power of the Community with the Establishment. What can be said is that its power is different, more diffuse and makes itself felt in more complex ways. For the old Establishment which was led by such men as Henry Stimson, Robert Lovett, and John J. McCloy, foreign policy was essentially a second career. Their main interest was the interests of business in and out of government. For most members of the Community being in government or second-guessing the government on foreign affairs is a whole-time job ...

The men of the Establishment were insiders, who knew the right person to telephone, meeting quietly, avoiding publicity. Most members of the community operate far more openly ... They talk to the President indirectly, through the articles they write for the journals, such as *Foreign Affairs* or

[19] Leslie H. Gelb, 'New US Establishment is called the Community', *Herald Tribune*, 22 December 1976.

Foreign Policy or in the 'op-ed' [*sic*] pages of the *New York Times* and other newspapers, or in testimony to congressional committees, through attending conferences with high government officials at the Brookings Institution in Washington or the Council for Foreign Relations in New York ...

These men, and particularly their students and protégés, were not cut from a single socio-economic mould. The Establishment was wealthy, almost pure WASP, and their views were centrist, cautious often non-partisan, with a slightly Republican tinge. The denizens of the Community are Republicans and Democrats and are often highly partisan.

Henry Kissinger, who had arrived in New York as an adolescent German Jewish refugee from Hitler in 1939 and, while serving in the US Army, had seen at first hand the devastation of his native Germany and of all Central Europe by the effects of Europe's last civil war, was a particularly striking example of how the 'community' had come to supersede the 'establishment'. Excluded, after a brief period of collaboration, from the brain-storming elements of the Kennedy staff, he had developed during the 1960s into a noted maverick within the 'community'; distinguished by his European orientation, his attempts to convince his fellows that Gaullism and de Gaulle were a genuine historical phenomenon which could neither be broken nor ignored, had made him uncharacteristic even by the standards of the new 'community'. Access to Nixon was achieved via Nelson Rockefeller on whose staff Kissinger had worked, while the future Vice-President was teetering on the verge of declaring himself a candidate for the Republican nomination in 1967–8. Although a familiar figure to the members of the unofficial British foreign policy establishment and, as it was to eventuate, considerably more 'European' than 'American' in his approach to foreign policy, Kissinger was in no sense a pan-Anglophone, felt no ties to Britain, had never visited a British university for more than a few days, and had none of the ties that had so often tied American 'experts' in with their British opposites. And the policy he chose to follow, which reserved repairing America's ties with her European allies until progress had been made with American–Soviet and American–Chinese relations, and the Vietnam issue was finally settled, was unlikely to improve matters. When he finally proclaimed 1973 the 'Year of Europe',[20] it turned out to be the year in which

[20] In his speech of 23 April 1973; see James Mayall and Cornelia Navari, *The End of the Post-War Era: Documents on Great Power Relations, 1968–1975*, Cambridge, 1980, pp. 360–7.

both the British and the West German governments barred the way to the movement of American troops to the Middle East at the height of the crisis which arose out of the Yom Kippur war between Israel and the encircling Arab countries.[21]

As for the 'special relationship', by a curious historical reversal, visits to Britain were to become for newly elected American presidents the touchstone by which they demonstrated their involvement in world affairs, at least as long as American presidents were to be conscious of, and worried by, their country's sense of diplomatic isolation. Nixon's first visit was thus to London. But he also took in Paris and Brussels. And though he paid lip-service to the 'special relationship' on arrival in Britain as no American President before him had done,[22] it was purely an act of theatre. Britain rates three mentions only in his account of his presidency[23] and he remarks of his first visit to Europe that it was his encounter with President de Gaulle which constituted the most exciting and rewarding experience. Mr Wilson devotes several pages of his memoirs to his two subsequent encounters with Nixon,[24] but with both men we are dealing with the politics of theatre rather than reality.

The only real common ground that Britain and the United States could still share was to disappear in the years 1969–71. So long as the Non-Proliferation Treaty was under negotiation, Britain as a nuclear power remained one of the 'inner circle', the 'top table'. But its signature transferred the search for balance between the nuclear armaments with which the senior partner in each alliance had equipped itself, or was planning to develop, from the nuclear explosives to the long-range delivery systems. With the opening of the Strategic Arms Limitation Talks, Britain, having abandoned its own missile programme in 1958–9 in favour first of 'Skybolt' and then of 'Polaris', ceased to have any *locus standi*. In the negotiations for the Berlin settlement of 1971, where Britain, as one of the

[21] Kelly, p. 392: for general surveys of Kissinger's record as Secretary of State by British scholars see Coral Bell, *The Diplomacy of Detente*, London, 1977; David Landau, *Kissinger: The Uses of Power*, Boston, 1972; D.C. Watt, 'Henry Kissinger: An Interim Judgment', *Political Quarterly*, 48, 1977; Bruce Mazlish, *Kissinger: The European Mind in American Policy*, New York, 1976; J.G. Stoessinger, *Henry Kissinger: The Anguish of Power*, New York, 1976.
[22] Wilson, *The Labour Government*, pp. 617–21.
[23] Nixon, *Memoirs*, pp. 371–5.
[24] Wilson, *The Labour Government*, pp. 580, 618–21.

occupying powers, still ranked, the main rôle of the British representative was to follow the American lead (so as to avoid presenting the Soviet leadership with the chance of exploiting any differences of opinion between them).[25] The British were, in fact, a good deal less than enthusiastic about the proposed treaty.[26] But West German pressure for the agreement, following its treaties with Poland and the Soviet Union, was so strong that none of the three occupying powers had much choice. Britain did perhaps play a larger rôle in urging the recognition of East Germany.[27] The main drive, however, came from Dr Kissinger.

Kissinger, it has been argued,[28] restored the President's power to take initiatives in foreign policy, outmanoeuvring the bureaucratic establishment which had developed considerable expertise in thwarting or blocking presidential advisers: the cost of his success, however, was the creation of 'an uninformed, sullen and at times sabotage-minded bureaucracy, a Congress determined to assert its eroded constitutional authority, without any sense of how far that authority could possibly extend, and, ultimately, the resignation of a President'.[29] The flexibility, the ability to manoeuvre, which both men sought, could never have been achieved among the excessively self-centred and fragmented bureaucracies of Washington. But if the desire to play their cards close to their chests inhibited the proper functioning of the American machinery of government, it made the cultivation of friendly relations with America's allies totally impossible.

There was, however, an élite element beyond the changes in the position of each country towards the other: President Nixon genuinely admired the British Conservatives and their leader, Edward Heath, as much as he disliked and distrusted the Labour leadership.[30] But Heath, though he was in many respects not unlike

25 Honoré M. Catudal, *The Diplomacy of the Quadripartite Agreement on Berlin. A New Era in East–West Politics*, Berlin, 1978, pp. 96–8.
26 Catudal, *Diplomacy*, p. 90; see also Michael Palmer, *The Prospects for a European Security Conference*, London, 1971, p. 39.
27 Catudal, *Diplomacy*, p. 246.
28 R. Morris, *Uncertain Greatness: Henry Kissinger and American Foreign Policy*, New York, 1977.
29 John Lewis Gaddis, *Strategies of Containment. A Critical Appraisal of Post-War American National Security Policy*, Oxford, 1982.
30 See the perceptive analysis in Henry Kissinger, *The White House Years*, London, 1979.

President Nixon, marked the culmination of the rise to power in Britain of a political generation that had been weaned away from the special relationship, indeed from any relationship (Heath was no admirer of the Commonwealth relationship, either) other than with the Europe of the Six. He remained unimpressed by President Nixon's courtship of him. He 'kept Washington at arms length': he did not immediately seek an invitation to Washington after his electoral victory in 1970. He made it clear that Britain's entry into Europe depended on the 'special relationship' being seen to be a thing of the past. In return, he was kept completely in the dark over Kissinger's revolutionary visit to Peking. The experience did nothing to reverse the conscious distance which Heath had deliberately chosen to put between London and Washington.

In so doing he was perhaps articulating a mixture of two rather different developments among different sections of the British élites. There was, among both the political right and substantial sections of the business and financial elements of the foreign policy élites, a residue of resentment of the United States for the rôle it had played in the dismantling of the familiar world of Britain's overseas connections with which anyone over forty in 1970 had grown up, and of the disorders of the years 1968–9 which had taken their origin in the American involvement in Vietnam. But there was more to the changes in British attitude to America than that. During the 1960s, the Atlantic identification, which so much of British élite opinion had used to link itself with the larger powers and issues outside the shrinking world of British attention and influence, lost any element of credibility it might have had. The 'Natonian', the mid-Atlantic spirit had nothing to do with South East Asia, or with a Texan president obsessed with the preservation of Saigon. Much of what went into the British drive towards Europe in the generation below the leaders of the élite sprang from the increasing conviction of its members that whatever they were they were not, and did not wish to be, American. This was a novel conviction in a generation who had come of age in the late 1940s and early 1950s, who had taken Truman's Fair Deal as America's equivalent of the Welfare State, in which they took such pride, and who in so many cases had spent time as students in *Wanderjahre* on American campuses. The incidence of American wives among them is also interesting. Heath, as it happens, was much more in touch with this element in the

Conservative party than Wilson was with the similar element in the Labour party: the ex-Gaitskellites, the Oxbridge-educated social reformers, the future Social Democrats of the 1980s. Heath promoted this element unashamedly; he needed their support against the new Tory right which was finally to overthrow him. Wilson feared and resented the drive of those who had been his enemies and whom he saw as a potential threat to party unity. Those whose standing was such that he could not avoid promoting them he took on board reluctantly and promoted only as the last resort. Those that he could avoid promoting, he did, regardless of their abilities.

How far Anglo-American relations had strayed from the assumption of common action was to emerge during the crisis which followed the Arab attack on Israel during the Yom Kippur festival in 1973. American requests to use bases in Britain and Germany as staging posts for American reinforcements for the Middle East, at a time when an American–Soviet confrontation seemed imminent, met with obstruction, if not outright refusal. Fear of a new boycott by Arab oil producers of the European markets paralysed the British and West German governments at what was a moment fraught with American intelligence reports that Soviet paratroop divisions were being alerted, possibly to intervene to prevent the destruction of Egypt's Third Army pinned against a Suez Canal Israeli forces had already crossed. British and German intelligence either could not confirm these reports or disbelieved them. The reputation of American intelligence agencies for trimming their reportage to suit their politics had destroyed much of their reputation with European opinion. The episode did little credit to European governments apparently made craven in a way unimaginable in 1967. But then America had not yet become a net importer of Middle Eastern oil.

Britain could no longer, it seemed, exert any influence in Washington adequate for the defence of British interests. The long march to the European Security Conference seemed to reinforce that view. Of all America's European allies and associates the Heath government was the most reluctant to yield to Mr Brezhnev's blandishments, the most insistent on substantial Soviet concessions in the area of mutual and balanced force reductions, and in the area of increased sub-governmental contacts, academic and newspaper exchanges, 'equal time' in propaganda, recognition of 'human rights': the whole contents of what came to be known as 'Basket

Three'. The opposition, the suspicion, the scepticism remained right up to the 1974 election. It was Harold Wilson who attended Helsinki and signed the final act of the European Security Conference.[31]

[31] Harold Wilson, *Final Term. The Labour Government, 1974–1976*, London, 1979, pp. 155–60, 165, 173–5.

8

Some tentative conclusions

It is difficult for any British historian contemplating the record of Anglo-American relations over the last eighty years to avoid one of two reactions: the more Atlanticist in sympathy, while taking pride in the undoubted achievements of British and American cooperation, will be left at the end with a feeling of failure and disappointment. The more nationalist in temperament and outlook will be left in a rage at the seductiveness of the myth of the special relationship and feel that American success was eased by British self-delusion.[1] Others may be equally critical of the American obsession with British imperialism and capacity for persuading themselves that the economic success which accompanied their vision of the international society is consequential rather than coincidental. *Sub specie aeternitatis* (the only respectable viewpoint for the profession of historian), these reactions are interesting only because they provide the reader with map references to the location in time, space and culture of the historian. But the illusion of timelessness can be achieved by individual historians only at the cost either of part or all of their humanity or of their ability to pass on their thoughts to humanity. The expression of such views is both unavoidable – since who can discipline their reactions – and unprofitable to our understanding of the historical process. But some pointers towards a more balanced judgment of the processes sketched in the preceding essays should have emerged even from so rapid and uncertain a survey as this.

[1] E.g. Max Beloff, 'The Myth of the "Special Relationship"', cited in Chapter 1, footnote 47 above.

The first must be to recognise that whatever the realities of the Anglo-American relationship, in the minds of participants on both sides of the Atlantic that relationship, in its development, was perceived as being different from other international relationships. The rationalisation of that perception varies in time and can be both positive and negative. Positively, in the sense that policy-makers tried to found policies on it, the rationalisation varies from the Social Darwinism of Mahon and Theodore Roosevelt, Cecil Rhodes and Joseph Chamberlain to the arguments of cultural linkages, Anglophonism, common historical traditions and so on of mid-century Pilgrim Society rhetoric. Others have sought to explain the relationship by geopolitical or humanistic factors; or by what can only be called the state of being embattled.[2] On the negative side, there is the obsession of American nationalists with Britain as the sole world power, whether enemy or friend, as the yardstick by which America's own great power status was measured, right down to the latest school who view Britain much as Shelley viewed Ozymandias: Britain is seen and used as the measure of America's uniqueness as a nation; for how can uniqueness be defined save by external comparison?

The question of perception ought therefore to provide a clue to understanding the relationship. Some historians have sought that understanding in studying the phenomena which illustrate it, especially what is measurable[3] – the sale of British books in America and vice versa, the frequency of transatlantic travel or communication, the degree of emigration in each direction and so on. For purposes of understanding the policies of the two nations towards each other, such phenomena are rarely indicative unless accompanied by prosopographical investigations at various stages in the careers of the policy-makers, beginning with the intellectual and educational milieux in which they entered into political awareness, and of the currents of opinion through which they piloted their way, or were drawn up to the levels where their opinions and perceptions can be shown to have played a perceptible rôle in the formulation and execution of policy. Over eighty years it might be expected that these milieux and the pattern of the currents will themselves have changed

[2] Kipling's 'ties of common funk'.
[3] Bruce M. Rusett, *Community and Contention: Britain and America in the Twentieth Century*, Cambridge, Mass., 1963.

— from the oligarchic to the meritocratic, for example. It is also for investigation whether the milieux in each country should be viewed as windowless monads, incapable of interaction or openness to common influence; or whether the currents of political and career advancement in each country do not encounter and interact upon each other — possibly even flow for a time together. Historically it would seem that there are periods and places of the closest intertwining, and groups of genuinely transnational actors, whose identification, loyalties and societal linkages are difficult to define in terms of the individual nation state; linkages at the level of common or interrelated educational options, family connections, ideological loyalties, etc., to the point that one can on occasion identify a genuinely transnational element at work seeking to influence the centres of decision-making in each country towards a common policy. If policy-makers are guided by mental maps,[4] it is permissible to ask whether and how far they use the same mapmakers, the same projections, study the same geographers or buy from the same commercial outlets.

Research into this kind of enquiry has hardly even begun. The difficulty is that research into attitudes tends to follow the methods of the sociologist whose samples tend to be cross-sections, holographical specimens of the entire body politic, taken at specific moments in time, rather than related to those individual players of parts in the decision-making structure in each country who can be shown to have taken a significant rôle as actors or critics in the historical sequence of specific happenings which governed the relationships between the two countries to each other and to the outside world.

Any points that can be made here must of necessity be impressionistic and unsystematic — advanced as hypotheses only: with that disclaimer it can be noted, firstly, that there is in the period examined a considerable degree of continuity in each country over time both in the individual membership and in the alternative poles between which policy-makers' perceptions of the courses of action open to them, and in terms of which particular courses are advocated, were to oscillate. This comes as no surprise in Britain; but it has not always been recognised by American historians as being valid for the United States.

5 Alan K. Henrikson, 'The Geographical "Mental Maps" ', work cited in Chapter 1, footnote 29 above.

Secondly, an *a priorist* approach, an insistence on casting debate and advocacy in terms of 'doctrine', is more apparent in American developments than in those in Britain where 'traditions' in the Oakeshottian sense are more commonly encountered. It is possible that the intellectual certainty provided by the common factor in all these periods would appear to be dissatisfaction, disillusionment or disappointment with the state of Anglo-American relations; this emotion, moreover, has tended in every case to focus on Britain's rôle in, or preoccupation with, factors, problems, interests, activities, etc., *outside* Europe. But when Britain was finally forced to withdraw from the wider range to Europe, American dissatisfaction was even greater. In British attitudes to America, by contrast, the driving factor has been the interaction between necessity and misperception. British policy towards the rôle of the United States in world politics has been governed by the search for and the failure to find a 'possible America' which would support or fulfil British ends. America at the élite level played a fantasy rôle akin to that which, under the impact of Hollywood and emigrants' letters, it played at the popular level, the land of last resort, where or through which failure could be redeemed, weakness remedied and ideals rehabilitated. Even where professional realism and clear-sightedness has prevented the individual from participating in such a search, its general grip on the minds of others has driven politicians and diplomatists to bitter rage and cutting comment, and writers to satire and caricature. Sir Warren Fisher and Evelyn Waugh, Stanley Baldwin and Graham Greene have this in common: that there is more to the savagery of the anti-American sentiments they expressed than their direct personal reactions to (and personal perceptions of) American reality.

At the heart of American perceptions of Britain there would appear to lie a complex of attitudes in which admiration for the rôle Britain has played in Europe and for British institutions *per se*, and hostility to Britain's overseas rôle, have been two sides often of the same coin. The dependence of the former on the latter; the non-European sources of British strength; the consequences of any change in British perceptions of their own rôle in the world upon their perceptions of the relationship with the United States: even the change in postures so that much of British comment on the United States today is an echo of past American comment on Britain, admiration for institutions and criticism of American power going hand in hand; these phenomena require much closer examination. The old 'special relationship' would appear to be at an end, to have gasped its last in 1970 or thereabouts; though a residual predisposition of each country towards the other may still be identified.

The last point to be made is one for my fellow historians. The historical examination of the Anglo-American relationship cannot be carried out without distortion by nationally minded historical schools, trained to see 'foreign policy' (whatever that is) as the external projection of domestic politics, without reference to the development of relations between the two countries as such, or without reference to the relationships of each of the two countries to other major powers. It is pre-eminently one for 'international historians' as defined in my introductory chapter. The interpenetration of each country's political, social, economic, financial, intellectual, cultural, educational and psychological processes by the members and concepts of the equivalent processes of the other is such as to render a purely nationalist or single-nation approach incomplete, if not positively distorted. The concept of the nation itself as actor is equally misleading. The study of Anglo-American relations in this country reveals the existence of a partially transnational élite in each country – and even a partially transnational opposition. Whether this is achieved by the historical equivalent of twinning, or simply by imitation or *mimesis*, is another question. A curious sidelight on this may be cast by examining the changeover in time between the rôle America played as a fantasy alternative society in British social thought and the rôle in the mid-1960s the supposed cult of 'civility' in Britain has played in American social fantasy. An examination of élite migration each way from Eliot and Henry James to Britain in the 1900s, through Auden and Isherwood to America at the end of the 1930s, to the American colony in Britain today would seem to be called for.

In the end, it is impossible to escape the melancholy conclusion that the policy-makers in the United States played a major part in bringing about the decline of Britain, although those who saw that decline consummated did not understand what they were doing and regretted it when they realised what they had done. Even the United States of America has not proved strong enough to dominate and guide the world towards peace and security on its own. But the restoration of Britain to the position of ally and critic of the United States on a basis of equality of strength and achievement or esteem must appear a historical impossibility. It is only as individuals that British citizens today can aspire to look Uncle Sam in the eye; and it is only in the Anglo-American family, in Anglo-American friendship, or in the Anglo-American intellectual community that the 'special relationship' can still exist. The deep, mutual and lasting satisfaction such relationships can still bring makes the failure of the policy-making élites on both sides of the Atlantic to achieve a relationship of similar durability in the sphere of politics the more striking and the more regrettable.

ADDITIONAL ESSAYS: THREE CASE STUDIES

9

Presidential power and European cabinets in the conduct of international relations and diplomacy; a contrast

In the aftermath of the Second World War, and in the opening years of the Cold War, the bulk of intellectual thinking on international relations in Western Europe was based on the assumption that there was a recognisable group of states bound together by a common historical experience, common traditions and a common culture which could be loosely called 'the West'. Most of its members were joined together by the common experience of being attacked by Nazi Germany. The revivified Germany (and Italy) of the post-war years, which by a desperate effort, not always given its proper value by its former enemies, had sloughed off and brought under control its authoritarian and aggressively nationalist past, joined them in an equally common anxiety about the military predominance in Central Europe of the Soviet Union. There was talk of 'Atlantic Union'[1] – and indeed, with the exception of Austria and Switzerland, the only European states which lay outside the great advance of Russian power to lines of influence it had not enjoyed since the end of the Napoleonic era, were, in fact, riparian states of the Atlantic or of its Mediterranean extension.

Parallel with these developments, at least from the late 1940s onwards, one can trace the beginning of a common 'European' consciousness. In its internal aspects it took various forms ranging from outright federalism through the administrative federalism of the Action Group for Europe to a reviving nationalism expressed within a European framework, 'l'Europe des patries'. But all its manifestations had one thing in common, an increasing awareness

[1] The 'Atlantic Declaration' was in fact signed on 19 January 1962.

that those who felt this consciousness of being 'European' were not 'American'; in some way, at first only ambiguously defined, there were distinctive American and European methods of doing things. This realisation was perhaps most clearly defined in France. But its elevation to the status of a doctrine within a generalised secular religion by that self-styled reincarnation of the humble Maid of Domrémy, President Charles de Gaulle, should not prevent the recognition that this consciousness of difference between 'European' and 'American' moves, beliefs, ethos and ways of doing things was very widespread throughout Western Europe even by the end of the 1950s, even among those who were opposed both to the Gaullist and to the nuclear disarmers' attempts to exploit it. Even in Britain, where 'Atlanticism' was only a thin veneer over a much longer established 'pan-Anglo-Saxonism', consciousness of the American failure to accept what 'Atlanticists' and 'Anglo-Saxonists' had assumed were the bases of their sense of community in quite the same way as their advocates on the eastern shores of the Atlantic had begun to make itself apparent around the turn of the 1950s. So that even in Britain, where old illusions die even harder than other kinds of lost causes, consciousness that Britain is, whatever this may mean, more 'European' than 'Atlanticist' is now fairly firmly rooted.

Since this consciousness of a 'European' identity, expressed at the lowest as a feeling that the American identity was in some way not 'European', grew out of a general experience of multilateral contacts with Americans at all levels of international activity, it is hardly surprising that the first fields in which these differences were perceived were in the style, the methods, the whole approach to international affairs of the Americans and their various European partners. What is surprising is that, on the whole, there has been remarkably little published work on these differences: and such as there is has stemmed more from the 'Nescafé school of instant sociology' and from the political advocates of national isolationism in the various European states than from academics.

It will be the main theme of this essay to argue that the chief differences between the American and the European approaches to international relations, defined here not as an intellectual discipline but as relations with the external non-American (or non-European) world, stem basically from two sources: the differing theories of 'the state' embodied in American and European constitutions; and the different perceptions of themselves and the external world embodied in the American and European traditions.

Before one proceeds with such a contrast one owes it to one's American, if not to one's European, readers and listeners to tighten a little more sharply one's definition of the Europe with which America is being constrasted. Since I am by discipline an historian, and this is a contrast which will be drawn over time, the kind of definition I will be using is ostensive, classificatory perhaps, rather than normative. My examples on the European side will be drawn from the European democratic rather than the European authoritarian ends of the spectrum of European political experience. This is basically because events have shown that, in the long run, hereditary authoritarianism has not given way in Europe to plebiscitary populist authoritarianism but rather to what might be called a mixed meritocratic–plutocratic limited democracy. The last authoritarian states in Europe that could in some way be regarded as part of the European tradition were those of the Iberian peninsula. And there is a good historical warranty for regarding them as having split away from the common path of European experience after 1830.[2] Their recent rejoining of the European tradition is, to judge from recent developments, still far from commanding the united support of their ruling élites. Neither post-Ottoman Greece nor post-Ottoman Turkey can be regarded as truly part of the West European tradition, the legacy of classical Greece and the modernism of Kemal Ataturk notwithstanding.

The basic contrasts in this essay are those to be drawn between the United States on one hand and Britain, France, Weimarian and Bonnisch Germany and non-Fascist Italy on the other. This is not to imply anything against the 'European' quality of the smaller countries of Western Europe, Belgium, the Netherlands, Luxemburg and the Scandinavian countries. It is just that studies of international relations of the kind this essay draws on have been greatly limited in Belgium and the Netherlands by the archival policy these countries have, until very recently, pursued; while I am debarred from all but the most superficial exploration of the Scandinavian literature by linguistic shortcomings.[3]

[2] See, for example, Raymond Carr, *Spain, 1808–1939*, Oxford, 1966.
[3] See, however, Nils Ørvik, 'From Collective Security to Neutrality: The Nordic Powers, the League of Nations, Britain and the Approach of War, 1935–1939', in

By far the greatest source of differences on the side of the administration of foreign policy lies in the unique nature of the American head of state. The Founding Fathers of the United States, unhampered by an hereditary monarchy with its attendant nobility, succeeded in solving the basic problem faced by all systems of government in Europe in the eighteenth century – how to legitimise the continuance of a system in which the head of state was the sole agent of government in a period when legitimisation by religious authority was no longer acceptable either to those who governed or to those who were governed. The President of the United States is an eighteenth-century benevolent despot legitimised by popular election, checked by a popularly elected assembly and a written constitution with a Supreme Court to interpret it – and this has the most far-reaching effects on the conduct and management of America's external relations.

The first and most obvious effect that the nature of the American Presidency as a temporary, elected, eighteenth-century enlightened (if limited) despot has upon the conduct of American external relations is in its dual effect upon the President's relations with the Department of State and with his chosen representatives abroad. The dual rôle stems from the dual nature of the Presidency – as being both despot and electee. As despot the departments of government are his servants. The members of his Cabinet are his advisers, recognised by the constitution in that they must be 'advised' and 'consented' to by the Senate, but in all other respects the American Cabinet is closer to the Cabinet of a Frederick the Great than to the Cabinets of Britain, of the Third, Fourth and Fifth Republics of France or those of the other European democracies. As electee, the President's Cabinet posts must go, as must his principal ambassadorships, as rewards to those who helped him to the nomination as his party's presidential candidate or in the presidential election itself.

It is thus in the nature of things that a President's relations with his Secretary of State, his other Cabinet ministers and his ambassadors abroad should reflect the nature of the political coalition which has secured his nomination and election. Some posts will go to his most faithful supporters; others to those whom he has had to placate or

K. Bourne and D.C. Watt (eds.), *Studies in International History*, London, 1967; Nils Ørvik, *Sikkerheitspolitikken, 1920–1939*, Oslo, 1961; Folke Lindberg, *Scandinavia in Great Power Politics, 1905–1908*, Stockholm, 1958.

win over. His chances of re-election and his influence on the nomination of his successor will depend on these uncertain alliances and ambitions. For if one has to go back to the eighteenth century to find analogies with the constitutional despotism of the American Presidency, one has no parallels, save that of the ill-fated crown of Poland, later than the seventeenth-century elections to the head office of the Holy Roman Empire, for an elected despot. And in, for example, Franklin Roosevelt's relations with Joseph Kennedy, his Ambassador to the Court of St James,[4] or with Woodring, his Secretary of War,[5] one can see again the clouded relations of the Emperor Ferdinand with Maximilian of Bavaria or the Great Elector.[6]

Thus the most stable relationships between Presidents and Secretaries of State in this century have existed between those Presidents who had no anxieties as to their election and have therefore picked their Secretaries as trusted advisers rather than as allies rewarded for their part in the electoral victory. The relationships between Theodore Roosevelt and Elihu Root, Harding and Charles Evans Hughes, Coolidge and Kellogg, Hoover and Stimson, Truman and Acheson, Nixon and Kissinger have all been more or less of this kind. The cases of Theodore Roosevelt, Truman and Nixon are proof that this relationship of confidence does not require, as is sometimes argued, that the President be a Louis XIII or a William I content to abide by the guidance of a Richelieu or a Bismarck.

There have on the other hand been Presidents who sought, so far as possible, to evade the problems of their 'over-mighty' allies by excluding them from office and by conferring the most important offices of state, as the Tudor monarchs did in Britain, on men whose position and stature in political terms depended entirely on the favour of the President. Woodrow Wilson's first Secretary of State, William Jennings Bryan, was just such an 'over-mighty' ally whose long leadership in disaster of the Democratic party Wilson felt obliged to reward. In all other respects he was as fitted for the

---

[4] On Joseph Kennedy see William W. Kaufmann, 'Two American Ambassadors: Bullitt and Kennedy', in Felix Gilbert and Gordon Craig (eds.), *The Diplomats, 1919–1939*, Princeton, 1953; Richard Whalen, *The Founding Father*, New York, 1965; Michael Beschloss, *Kennedy and Roosevelt*, New York, 1981.

[5] On which see John M. Blum, *From the Morgenthau Diaries*, vol. II, *Years of Urgency 1938–41*, Boston, 1965, p. 37.

[6] See C.V. Wedgwood, *The Thirty Years War*, London, 1938.

position of Secretary of State as the Emperor Caligula's horse was for that of consul. His second Secretary of State, Lansing, belongs much more closely to the Tudor models (though he was more a Wolsey than a Thomas Cromwell). For the full illustration of this development one has to turn rather to President Kennedy's choice of Dean Rusk and Robert McNamara. Rusk, a Georgian lawyer, Rhodes Scholar, soldier and State Department employee, was in no sense a political appointment – nor did he come from any of the milieux from which Presidents traditionally selected their Cabinet ministers or ambassadors. McNamara's case was only superficially different. Though he came from the Chairmanship of Ford Motors it was a post he had only just attained, and that by sheer merit. In no other respect can he be compared with industrial barons such as his predecessor as Secretary of Defence under Eisenhower, 'Engine' Charlie Wilson of General Motors.

Bad relations between President and Secretary of State or ambassador can thus stem from either of the two aspects of his office in which the President is unique. They may arise because the President does not trust or cannot work with a political ally with whom for political reasons he would prefer not to break. This is the basic reason for the appalling relations which existed between Wilson and Bryan, between Franklin Roosevelt and Cordell Hull, and between Truman and Stettinius. But they may also arise because of the character of the President and from the fact that it lies within his power to employ the machinery of state in whatever way best suits his own personal style of governance. To decide why Roosevelt and Kennedy placed as much reliance on the employment of personal emissaries as they did requires a detailed analysis of both the domestic political and politico-managerial factors in each case. With Roosevelt his use of a Norman Davis,[7] a Murray of Elibank[8] or a Harry Hopkins[9] stemmed basically from his secretiveness, his distrust of political allies, and his need to establish as close a personal

---

[7] See on Norman H. Davis, Thomas C. Irwin, 'Norman H. Davis and the Quest for Arms Control, 1931–1938", Ohio State Univ. Ph.D., 1963; Dorothy Borg, *The United States and the Far Eastern Crisis*, Cambridge, Mass., 1964, p. 403; D.C. Watt, *Personalities and Policies*, London, 1965, pp. 83–99, 'Britain, the United States and Japan in 1934'.

[8] See Lord Murray of Elibank, 'Franklin Roosevelt, the Friend of Britain', *Contemporary Review*, 138, 1955.

[9] Maurice Waters, *The Ad Hoc Diplomat*, The Hague, 1963.

relationship as he could with foreign statesmen whose cooperation was necessary to him. On the rare occasions where he used a political appointee, as he did with Ambassador Dodd in his soundings in Berlin on the possibility of a conference on economic disarmament in the fall of 1936,[10] it was an appointee with whom he was in emotional sympathy and who, in any case, carried very little weight in domestic American politics. To see things in perspective one should compare Roosevelt's instructions to Murray of Elibank that on no account should Ambassador Kennedy be informed of his clandestine contacts with Neville Chamberlain[11] in the last three months of 1938 and the assurances he conveyed to Chamberlain that America's economic resources would be made available to support Britain if it were engaged in war with Germany, whatever the state of America's neutrality legislation.

The case of John F. Kennedy is different. Technological means had made the employment of a personal emissary much easier in his day than it was in the time of Roosevelt. It took Norman Davis a week to reach Britain or Brussels in 1937. He could, it was true, converse with his President by transatlantic telephone, though this was not entirely satisfactory. By 1961 a George Ball or a McNamara could be in London in eight hours and fly back the next day, if needs be, to inform his President and confer with him on what had transpired. Kennedy tended therefore to use whoever seemed the most appropriate man to hand. To negotiate with Mr Khrushchev on Berlin, a long slow process dependent on the establishment of personal respect between the two, he used his Ambassador in Moscow.[12] To deal with crises such as 'Skybolt', the original multilateral force proposals or the negotiations on Britain's entry into Europe, he turned rather to the man whom he had chosen to act as his principal adviser, as it might be a McNamara for 'Skybolt',[13] a George Ball for Europe,[14] or an Arthur Schlesinger Junior for Latin America,[15] irrespective of whether the individual concerned came from his appointments to

[10] See Francis L. Loewenheim, 'An Illusion that Shaped History', in Daniel R. Beaver (ed.), *Some Pathways in the Twentieth Century*, Detroit, 1969.

[11] Murray of Elibank Papers, National Library of Scotland, Folio 8809, Memorandum of 21 October 1938.

[12] D.C. Watt (ed.), *Survey of International Affairs, 1961*, Oxford, 1966, pp. 213, 217–18.

[13] D.C. Watt (ed.), *Survey of International Affairs, 1962*, Oxford, 1970, pp. 162–3.

[14] George Ball, *The Discipline of Power*, London, 1968, pp. 81–2.

[15] Arthur Schlesinger Jr, *A Thousand Days*, Boston, 1965, pp. 158–67.

the bureaucracy or from his own kitchen Cabinet, the White House staff.

If one turns to the European states chosen as comparison, one has to recognise at once that with the European dependence on the parliamentary Cabinet commanding a majority in the National Parliament, whether that majority is achieved by the comparatively monolithic parties of Great Britain, or the shifting political coalitions of the Third Republic, the Cabinet is an alliance of political figures, elected and representative, with no term other than electoral strength set on their office and commanding political power not in the once-and-for-all delivery of votes in an election but in the continuous delivery of support in Parliament. The British Foreign Secretary, His (or Her) Majesty's Principal Secretary of State for Foreign Affairs, may share with the Secretary of State that curious eighteenth-century nomenclature which placed as the first duty in the affairs of state on the Sovereign's servants, after that of managing his Treasury, that of conducting his relations with other monarchs. But he is much more than the Monarch's first servant after the Premier. He is usually one of the two or three most powerful political figures in the Cabinet. The sole cases where this has not been so have been where the Prime Minister wished effectively to be his own Foreign Secretary without having to incur, as MacDonald did in 1924, the added burden of managing the day-to-day work of the Foreign Office. The most recent case of this sort was the relationship between Sir Anthony Eden and Mr Macmillan, his successor, with Mr Selwyn Lloyd. This is a relationship still virtually unexplored by contemporary historians. That it was not a happy one and that it came to a disastrous end is, however, a matter of record. The relationships between Churchill and Eden during the years 1940–5 and between Chamberlain and Halifax in the years 1938–40 have also been put in the same category, but recent evidence has made it clear that their relations were less a matter of rider and horse than of a closer and rather different kind of symbiosis.[16]

Indeed for the closest parallels one has to go to the period of *Kanzlerdemokratie* in post-war Western Germany or the Gaullist experiment in presidential democracy in the French Fifth Republic.

---

[16] D.C. Watt, *Personalities and Policies*, pp. 177–86, 'Divided Control of British Foreign Policy – Danger or Necessity?'; Max Beloff, *The Intellectual in Politics*, London, 1970, pp. 19–34, 'Prime Minister and President'.

What is interesting in Bonn is that the years of Adenauer's dotage showed that the relationship between, for example, himself and Heinrich von Brentano was a deviation from the norm rather than, as was feared at the time, the re-establishment under the patina of parliamentary democracy of the *Bismarckischen Geist.*[17] He was forced by the collapse of his parliamentary majority to accept a Foreign Minister, Dr Schroeder, whose methods and views he detested. Since that date the difficulties that have arisen, as between Brandt and Kiesinger at the time of the *Grosse Koalition* or between Brandt and Scheel after the 1968 elections, are those inseparable from any coalition, despite the fact that constitutionally the *Bundeskanzler* is a more powerful figure than a British or a French Premier. One need look no further than the tensions existing between Chamberlain and Eden, or between Lloyd George and Curzon for a parallel. In brief the difficulties that have arisen in European practice between heads of government and their Foreign Ministers have stemmed either from conflicts of personality or from the strains of a coalition of equals rather than from the complicated system of one-way rewards and spoils inherent in the President's relations with his Secretary of State and his ambassadors.

The employment of political appointees in diplomatic positions and of personal emissaries by the West European parliamentary democracies has been quite different. It is true that in the past, for a comparison to be really valid, the number of British political appointees in diplomatic posts needs to be augmented by the Viceroys, Governors-General of Dominions, Governorships of Colonies and High Commissionerships, as well as holders of that curious British institution, developed during the Second World War and applied occasionally thereafter, the Minister of State stationed permanently abroad. Even then while a Royal Duke could be sent to govern the Bermudas or to act as Governor-General of an antipodean Dominion for a time, this was the exception rather than the rule. Colonial Governors were usually career men. Governors-General of Dominions were not infrequently retired soldiers of considerable personal ability, still able to contribute something to the state and lacking in any overt party attachment. And the position they filled, while being more than merely honorific, did not make them direct instruments of

[17] Arnulf Baring, *Aussenpolitik in Adenauer's Kanzlerdemokratie*, Munich, 1969, esp. pp. 1–48.

British external policy subject to continued directives from London. Direct political appointments such as that of Lord Head, a Conservative War Minister, to Nigeria, or of Malcolm MacDonald, son of Ramsay MacDonald and a Cabinet minister before 1939, as High Commissioner for South East Asia, have in them an element both of respect for the judgment of the men concerned and of political exile.

Setting these cases aside the bulk of British political appointments to ambassadorial posts abroad fall into two quite separate categories. Some stem from problems of coalition warfare, and are indeed carried over into the field of coalition peacemaking. Such appointments as those of Lord d'Abernon in Berlin, Sir Auckland Geddes in Washington and Lords Derby and Crewe in Paris have an element of this (though it is to be noticed that they date from the only period in British politics in which an individual was trying to build his own political party by methods which reportedly included the sale of honours and the employment of a personal spoils system). The appointments of Sir Stafford Cripps in Moscow (1940–2), Lord Halifax in Washington (1942–6), Duff Cooper, Lord Norwich, in Paris (1944–7), Sir Samuel Hoare, Lord Templewood, in Madrid (1940–5) certainly come into this category. There have, of course, been deliberate attempts to politicise some posts, most notably by the first Wilson government, with its appointment of Lord Caradon as head of the British delegation to the United Nations and John Freeman, first to New Delhi and then, in mistaken anticipation of a Democratic victory in the 1968 elections, to Washington. Such posts, however, have a natural tendency to depoliticise themselves either by the resistance of the professionals to the process (which was, for example, to result in Lord Caradon's replacement by his professional deputy) or by the transformation of a political appointment into a career one after the change of government. Duff Cooper, a Conservative First Lord of the Admiralty (1937–8), continued to serve as Ambassador in Paris under a Labour government – and the Conservative government of Mr Edward Heath took its time in finding a replacement for John Freeman in Washington, despite his former editorship of the *New Statesman*.

It is when one turns to the employment of personal emissaries by the West European democracies that one can see how the exigencies of external relations exercise an effect far beyond that of problems of domestic political management. None of the West European bureaucracies like the personal emissary, who is by their definition nearly always an amateur, even where, as with Neville Chamberlain's employment of Sir Horace Wilson, the Permanent Under Secretary of the Treasury, he is, in his own field, a professional. Nevertheless one has to be pragmatic. Whereas Chamberlain's employment of Wilson and others is widely condemned as an inefficient deviation from the norm, where Britain is dealing with an authoritarian régime, where personal relations to the head of state or government are important, the British have shown themselves ready to use whatever means they have to hand. The leaders of the Secret Intelligence Service are not beyond a little personal diplomacy (most marked in the cases of Sir William Wiseman and Sir William Stephenson in Anglo-American relations in the two world wars).[18] In the case of Lord Harlech's embassy to the United States it was less his political eminence than his long-standing friendship with President Kennedy which made him the obvious choice.

France has not been behind Britain in the use of personal emissaries, though the peculiar nature of French politics has procured very few political figures willing to accept the exile of a permanent embassy; they prefer to be *anciens ministres* in Paris rather than servants of the Quai d'Orsay abroad. The use of the personal emissary moreover came naturally to those accustomed to the personal *Cabinets* of the leading political figures and the great rôle played by intermediaries in the construction, if not in the maintenance, of those ever-changing coalitions. Especially in relations with the dictators, missions such as those of Lagardelle in 1935[19] and Baudouin in 1939,[20] between the governments of the day and Mussolini, were a natural outgrowth of the problem of relations with personal dictators.

Behind the differing natures of the American system of elective limited absolutism and the various European parliamentary Cabinet systems there are further complications that need exploration. These

---

[18] On Sir William Wiseman see Arthur Willert, *The Road to Safety*, London, 1952; W.B. Fowler, *British–American Relations, 1917–1918. The Role of Sir William Wiseman*, Princeton, 1969; on Sir William Stephenson see H. Montgomery Hyde, *The Quiet Canadian*, London, 1962; see also the memoirs of the Chief of Air Intelligence in the 1930s, Group Captain F.W. Winterbotham, *Secret and Personal*, London, 1970.

[19] Hubert Lagardelle, *Ma Mission à Rome*, Paris, 1955.

[20] Paul Baudouin, 'Un voyage à Rome,' *La Revue des Deux Mondes*, 1 May 1962, pp. 69–85.

have to do with the nature of the foreign-policy-making élites in America and Europe. In Europe these élites tend to be long-serving, their members so continuously in service that whatever their individual social origins they tend to grow together as a group and their shared assumptions become backed by a network of social contacts and relationships such as to give the élite to which they belong a fairly permanent character. Theoretically this should be modified by changes in office among the political members of the élite – but in practice, even among the various political parties, there tend to develop long-term experts in external relations with its allied fields of defence, international economics and finance, and overseas aid and investment. This tendency is noticeable even in Britain, where the development of specialist parliamentary committees is in its infancy. In the continental European powers where parliamentary committees on foreign affairs play an important part in the legislative process this tendency is greatly strengthened.[21] It is reinforced by the development of international parliaments and gatherings of parliamentarians on the one hand and institutes and associations for the study of international affairs on the other. The rôle this is playing in the emergence of élite groups common to the European states has not so far been examined by any political scientist, to the best of the author's knowledge.

This continuity in élite group membership is of particular importance where the balance between political and professional bureaucratic status and influence is disturbed. It is, however, to be mentioned that these élites also include political commentators and academics, both of whom play an important rôle in the ventilation and analysis of disagreements within the élite and in the maintenance of consent to and acceptance of élite leadership in the field of foreign relations among the general mass of those politically involved in their particular societies. As with the political and professional bureaucratic members of the élite, its academic and journalistic membership tends to be long-serving, moving perhaps from one mode or organ of communication to another and from all of these into the field of foreign correspondent and back to their own countries. The same is true of a fifth element, those in positions of

---

[21] On the French parliamentary committee for Foreign Affairs under the Third Republic see J.E. Howard, *Parliament and Foreign Policy in France*, London, 1948.

responsibility in private industry, finance, trade and shipping, etc., whose main work lies in the field of overseas economic and financial relations. Even with the addition of this last group their length of service, their concentration in, at most, two or three centres of activity, and their numbers make for a degree of collective agreement that is the more surprisingly strong for its habitual understatement.

When one turns to the United States, the picture is changed very radically by three factors. The first is the sheer size of the country, the decentralisation of economic activity caused by its regional differences in industry, markets overseas, outlook on foreign affairs, etc. The second is the number of those whose positions in industry, politics, journalism, academic life and in the administrative bureaucracy would make their European equivalents at least candidate members of the foreign-policy-making élites in their own country. The third is the distorted balance between its political members, their permanent division into parliamentary and political administrators, and the disparity in power between this second group and the professional bureaucrats brought about by the system of elective limited absolutism already referred to.

The effect of this is to introduce a number of distortions. The first is to deprive the parliamentarians of any but the most public and indirect influence on the formation and conduct of external relations save in a critical and destructive sense. As a result only that handful of Senators and Representatives who enjoy the President's confidence (and they, of course, change somewhat as one elected absolutist succeeds another) are members of the American foreign-policy-making élite in any sense comparable with their European equivalents. A second is to devalue the long-term professional members of the civilian side of the American bureaucracy and to make them hesitant and reserved *vis-à-vis* their political mentors. They are effectively denied access to all but a handful of the top policy-making jobs within both the State Department and the overseas embassies, save in so far as they become identified with a particular party.

By a curious paradox, however, the long-term military members of the bureaucracy enjoy no such devaluation, save where the general character of civilian attitudes to the military prescribes it. Traditionally the advisory bodies of senior military and naval figures acted as military advisers not only to the absolutist and his administration but also to the congressional committees charged with keeping the absolutist's actions in the field of defence and the armed services under constant scrutiny. Thus, whereas British, French and other West European military figures have constantly campaigned individually and collectively with considerable force to obtain the policy which seemed most advisable to them, they have rarely if ever campaigned as an organised body to attempt to persuade their parliaments to reject a treaty signed by their own government as, for example, the General Board of the US Navy campaigned in Congress to secure the rejection of the 1930 London Naval Treaty.[22] This was elsewhere a phenomenon confined to those absolutist states where military and civilian authorities existed as coequals in theory, the civilians being slightly subordinate in fact, as in Czarist Russia or Bismarckian Imperial Germany. They do not always campaign effectively; the General Board was defeated in 1930 as was MacArthur in 1951. But apart from Foch's attack of *folie de grandeur* at Versailles[23] and the Beresford–Fisher row in Edwardian Britain,[24] Europe has no recent parallels save in France in 1958–61, where what was at issue was not the use of parliamentary methods to defeat an administration's policy but a *coup d'état*.

So far as the politico-administrative élite in the United States is concerned, one has to note one element, now superseded, of continuity among its number. This was provided by the East Coast Ivy League wealthy patrician element, the product of a limited number of private schools and universities. The existence of such figures as Acheson, Harriman, Christian Herter, David Bruce and others, whose service as foreign affairs experts for their chosen parties goes back their full working careers, and who moved back into banking, the law, the universities or state politics, remaining available to serve either administration if their service was requested, has provided an element of continuity and authority in the conduct of American foreign policy which to some extent offset the lack of power and influence of the professional bureaucrats of the State Department and the Foreign Service. Against these one has to set the gradual

---

[22] See Raymond O'Connor, *Perilous Equilibrium*, Lawrence, Kansas, 1962.
[23] See Jere Clemens King, *Foch versus Clemenceau: France and German Dismemberment, 1918–1919*, Cambridge, Mass., 1960.
[24] See Arthur Marder, *Fear God and Dreadnought*, vol. II, London, 1916, pp. 39–45.

decline in power, influence and authority of this group in both parties, as the balance within the parties moved westwards and southwards.

So far, in this comparison between America and the European countries, attention has been focused on the differences between the governmental aspects of the different foreign-policy-making processes. It has been argued that these stem basically from the fact that, lacking the obstacle of a hereditary monarchy, the Founding Fathers of the United States were able to solve the problems of legitimising authority, as these were seen in the eighteenth century, by basing that authority on an elective process, albeit an indirect one. In other respects, however, the principal bearer of authority remained as the eighteenth century had conceived him, an absolute monarch whose absolutism and whose exercise of power was limited by the rule of law, embodied in a written constitution, safeguarded by an independent judiciary and watched over by an elected assembly which retained the power of the purse.

It need hardly be said that an assembly, even one elected to be both federal and national, which has to operate within this general framework is a very different kind of assembly from those which function in the various European countries. Whether these fall into the French republican tradition of an assembly which is itself the final repository of sovereignty, or whether they follow the British, Scandinavian, Dutch and Belgian models whereby sovereignty resides with the King's ministers in Parliament, the rôle the elected assembly plays in the field of foreign policy is bound to be totally different from that of the US Congress. In eighteenth-century terms the state was still very much the territorial extension of the monarch's personality. External relations were conducted between monarchs and their courts. They were pre-eminently a field reserved for the monarchical prerogative. This did not change, and was not changed by making the monarch elective. The only changes introduced were those which limited his powers to make war, his powers to make treaties and his powers to make appointments. Of these the first and the third at least stemmed much less from a distrust of the way in which the presidential prerogative might be exercised than from the process by which the founding states abandoned their thirteen separate sovereignties only piecemeal and with reluctance to the new federal power. The second was inherent in the separation of powers, since treaties become part of the domestic law of the countries which conclude them.

The effect of this is that, save where the conduct of foreign policy requires the voting of funds or the ratification of treaties, the President of the United States is absolved from the necessity of seeking parliamentary or popular support for his actions in a way for which there are few parallels in the European democracies. America offers few parallels to the reversal of the Hoare–Laval plan by the British and French governments of the day, or the Suez débâcle in 1956. The closest American parallel to the first is the abandonment of their big Navy plans by Harding's administration and the Congress elected in 1920 in the face of organised pressure by American religious and civil organisations advocating naval arms limitation.[25] The Kennedy régime survived more or less unharmed the collapse of the Bay of Pigs assault on Cuba in 1961. And the general consensus of historians regarding Wilson's failure to obtain the necessary two-thirds majority in the Senate for the ratification of the Treaty of Versailles centres on his lack of competence as a manager of Congress, not on the inherent impossibility of the task. It is interesting to note that attempts to extend congressional control over the presidential exercise of the prerogative have been defeated, as were the Ludlow amendment in 1938[26] and the more recent attempts, made in the aftermath of the use made by President Johnson of the congressional resolution passed in 1964, after the alleged attacks by North Vietnamese naval craft on ships of the American Navy.

Where the Senate exercises more power than its British, French or West German equivalents is in its powers of investigation. The weakness of the British position arises from the general weakness of the British Parliament as against the executive, though the effectiveness of the parliamentary question and the emergency debate is often underestimated, while that of the Senate Foreign Affairs Committee, where legislation is *not* in question, is frequently exaggerated.

So far attention has been focused on those contrasts between the American and European approaches to external international affairs

[25] See Adelphia Jan Bowen Jr, 'The Disarmament Movement, 1918–1935', Columbia Ph.D., 1956, pp. 20–33.
[26] On the Ludlow amendment see Robert A. Divine, *The Illusion of Neutrality*, Chicago, 1962, pp. 219–21.

which arise from the differences between the foreign-policy-making machines in America and Europe. It has been argued that the American system in practice leaves far more to the prerogative of the elective co-head of state and government than the European system does to the head of government. In practice the conduct of foreign policy in America is in many respects more absolutist and more authoritarian in the United States than in the democracies of Western Europe.

This may at first sight seem a very startling statement: but the degree to which it contravenes the view generally accepted, especially by American writers, about the conduct of and approach to foreign affairs of the United States is the measure of the strength of the second main source of contrasts between the American and European democratic approach to foreign affairs, diplomacy and international relations. This contrast lies in the differing perceptions of the nature of their own system of government (and of all other systems of government, with which they have to have contact if they are to be involved in international relations and diplomacy) held by the leading writers and practitioners in the field on either side of the Atlantic.

The dominant school of thought in the United States, since the elections of 1912 and 1916 welded Populists and Progressives into a single coalition behind Wilson, has laid particular stress on the strength and importance of public opinion and of the influence of the public on the formation of foreign policy. For a brief period, roughly from the Republican victories in 1892 and 1896 to the débâcle of the Bull Moose party in 1912, it looked as if the United States might develop the same élitist attitude to international relations as prevailed in Europe. The possibility was never very high – but it existed. The election of Wilson (for all his admiration of the English political tradition in domestic politics), and his appointment of Bryan as his Secretary of State, put paid to that prospect for ever.

This prevalence of a 'populist' approach to international relations and diplomacy manifests itself in all kinds of ways. In the academic world it is revealed in the manner in which the study of diplomacy, or still more the foreign policy, of a particular country or at best a region, seen as the external aspect of its domestic history, is institutionalised throughout the American academic world, whereas posts in the history of international relations such as those which predominate in France, Italy or Britain are found only as adjuncts to the theoretical study of contemporary international relations, if they are found at all. It shows equally in the extraordinary prevalence, in the study of the contemporary international scene, of abstract theories and models which rest on a polarised abstraction from purely American experiences. In 1964 I attended a two-day conference on the Marshall Plan as a field for historical research. The first day was devoted to the discussion of subjects to be investigated on the American side, the second day to those worthy of investigation on the European side.[27] The American diplomatic historians attending the conference thought and spoke almost exclusively of the influences of sections of American opinion, interest groups, minority groups and the like on the formulation of opinion, topics which the bulk of European historians would investigate only after all efforts to penetrate the processes of policy formulation at the Cabinet, ministerial and bureaucratic levels had been abandoned for lack of access to archival materials or participant's testimony.

These attitudes are the reflection of a dominant doctrinal approach to problems of America's external relations, which has distinct analogies to the ideologies of the Eastern powers. When crossing to Europe in 1918 on the *George Washington*, President Wilson bade his entourage remember that the statesmen of Europe with whom they were about to negotiate were in no way representative of their peoples.[28] He is said to have remarked, on returning from the tour of Europe he embarked on before the Versailles Conference opened, that the dumb eyes of the people haunted him.[29] He came to believe that the hopes of the peoples of Europe, whom he separated entirely in his mind from their elected representatives, so recently elected and by margins much greater than his own in 1916, were pinned on him rather than on their own leaders. This concept of the people, dumb, inarticulate, managed by the self-promoted élites who govern them, at once innocent, positively good, primevally naïve, is not unknown in Europe. Indeed it is the stock in trade of the European radical tradition, although that tradition is

---

[27] For a record of the proceedings of this conference see Robert H. Ferrell and Jerry N. Hess (eds.), *Conference of Scholars on the Marshall Plan, 1964*, Independence, Missouri, 1964.

[28] Notes of Dr Isaiah Bowman, 10 December 1918, cited in James T. Shotwell, *At the Paris Peace Conference*, London, 1957, pp. 75–8.

[29] Harold Nicolson, *Peace Making 1919*, London, 1964, p. 50.

usually voiced not by the people themselves but by the *déraciné*, alienated intellectuals at the fringes of the ruling élites, as it was, for example, by the English radicals of the Union of Democratic Control from whom Wilson obtained so many of his ideas.[30] What is important to note is that, whereas in Europe this is a deviant tradition, in the United States, certainly since 1912, it has become the dominant tradition, not in the least invalidated by those who point out its inconsistencies with the evidence or its actual irrelevance. The whole bitter debate over Vietnam in the United States turned frequently on allegations that one or the other side represented the Vietnamese people and that, *ipso facto*, their victory was morally ordained. The few European voices which pointed out that this argument was essentially nonsensical, in that there is no such entity, in the political sense in which both sides employ the term, as the 'Vietnamese people', remained largely unheard.[31]

By a curious paradox this doctrinal approach to international politics has infected even those who think of themselves as realists. A realistic foreign policy is judged as much by its accordance with the abstract canons of 'realism' as any other of the alternative doctrines. It is a remarkable experience to find a discussion of American foreign policy of any era in this century, either contemporary or historical, which focuses on its degree of success in attaining its ends or its degree of accuracy in perceiving the actual outlines of the problems with which it had to deal. As a result those Presidents and Secretaries of State whose policy was actually successful and whose perceptiveness clear, acute and accurate, people such as Theodore Roosevelt, Henry L. Stimson, Dean Acheson for example, figure as the villains and failures in a historiography whose heroes are Wilson, Charles Evans Hughes and Franklin Roosevelt. John F. Kennedy is still regarded with considerable ambivalence. But if he is, as current trends would indicate, in process of being sent to join the villains, it will be for his success in Cuba, South East Asia, the Congo, the Test Ban Treaty and Berlin rather than for his failures in relations with Britain and Western Europe. Dean Rusk has already been disowned, even by Kennedy's defenders.[32]

[30] See Lawrence W. Martin, *Peace Without Victory*, New Haven, 1958; Arno J. Mayer, *The Political Origins of the New Diplomacy, 1917–18*, New Haven, 1959.
[31] See, for example, Dennis Duncanson, *Government and Revolution in Vietnam*, Oxford, 1968; see also Chapters 10 and 11 below.
[32] See, for example, Arthur J. Schlesinger Jr, *A Thousand Days*, pp. 334–87.

Together with the populist ideology there goes a considerable ambivalence over the limits of national interest. Isolationists, who set very narrow limits on the national interest, do it in essentially populist terms, limiting the 'people' to the American people whose sons must not, for example, be sent to die in 'foreign wars'. Their opponents, however, echoing Wilson, would deny that the 'people' have to have been born under the American flag or to have taken out naturalisation papers. A century of mass immigration has made such arguments 'nativist', an ugly word for what in other countries could well have been once called patriotic. The problem is complicated by the difficulty of defining an American except in ideological terms by relation to his activities. No doubt the Protestant ethic of salvation through good works rather than grace enters into this too. But in practice this attempt to define citizenship by relation to abstract qualities, an attempt whose darker side is the obsession with symbols such as 'the flag' or the loyalty oath, is without parallel in the history of Western Europe after the end of the seventeenth century, when attempts to define citizen loyalty in terms of religious faith withered with the onset of the Age of Reason.

What this means in practice is that Americans have the utmost difficulty in delineating their concepts one from another. Supporters of the main line of American policy since 1954 move easily in their discussion of world affairs between concepts such as 'America', 'the West', the 'Free World' as groups holding policies, sharing the same interests, involved in the same decision-making processes, as though the terms were virtually interchangeable.[33] While, by contrast, Americans who oppose this viewpoint saw nothing inconsistent in the exaltation of Che Guevara or Ho Chi Minh, as representative leaders of the Peoples International, the *Weltvolk* as it might be, whom the American ruling élites, the barons of the 'military–industrial complex', are oppressing. They see nothing wrong, any more than Wilson did in 1914 in Mexico, in imposing a leader on a foreign country, providing his credentials are recognisably 'democratic'; if his actions are rejected by his own people, this is merely a temporary aberration. The degree of persistent anti-Germanism in America, like the deep-rooted antipathy which used to obtain towards President de Gaulle, stems from the logical dilemma that

---

[33] See, for example, Walter C. Clemens Jr, 'The Soviet World Faces West', *International Affairs*, 46, no. 3, July 1970.

Hitler's popular support in Germany or de Gaulle's refusal to accept France's rôle as an outlying part of a *Weltvolk* centred on Washington imposes on them. If Hitler was popular in Germany this must argue something basically evil, *unmenschlich* or *unweltvölkisch*, in the German people. If de Gaulle denied the universal applicability of the American scale of values, then he too was clearly evil, *unweltvölkisch*, and his French supporters with him.

At a rather different level this universalist approach leads to a considerable impatience with the sovereignty and interests of America's smaller allies. One can see this manifested in the callousness with which the Papuans of Dutch New Guinea were sacrificed to the cause of good relations with Indonesia by the Kennedy régime in 1962;[34] in the inability of the Kennedy régime to understand the implications for the sovereignty of America's allies of Mr McNamara's remarks at Athens and at Ann Arbor in 1962 on the military irrelevance of small deterrent forces,[35] a speech which, together with the cancellation of the Skybolt missile programme, did more to defeat President Kennedy's Grand Design than any of President de Gaulle's evocations, in his execrable German, of Germany's past; in the use of American financial pressure to bring about a dismantling of the sterling area in 1946–7 and to attempt to force the pace of development in Europe in 1949–50.[36] In each case the American action has been justified and defended in terms which carry conviction only if it is accepted that the US government in some sense is super-sovereign, super-representative of the interests of the peoples of its allies.

The belief that foreign policy has to be conducted in accordance with a universalist 'doctrine' and that the decisions and actions out of which a foreign policy is constructed are justifiable only in relation to their degree of accordance with the principles of that doctrine has further implications. By contrast with the limited pragmatism with which European theorists and practitioners in the field of international politics have approached their subject, their

---

[34] See Watt (ed.), *Survey of International Affairs, 1962*, pp. 376–403, and the sources there cited. See also Chapter 10 below.

[35] *Survey of International Affairs, 1962*, pp. 82–4. For the text of the Ann Arbor speech see *Documents on International Affairs, 1962*, pp. 369–76. See also William W. Kaufmann, *The McNamara Strategy*, New York, 1964.

[36] See D.C. Watt, *Personalities and Policies*, pp. 53–80, 'American Aid to Britain and the Problems of Socialism'.

American opposites have been interested, often to the point of obsession, with the nature of political power, or at least that part of political power which relates to international politics. Where European writers on international politics, from Grotius onwards, have concerned themselves mainly with the legitimisation of power, leaving discussion of its nature and employment basically to the school of military theorists of which Jomini, Clausewitz and Douhet are the most distinguished,[37] Americans face no such problems. Legitimacy in the use of power is supplied by the moral basis of the general universalist doctrine which inspires their approach to international politics. Instead, from Admiral Mahon to the Rand Corporation's theorists, their interest has been directed to the nature and best means of employing power in international politics. In this field and in this alone, the much vaunted pragmatism of the American approach to life for a moment asserts itself. But the arguments which follow are again far from pragmatic, being at best abstractions from experience, where they are not theoretical inferences from a set of principles adopted *a priori*.

Four separate approaches to political power can be easily distinguished. There are the theoreticians of military and sea power from Admiral Mahon to the theorists of warfare in the nuclear age, from Bernard Brodie to McNamara and Kissinger.[38] There are the believers in moral power from Wilson and John Foster Dulles to President Jimmy Carter, whose techniques, rhetorical and legalistic, lead to the final section of this essay, a comparison of European and American methods of diplomacy. There are those who attempted to refine these by developing other non-violent forms of power, of whom Franklin Roosevelt's ideas on quarantining aggressors,[39] George Kennan's containment and Dean Acheson's rôle in the conception of the Marshall Plan[40] are perhaps the most interesting examples. And there is the new school of sociological engineers who lack a major figure, save perhaps in Walt Rostow's theories of

[37] See Michael Howard, *Studies in War and Peace*, London, 1970, pp. 21–36, 'Jomini and the Classical Tradition in Military Thought'.
[38] Howard *Studies*, pp. 154–83, 'The Classical Strategists'.
[39] See John McVickar Haight Jr, 'Roosevelt as Friend of France', *Foreign Affairs*, April 1966, and Lawrence W. Pratt, 'The Anglo-American Naval Conversations on the Far East in January 1938', *International Affairs*, 47, 1971.
[40] See Joseph Jones, *The Fifteen Weeks*, New York, 1955; Dean Acheson, *Present at the Creation*, New York, 1970.

economic development,[41] but whose doctrines have been put into action in development aid projects from Point Four to the Alliance for Progress,[42] in the whole body of CIA practice from the subsidising of existing non-Communist international fronts such as the International Confederation of Free Trade Unions (ICFTU), the Congress for Cultural Freedom and the International Union of Students, to the whole, much more un-American, range of 'dirty tricks' of the militant anti-Communist organisations involved in Teheran in 1953, in Guatemala in 1954 and in the Bay of Pigs débâcle. To this one must add such projects as the Peace Corps,[43] and the various crash programmes designed to produce as rapidly as possible American-trained, American-oriented and pro-American élites in the newly emergent states of Africa and South East Asia,[44] and the ill-fated project for the academic study of the promotion of revolution in Chile exposed in the mid-1960s.[45]

It is, however, from the early believers in moral power through the appeal to the people that the greatest difference has opened between American and European diplomatic methods. This lies eventually in the development of 'open diplomacy' to a point where public oratory and the open press conference become themselves major methods of international communication. To this one must add the development of parliamentary lobby-style diplomacy in which the methods by which majorities are sought and obtained in the United States Congress are applied to the organisation of majorities for resolutions introduced into the General Assembly of the United Nations.

These are not of course methods which have remained private to the Americans, and their definition needs to be refined. Diplomacy by oratory falls into two basic categories, that designed as a form of communication with other governments and that designed as a form

---

[41] Walt W. Rostow, *The Stages of Economic Growth: A Non-Communist Manifesto*, Cambridge Mass., 1960.

[42] David M. Baldwin, *Economic Development and American Foreign Policy 1945–1962*, Chicago, 1966.

[43] David Hopgood and Meridian Bennett, *Agents of Change. A New Look at the Peace Corps*, Boston, 1964.

[44] Robert Ellsworth Elder, *The Foreign Leader Program: Operations in United States*, Washington, Brookings Institute, 1961.

[45] Irving Louis Horowitz, *The Rise and Fall of Project Camelot: Studies in the Relationship between Social Science and Practical Politics*, Cambridge, Mass., 1967.

of propaganda aimed at the domestic support enjoyed by other governments. The distinction is basically one of motivation. Wilson's speech of January 1918, embodying his famous Fourteen Points, was intended essentially to fall into the second category. It was the action of the German government in October 1918 which made it into the first. It was thus an extension by accident rather than intention of the technique Wilson had developed with the Peace Notes of 1916, documents couched in the form of traditional diplomacy but transformed in practice into instruments of the New Diplomacy by their simultaneous publication. The technique puts Wilson slightly ahead of his Soviet rivals. (President Cleveland's Venezuelan message of 1895 and William II's famous telegram to President Kruger of the Transvaal are much earlier examples. The Monroe Doctrine itself is perhaps the earliest.) But Trotsky's famous comment, on assuming control of the Soviet commissariat for foreign affairs, that all he intended to do was to issue a few manifestos and then shut up shop, is perhaps the most extreme statement of the techniques of open diplomacy these two superpowers of the future were developing.

There are of course earlier examples of the speech intended as warning rather than communication. Lloyd George's Mansion House speech of 1912, made at the height of the Agadir crisis, and the Kaiser's famous Tangier speech of 1905 which opened the first Moroccan crisis are examples of this technique. It was, however, one which has been sparingly employed, and then only as a means of overt diplomatic pressure coordinated and orchestrated with more traditional forms of diplomatic communication as well as the traditional military methods of manoeuvre, partial mobilisation, naval concentrations, etc. What was new with Wilson and Lenin was this preference for the manifesto over all other forms of diplomatic communication, an example which was to be eagerly adopted by the European plebiscitary autocrats of Nazism and Fascism, by the Vatican (some of whose earlier encyclicals, especially that of 1871 on Papal infallibility and Leo XIII's *De Rerum Novarum*, could perhaps be regarded as prototypes of this form of communication), and by the representatives of the lesser powers seeking on the podium of the League of Nations a means of universal communication which their otherwise exiguous diplomatic resources denied to them.

When one turns to the use of the press conference as an instrument of open diplomacy, problems of definition loom rather larger. The use of individual organs of the press as semi-official channels of communication is a nineteenth-century device, and the use of an official press is at least as old as Napoleon. Bismarck's famous instigation of the *Krieg in Sicht* articles in the *Kölnische Anzeiger* and the Berlin *Post* in April 1875 shows that the technique was already well established in the 1870s, though in this case the exercise rebounded on the head of its initiator. The Kaiser's *Daily Telegraph* interview of 1908 represents a widening of the technique, since it involved an element absent in the earlier examples, that of relying on the news value of the action itself rather than control of the journal involved as the principal means of obtaining publicity for the action.

The press conference itself is, however, a newer and more recent development. It became a necessity as a result of the development of an international press that was commercially viable and therefore in itself beyond the control of particular governments. Again there is a gap in the historical study of this instrument of communication. Regular conferences were given, on and off the record, by statesmen in the 1920s and 1930s though they were rarely used as instruments of international communication even by Franklin Roosevelt. Roosevelt was not unskilled in the use of the press interview or the selective leak as witness, to give two examples, his use of the *Times* Washington correspondent in October 1934 to warn the British government against a *rapprochement* with Japan,[46] and his use of Arthur Krock of the *New York Times* in August 1936 to float the idea of an international conference on peace through world trade.[47] But for the full development of the press conference as an instrument of diplomatic communication one has to wait until John Foster Dulles, an example developed by President Kennedy but encountered in its fullest and most stylised forms in the press conferences given by Europe's most distinguished admirer and imitator of the American model of elective absolutism, President de Gaulle. It is, however, fair to point out that President de Gaulle's model has been followed by no other European head of government, not even by Mr Harold Wilson, who experimented very widely with various forms of public communication during his nine years as Prime Minister of

[46] See D.C. Watt, *Personalities and Policies*, p. 95.
[47] See Arthur C. Krock, *In the Nation, 1932–1966*, New York, 1966, p. 63.

Britain, without, however, hitting on any very new variant of the original techniques of open diplomacy. With Mr Dulles and President de Gaulle the press conference became a means of evading as well as augmenting normal methods of diplomacy.

The last form of populist diplomacy to which reference has already been made is that of lobby diplomacy as practised today at the General Assembly of the United Nations. There has been disgracefully little study as yet of the methods by which majorities were sought in the League of Nations. Such evidence as is available suggests that Britain and France concentrated basically on voting their client states in the Dominions on one hand and through the mechanisms of the French alliance system in Eastern Europe on the other. In the case of Germany the one case which is most extensively documented is the pressures brought to bear on what would now be called the 'non-aligned' members of the League Council at the time of the Rhineland crisis of March 1936.[48] Here all the pressures were applied not in London when the Council was meeting but in the respective capitals of the states concerned using normal diplomatic channels. The only real novelty lay in the number of states against whom pressure was simultaneously orchestrated.

The techniques used first by the United States in the General Assembly of the United Nations seem to have been developed at the pan-American conferences, especially those of 1936 and 1938, as a substitute for the cruder forms of pressure abandoned by the proclamation of the Good Neighbour policy.[49] Again they require far more precise study and documentation than is at present available. What is significantly American in this is the effort put into and the importance attached to the securing of a regular majority behind American-sponsored resolutions as a means of pressure to be employed against the Soviet Union.[50] This too is a post-Rooseveltian phenomenon, embodied in its ultimate form in the Uniting for Peace Resolution of 1950. The United States was to find the Soviet Union an apt pupil – and has come, correspondingly, to attach less importance to resolutions of the General Assembly. But the facts that the

---

[48] *Documents on German Foreign Policy*, London and New York, 1966, Series C, vol. V, *passim.*

[49] See, for example, Julius Pratt, *Cordell Hull*, New York, 1964, vol. I, pp. 168–76, on Hull's rôle at the Lima Conference in December 1938.

[50] For a characteristically unsympathetic note on this see Conor Cruise O'Brien, *To Katanga and Back*, London, 1962, pp. 18–25.

US delegation to the United Nations is regularly headed by a political figure of at least Cabinet status, if not rank, and that its size and organisation has led to its being called the 'other State Department' show the importance it still holds in American eyes.[51]

To sum up the principal differences between the American and the Euro-democratic approaches to diplomacy and international relations: America combines a system of government which, even if its head is elected and limited by a written constitution and an elected assembly, is basically akin to the systems of monarchical rule obtaining in eighteenth-century Europe, with an ideological attitude to the problems of foreign relations which judges actions by their accordance with the values of the ideology and which seeks to influence the widest possible range of opinion in the countries with whose actions it is concerned. Its methods of diplomacy accord with the populist and universalist nature of its ideology. Common to the Euro-democracies is a system of government which basically has at its head a career political oligocracy which is allied with an élite which is sufficiently cohesive and sufficiently continuous in its membership over time to be only intermittently open to American populist methods and is progressively if slowly regaining its consciousness of its difference from the United States and its own common European identity. The kind of populist, universalist approach which the United States embodies is in Europe basically a heresy, a deviation from the European norm, as it has been ever since a misreading of Montesquieu and the revolutionary ardour of a Tom Paine finally divided what was essentially a culture founded by refugees from Europe from its European roots.

[51] See Arnold Beichman, *The 'Other' State Department. The United States Mission to the United Nations – Its Roles in the Making of Foreign Policy*, New York, 1968.

10

Britain, America and Indo-China, 1942–1945

Second only to India among the problems Roosevelt's anti-colonialism set for his British allies in the years of the Grand Alliance was that of French Indo-China. It was not so much that Roosevelt's antipathy to de Gaulle and all he stood for expressed itself peculiarly strongly in relation to the question of the establishment of Gaullist troops in Indo-China, though that was undoubtedly a complicating factor. Nor was it only that so long as the Third Republic continued, even in its Vichy form, to exert its attraction on some of Roosevelt's entourage, Admiral Leahy for example, what was promised to Pétain could be ignored in relations with the French Committee of National Liberation. Nor was it only that the Indo-Chinese nationalist movement on the whole resisted the Japanese where the Indian nationalist movement remained neutral and those of Burma and Indonesia lent themselves to the propaganda purposes of the New Order of Japan. It may be that, hemmed in by political inhibitions elsewhere, Roosevelt's anti-colonial sentiments broke out with redoubled strength on the Indo-Chinese issue. But that he expressed himself on the subject of French rule with a violence, an extremism, an irrational vehemence that ignored justice, past professions and any pretence at objectivity, cannot be denied. Wherefrom came this vehemence, this bitterness, is still largely unexplained by any of the American historians who have so far examined his record.[1] Equally unexplained is the source of the reports on which he

[1] Lloyd C. Gardner, *Economic Aspects of New Deal Diplomacy*, Madison, 1964; Edward R. Drachman, *United States Policy Towards Vietnam, 1940–45*, Rutherford, New Jersey, 1970. See also on the period covered by this Walter LaFeber,

based his repeated denunciations of the French colonial record in Indo-China.[2] But, holding the views he did, expressing them as openly as he did, he imposed a considerable burden on British patience as on British policy-making. Had it been left to the Foreign Office, to Mr Eden or to the embattled political advisers of the South East Asia Command, Anglo-American relations would have become more than a little strained. But Winston Churchill retained both balance and judgment. The Anglo-American relationship was more important to him than anything else. Repeatedly it was his refusal to act or to sanction action that prevented a head-on collision. No one was second to him in his refusal to accept the American anti-colonialist urge as the dominant force in the post-war settlement. But his instinct was to see Roosevelt's views on Indo-China as a personal aberration, fed, it was true, by the starry-eyed Sinophiles and the more bellicose American imperialists in his service in Washington as in Chungking. And Churchill's instinct was the governing factor in British policy up to Roosevelt's death.

One should perhaps begin by citing a few of Roosevelt's choicer remarks on the subject of French rule in Indo-China to illustrate the strength of his views and the lack of inhibition with which he expressed them.

His son, Elliott Roosevelt, records him as saying: 'The native Indo-Chinese have been so flagrantly downtrodden that they thought to themselves: anything must be better than to live under French colonial rule ... Don't think for a moment that Americans would be dying tonight if it had not been for the short-sighted greed

'Roosevelt, Churchill and Indo-China, 1942–1945', *Am. Hist. Rev.*, 80, 1975; C. Thorne, 'Indo-China and Anglo-American Relations, 1941–1945', *Pac. Hist. Rev.*, 45, 1976.

[2] Professor Walter LaFeber put this down to reports from the private research staff maintained for him by Henry Field. But the summaries of the reports produced by Henry Field's 'Project M' published in Henry Field, *M Project for FDR. Studies on Migration and Settlement*, Ann Arbor, 1962, show that of the seven reports on Indo-China, two were factual summaries of reports of resettlement projects carried out in 1943 by the Vichy administration, monitored from Saigon radio, three were based on translated excerpts from standard French texts, Pierre Courou, *L'Utilisation du sol en Indo-Chine française*, Bordeaux, 1936, and Charles Robequin, *L'Evolution economique de l'Indo-Chine française*, Paris, 1939, one dealt with the demographic imbalance between northern and southern Indo-China and one with the wartime population movements in South East Asia. There is no actual evidence that Roosevelt with all his other duties ever read these reports, none of which would for a moment seem to justify the views he held on the iniquities and indolences, alleged, of French colonial rule.

of the French, the British and the Dutch.'[3] To Stalin at Teheran he said that: 'After 100 years of French rule in Indo-China, the inhabitants are worse off than before.'[4] To Lord Halifax, according to his own record, he said: 'France has had the country, thirty million inhabitants for nearly one hundred years, and the people are worse off than they were at the beginning.'[5] And at Yalta again he repeated himself to Stalin: 'The Indo-Chinese people were of small stature like the Japanese and Burmese and were not at all warlike... France has done nothing to improve the natives since she had the colony...'[6] Up to the beginning of 1943 Roosevelt's attitude towards Indo-China was governed by the desire not to offend the Vichy régime. A State Department memorandum of 7 January 1944[7] listed ten occasions on which American officials had expressed the desire to maintain the integrity of France and its empire; four of these statements were made by Roosevelt himself to Pétain or his representatives. In addition, Mr Murphy had made a precise pledge to General Giraud as part of the negotiations which were supposed to ease the American invasion of French North Africa. But from then on Roosevelt's attitude changed. It began even before Roosevelt's visit to North Africa with Roosevelt stating outright to the US Chiefs of Staff[8] that Murphy, in promising to General Giraud the return of French colonial possessions, had exceeded his authority: 'There were some of the colonial possessions which he was sure would not be returned to France and he had grave doubts as to whether Indo-China should be. He thought the Chiefs of Staff in their discussions in North Africa should make this plain to both Mr Murphy and General Eisenhower.' He also maintained that French sovereignty over all her colonial territories had ceased in June 1940 when President Lebrun resigned.

3 Elliott Roosevelt, *As He Saw It*, New York, 1946, p. 115; surely an odd explanation for Pearl Harbour. One recollects that it was an American, Commodore Perry, who 'opened' Japan.
4 Bohlen minutes, *Foreign Relations of the United States. The Conference at Cairo and Teheran 1943*, pp. 183–6.
5 Roosevelt to Hull, 24 January 1944, *FRUS 1944*, vol. III, p. 773.
6 Bohlen minutes, 8 February 1945, *FRUS, The Conferences at Malta and Yalta, 1945*, p. 770.
7 Enclosure to Hull memorandum for Roosevelt, 7 January 1944, *FRUS 1944*, vol. III, pp. 770–2.
8 On 7 January 1943, Joint Chiefs of Staff minutes meeting at White House, *FRUS, The Conference at Washington, 1941–42, and at Casablanca, 1943*, pp. 505–16.

In March 1943, Roosevelt told Anthony Eden that in his view Indo-China should be made an international trusteeship. A later State Department memorandum prepared in the Far Eastern Division recorded Eden as indicating his favourable impression with the idea.[9] The American Ambassador to Britain, James Winant, had a rather different recollection, telling Matthews of the Office of European Affairs at the State Department that Eden had advocated a national administration (i.e. French) for Indo-China.[10] 'There was considerable inconclusive discussion as to the degree to which governments other than the one having sovereignty or administrative responsibility for a particular area might properly intervene in matters involving the administration of the area or its relations with the other areas.' Eden's own telegram[11] dealt with the matter only cursorily. 'I remarked that the President was being very hard on the French from whom the utmost opposition was to be expected. He admitted this ... '

The minutes kept by Sir William Strang were fuller and more revealing:

The President: An international trusteeship to be set up for Korea and Indo-China ... also the United States to act as 'policemen' at Dakar ... Great Britain at Bizerta.

Eden: The President being very hard on the French who would oppose his suggestions.

The President: France will need assistance after the war and might be willing in return to place certain parts of her territory at the United Nations' disposal.

Sumner Welles: reminded the President of United States promises of restoration of her territories to France.

The President: thought this referred only to North Africa.

Welles: No such limit clear ...

The President: Matters of this kind can be settled in the general ironing out after the war.[12]

These notes are revealing. They show Eden's immediate opposition

---

[9] London memorandum, 10 July 1944; House Committee on the Armed Services, *United States–Vietnam Relations 1945–1967. Study Prepared by the Department of Defence* (Washington, 1971), Book 7, Part V, pp. 32–3. hereinafter cited as *House, Pentagon Papers*. This echoes Howe's memorandum of 27 March 1943, *FRUS 1943*, vol. III, pp. 777–8.

[10] H. Freeman Matthews memorandum, 2 November 1944, *FRUS 1944*, vol. III, pp. 777–8.

[11] Telegram 1470 of 28 March 1943, PRO WP 43(130) CAB. 66.

[12] PRO, FO 371/35366, U 1430/320/70.

to Roosevelt's proposal, the President's willingness to use American economic predominance after the war, his obsession with the idea of the Four Super-imperialist Policemen as keepers of the post-war peace, and the reasons for the lack of any further British reaction for the time being, that is Roosevelt's apparent willingness to postpone the matter until later.

There was thus no very marked reaction when the President trotted out the same idea at the Pacific War Council in Washington in July.[13] When Dr Stanley Hornbeck, head of the US State Department Far Eastern Division, repeated the idea to his British opposite number, Ashley Clarke, in October,[14] the Foreign Office began to sit up. Minutes attached to Clarke's note of the conversation record the official awareness of Mr Murphy's pledges to General Giraud. The President's views were not based, in the Office's opinion, on any real knowledge of the facts but arose largely out of his prejudices with regard to the colonial policies of the Western powers. The proposal was unsatisfactory since it would allow Chinese and ultimately Japanese intrigues. Direct Chinese control was not, in the Office's view, wanted by the local inhabitants and would probably be hostile to British interests. No representations were made in Washington, probably as a result of the Foreign Office's mistaken belief that Murphy's written pledges to General Giraud could not have been given without Roosevelt's knowledge. The Office did, however, begin to consider its own policy on Indo-China.

Roosevelt was in fact in full cry, as he was to show in Cairo and Teheran. At Cairo he extended the bait of a joint trusteeship over Indo-China, Korea and Thailand to Chiang Kai-shek. The bait was not taken in the form offered. Instead Chiang proposed agreement on joint American–Chinese cooperation 'to help Indo-China achieve independence after the war'.[15] Five days later at Teheran he discussed the matter with Stalin. The discussion took place in the context of France's future, a discussion which arose in turn out of the clash between Britain and America and the French Committee of National Liberation over the future of the Lebanon. According to Bohlen's minutes,

[13] *FRUS 1944*, vol. III, p. 769, footnote thereto: PRO, FO 371/35921, F 4646/1422/61.

[14] Clarke memorandum, PRO, FO 371/35921/F 5379/1422/61, 18 October, 1943.

[15] Minutes of meeting of 23 November 1943; *FRUS, Conferences at Cairo and Teheran, 1943*, pp. 322–5.

The President said that Mr Churchill was of the opinion that France would be very quickly reconstructed as a strong nation, but he did not personally share the view since he felt that many years of honest labor would be necessary before France would be re-established. He said the first necessity for the French, not only for the Government but for the people as well, was to become honest citizens.

Marshall Stalin agreed and went on to say that he did not propose to have the Allies shed blood to restore Indo-China, for example, to the old colonial rule ... He said that in the war against Japan, in his opinion, in addition to military missions, it was necessary to fight the Japanese in the political field as well, particularly in view of the fact that the Japanese had granted at the least nominal independence to certain colonial areas. He repeated that France should not get back Indo-China and that the French must pay for their criminal collaboration with Germany.

The President said that he was in 100% agreement with Marshall Stalin ... He said that Chiang Kai-Shek had told him that China had no designs on Indo-China but the people of Indo-China were not ready for independence ... He added that he had discussed with Chiang Kai-Shek the possibility of a system of trusteeship for Indo-China which would have the task of preparing the people for independence within a definite period of time, perhaps 20 to 30 years.[16]

In passing, Stalin's own diplomatic skill should be noticed.[17] He, not Roosevelt, broached the question of Indo-China. He played most effectively on the President's ill-considered and, as it proved, unwarranted fears of post-war French stability and resentment against General de Gaulle. He also played very effectively on Roosevelt's Wilsonian beliefs in national self-determination and sensitivity to Japanese anti-colonialism although both he and Roosevelt were, if they took a moment's thought, well aware that French Indo-China was one area where the Japanese had not overthrown the local colonial administration in the name of independence within the New Order and had encouraged local nationalism only in secret.[18] Roosevelt had in fact shown his hand to the Russians as early as June 1942, on the visit to Washington of the Soviet Commissar for Foreign Affairs, M. Molotov. On that occasion, according to the notes of Samuel H. Cross, the American interpreter:[19]

[16] *Conferences*, pp. 482–5.
[17] The Russian record of this conversation agrees at all essential points with Bohlen's minutes.
[18] It was very largely pro-Chinese, a fact of which the Japanese were well aware.
[19] Memorandum of meeting of 1 June 1942, *FRUS 1942*, vol. III, pp. 578–83.

Turning to the question of colonial possession, the President took as examples Indo-China, Siam [sic] and the Malay states or even the Dutch East Indies ... Each of these areas would require a different lapse of time before achieving readiness for self-government, but a palpable surge towards independence was there all the same and the white nations thus could not hope to hold these areas as colonies in the long run ... General-issimo Chiang Kai-Shek therefore had the idea that some form of interim international trusteeship would be the best mode of administering these territories until they were ready for self-government ...

On his return from Washington, Roosevelt took the extra-ordinary step of summoning a clamjamphrie of ambassadors to the White House,[20] ostensibly to thank them for the hospitality he had enjoyed during his visit to the Middle East. At the reception, prefacing his remarks[21] with a request that what he was about to say should be kept secret, he stated that he had been working to prevent the restoration of Indo-China to France. Since, in his belief, the Indo-Chinese were not ready for self-government, they would have to be placed under United Nations trusteeship which would teach them how to govern themselves. This was the more important in that recent international meetings had decided that peace would have to be kept by force. Force required international policemen who would need to occupy certain important strategic areas so that they could make that force available without worrying about changes in sovereignty. Indo-China was just such an area. France would therefore have to abandon Indo-China.

How the other ambassadors received this curious manifesto, virtually the last positive step taken by Roosevelt on the issue of Indo-China, is not as yet on public record. In London and in Delhi it aroused a storm of imperial opposition. Mr Cavendish-Bentinck minuted:

This provokes the impression that President Roosevelt is suffering from the same kind of megalomania which characterised the late President Wilson and Lloyd George at the end of the last war and proved the former's

---

[20] They included the Chinese, Turkish, Egyptian, Iranian and Soviet ambassadors and the Counsellor to the British Embassy.

[21] Report by the British Minister, 20 December 1943, FO 371/35921, F 6656/1422/61. It is characteristic of Roosevelt's somewhat peculiar way of doing things that there is no State Department record of this occasion. The editors of the Series, *Foreign Reactions of the United States*, lacking any State Department record, wrongly attribute subsequent references to this speech to his address in 1943 to the Pacific War Council (see footnote 13 above).

undoing. I trust that we shall not allow ourselves to quarrel with the French without being on very strong ground, for the benefit of an American president who in a year's time may be merely a historical figure . . .

If Indo-China is not restored to France on the grounds that the 'poor Indo-Chinese' have had no education and no welfare (I have never heard that the Indo-Chinese were any more unhappy than the share-croppers of the southern United States), the Dutch and ourselves may later on be told that the oil resources of the Netherlands East Indies and Borneo had not been properly developed, nor the rubber resources of Malaya and that the natives are insufficiently educated by Washington standards and that their territories must be placed under UN trusteeship (perhaps with American oil and rubber controllers).[22]

Discussion of Indo-China within the Foreign Office tended to be very much governed by these kinds of reaction, that of believers in Britain's great power status and imperial mission whose beliefs were being challenged by another and different morality with power to back it. Although the Far Eastern section of the Foreign Office may have shared some of Roosevelt's distrust of the French, the *de haut en bas* tone of American strictures and a long experience of the coincidence of American moral principles with American commercial interests aroused both their patriotic ire and their professional cynicism. Much the same could be said of the reactions of the Permanent Under Secretary of the Foreign Office, Sir Alexander Cadogan, and of Anthony Eden himself.

Within the Foreign Office, however, there were arguments other than the merely cynical for opposing the President's views. The Office was still largely dominated by the generation of diplomatists whose training, social origins and experience made them European in outlook, concerned most of all with the future of the balance of power in Europe. The Atlanticist view, so often encountered in the Office in the 1950s, with its reminiscences of the pan-Anglo-Saxonism of earlier days, is encountered only in the occasional interventions of the American section and of Sir Harold Butler, the Assistant Under Secretary of most American experience. Other voices, from the Chiefs of Staff, from South East Asia Command, and from the Special Operations Executive (SOE), or Force 136 as it was known in its South East Asian manifestations, added to the strength of opinion arguing for positive counter-action to thwart

[22] Minute on F6656/1422/61.

Roosevelt's policies. Only Churchill restrained them – and in this, as in everything, Churchill was paramount.

His first reactions were characteristic. On 21 December 1943 he replied to Eden's query that

he had often heard the President express his views about Indo-China and Dakar and that he had never given his assent to them. He did not think the Americans have the intention to take territory from France forcibly and without agreement with the French after a French government has been formed on the basis of the will of the French people. If we were informed officially of the statements made by the President, we should state clearly and at once that we had no part in them.[23]

The Foreign Office in the meantime instructed Lord Halifax to enquire[24] whether the President had considered his proposals in relation to America's pledges to France and whether the policy they represented had been agreed with the State Department.

Halifax saw Hull on 3 January 1944. According to Hull's note to Roosevelt[25] (in which he thoughtfully enclosed a list of no fewer than eleven American promises to various French official figures), he pleaded ignorance as to whether Roosevelt had reached any final conclusions. Halifax reported[26] him in this sense, leading the Foreign Office to infer that Roosevelt's remarks did not represent any settled policy. This provoked Churchill to his one positive step, a minute to Eden[27] of 12 January 1944, suggesting that the Foreign Office 'should develop a very strong movement on this issue through the State Department' and leave to a later stage any direct communication between himself and the President. Halifax's inference proved to be ill-founded. On 18 January he had a long talk with Roosevelt, who was at his most infuriating. The President 'gaily interjected'[28] that his remarks did represent his considered opinion. He did not mind if they were repeated to the French. He did not think his pledges to France were of importance. Murphy had committed himself more definitely than he should. Halifax interrupted to say

---

23 Minute of 21 December 1943, FO 371/35921 F 6815/1422/61.
24 FO 371/35921, F 6656/1422/61, F 6656/1422/61.
25 Hull to Roosevelt, 14 January 1944, *FRUS 1944*, vol. III, pp. 769–73; Hull memorandum of 3 January 1944, *FRUS, Conferences at Cairo and Teheran, 1943*, p. 864.
26 FO 371/41723, F 66/66/61.
27 F 118/66/61 of 12 January 1944, FO 371/41723.
28 Halifax to Eden, 18 January 1944, F 360/66/61, FO 371/41723.

that this was all very well but Roosevelt 'might one of these days have the bright idea that the Netherlands East Indies or Malaya ... should go under international trusteeship. The President interrupted to say that the cases were quite different. Both we and the Dutch had done a good job, but the French were hopeless ... The President was not taking it all too seriously ...'[29]

The matter became thus sufficiently serious for the Foreign Office to feel obliged to refer it to the Cabinet. A long paper was prepared and sent to the Cabinet on 16 February.[30] The Foreign Office's recommendations were a compendium of five different ingredients: an internal paper produced the previous August as an exercise in internal mind-clearing;[31] the reactions of the South East Asia Command to the reports of Roosevelt's address to the Teheran ambassadors, reactions which betray the hand of Force 136;[32] the views of the Chiefs of Staff;[33] a lengthy memorandum introduced by Professor Geoffrey Hudson of the Foreign Office Research Department on French rule in Indo-China;[34] and representations from the French National Committee. They were to carry conviction with the Cabinet, but not, as it proved, with Churchill.

In September 1943, the main Foreign Office anxiety was the danger of a clash between the French Committee of National Liberation and Roosevelt. British policy, the memorandum recommended, should be agreed with the Dominions. It should promote the strategic security of the Commonwealth and Empire in the Pacific. It should encourage the United States to participate in collective security. It should avoid any adverse reactions on the French strength in Europe and on the close Anglo-French relations so essential to European security. Fears were expressed in this context of a new Franco-Czechoslovak-Soviet bloc or of a continental bloc in contraposition to a group formed by the United States and the British Commonwealth. One way, it was argued, of

---

[29] For Roosevelt's version of his remarks on this occasion see Roosevelt to Hull, 24 January 1944, *FRUS 1944*, vol. III, p. 773; 'I see no reason to play with the British Foreign Office in this matter. The only reason they seem to oppose it is that they fear the effect it will have on their own possessions and those of the Dutch.'

[30] FO 371/41723, F 980/66/61; WP(44) III; PREM. 3, 178/2/53.

[31] FO 371/35921, F 4646/1422/61.

[32] FO 371/41723, F 79/66/61. Dening to Cadogan, 3 January 1944.

[33] PHP(44)2(0), FO 371/41723, F 260/66/61.

[34] FO 371/41723, F 478/66/61.

keeping France 'loose from such a bloc' would be 'to give them as far as possible a sense of common interests with this country as a colonial power'. British policy, it was recommended, should aim at the continuation of French sovereignty on condition that France accepted the same international arrangements for peace and security as did Britain, 'that she agrees to the establishment of international bases at strategic points'. An international trusteeship should be opposed. 'It would open the door wide to Chinese intrigues and we should expect the Japanese to start fishing in the troubled waters at the first opportunity.' But, the memorandum concluded, this should be changed 'If it become clear that the United States are determined to insist on the termination of French sovereignty as the price of their participation in security measures and that their attitude is approved by the dominions ... We cannot be expected to fight for the future of the French Empire at the price of splitting our own.'

In this last phrase we can detect the hand of the American section of the Foreign Office. Cadogan himself took the view that the colonial powers should stick together in the Far East,[35] a view shared by Dening, the political adviser to the South East Asia Command (SEAC). In September 1943, SEAC had opposed the French request for the attachment of a military mission to SEAC.[36] But the chance of acquiring a French *corps léger*, a commando-style unit of five hundred to six hundred strong, to operate across the Japanese lines of communication from Burma to Indo-China was a different matter. 'We could not employ Frenchmen for our own purposes and then refuse to give them back their territory', Dening cabled.[37]

The view of the Chiefs of Staff was more Eurocentric. They wrote that it was, of course, important that the United States should be directly involved in the event of a (future) attack on Indo-China. But

any suggestion that we should support the United States in depriving France wholesale of such an important possession as Indo-China would be most strongly resented by the French and would seriously endanger our post-war co-operation with them ... as long as there is any threat of aggression by a European power our policy should aim at maintaining a strong and friendly France and even if she remains weak, she should at least be friendly ...

In order to provide a greater measure of security in the Far East it is

[35] See his minute to Churchill of October 1943, FO 371/35921, F 5608/1422/61.
[36] General Pownall to Foreign Office, FO 371/35921, F 4870/1422/61; this document has been removed from the file since I saw it and noted its contents.
[37] F 79/66/61.

essential to have American participation; but we should try to do this without antagonizing France since to do so would be to insure against one danger at the cost of exposing ourselves to another more immediate and vital to the Empire as a whole ...

The Foreign Office Research Department was principally concerned to provide material with which to counter President Roosevelt's attempts to plead immorality and incompetence by the French administration as the principal justification for ending French rule over Indo-China. In his cover note[38] Professor Hudson wrote that 'the Indo-Chinese Union ... has no geographical, ethnographical or religious unity and no political cohesion apart from that conferred by the French administration'. There had been 'no serious troubles apart from the Communist risings in 1930–31', in his view, and the French had set 'a notable record in the building of road and rail communications, dyke construction and irrigation and agricultural and industrial development. Exports and imports have risen remarkably and the population has increased considerably ... the standard of health has been much raised since a service of direct medical assistance began in 1904.'

The view of the Foreign Office's senior staff on these various opinions was, as always, carefully balanced, as much through the competitive xenophobia that senior Foreign Office officials reveal in their minutes as on the more general issues. Sir Maurice Peterson summed it up most fully in his minute on the paper presented to the Cabinet:[39]

Despite this paper, I should still be of the opinion that, if other things were equal, there would be great advantage in restricting post-war France to the rôle of a European and North African power. But other things are not equal. In the first place we do not know where the US would stop if they were encouraged to imagine that the concept of 'parent states' in the Pacific might be discarded; and in the second place, apart from the establishment of United Nations military bases in Indo-China ... it is very difficult indeed to suggest any alternative to the French régime than that of China which has even less to recommend it.

To both this, and Cadogan's comment that this was 'one of the President's most half-baked and most unfortunate dicta', Eden minuted 'I agree.'

[38] FO 371/41723, F 478/66/61.
[39] Minutes on 980/66/61.

The War Cabinet shared that agreement and recommended consultation with the Dominions.[40] Churchill did not. He minuted:[41]

I think it a great mistake to raise the matter before the Presidential election. I cannot conceive it is urgent. On this point the President's views are peculiar to himself. The war in the Far East may go on for a long time. I do not consider that chance remarks which the President made in conversation should be made the basis for setting all this ponderous machinery in motion. Nothing is going to happen for a long time.

This was no passing or momentary pig-headedness. Churchill continued to oppose any approach to Roosevelt for the rest of 1944. On 21 May 1944 he minuted to Eden:[42]

1. It is hard enough to get along in South East Asia Command when we virtually have only the Americans to deal with. The more the French can get their finger in the pie, the more trouble they will make to show they are not humiliated. You will have de Gaullist intrigues there just as you have here in Syria and the Lebanon.
2. Before we could bring the French officially into the Indo-China area we should have to settle with President Roosevelt. He has been more outspoken to me on Indo-China than on any other colonial matter, and I imagine it is one of his principal war aims to liberate Indo-China from France. Whenever I have raised it, I have repeatedly reminded him of his pledge about the integrity of the French Empire and reserved our position. Do you really want to go and stir all this up at such a time as this?

On this note, and the idea of postponement until after D-Day,[43] the matter rested until August when the Chiefs of Staff, who had under consideration the more general issue of French participation in the war against Japan, requested the Joint Staff mission in Washington to raise the issue with the US Chiefs of Staff, and secured from the latter their agreement to French participation at least so far as the area covering the allied South East Asia Command was concerned. Participation inside Indo-China, however, was ruled out on the grounds that this belonged to the China theatre of war.[44] The Chiefs

---

[40] Cabinet conclusion WM(44)25, FO 371/41723, F 1075/66/61, 24 February 1944.
[41] FO 371/41723, F 1176/66/61.
[42] FO 371/41719, F 2502/9/61.
[43] Although Eden and Cadogan thought this indicated 'some progress' in the Prime Minister's views, Churchill deferred the issue again in June. F 2718/9/65. Cadogan confessed himself baffled: 'I cannot follow the purpose of a policy of estranging progressively and often to our disadvantage the only French authority that at present exists. I don't understand it. I don't know what is at the back of it.' (Minute on F 2223/66/61, FO 371/41723.)
[44] FO 371/41720, F 4261/9/61, 9 September 1944.

of Staff were not acting on their own, as the same month marked the opening of a new French diplomatic offensive aimed at the re-establishment of the French presence in South East Asia. M. René Massigli, the Ambassador in London of the new provisional French government, in early August enquired politely of the Foreign Office for agreement to the attachment of a French military mission under General Blaizot to Lord Louis Mountbatten's command, and for the dispatch to the war theatre of the French *corps léger* offered the previous October. To their embarrassment the Foreign Office officials were forced to temporise with M. Massigli,[45] and General Blaizot remained for the time being in Algiers; their embarrassment was somewhat tempered by the discovery that M. Massigli's description of General Blaizot's mission and purpose did not altogether correspond with that issued by General Blaizot himself.

Pressure continued from South East Asia Command, which had raised as early as March the bogey of a Franco-American *rapprochement* based on joint hostility to the British position in South East Asia and expressed in the dispatch of General Blaizot to Chungking rather than Delhi.[46] Eden proposed that the matter should be raised at Quebec but Churchill again refused to raise the question until 'other more urgent matters have been settled', giving as his reason that 'the present position of South East Asia Command shows no hope of advancing before the beginning of 1946'.[47]

Ten days later, however, presumably after seeing Lord Mountbatten who was in London, Churchill had changed his mind and approved the dispatch of the Blaizot mission, of the French *corps léger* and of French help in political warfare in South East Asia. 'There is no need to telegraph the President', he minuted. He had not, it was soon to be evident, changed his basic attitude to the whole issue; this change of mind developed out of two rather misleading assurances. The first of these was the qualified agreement of the US Chiefs of Staff; the second was Lord Louis Mountbatten's statement that he had agreed with Chiang Kai-shek that both Chinese and SEAC Commands were free to attack Indo-China and that this agreement could be taken to cover 'pre-operational activities'.[48] The

Foreign Office had already agreed on 2 October to General Blaizot going on a 'temporary personal visit' to Mountbatten; this seemed the least objectionable way of evading M. Massigli's polite but continuous pressure and the Foreign Office's own inability, in the face of Churchill's persistent refusal to tackle Roosevelt, to plead the American refusal to reply to their approach on French participation in the war against Japan.[49]

South East Asia Command continued to press for the *corps léger*. The motive force was provided by SOE/Force 136. SOE planned to operate in three phases: firstly, pure sabotage directed against Japanese lines of communication with Burma; secondly, wider developments 'involving certain elements in the French army' in Indo-China; thirdly, substantial support for the French regular troops in Indo-China in widespread risings with the main elements in north-west Indo-China.[50] Such plans required both the *corps léger* and a considerable increase in their own resources of aircraft and other supplies. None of these was forthcoming. Despite Churchill's OK the *corps léger* remained in Africa.

The main fault for this must be laid at the door of the Foreign Office, which found itself unable or unwilling to evade the issue of American agreement to the dispatch of the *corps léger* to India. SOE professed to believe that the French, yet again, were being tempted to base their activities in Indo-China on Chungking and on American control.[51] The Foreign Office felt that the arrival of the *corps léger* in the area of SEAC might well be followed by a refusal by the American element in Lord Louis Mountbatten's inter-Allied staff to cooperate any further. It therefore instructed Halifax to raise the matter again[52] with the State Department, as he did on 22 November.[53] Roosevelt was, however, already in receipt both of direct

[49] FO 371/41720 F 4681/9/61.
[50] Keswick to Ashley Clarke, FO 371/41724, F 3554/66/61, 15 July 1944.
[51] They were not altogether wrong; see Hull to Roosevelt, 13 October 1944, *FRUS 1944*, vol. III, pp. 776–7.
[52] He had raised the matter on 25 August with Hull, *FRUS 1944*, vol. III, pp. 775–6.
[53] Eden to Halifax, 16 November 1944, FO 371/41721, F 5303/9/61. Halifax to Eden, 22 November 1944, FO 371/41721, F 5575/9/61; Halifax to Stettinius, 23 November 1944, *FRUS 1944*, vol. III, pp. 781–3.

French representations[54] and of a variety of largely inaccurate and prejudicial reports about alleged British attempts to exclude the American Office of Strategic Services (OSS) and Office of War Information agencies from operations in South East Asia and even more inaccurate allegations of a joint Franco-British–Dutch agreement on the setting up of a joint 'Imperial Command' in Ceylon to coordinate the establishment of colonial rule in South East Asia.[55] Nothing could have been more calculated to make Roosevelt's flesh creep. In October he had ordered that nothing should be done 'in regard to resistance groups or in any other way in relation to Indo-China'.[56] He repeated this on 3 November.[57] And he authorised a strong note of warning to Britain that the United States expected to be consulted about any arrangements for the future of South East Asia. The State Department linked this with the reports it admitted receiving of an Anglo-Dutch agreement with French participation. Foreign Office minutes noted this communication as an example of the American suspicions which were Britain's greatest potential difficulty in the Far East.[58] No such agreement in fact existed,[59] the Americans being well aware of the only Anglo-Dutch agreement so far concluded, one relating to the question of civil affairs in the Netherlands East Indies.

This episode takes one into the murky waters of competitive intelligence, a subject carefully excluded from those files available to researchers in the British Foreign Office. From the few indications of SOE evaluations and plans, it is clear that the main weight of British

---

[54] Caffery (Paris) to Hull, 4 November 1944, *FRUS 1944*, vol. III, pp. 780–1. Admiral Ferard to General de Gaulle, 12 October 1944. Charles de Gaulle, *War Memoirs, vol. III, Salvation, Documents*, London, 1960, pp. 39–42.

[55] Hull to Roosevelt, 10 October 1944 and 13 October 1944; Stettinius to Roosevelt, 2 November 1944, *FRUS 1944*, vol. III, pp. 775–7, 778–9; General Wedemeyer to Washington, 15 November 1944; Roosevelt to Hurley, 16 November 1944; Allan W. Cameron, *The Vietnam Crisis: A Documentary History*, Ithaca, 1971, vol. I, pp. 18–19, citing Wedemeyer papers; Hurley to Roosevelt, 26 November 1944, cited from Hurley papers, by Drachman, p. 65.

[56] Roosevelt to Hull, 16 October 1944; *FRUS 1944*, III, p. 777.

[57] Roosevelt to Stettinius, 3 November 1944; *FRUS 1944*, vol. III, p. 780.

[58] FO 371/41724, F 5868/168/61.

[59] The origin of such reports being with the OSS office in Ceylon (i.e. within the British led South East Asia Command area, where intelligence and subversive activities were dominated by the British military intelligence and SOE/Force 136 organisations) suggests an inter-intelligence agency intrigue.

clandestine operations into Indo-China was based on the Gaullist resistance, and that there was little or no contact with either Vietnamese or other Indo-Chinese resistance groups.[60] The American OSS groups operating out of Southern China, which had since 1944 been using the apparatus carefully built up in the 1930s by the Indo-Chinese Communist party and reactivated by Ho Chi Minh in 1942–3,[61] professed to believe that SOE had been specifically forbidden to have anything to do with the Chinese sponsored Vietnam Dong Minh Hoi, behind which Ho sheltered.[62] The British were well informed as to the activities of the Vietnam Dong Minh Hoi and its dependent relationship with the Chinese; their information was that the Chinese were actively persecuting all Annamite refugees who made any attempt to get in touch with the French Consulate in Kunming, and that the French observers on the Chinese frontier with Indo-China were kept in complete isolation by the local Chinese authorities and not allowed to see anyone. It was the British belief that, with high level American encouragement, the Chinese were preparing to set up an Indo-Chinese 'puppet government'. OSS subversion of a French intelligence group operating with Indo-China was also reported.[63]

Lord Halifax's note thus remained unanswered, despite a reminder in late December. Halifax finally succeeded in breaking Roosevelt's reserve on 4 January 1945. Three days earlier Roosevelt had again noted his unwillingness to see America in any way involved militarily in the liberation of Indo-China, and that he had made this clear to Churchill at the Second Quebec Conference in September 1944.[64] In this his memory misled him. For their own different reasons neither Churchill nor Roosevelt had made any reference to Indo-China at Quebec. If Roosevelt made a record of his conversation with Lord Halifax, it has so far eluded historical discovery. Halifax's record is thereby doubly interesting.[65] Halifax records himself as telling Roosevelt that he was not in the least

[60] See the SOE report of 15 July 1944 cited in footnote 50 above.
[61] Dennis J. Duncanson, *Government and Revolution in Vietnam*, Oxford, 1968, pp. 146–8, 153–4, 157.
[62] *FRUS 1944*, vol. III, pp. 778–80, Stettinius memorandum for Roosevelt, 2 November 1944.
[63] Chungking dispatch enclosing report by Brewis, acting Consul-General in Kunming, of 18 July 1944, FO 371/41724, F 3713/66/61.
[64] *FRUS 1945*, vol. VI, p. 293.
[65] Halifax to Eden, 9 January 1945, FO 371/46304, F 190/11/61.

concerned with the President's views on the general future of Indo-China but with the concrete issue of getting Frenchmen into Indo-China to do sabotage to hamper Japanese communications with Burma. Roosevelt replied, in Halifax's words: 'if we felt it was important we had better go ahead and do it and ask no questions. He did not want in any way to be committed to anything that would seem to prejudge political decisions about Indo-China in a sense favourable to the restoration of the French *status quo ante* which he did not wish to see restored . . . ' 'I suggest', added Lord Halifax, 'we should let sleeping dogs lie.'

This advice coincided with an SOE report of a most secret character from Washington[66] ascribing Roosevelt's refusal to modify his position to Admiral Leahy's influence. Leahy, the former American ambassador to Vichy France, was reported to be determined to get Indo-China out of the theatre covered by South East Asia Command and did not want anything to happen to make this more difficult. The London office of SOE added drily: 'I do not think the Americans realize anything like the extent to which our own penetration of French Indo-China jointly with the French has already progressed.'

Lord Halifax's advice was echoed by Lord Mountbatten and by his political adviser, Dening.[67] The French allayed Dening's fears that despair would make them sell out to Chungking and Wedemeyer. Mountbatten was about to open 'pre-operational activities' in Indo-China to coincide with the beginning of the Burma liberation campaign and feared that any new decision by Roosevelt might destroy matters.

The Foreign Office were thus deprived of their major allies. Nevertheless they still felt that it was necessary to bring the matter into the open, and prepare a joint position with the Dominions as had been agreed in February 1944, in case Roosevelt sprang the issue on Churchill at the forthcoming Yalta Conference. On 8 February, the Foreign Office intervened in great anger to thwart an SOE attempt to ship the unhappy *corps léger* to Ceylon.[68] Their point was almost immediately underlined by a major intervention by General Wedemeyer to prohibit any SEAC intervention into Indo-China

[66] Sporborg to Foreign Office, 5 January 1945, FO 371/46304, F 163/11/61.
[67] Dening to Eden, 7 January 1945, FO 371/46304, F 163/11/61.
[68] Sterndale-Bennett memo, 8 February 1945, FO 371/46304, F 741/11/61.

without his previous consent.[69] The matter unleashed a major row in Washington and re-awoke the internal debate in the Foreign Office as an exasperated Dening demanded from the Foreign Office a definition of British policy towards Indo-China.[70] The usual notes of anxiety over Roosevelt's idea that the restoration of French rule 'depends on the United Nations (or rather the United States) satisfying themselves that the French record in Indo-China justifies the restoration of French authority' and that 'there seems no reason why the French should not fight their own battles on Indo-China' were sounded in the Foreign Office minutes. The most authoritative came from Speaight for the European view and Butler for the pro-American view. Speaight minuted:

We regard a strong and friendly France as an essential factor for our post-war security: (i) because it is vital that her northern ports and air bases should be in strong and friendly hands; (ii) because we must rely on France to play the major rôle in containing Germany from the west; (iii) because with the many European and imperial interests which she has in common with us, France should prove a useful ally on occasion in the councils of the Great Powers.

In pursuance of this policy we have tried progressively to build up France as a European great power. It was we who pressed the Americans to agree to recognize the provisional government. We took the lead in bringing France into the European Advisory Commission and in getting her a zone of occupation in Germany and a seat on the German Control Commission.

To this Butler replied:

I think we have to face the fundamental question of whether we want to have the United States as a partner after the war, which has, as I understand it, hitherto been our policy; or whether we have become so convinced of the recuperative capacities of France and of the instability of the United States that we are only going to consult the latter when it suits us. Our Service and our Treasury advisers both assure us that it is essential to carry the Americans with us. We shall not succeed unless we bring them in on the ground floor in all our dispositions where they are concerned.

A reluctant Wilson, confronted with the facts, finally agreed on 6 March 1945 to approach Roosevelt at least on the issue of Mountbatten's understanding with Chiang Kai-shek. He delayed even this for a vital ten days.[71] By then the Japanese had rendered the matter largely academic.

[69] Dening to Eden, 8 February 1945, FO 371/46034, F 888/11/61.
[70] Dening to Sterndale-Bennett, 16 February 1945, FO 371/46304 F 1269/11/61.
[71] Sterndale-Bennett minute FO 371/46035, F 1563/11/61.

On 9 March, Japanese forces attacked the French garrisons in Indo-China and overthrew the French colonial authorities. In the south the garrisons were largely overwhelmed. But in the north, the French colonial troops were more prepared. General de Gaulle's provisional French government had been in touch with the French forces in Indo-China since the secret mission of Baron de Langlade the previous October.[72] General de Gaulle had appointed General Mordant, his delegate-general, in Indo-China and planning was going forward for a *coup de main* by the French forces in Indo-China to coincide with an Allied invasion.[73] If the Japanese anticipated this, French forces were to fight, and in no case to allow themselves to be disarmed without resistance.

In preparation for this latter possibility the French military attaché in Chungking saw General Wedemeyer on 2 February, and asked for aid in the event that French forces were forced to disperse into the hills for guerilla activity.[74] Unfortunately for any chance they might have had of obtaining a sympathetic hearing, the French Embassy in Chungking had already felt obliged to read their American colleagues a lecture on the French position in Indo-China, in a note of 20 January.[75] The note itself brought General Hurley close to apoplexy,[76] and caused the State Department some amusement.[77] The Embassy was, however, instructed on 16 February that they could be 'helpful to the French wherever feasible',[78] instructions which almost certainly went beyond Hurley's understanding of the President's point of view. On 22 February, the French protested again, this time at reports of American military assistance in the organisation of a Chinese expeditionary force for use in Indo-China.[79] Both

---

[72] For Baron de Langlade's report on his mission, made on 15 January 1945, see Charles de Gaulle, *Salvation, Documents*, pp. 211–12; *FRUS 1944*, vol. III, pp. 778–9, Stettinius memorandum, 2 November 1944.

[73] *FRUS 1944*, III, pp. 783–4; Stettinius memorandum, 27 December 1944; Charles de Gaulle, *Salvation, Documents*, de Gaulle to Mordant, 21 February 1945, p. 216.

[74] *FRUS 1945*, vol. VI, pp. 296–7, Hurley to Washington, 6 February 1945.

[75] *FRUS 1945*, vol. VI, pp. 295–6. Fears of American action 'not in agreement' with that of France may have provoked this action. De Gaulle, *Salvation, Documents*, p. 212.

[76] *FRUS 1945*, vol. VI, p. 294, Hurley to Washington, 31 January 1945.

[77] Memorandum of 14 February 1945, *House Pentagon Papers*: 'I fear there is a lump in the General's mashed potatoes.'

[78] *FRUS 1945*, vol. VI, pp. 50–1.

[79] *FRUS 1945*, vol. VI, pp. 55–6.

Wedemeyer and Hurley were on their way to Washington, so the French complaint was sent on for their comment. It can be imagined therefore that the American conclave in Washington were not entirely of a mind to be sympathetic towards the French at the time of the Japanese attack. They were already at odds with Admiral Mountbatten and SEAC for intrusion into General Wedemeyer's command area. French contacts with Indo-China were largely being organised via the British aircraft of Force 136, Lend-Lease aircraft (a fact which particularly offended General Hurley, since he persisted in thinking of any Lend-Lease material as still formally American).[80] And General Wedemeyer and the President were convinced that the British, French and Dutch were working to a closely coordinated plan to 'ensure recovery of their pre-war political and economic positions in the Far East'.[81]

The French military resistance movement in Indo-China had long been aware that in the event of Japanese action there was little that could be done in the south. In the north, however, Generals Sabattier and Alessandri had established themselves with some ten thousand men around Dien Bien Phu. Contact was established almost immediately with General Chennault, commanding the American Air Forces in China. Liaison officers from his Command were dropped from light aircraft and air-drops of arms, supplies, medical stores, etc., arranged. Chennault felt himself unable to act without authorisation.[82] This was slow in coming, apparently as a result of previous French protests about American arms-drops to the Vietminh. Moreover, the limited missions flown by British aircraft at the disposal of SEAC were made the subject of protest by Brigadier Gross,

---

[80] See his report of 29 May 1945 to President Truman of his conference with Roosevelt on 24 March 1945 cited in undated Elsey memorandum, *FRUS, Conference of Berlin (Potsdam)*, vol. I, pp. 915–21 at p. 917.

[81] Wedemeyer report of 15 November 1944, cited from the Wedemeyer papers by Cameron (ed.), *The Vietnam Crisis: A Documentary History*, vol. I, pp. 18–19.

[82] Claire L. Chennault, *The Way of a Fighter*, New York, 1949, p. 342; Albert C. Wedemeyer, *Wedemeyer Reports*, New York, 1958, pp. 343–4; Charles F. Romanus and Riley Sutherland, *Time Runs Out in CBI*, Washington D.C., Department of the Army 1959, pp. 259–60; Wedemeyer to Drachman, 19 January 1967, cited in Drachman, p. 84; SOE report 16 March 1945, FO 371/46305, F 1715/11/61; Joint Staffs Mission, Washington to London, FO 371/46305, F 1720/11/61.

Wedemeyer's military deputy in China, as the 'employment either directly or indirectly of American resources'.[83]

French appeals were made to both Britain and the United States on 12 March 1945.[84] Their action provoked one of Churchill's rare positive acts. That day he appealed to Ismay for a one-page briefing, writing[85] 'I have not followed affairs in this country for some time', an odd comment in the light of his agreement to approach F.D.R. on the question of SEAC operations in Indo-China, but one which sufficiently illustrates the irksome nature of the entire subject to him. And on 19 March he addressed Field Marshal Wilson, head of the British military mission to Washington:[86] 'The Prime Minister feels that it would look very bad in history if we were to let the French forces in Indo-China be cut to pieces by the Japanese through shortage of arms, if there is anything we can do to save them. He hopes, therefore, we shall be agreed in not standing on *punctilio* in this emergency.'

It should again be noted, however, that Churchill refused to approach Roosevelt directly on the matter, telling Wilson to talk instead to his Chief of Army Staff, General Marshall.[87] In fact instructions were sent by Wedemeyer to Chennault the same day[88] to undertake operations against the Japanese but with the highly limiting proviso that assistance to the French 'should not interfere with operations now planned'. That same day four P 38 aircraft of the US Fourteenth Air Force attacked Japanese forces in the Hoa Binh area.[89]

The wisdom of Churchill's approach was shown by two events. The first was the fate of a proposal by Stettinius, put to Roosevelt on 16 March, to issue a statement[90] designed to counter de Gaulle's

---

[83] Joint Staffs Mission Washington to London, 18 March 1945, FO 371/46305, F 1787/11/61. Six Liberators were employed with limited success owing to weather conditions, FO 371/46305, F 1461/11/61. Mountbatten subsequently reported, 21 March 1945, that in the month 6 February–6 March, owing to weather conditions, only 28 of 78 Liberator sorties were successful.

[84] Eden note on conversation with Massigli, FO 371/46305, F 1563/11/61; *FRUS 1945*, vol. IV, pp. 297–9, Bonnet to Stettinius, 12 March 1945; p. 300, Caffery to Stettinius, 13 March 1945.

[85] FO 371/146305, F 1648/11/61: PREM 3, 178/3/202.

[86] FO 371/146305, F 1790/11/61; PREM 3, 178/3/166.

[87] Churchill to Wilson, 17 March 1945, PREM 3, 178/3/172.

[88] *House, Pentagon Papers*, p. 71.

[89] FO 371/46305, F 1795/11/61 of 23 March 1945. Marshall told Chennault that ammunition could be flown in; FO 371/46305, F 1824/11/61 of 21 March 1945.

[90] *House, Pentagon Papers*, pp. 66–7.

bitter (and public)[91] complaint that America had abandoned its French ally, that the American government 'in accordance with its constant desire to aid all those who are willing to take up arms against our common enemies' would 'do all it can to be of assistance in the present situation consistent with the plans to which it is already committed'. Roosevelt quashed the proposal as 'inadvisable'.[92]

Three days later a very strongly worded telegram was dispatched to Churchill from Washington over Roosevelt's signature.[93] It is alleged that Chiang Kai-shek had insisted that all clandestine operations in Indo-China should come under his own control and command.

It seemed to me the best solution at present is for you and me to agree that all Anglo-American–Chinese military operations in Indo-China regardless of their nature be coordinated by General Wedemeyer as Chief of Staff to the Generalissimo at least until any major adjustment of theatre boundaries is made in connection with an advance by Mountbatten's forces into Indo-China from the South.

This version of Generalissimo Chiang Kai-shek's views differed so markedly from what he had said to Admiral Mountbatten as to lead the Foreign Office to assume the telegram had been drafted by General Wedemeyer himself, a view which Winston Churchill echoed in a rather different sense in assuming, in a minute of 31 March, that Roosevelt had had nothing to do with its wording.[94] He proposed instead that the matter be taken up again at the staff level. 'I feel a little shy of overburdening the President at this moment with these directives ... I hear he is very hard pressed and I like to keep him as much as possible for the big things.'

Churchill was, however, being more than a little charitable. Hurley and Wedemeyer had been specifically recalled to discuss Indo-China among other matters with the President and the telegrams sent both to London and to Chungking went out on his authority. General Wedemeyer went on attempting to maintain a veto over all operations in Indo-China, despite a verbal agreement to differ reached on 8 April 1945 with Admiral Mountbatten in

[91] In a broadcast of 14 March 1945; see de Gaulle, *Salvation. Documents*, pp. 217–19.
[92] Admiral Leahy to Stettinius, 19 March 1945, *House, Pentagon Papers*, p. 68.
[93] FO 371/46305, F 1829/11/61; PREM 3, 178/3/152.
[94] FO 371/46036, F 2140/11/61; PREM 3, 178/3/124.

Ceylon.[95] The crowning ignominy on the American record had already been committed on 29 March when the American aircraft flew empty in to a French-held airstrip in North Vietnam and evacuated the six American liaison officers.

During all this period the French *corps léger*, whose transfer to South East Asia had originally been proposed by the French in 1943, were still no nearer than French Somaliland. Despairing of American agreement the British Chief of Staff finally agreed to its move to the SEAC area on 22 April 1945.[96]

By this date the dying Roosevelt had finally abandoned his opposition to the re-entrenchment of French rule in Indo-China. At Yalta he had boasted to Stalin that his inability to find the necessary shipping space had prevented the French from transferring to the Pacific the two divisions General de Gaulle had offered.[97] Signs of his weakening had become apparent in mid-March in a discussion devoted to the evolution of American views on trust territories. After a review of the absolute demands by the American service chiefs for American sovereign control over the former Japanese mandated islands in the Pacific (of which Roosevelt was critical) and of the American bases in the West Indies (which Roosevelt felt should remain entirely American), Roosevelt agreed that France should be granted trusteeship over Indo-China (and New Caledonia) provided that the French undertook to prepare the areas for independence.[98] This was still a long way away from the French refusal to admit of any American or other interference; but it has been severely criticised by American historians as the betrayal of the President's ideals.

The month of April was to prove critical in the resolution of the British dilemma between Roosevelt's Francophobia and their own need to strengthen France in Europe. Their delegation attended the San Francisco Conference at which the final draft of the UN Charter was to be evolved, including its vital trusteeship clauses, with a brief which came down very definitely but reluctantly on the French side:[99]

[95] FO 371/46306, F 2230/11/61.
[96] FO 371/46306, F 2668/11/61.
[97] *FRUS The Conferences at Malta and Yalta 1945*, p. 770. Bohlen minutes of Roosevelt–Stalin conversation, 8 February 1945.
[98] *FRUS 1945*, vol. I, Taussig memorandum of 15 March 1945, p. 124.
[99] FO 317/46306, F 2031/11/61 memorandum of 16 April 1945. This document has been removed from the file since I noted its contents.

What is most likely to be lacking in the Far East after the defeat of Japan is stability and it is in our interests to support those elements of stability in the Far East which are capable of preserving law and order. So far as Indo-China is concerned we do not believe there is any satisfactory alternative to the French as a stabilising element. Indo-China has no geographical or ethno-graphical unity and no political cohesion apart from that conferred by French rule. It is a mixture of peoples, tongues and cultures and its history prior to the French conquest was one of constant warfare. The French administration before the war may have been open to criticism, but there is evidence that the French are conscious of this themselves and are planning to introduce extensive reforms after the war.

France is our nearest neighbour and we have a vital interest in her restoration as a strong and friendly power ... Any attempt to interfere with French sovereignty over Indo-China ... would be passionately resented by the French and would have incalculable results not only in the Far East but across the Channel ... We should profoundly regret a Franco-American controversy over this issue since we might find ourselves forced to side against the United States, an eventuality we should naturally prefer to avoid.

Fortunately for the British the American position was already changing. On 3 April, Stettinius issued a statement indicating that American policy on trusteeship was limited to territories 'taken from the enemy in this war ... and also such other territories as might be voluntarily placed under trusteeship'.[100] This was followed by a discussion in the State–War–Navy Coordinating Committee on 13 April on the 'use of Indo-Chinese resistance forces' which led to a request that the State Department should take up the question of clarifying American policy towards Indo-China. The ensuing debate, in which the European and Far Eastern Bureaux of the State Department found themselves very much at loggerheads,[101] was still unresolved at the time of Roosevelt's death. The way was then clear for Mr Stettinius to assure M. Bidault, the French Foreign Minister, in words which are an equal compound of ignorance and misre-presentation that 'the record is entirely innocent of any official statement of this government questioning, even by implication, French sovereignty over Indo-China'.[102]

Generals Hurley and Wedemeyer maintained a rearguard action in favour of Chiang Kai-shek's hopes of a Chinese sphere of influence in Vietnam and the local OSS continued to give the

---

[100] Department of State Bulletin, 8 April 1945.
[101] Documented in *House, Pentagon Papers*, pp. 5–6.
[102] *FRUS 1945*, vol. VI, p.307.

Vietminh all aid and assistance, especially during the vital interregnum between the Japanese surrender and the return of the French, when northern Indo-China was placed under Chinese occupation. But the threat to Anglo-American cooperation previously presented by Indo-China was temporarily interred, to be resurrected in a very different metamorphosis in the spring of 1954. At Potsdam, to General Hurley's rage and fury, southern Indo-China was formally placed under Admiral Mountbatten's South East Asia Command. But his rage passed without effect over the face of a Washington concerned much more in political terms with the balance of power in Europe, even though the Japanese surrender lay less than six weeks away.

11

American anti-colonialist policies and the end of the European colonial empires, 1941–1962[1]

The New Left school of historians in the United States, who have concerned themselves with the origins of the war in Vietnam in particular, and of the Cold War in general, have come perilously close to enunciating a variant of the myth of the expulsion from the Garden of Eden. According to them America once lived a pure anti-colonialist anti-imperialist life. America did not dabble in imperialism. It had no truck with Europe. In the words of one of their earlier practitioners, Lloyd C. Gardner:

> Political leadership in the anti-Axis alliance suddenly brought the United States into new and sometimes uncomfortably close relations with the colonial empires of its allies ...
>
> America's historic disassociation from European rulers, and its own revolutionary heritage, had created reservoirs of good-will in Asia and Africa. Native leaders and potential revolutionaries from these places had studied with admiration the thought and deeds of the first American revolutionaries, Tom Paine and George Washington, along with those of the next century, Henry Thoreau and Abraham Lincoln.
>
> The image of America which they carried back to their fellows was generally happy, one on which Americans liked to pride themselves. How crushing then that so many Asians and Africans held up to America after World War II a new image in which Uncle Sam had become corroded and evil ...[2]

A more recent study of American wartime policy towards Vietnam concludes:

> One of the most serious criticisms that has been directed against American policy towards Vietnam at the end of World War II was its

[1] An earlier version of this paper was published in the proceedings of the 1971 Conference of the European Association of American Studies, A.N.J. den Hollaender (ed.), *Contagious Conflict. The Impact of American Dissent on European Life*, Leiden, 1973.
[2] *Economic Aspects of New Deal Diplomacy*, Madison, 1964, p. 175.

failure to support the Viet Minh quest for independence. In retrospect, this was one of the most important failures in American diplomatic history ... Vietnam was initially lost in the post-war shuffle of events and the United States began to stumble into a course of backing French colonialism.[3]

The standard explanation for this failure is that America was caught in a dilemma between its obligations or interests in Europe and its traditional hostility to colonialism. As Julius Pratt put it, the United States[4] 'traditionally ... sympathised with peoples seeking independence. Furthermore, it seemed clear that old-fashioned colonialism was dead, that the aspirants for independence made the "wave of the future" ... On the other hand ... the United States could ill afford to antagonize its European allies by helping divest them of their valued overseas possessions.'

America in fact chose Europe first. As Joseph Ballantyne, special assistant to Byrnes during the latter's tenure of the Secretaryship of State, and former director of the department's Office of Far Eastern Affairs, put it in the autumn of 1945:[5] 'We have to think not only of our relations with Asiatic peoples but of our relations with the Europeans. There is a balance which we have to strike there.'

It is not the purpose of this essay to chew again the rags of this particular controversy, which is very largely an exercise in the gladiatorial–theological approach to American history. One can put it in its proper perspective by noting the existence of a Gaullist alternative. As usual it was set out most clearly by Charles de Gaulle himself in relation to Indo-China:[6] 'President Roosevelt, under cover of proclamations to the contrary intended that French affairs should fall within his own sphere of influence, that the leading strings of our divisions should end up in his hands and that the public powers eventually emerging from this disorder should derive from his arbitration.'

De Gaulle was no doubt reflecting on that extraordinary interview he had with President Roosevelt during the Casablanca

[3] Edward R. Drachman, *United States Policy Towards Vietnam, 1940–1945*, Rutherford, New Jersey, 1970, p. 165.
[4] Julius W. Pratt, 'Anti-Colonialism in United States Policy' in Robert Strausz-Hupé and Harry Hazard (eds.), *The Idea of Colonialism*, New York, 1958, pp. 133–4.
[5] Cited in Drachman, *US Policy Towards Vietnam*, p. 125.
[6] Charles de Gaulle, *War Memoirs*, vol. II, p. 355.

Conference in which Roosevelt claimed that the Allied nations[7] 'should hold the political situation in trust for the French people'. France, the President continued, 'is in the position of a little child unable to look out and fend for itself, and in such a case a court would appoint a trustee to do the necessary'.

De Gaulle would have been reinforced in his suspicions of the President had he known of Roosevelt's remarks to the Joint Chiefs of Staff only a fortnight earlier, to the effect that Robert Murphy, in promising General Giraud that France's colonial possessions would be restored after the war, had exceeded his authority. The President said that he,[8] 'as President, was not prepared to make any such promises. There are some of the colonial possessions which he was sure would not be returned to France and he had grave doubts as to whether Indo-China should be.'

The aim of this essay is to examine the basic assumptions, political and social, which were contained in American anti-colonialism during and after the Second World War, and to compare them with the political and social realities of the countries on which that anti-colonialism expressed itself. The particular cases it is proposed to study are India, Indonesia and Indo-China.

One should perhaps begin by quoting some examples of the anti-colonialist statements it is proposed to examine. American political rhetoric being what it is, it is only too easy to find statements that would give the impression almost of selection for their ludicrous qualities. But consider the following examples. First, the Atlantic Charter, which bound its signatories to[9] 'respect the right of all peoples to choose the form of government under which they will live', and according to Roosevelt's view of it,[10] 'applied to all humanity ... I think that is a matter of record'. Elliott Roosevelt reports his father as saying:[11] 'When we've won the war, I will work with all my might and main to see to it that the United States is not wheedled into the position of accepting any plea that will further

[7] Note by Lt Commander McCrea, USN, 22 January 1943; *Foreign Relations of the United States, the Conferences at Washington 1941–42 and Casablanca, 1943*, pp. 694–6.

[8] Joint Chiefs of Staff minutes, 7 January 1943; *FRUS 1943*, pp. 505–14.

[9] Joint statement by President Roosevelt and Prime Minister Churchill, 14 August 1941, *FRUS 1941*, pp. 367–9.

[10] Press Conference of 27 October, 1942, Samuel J. Rosenmann, *The Public Papers and Addresses of Franklin D. Roosevelt*, New York, 1938–50, vol. XI, p. 437.

[11] Elliott Roosevelt, *As He Saw It*, New York, 1946, pp. 114–16.

France's imperialistic ambitions or that will aid and abet the British empire in its imperial ambitions.'

Many have questioned the reality of Elliott Roosevelt's record. But the evidence of Roosevelt's views on French colonial rule in Indo-China and on Britain's own selfish imperial ambitions, now available from official American records, is such that there can be little doubt that Elliott Roosevelt reported his father's sentiments accurately. Moreover, as Roosevelt's sense of American power grew from 1942 onwards, the idea of using that power to dictate a new settlement of the European colonies after the war came more to the fore in his conversations with the Russians and the Chiang Kai-shek régime, two systems of government which by virtue of their allegedly revolutionary origins appeared to be free from the taint of desire to dominate other peoples. Thus in June 1942, meeting Molotov in Washington, he spoke of a number of islands and colonial possessions which 'for our own safety' ought to be taken away from 'weak nations', and put under 'international trusteeship'. As examples of the latter category he instanced Indo-China, Siam [*sic*] (then, as now, independent) and the Malay States, and even the Dutch East Indies, in all of which there was a 'palpable surge towards independence' and all of which might be ready for self-government in twenty years.[12] In July 1943, speaking to the 33rd meeting of the Pacific War Council, he repeated the view that Indo-China should be placed under international trusteeship until it was ready for independence.[13] Meeting Chiang Kai-shek at Cairo in November 1943 he agreed with Chiang's suggestion for a joint effort to aid Indo-China to obtain independence after the war.[14] At Teheran he told Stalin that 'after 100 years of French rule in Indo-China, the inhabitants were worse off than they had been before', and agreed with Stalin's remark that 'France should not get back Indo-China'. He repeated this view to Lord Halifax, the British Ambassador, early in 1944 and added for his Secretary of State's benefit:[15] 'I see no reason to play with the British Foreign Office in this matter. The only reason they seem to oppose this is that they fear the effect it would have on their own possessions and on those of the Dutch.' He was still main-

12 *FRUS 1942*, vol. III, pp. 578–83, notes by Samuel H. Cross, 1 June 1942.
13 *FRUS 1943*, vol. III, p. 769.
14 *FRUS Conferences at Cairo and Teheran*, 1943, pp. 322–5.
15 Roosevelt to Hull, 24 January 1944, *FRUS 1943*, pp. 872–3; *FRUS 1944*, vol. III, p. 773.

taining the same view at Yalta in conversing with Stalin,[16] though he was to modify it a month later in conversation with Charles Taussig, his adviser on Caribbean affairs,[17] in so far as he was prepared to allow a French trusteeship over Indo-China, provided they accepted that independence rather than self-government or dominion status was the goal. This combination of populism[18] and arrogance is to be found in statements by other US agencies and by Roosevelt's personal appointees. Over India, Breckenridge Long, then Assistant Secretary of State, noted on 25 February 1942 the feeling of the Senate Foreign Affairs Committee that something should be done about India:

Even if they [the Indians] had equipment in their hands and capable American officers to direct them, the Indians would not have the desire to fight just in order to prolong England's mastery over them ...

Concerning India, the argument was that we are participating on such a large scale and had done so much for England in lend-lease that we had now arrived at a position of importance to justify our participation in Empire councils and such as to authorize us to require England to make adjustments of a political nature within the framework of her Empire. We should demand that India be given a status of autonomy. The only way to get the people of India to fight was to get them to fight for India.[19]

India, next to China, was, of course, the area on which American populist anti-colonialism most centred during the wartime years. Both of Roosevelt's special representatives to visit India, Louis Johnson, the naïve and unsophisticated Texan, and William Phillips, the long-time professional diplomatist and Anglophile, transferred their populism on to the Indian scene. Johnson, for example, saw events in India at the time of Sir Stafford Cripps's mission entirely in terms of a clash between the Indian people as represented by Churchill and the Viceroy. Jinnah and the Muslim League he saw entirely as puppets of the British.[20] 'The magic name over here', he cabled Hull,[21] after Congress had rejected the Cripps proposals

---

[16] Bohlen notes, 8 February 1945, *FRUS The Conferences at Malta and Yalta 1945*, pp. 766–71.

[17] Taussig memorandum, 15 March 1945, *FRUS 1945*, vol. I, pp. 121–4.

[18] For the sense in which the author has used the words 'populism' and 'populist' in the present article, see p. 250 below.

[19] Long memorandum, 25 February 1942, *FRUS 1942*, vol. I, pp. 606–7.

[20] *FRUS 1942*, vol. I, p. 642, Johnson to Hull, 25 April 1942.

[21] *FRUS 1942*, p. 630, 9 April 1942.

unanimously, 'is Roosevelt. The land, the people would follow and love, America.'

Phillips, for all his doubts of official American policy, found himself eventually expressing the same sentiment.[22] 'India, China and Burma', he wrote to Roosevelt on 19 April 1943, 'have a common meeting ground in their desire for freedom from foreign domination.' Phillips in his final report wrote that:

The peoples of Asia cynically regard this war as one between fascists and imperial powers. A generous British gesture to India would change this undesirable political atmosphere. India itself might then be expected more positively to support our war effort against Japan. China, which regards the Anglo-American bloc with misgiving and mistrust, might then be assured that we are in truth fighting for a better world. And the colonial peoples conquered by the Japanese might hopefully feel that they have something better to look forward to than simply a return to their old masters.[23]

General Hurley was more direct: 'So far as I am concerned', he cabled Hull from Chungking, early in 1945,[24] 'I have let the diplomatic representatives of the so-called imperialist governments with interests in South East Asia know that I am personally opposed to imperialism – I have remarked to them that the United States is committed to the proposition that governments should derive their just powers from the consent of the governed.' Hurley was to resign in violent protest over what he regarded as American official pandering to both imperialism and Communism.

The State Department summed up the philosophical basis for this populist approach to the problems of South East Asia in June 1945.[25] A policy paper on conditions in Asia at the close of the Pacific war declared:

The American People ask for a reasonable assurance of peace and security in this great area ... Peace and security ... depend on a number of conditions.

One of those conditions is the right of all peoples to choose the form of Government under which they will live. The United States therefore has a definite interest that there should be a progressive enlargement of the political responsibilities, both as individuals and groups, of all the peoples of this region, in order that they may be prepared and able to assume the responsibilities of freedom as well as to enjoy its rights ... the largest possible measure of political freedom for the countries of Asia consistent

[22] William Phillips, *Ventures in Diplomacy*, London, 1955, p. 248.
[23] Phillips, *Ventures*, p. 252.
[24] FRUS 1945, vol. VI, 294.
[25] FRUS 1945, vol. VI, pp. 565ff.

with their ability to assume the responsibility thereof is probably necessary in order to achieve the chief objective of the United States in the Far East and the Pacific: continuing peace and security.

One could add to these statements similar views from more recent American official statements. There is Mr John Foster Dulles's famous press conference of 2 October 1956, during the Suez crisis, referring to the 'problem of colonialism' as one in which the American approach was not identical to that of the 'so-called colonial powers'.[26] There is President Kennedy's inaugural[27] and the singularly unfortunate statements of his African appointment, the former governor of Michigan, G. Mennen Williams, made during his 1961 tour of Africa.[28] Throughout all of them can be traced a fairly consistent political doctrine which might be summarised as follows.

Governments should derive their powers from the consent of the governed. The form of government should also be that which the governed desire. All other forms of government are tyrannous and imperialist. It is assumed that no one would voluntarily choose to be governed by foreigners. Tyrannous and imperialist governments are naturally competitive, monopolistic and aggressive. Peace and international security therefore can only be based on the universal adoption of one of the various forms of popular democracy. Popular democratic governments are not competitive, nor monopolistic nor aggressive; though conflicts between them may arise, they result from misunderstandings and failures of communication and can be resolved by negotiation among men of goodwill.

These are, even if baldly stated, political principles which would command a good deal of support in the abstract throughout the countries of Western Europe and America. As guides to policy-makers faced with the countries of Eastern Asia under European rule before 1941 and conquered, or under threat of conquest, by the Japanese, they were to prove a good deal more than merely misleading. The statements of American policy already quoted are all

---

[26] His remarks are cited verbatim from the record preserved in his papers by Carey Joynte, 'John Foster Dulles and the Suez Crisis', in Gerald N. Grob (ed.), *Statesmen and Statecraft of the Modern West*, Barre, Mass., 1967.

[27] *Public Papers of the Presidents of the United States: John F. Kennedy, 1961*, Washington, DC, 1962, 1–3.

[28] See D.C. Watt (ed.), *Survey of International Affairs, 1961*, Oxford, 1965, pp. 391–2.

predicated on there being 'peoples' of the countries of East and South East Asia. The word 'people' or 'peoples' clearly hid a confusion of two quite separate concepts, the two being taken as synonymous. It was assumed that, as there was clearly a numerical group in each country, native to that country not merely by birth but by ethnic grouping, language and culture, and much more numerous than those of the country's inhabitants who could be recognised as being European in race, this group was so politically self-conscious, habituated to the exercise of political choice and responsibility and desirous of exercising those powers for self-rule in the best collective interests that it could be regarded as a 'people' in political terms.

These assumptions led to other further assumptions. Where there were individuals who claimed to speak for the native peoples and to exercise the sovereign rights of self-government in their name and who, by advancing that claim, came into conflict with the colonial authorities, it was assumed, firstly, that those claims were automatically justified, since the colonial authorities, not being native born, could not enjoy the confidence or act in the best interests of the people they governed; secondly, it was assumed that the resultant conflict was a popular struggle of 'people' against alien overlords and not simply the struggle of a native group of would-be authoritarians struggling to replace a European group of actual authoritarians. Since colonial rule, even if benevolent, is inevitably authoritarian, it was assumed that the alternative would, as a matter of course, be populist and democratic. Lastly, it was assumed that, being populist and democratic, the native movements would inevitably be drawn to like and admire the American government and people. If they turned against the Americans this was either the result of wilful misdirection by evil people – Communists for example – or the result of the American government mistakenly putting itself on the side of the oppressors. That this interpretation was, until recently, still inherent in the American approach can be seen very clearly in the 1970s debate in the United States over the war in Vietnam in which the obviously authoritarian nature of the governing authorities in Saigon was clearly adduced as proof of the populist and democratic character of their opponents, whether Vietcong or from North Vietnam.

The interesting point is that this compulsion to talk in terms of a popular will, almost of a *volonté générale*, in relation to countries such as India, Indonesia and Indo-China, persists even where the complexity of the political picture on the ground is admitted. On the whole, for example, the State Department did not share Colonel Johnson's belief that Congress spoke for the Indian people. Indeed he was warned by Hull to be careful[29] 'not to identify yourself too closely with any particular group or groups in Indian national life'. But Hull's own words revealed the assumption that there was such a thing as 'Indian national life' and that the Congress movement could be regarded as a faction within it, a party such as American history had known.

Yet any examination of the social, sociopolitical and political groups over which colonial rule was being exercised by the European colonial powers shows that the criteria which would be used to identify parties, factions within parties or movements in Western Europe or in North America are almost completely lacking. Whether objective criteria like language, law, religion, hierarchical organisation and the like or subjective criteria such as group identification, loyalties, sense of community or the like are applied, the picture that emerges is irreconcilable with that postulated by the language of American populist democracy. In brief, to maintain that there was in any political sense an Indian 'people', an Indo-Chinese 'people' or an Indonesian 'people' was to make a statement which did not correspond with reality. To maintain that those who claimed to represent those people in fact did so was to mistake a weapon of persuasion for a statement of fact.

After the tragic history of the partition of India, the break-up of Pakistan and the sufferings, still unended, of the Bihari minority in Bangladesh, with civil wars in Laos and Cambodia and the war between North and South Vietnam, after the widespread massacres that accompanied the fall of President Sukarno from power and the truly appalling record of the Cambodian régime of Pol Pot, these statements may seem somewhat less questionable than they would have been in the years 1939–45. It was, of course, one of the ironies of history that, when they were made, they were made inevitably by those who knew the local society best, that is by those whose job it was to maintain order and administer justice between the various separate elements which American opinion lumped so readily together as the Indian, Indo-Chinese or Indonesian 'peoples'. These

[29] Hull to Johnson, 27 April 1943, *FRUS 1942*, vol. I, pp. 644–5.

men were, however, colonialists. And their obvious interest in the continuation of colonial rule was taken as disproving their arguments.

This is not really the place for a lengthy discussion on the very different forms of social organisation to be found in the mixture of Hindu, Buddhist and Muslim cultures which flourished in the three European colonial territories on which American disapproval was bent during the Second World War except to note three factors which entirely vitiate the American populist approach to and interpretation of their sociopolitical condition. The first is that the only known forms of sociopolitical organisation to flourish in these territories before the Europeans came were religious in character and entirely hierarchical–deferential in nature. The second is that the predominating form of socioeconomic organisation was small-scale agrarian in character. The model of success for the vast bulk of the population was the peasant landholder of large family. The unit of social identification was not the nation but the village. The third factor, which stems naturally from this, is the existence in all three societies of *two* kinds of current of opposition to European rule rather than the single type of secular nationalism which Americans recognised, wrongly it is here argued, as conforming to their own populist–secular stereotype of the anti-colonialist independence movement.[30] The first of these rejected European rule because of the threat posed by European example and mores to the traditional religious principles on which local society was organised and held together. The second rejected the traditional religious basis of society and turned deliberately to Western secular forms of organisation, seeing in them a more potent form of power and authority than anything traditional society could offer. The members of this second group were often impelled to join it by virtue of the low status socially and politically their own society afforded them. Some tended also to come from marginal groups already desocialised by their differing experiences. Their leaders had often spent their formative political years totally outside their own cultures, as did Gandhi in South Africa, Ho Chi Minh in France and Sutan Sjahrir in the Netherlands, for example. The implication of this for the

---

[30] Students of Indonesia distinguish three groups, the traditional élites (the *priyahi*), the Islamic and the secular nationalists. See H.J. Benda, 'The Beginnings of the Japanese Occupation of Java', *Far Eastern Quarterly*, 15, 1956.

American populists was that the group which they most easily encountered, which most sought them out, which most fitted their stereotypes of populist nationalist leadership was that which most separated itself from the traditional culture, was least integrated socially into the 'people' it claimed to lead and represent and was therefore most unrepresentative; while the traditional aristocratic leadership with which, at least in India and Indonesia, the colonial powers had concluded a concordat and through which they ruled was, despite its antique traditional feudal nature, much more the real embodiment of local political loyalties. Where this was not so, it was because the nationalist leader had successfully cast his own appeal in terms of local traditional political models. American observers during Gandhi's fast and civil disobedience campaign in 1943–4 often commented that he was regarded by the Indian people as a god without in any way realising the implications of their comments for their own stereotypes. Sukarno's success in Java lay in his appeal as a Messianic figure of an Islamic type at a time when traditional society and values had been almost completely overthrown by the collapse of Dutch rule and the conquest by Japan, with all its economic as well as political disintegrative effects on Javanese society. Ho Chi Minh adapted to the use of his Communist principles the religious-sect cum bandit-protective-racket cum secret-society model with which Vietnam was familiar, at least since the eleventh century, and which is part of Vietnam's cultural heritage from China.[31] A classic example is that of the Mafia-like Triad society which spread into Vietnam from Fukien with the Manchu conquest of the Ming Dynasty in the 1640s. The inter-war years in Vietnam saw the growth of two other examples, the Cao Dai and the Hoa Ho, both in the south. The other main 'nationalist' movement, the VNQDD (Vietnam Quoc Den Dong), like Ho Chi Minh's Indo-Chinese Communist party, originated in the north and was organised equally conspiratorially. Significantly, membership in both the VNQDD and the Indo-Chinese Communist Party (ICP) was not by application but by invitation – a far cry from the populist ideal of the nationalist independence movement.

It is a popular argument, noted above, that the United States has been faced in South East Asia by a conflict of aims between its desire

[31] See Dennis J. Duncanson, *Government and Revolution in Vietnam*, Oxford, 1968, pp. 49–51.

to see Western Europe strong, peaceful and able to stand on its own feet, and its traditional sympathies for the aspirations of so-called dependent peoples. Revisionist critics of American policy imply that America's confrontation with national defeat in South East Asia in the 1969–75 period was largely due to its choice of the first rather than the second of these aims – though it should be remarked in this context that in South East Asia this applies uniquely to Vietnam. Such critics ignore the American record in relation to Indonesia and the Netherlands. In the larger context their criticism applies neither to the Middle East, where America has long faced a similar near disaster, nor to Africa. Nor does it really apply to India, where American intervention was rebuffed by Britain during the war years and overtaken by events in the years 1945–7. This would tend to suggest that while the conflict of aims clearly existed in American minds, the failure of American ambitions cannot be ascribed to this conflict but must be sought elsewhere. Much of it, it could be suggested, stems precisely from the rigidly doctrinal nature of American political thinking as applied to the political conflicts of the area.

What fewer critics have noted is that much of the present difficulty in American relations with Western Europe, particularly in the financial and economic sphere, can be traced back not merely to a European consciousness of the existence of the American dilemma, but to the feelings of resentment awakened by those occasions on which, to European eyes, America seemed to be following the interests of the nationalist movements of the former colonies rather than those of their European overlords. A contemporary historian who seeks to explain his view of present events in terms of the immediate past should be aware of the unusually thin ice on which he treads. But in the attitudes of European bankers on the Group of Ten during the 1960s and early 1970s towards the American imbalance of trade and payments, in the loudly expressed fears of the *défi américain*,[32] the American industrial takeover of the growth areas in the European industrial economy which this vast and forced injection of dollars into the world financial system made possible, as well as in the almost universal *Schadenfreude* with which American's failure in Vietnam was greeted in Europe, it is impossible to exclude a very strong current of resentment traceable to those

[32] J-J. Servan Schreiber, *Le Défi américain*, Paris, 1967.

sentiments of economic imperialism which American revisionists now profess to be able to document. It is also a very strong suggestion that the growth of a European consciousness in the countries of the Six, as in Britain, has been enhanced by the destruction of European beliefs in the identity of the West European and American approaches to the current problems of world politics in the 1950s embodied in the British belief in the 'special relationship', so-called, and in the Atlantic unity movement, a destruction to which the experiences of decolonisation and American policy since 1945 and the increasing evidence of lack of harmony on such issues even between America and her British ally before 1945, now available to European readers, have made a significant contribution.

Such a consciousness focuses particularly on two sets of experiences to which it is proposed to devote the remainder of this essay. The first is the evidence of willingness to use American power to *impose* solutions upon European states during and after the years of the Second World War. The second comprises the examples where that power was deliberately used by America to force her European allies into positions of national humiliation, defeat and withdrawal analogous to that now advocated by critics of American involvement in Vietnam.

To take the first of these first; it should be pointed out that since the Congress of Vienna put an end to the experience of the Napoleonic and French revolutionary wars, European security systems have embodied the convention by which the use of power against a fellow European state was, if used at all, to be severely limited in both time and effect. This is not to say that the convention has always been observed; but to point out that the peculiar horror of the two world wars to their European participants was the breach they involved of this fundamental convention. Civilised states might fight; but they did not conquer and, save for small frontier adjustments, they did not annex. The Berlin Conferences of 1878 on the Balkans and of 1884–5 on West Africa added a further corollary to this convention: that they should not aggrandise themselves outside Europe without compensation being awarded to their fellows. These conventions were seen as being essential to the maintenance of peace and the avoidance of the far-reaching social and political destruction total war of the Napoleonic kind brought with it on all participants.

It should be pointed out that no such convention is part of the

American political experience in international relations. The nearest equivalents are the Good Neighbour policy and the Stimson doctrine, both products not of a balance of power system but of one of overwhelming imbalance, since both are part of United States relations with Latin America. The first involved a self-denying ordinance on the part of the only major power in the two American continents by which it bound itself not to use its military predominance against its neighbours so as to intervene in their domestic political affairs. The second[33] involved the non-recognition of changes brought about by force, a doctrine again which only carries political conviction if the economic and political effects of non-recognition can be felt by those against whom it is directed, by virtue of their dependence on the goodwill of those practising the doctrine against them.

The use of power either negatively to withhold aid or positively to impose a settlement upon weaker states is thus something which in American thinking is seen as wrong not in itself but only by virtue of its effects on the local political situation. From this arises the paradoxical contrast between Roosevelt's pride in the enunciation of the Good Neighbour policy of non-intervention in Latin American affairs and the arrogant assertion of American power towards her European partners in the war against Hitler. Such inhibitions as were observed by Roosevelt *vis-à-vis* his European partners were imposed by the relative strength of their positions. Thus in India, and faced as he thought with Winston's old-fashioned imperialism, Roosevelt trod very circumspectly – although he allowed himself a good deal of indiscretion *vis-à-vis* his radical supporters and the press; perhaps the most far-reaching example being the press conference given aboard the USS *Quincy* on the return from Yalta in which he called Churchill's attitude 'mid-Victorian' and remarked patronisingly: 'Dear old Winston will never learn on that point.'[34] He had earlier assured General Hurley that 'I can change all that at the proper time as easily as this', turning his palm over on the last word.[35]

These indiscretions should be contrasted with Churchill's reactions to Roosevelt's attempts to intervene in the Cripps mission.

---

[33] Though applied to the Japanese action in 1931–2 against China, the Stimson doctrine was borrowed from American experience with Latin America.

[34] Rosenmann, *Roosevelt's Public Papers*, LXIII, pp. 562–64.

[35] Cited in Gardner, *Economic Aspects of New Deal Diplomacy*, p. 177.

On 11 April 1942, after Congress's unconditional rejection of the Cripps proposals, Roosevelt sent a long message to Churchill asking that Cripps's departure from India be postponed until one final effort had been made to avert a breakdown in negotiations. His message[36] threatened a prejudicial reaction by American public opinion if the negotiations were allowed to collapse and a Japanese invasion of India were to follow, alleged that American opinion put the blame for the breakdown entirely on British intransigence and repeated the curious analogy he had drawn earlier[37] with the governmental system employed by the Thirteen Colonies under the Articles of Confederation. Nowhere in the message did he indicate that he was prepared to counter these illusions, which he alleged to be held by US public opinion, or even that he regarded them as in any way mistaken.

Churchill's reply[38] made it clear that it was too late to postpone Cripps's departure from India as he had already left, and added that he could not take responsibility for the defence of India 'if everything has again to be thrown into the melting pot at this juncture'. He added that he proposed to keep the telegram purely private and did not intend to bring it before the Cabinet.

'Anything like a serious difference between you and me', he concluded, 'would break my heart and surely deeply injure both our peoples at this juncture.' To this undertaking he remained entirely true. When the Viceroy tried to discover the content of Roosevelt's communications with Churchill, the Secretary of State for India, Leo Amery, was forced to tell him that Churchill was keeping the content strictly to himself.[39] It was only after Roosevelt had invoked the extension of the Atlantic Charter to Asia, under the needling of his Republican opponent, Wendell Wilkie, in the 1940 election, that Churchill was driven to his famous public statement: 'I have not become the King's First Minister to preside over the liquidation of the British Empire.'[40]

---

[36] Roosevelt to Hopkins for Churchill, 11 April 1942, *FRUS 1942*, vol. I, pp. 633–4.

[37] Roosevelt to Churchill, 10 March 1942, *FRUS 1942*, vol I, pp. 615–16.

[38] Churchill to Roosevelt, 12 April 1942, *FRUS 1942*, vol. I, pp. 634–5.

[39] Clauson to Laithwaite, 20 April 1942; Nicholas Mansergh (ed.), *Constitutional Relations between Britain and India, The Transfer of Power 1942–1947*, I, no. 656.

[40] Rosenmann, XI, 437; *The Times*, 11 November 1942.

One might comment[41] on the curious outlook of a man who could find Churchill's attitude Victorian while recommending to him a model taken from the third quarter of the eighteenth century. For the example was an obsession with Roosevelt. He used it to Chiang Kai-shek.[42] He even urged it on the Indian agent-general in Washington, Sir Girja Shankar Bajpai, who attempted to point out the difficulties in applying such an analogy to India, but in vain. 'The President', he reported,[43] 'is not a good listener.'

But behind these interventions there lay a series of other illusions. The first of these was the representative character of the Indian National Congress and has already been referred to. The second was the availability of Indian manpower for military purposes once an appeal to Indian patriotism had been made possible by the grant of self-government, an argument greatly urged upon Colonel Johnson by Pandit Jawaharlal Nehru at the time when, as Congress documents which later came into British possession made clear, a successful Japanese invasion of India was expected. Other illusions were that there was no British intention to defend India,[44] that the British would be unable to contain Gandhi's campaign of civil disobedience or, a year later, the consequences of Gandhi's fast. They allowed these fears to cause the abandonment of the recommendations of the Grady mission on the establishment of a war industry in India.[45] But most striking of all was the failure to realise that Indians, whether congressional leaders[46] or industrialists,[47] inevitably saw the United States as a power factor which, by professing the appropriate sentiments whether of enmity, as in June–August 1942,[48] or friendship, could be used as a means of pressure against Britain.

Under the circumstances, the somewhat craven announcement issued on 12 August 1942,[49] that the primary aim of the US government in sending American troops to India was to aid China,

---

[41] As Churchill did, *The Second World War*, vol. IV, *The Hinge of Fate*, London, 1950, p. 219.
[42] Roosevelt to Chiang, 12 August 1942, *FRUS 1942*, vol. I, pp. 715–17.
[43] Bajpai to Viceroy, 2 April 1942, *The Transfer of Power*, I, no. 508.
[44] State Department memorandum, 26 May 1942; *FRUS 1942*, vol. I, pp. 657–9.
[45] Basle memorandum, 2 October 1942, *FRUS 1942*, vol. I, p. 735.
[46] Especially by Nehru on Colonel Johnson. *FRUS 1942*, vol. I, pp. 626–7, 635–7, 657–79, 660–2.
[47] See Johnson's report of the alleged views of Indian industrialists, Johnson to Hull, 25 April 1942, *FRUS 1942*, vol. I, pp. 643–4.
[48] See *FRUS 1942*, vol. I, pp. 667–9, 712–14.   [49] *FRUS 1942*, vol, I, pp. 720–1.

did nothing to end Congress tactics in this regard. The cessation of such pressure came mainly as a result of the paralysis of the Congress leadership by the arrest of their principal figures on 9 August 1942. They led directly to the fiasco of the Phillips mission. It should be admitted in advance that Phillips himself regarded his instructions as 'slightly naïve'.[50] What was even more naïve was to expect that a senior American diplomatist, a former ambassador to Rome, who still held the personal rank of Ambassador, could be sent to India without being placed in an entirely false position. Since Indian policy was made in London, the government of India being subordinate to the Cabinet, Phillips was simply in no position either to represent American interests in India or to act as anything more than a reporter on Indian affairs. Since the major problem on which the Cripps proposals had broken down was the disparity between Congress's claim to be the sole representative body for Indian affairs and the reality of communal divisions, and Cripps's failure to reconcile these divisions, Phillips was totally unable to come to grips with the main problem. Since Gandhi was in jail for what in anyone but Gandhi would have been regarded as defeatism, and being a threat to the security and domestic peace of India, Phillips was debarred from contact with him. And once Congress opinion had realised that he could not serve as a new form of pressure on the Viceroy or the British government, Phillips's scope for influence was at an end. The Viceroy, who, foreseeing all these difficulties, had objected to Phillips's appointment, was led to plead for the substitution of a less diplomatic figure.[51] The unauthorised publication by Drew Pearson of Phillips's final report, with its libellous reflections on the low morale of the Indian Army (stigmatised as 'mercenary') and its allegations that Britain was unwilling to do anything to fight the war in the Far East, led the Indian government to declare him eventually *persona non grata*.[52] Americans, unable to understand the neutralist and anti-American stance followed by the Indian government after independence, would have done well to reflect on the consequences of the dispatch, let alone the failure, of such missions as those of Johnson and Phillips.

[50] Phillips, *Ventures*, p. 218.
[51] *Transfer of Power*, vol. III, nos 485–9, 493, 726, 755.
[52] Hull to Winant, 25 July 1944; Hull to Roosevelt, 15 August 1944; F. Breckenridge Long memorandum, 2 September 1944; Merrell (Delhi) to Hull, 4 October 1944; *FRUS 1944*, vol. V, pp. 239, 241–2, 243–6, 247.

The frustration of American attempts to have it both ways in India by bringing about a reconciliation between a Congress unable, even with the Japanese at India's door, to look beyond a purely Indian frame of reference or to abandon claims to a monopoly of Indian opinion which they were unable to substantiate, and a British government aware that the main problem in India was not the aspirations of the élites but the communal violence that lay so marginally beneath the surface of Indian politics, can be ascribed basically to the strength of British resistance rather than to the actual unrealities of the American situation. It was James Thurber who, in *Fables of Our Time*, drew as the moral of his fable of the owl as the leader of the animals that 'You can fool too many of the people too much of the time'. It is equally true that the illusions of the mighty can assume a pseudo-reality by virtue of the strength of those who hold them. Evelyn Waugh, in his satirical novel on the Italo-Abyssinian war, *Scoop*, tells the story of the American correspondent who, sent to cover a revolution, got off the train in the wrong Balkan state, and brought about an actual revolution simply by his vivid reportage of a revolution he alleged was already in progress. Roosevelt's illusions were to have equal force where the former colonial power, France, was in no position to resist them.

French Indo-China was exposed to Japanese pressure from the summer of 1940. Its home government had passed under German influence with the French armistice and French forces in Indo-China amounted in all to some 35,000 men. America remained in diplomatic relations with Vichy France; but the main reaction to France's fall was an extraordinarily deep-rooted revulsion to all things French and to any French claims to continuing great power status. Where Churchill and British opinion, and much of the American press saw in General de Gaulle a continuing symbol of all that was best in France, and regarded the events of 1940 as a military defeat rather than the passage of an imperial power into the limbo of history – something like the fall of Carthage – Roosevelt and his entourage saw the French collapse as the final illustration and outcome of the historical decadence of European power.

Thus it was that when the Vichy régime approached the Americans to ask for aid and encouragement to resist the Japanese demands, the American reply was in essence a plea of *non possumus*. The American government would not aid the French militarily, since they believed this would not be supported by American opinion. They would not press Tokyo only to ask for a temporary occupation of Indo-China since this would by implication recognise a change in the *status quo*. And they would not supply arms to Indo-China.[53] As a result, after the border fortresses of Lang-son and Dong-dang had been taken by the Japanese and after losing eight hundred dead defending the latter to the last cartridge,[54] Admiral Decoux, the French military governor of Indo-China, was forced to concede to the Japanese the right to pass 25,000 men through northern Indo-China and to station some 6,000 in Indo-China to maintain their lines of communication. In January 1941 French forces met and defeated a Japanese-inspired attack by the Thais on Cambodia; the war ended only with the offer of Japanese good offices, the beneficence of which inclined much more markedly towards Thai claims than towards the French. In July 1941 therefore, after the German attack on the Soviet Union had led a Japanese imperial conference to the decision to achieve its objectives in the south, the Japanese concluded an agreement with the Vichy government authorising the military occupation of southern Indo-China. American diplomatic protests and counter-pressures of an economic character led the Japanese, on 20 November 1941, to offer an interim proposal by which southern Indo-China would be immediately evacuated in return for the abandonment of these pressures.[55] This proposal the American government rejected.

These facts are worth reflecting upon when considering Roosevelt's later statements. Hull recorded that[56] 'The President entertained strong views on independence for French Indo-China ... It stuck in his mind as having been the springboard for the Japanese attack on the Philippines, Malaya and the Dutch East Indies. He could not but remember the devious conduct [of the French], the [concession of the] right to station [Japanese] troops there without any consultation with us.' Now it is true that the American reaction to the Japanese agreement with Vichy was to

[53] See Fall, *Two Vietnams*, pp. 41–3; Drachman, pp. 12–20.
[54] Fall, *Two Vietnams*, p. 43.
[55] *FRUS, Japan, 1931–1941*, vol. II, pp. 755–6.
[56] Hull, vol. II, p. 1595.

see in this a movement which outflanked and 'completed the left curve of a strategic horse-shoe around the Philippines'.[57] But in actual fact neither the Japanese invasion of the Philippines nor that of Malaya was mounted from Indo-Chinese territory, though the attack on Malaya was supported in the air by Japanese aircraft based on Saigon. Apart from this, Roosevelt's views, as reported by Hull and his son, are entirely without basis in fact and ignore the total failure of the United States to offer any practical help or assistance to Admiral Decoux in 1940.

This, however, cannot excuse President Roosevelt's abandonment of the French in Vietnam in 1944–5, when he apparently sought to evade and prevent any French participation in the liberation of Indo-China. This episode has already been dealt with in the preceding essay, at least in its Anglo-American aspects. What remains to be said is that the order to Wedemeyer and Chennault that under no circumstances were they to provide arms and ammunition to the French[58] was not rescinded until the end of March after the withdrawal of the American liaison officers. By this time the French generals, Sabattier and Alessandri, who had been holding some 10,000 French troops under arms at Dien Bien Phu, were forced into what was to prove an 800-mile march into Yunnan, where some 5,500 men finally joined the Chinese nationalist forces, who interned them. The garrisons of Lang Son, and the other French stations which offered resistance, were massacred. On a much smaller scale admittedly, President Roosevelt's action can only be compared with that of the Russians towards the Warsaw rising the year before. The dishonour he brought in his dying days on America has been compounded ever since by American historians.

Roosevelt's death was not the end of American illusions about Vietnam. Ho Chi Minh moved into northern Indo-China together with the guerilla forces which, under the command of General Giap, had been earlier established on the Chinese borders with Annam. In July 1945, he entertained an OSS mission. Ho's first contacts with

[57] Samuel Eliot Morison, *History of US Naval Operations in World War II*, vol. III, Boston, 1968, p. 62.
[58] Claire L. Chennault, *The Way of a Fighter*, New York, 1949, p. 342; Albert C. Wedemeyer, *Wedemeyer Reports*, New York, 1958, pp. 340–3; Charles F. Romanus and Riley Sutherland, *Time Runs Out in CBI*, Washington, DC, Department of the Army 1959, pp. 259–60; Wedemeyer to Drachman, 19 January 1967, cited Drachman, *US Policy Towards Vietnam*, p. 84.

the OSS, apparently in the winter of 1944–5, had been inconclusive. By the time the OSS mission was landed, Ho already had two unidentified American liaison officers. The mission, which included one French intelligence officer and two other ranks, was led by Major Thomas whose main mission was sabotage. He became, however, the main source of OSS information on Ho Chi Minh's Vietminh forces which, on Ho's authority, he reported to be 'not Communist or Communist-controlled or Communist-led'. He also alleged that the French had taken away 'Ho's wife and children' and 'burned his lands' (which would appear to be total invention).[59] Major Thomas took it upon himself to report that all the French, and French sympathising Annamese, with whom the OSS had been collaborating would have to be abandoned and that Ho commanded the loyalty of 85% of the Annamese people. This remarkable judgment, made by a man who spoke no Vietnamese, and had no access to any source of information other than that provided by Ho and the Vietnamese, was apparently immediately accepted by Major Thomas's superiors. The 'French' were eliminated and Major Thomas settled down to train the Vietminh troops against America's allies.

Trading on these carefully fostered illusions, Ho Chi Minh adroitly seized the interregnum between the Japanese surrender and the occupation of Indo-China by British and Chinese forces to seize power in Hanoi immediately on the Japanese surrender and to proclaim the establishment of the Democratic Republic of Vietnam. His supporters also took over Saigon in pursuit of the Indo-Chinese Communist party policy of establishing themselves as the 'people's power' to welcome the Allied forces which came to disarm the Japanese forces stationed in Indo-China. Saigon, however, lay in the British zone of occupation and Ho's supporters got little grace from General Gracey, the British officer commanding who, in his own words, 'promptly kicked them out'.[60] Gracey released the survivors

---

[59] This passage on the 'Deer' mission, headed by Major Allison K. Thomas Special Operations Team No. 13, is based on the mission reports printed in US Congress, Senate, 92nd Congress, Second Session, *Hearings before the Committee on Foreign Relations... on the Causes, Origins and Lessons of the Vietnam War, May 9, 10 and 11, 1972*, pp. 244–72. See also *The United States and Vietnam 1946–1947. A Staff Study based on the Pentagon Papers Prepared for the Use of the Senate Committee on Foreign Relations*, Study No. 2, Washington, 1972.

[60] Cited in Fall, *Two Vietnams*, p. 65. See also the report of Captain Bluechel and Major Small of the OSS of 20 September 1945. *Hearings on the Causes, Origins and Lessons of the Vietnam War*, pp. 283–4.

of the French army interned by the Japanese in March and handed over responsibility for law and order to them.

The Vietminh forces in Saigon then attacked all Europeans indiscriminately including several OSS officers. In two separate incidents one officer was badly wounded and one killed. The survivor of this second incident was pursued to the OSS headquarters in Saigon, which was assaulted under the eyes of two American war correspondents, who were themselves so infected with the idea of popular revolution that they chose to pick a quarrel with the British officer commanding a platoon of Gurkhas who came to their rescue! The episode cost the OSS some little trouble to explain away, a task they succeeded in doing mainly by laying the blame on General Gracey.

In the north neither the Chinese nor their American advisers were prepared to do anything very much for the French. Ho devoted himself and his ministers to cultivating the various American bodies, the OSS, General Gallagher of the Military Advisory and Assistance Group, charged with aiding the Chinese to repatriate the Japanese troops, and the Military Governors group under the French-speaking Colonel Nordlinger, as well as American diplomatists and journalists. A Vietnamese–American friendship society was formed, the Vietnamese adopted a Declaration of Independence deliberately patterned on that of 1776, the ICP was ostentatiously dissolved and Ho sounded the possibilities of an American trusteeship. In the short run there was little advantage to Ho in these manoeuvres; in the long run, however, he had laid the basis of that extraordinarily prevalent myth in contemporary America and Europe which depicts him as the populists' folk hero.

In the course of the brief American stay in Hanoi, the OSS succeeded in storing up a degree of resentment among the French in Indo-China which was to have long-standing consequences. Pierre Messmer, de Gaulle's Minister of Defence in the 1960s, was left unrescued in a Japanese prison camp. General Sainteny, de Gaulle's Minister for Veteran Affairs, was excluded from the surrender ceremonies and evicted by Chinese action from the office of the French Governor. And General de Gaulle himself was strengthened in his conviction that the United States should be counted as an enemy of France.

After so long a disquisition on Indo-China during the war and the strains with which American populism seeded the ground of future

Franco-American relations, it would be superfluous to add to the catalogue. But the intervention of John Foster Dulles in 1954 into the French efforts to extricate themselves from Indo-China must be mentioned as evidence of the continuance of American colonialism noted above.

Superficially the case seemed entirely different. By 1954 the French had been at war with the forces of the Vietminh for seven years. They had chosen to fight the war with regular troops rather than conscripts. And they had chosen to fight the war with modern military methods against an enemy they could not bring to battle. Since 1949 the Vietminh had enjoyed support from and sanctuary among the victorious Chinese Communists. Since the outbreak of the Korean war the United States had supported France with arms and money. In 1948 France had established the former emperor, Bao Dai, as chief of state of a Vietnamese state, an Associated State within the French Union. For American opinion, however, this was not enough. The old argument was heard that had been used in the case of India – men will fight only in their own cause. 'Until the peoples of the Associated States are assured of receiving their ultimate independence, success in driving out the Communist invaders will be impossible to achieve.' So the Committee on Foreign Affairs of the US House of Representatives reported in June 1953.[61] By early 1954 the French were weary of war. French politics were dominated by two questions – the war in Vietnam and the ratification of the treaty of 1952 allowing the rearmament of Western Germany within the framework of the European Defence Community. To secure this ratification had become a major aim of US foreign policy. In his speech to the NATO Council in December 1953, John Foster Dulles had threatened 'an agonizing reappraisal of basic US policy' if the treaty was not effective.[62]

It was at this stage that an ill-chosen riposte to a Vietminh invasion of Laos placed a large contingent of French troops, across the Vietminh invasion route to Laos, at Dien Bien Phu deep in Vietminh-held territory. The Vietminh brought the garrison to siege and rendered its airfield unusable by long-range mortar and artillery fire. The guns came from China. Chinese MIG aircraft were seen

---

[61] United States Congress, House of Representatives, 83rd Congress, 1st Session, *Report on HR 5710, HR Reports 569*, 16 June 1953, p. 37.
[62] *New York Times*, 15 December 1953.

over Vietnam and a full-scale Chinese intervention seemed possible. As the situation deteriorated, British and Soviet pressure brought America and France together with China at the conference table. And the French began to appeal to America desperately for aid and intervention to save the beleaguered garrison of Dien Bien Phu, whose defeat and surrender would, it was felt, so break morale in France that a complete collapse of the French position in Vietnam would follow.

Mr Dulles began by arguing that American intervention would be an act of war requiring congressional authorisation. This, he said, would be forthcoming only if America was assured that it would be supported by its allies. Britain was not prepared to give such assurances. Desperate, the French returned to the charge. And Dulles turned to anti-colonialism. France must grant independence to the Vietnamese, he declared in a speech to the Overseas Press Club in Washington on 29 March 1954.[63] And on 4 April, President Eisenhower, Dulles and Admiral Radford, the Chairman of the Joint Chiefs of Staff, decided that any US intervention had to be based on the grant of independence to Vietnam, Laos and Cambodia.[64] Six other conditions were included in an American note given to Robert Schuman on 15 May,[65] but the stipulation that the French 'must make good their declaration of intention to grant complete independence' was, in Dulles's words of 10 June 1954,[66] 'at the head of the list'. 'The United States', he added, 'will never fight for colonialism'. No American aid was in fact forthcoming. Dien Bien Phu surrendered. The French government fell, to be succeeded by a capitulationist government under Pierre Mendès-France. France accepted the *de facto* partition of Vietnam in the Geneva agreements and the South Vietnamese government did not. Dulles continued to maintain that the loss of northern Vietnam to the Vietminh forces was the result of France's failure to win the support of the Vietnamese people by granting them genuine national independence.[67] And he welcomed the refusal of the South Vietnamese to accept the settlement.

[63] R.J. Randle, *Geneva 1954: The Settlement of the Indo-China War*, Princeton, NJ, 1971, p. 112.
[64] Randle, *Geneva 1954*, pp. 113–14.
[65] J. Laniel, *Le Drame indochinois*, Paris, 1957, p. 110; Anthony Eden, *Full Circle*, London, 1960, p. 134.
[66] Cited in Randle, *Geneva 1954*, pp. 257–8.
[67] Randle, *Geneva 1954*, pp. 351–2.

'Now', he said, 'we can make a new start.' And, secure in the belief that the only problem South Vietnam would now face was the economic weakness which was allegedly the legacy of years of French colonial rule, America accepted the personal tyranny of Ngo Dinh Diem. The French assembly duly rejected the European Defence Community. German rearmament was saved within the limits of the much looser control of the West European Union. And the way was clear for the European – and as it was to prove profoundly anti-American – *relance* embodied two years later in the signature of the Treaty of Rome.

The subsequent American experience with Vietnam was to prove profoundly disillusioning in everything save the populist belief that victory belongs to 'the people'. The strength of opposition to American support for the successive régimes in the south was based on the clear absence of anything resembling a democratic base for these governments. The entire absence in South Vietnam of any sociopolitical entity analogous to the Greek *demos* passed unremarked. The victories of the North Vietnamese and the Vietcong were taken as proof that they were the embodiment of the *volonté générale vietnamienne*. The political realities of both countries were too alien and too complex to carry much understanding when the real issue in American eyes was the justification for sending young American citizens to death or moral degradation in Vietnam. *Raison d'état* was not enough.

The American experience with Indonesia afforded another, even more striking example of the extraordinary positions into which the application of this kind of populist yardstick was to lead American governments to adopt *vis-à-vis* their European allies. And it underlines another factor which we have left uncommented upon, though it is present in the cases of both India and Indo-China. This is the extraordinarily naïve assumptions about political geography that underlie it. The British imperium in India spread its rule over the whole of the Indian sub-continent. It comprehended seventeen major languages, three major and opposed world faiths (besides Christianity and Parseeism), a number of states with whom Britain had treaty relations, and numerous separate racial stocks produced by successive waves of invasion from Central Asia and imposed upon the aboriginal Dravidian inhabitants. Yet since 'British India' existed, there must be an Indian people. Vietnam is a land of many races, differing religions, only unified twice in its history, in both cases with foreign aid and under foreign rule. Yet there must be a Vietnamese *people*. But Indonesia? Not only do all the different-iating factors seen in the Indian and Indo-Chinese examples exist in Indonesia. The territories are not contiguous, but consist of islands scattered over more than 1,000 miles of sea. By some curious geographical accident they included the Melanesian inhabitants of northern New Guinea but not their relatives who live in the Australian-governed eastern part of the island. In fact what American populism took as the Indonesian people were merely the modernising élites of the most heavily populated island, Java; indeed America aided and abetted the suppression by force of the indepen-dent Republic of the South Moluccas in 1949 and of the native Papuan nationalist movement in Dutch New Guinea in 1962, simply on the ground of geography.

The Indonesian example underlines another factor present in the Indian example but not hitherto commented on. This is the threat of the use of American aid, given originally in a generous manner intended to be free from strings, from a belief that American interests demand the recovery of the recipient, as a form of pressure on the recipient. In the British case in India it was Lend-Lease aid; in the case of the Netherlands it was Marshall Aid. But in each case the threat not only marred what Churchill once called the 'most un-sordid' act, but also made nonsense of the arguments of enlightened self-interest which were used to persuade the American political élites and public to accept the large-scale diversion of American resources to build up the military and economic strength of foreign states.

The case of Indonesia was particularly odd in that, whereas in Vietnam the leaders of the Indo-Chinese Communist party whom the Americans took to be the spokesmen for the nascent Vietnamese independence movement had collaborated with the OSS against the Japanese, while their French opponents were at least tarred with the stigma of defeat and collaboration with both Germany and Japan, the leaders of the Indonesian nationalists had collaborated with the Japanese. They had seized power with Japanese aid and arms, while the Dutch had fought valiantly to defend the East Indies against Japan and had stood up to the severest Japanese diplomatic pressure before the attack had begun. Moreover, the Indonesian 'nationalists', so-called, enjoyed popular support on any major scale only on Java and Sumatra. The Republic of Indonesia which they proclaimed was in fact a Javanese-dominated centralised state. They were, moreover, with a few exceptions, unwilling to submit themselves to the main process of democracy, popular election. Of the original leading figures, three – Sjarifuddin, Musso and Tan Malakka – were Communists: Musso in fact spent the war in Moscow. Of the remainder both Sukarno and Mohammed Hatta, his vice-president, had been flown to Tokyo in 1943 to thank the Japanese for setting up a Javanese representative council.[68] Records of their activity were in fact produced at the Tokyo War Crimes Trial.[69]

Furthermore Sukarno's programme was unashamedly expansionist. The BPKI (Badan Pendjelik Kemerdekaan Indonesia or Body for the Investigation of Indonesian Independence) was set up by Japanese proclamation on 1 March 1945. Consisting of 66 leading Javanese political figures, it held two plenary sessions at the end of May and in mid-July 1945. On the morning of 11 July 1945, it voted by secret ballot on three alternative versions of the territory to be claimed by the future Indonesian state. The first alternative included the whole of the Netherlands East Indies, all of New Guinea plus North Borneo, Sarawak, Portuguese Timor, Malaya and Singapore: it won 39 votes; the second, which limited the state simply to the territories of the Netherlands East Indies, won 19 votes; the third, basically a pan-Malay position, claiming the Dutch East Indies and Malaya without New Guinea, won only six votes. Mohammed Hatta spoke for this last view, arguing that to claim New Guinea with its Melanesian population would be to give the outside world the impression of imperialist ambition. Sukarno spoke for the first alternative – the Papuans could not understand politics, he said. Greater Indonesia, *Indonesia Raja*, was his goal.[70]

Sukarno's draft constitution moreover envisaged an elective President, kept in check by an elected Congress which was to meet only once every five years, but otherwise totally unlimited in the exercise

---

[68] W.H. Elsbree, *Japan's Role in South-East Asian Nationalist Movements, 1940–1945*, Cambridge, Mass. 1953, p. 49.

[69] *IMT FE*. Exh. 1344.

[70] Hadji Mohammed Yamin (ed.), *Hashab-Persipian Undang-Undong Dasar 1945*, Djakarta, 1959, pp. 213–14, cited Gareth Jones, 'Sukarno's Early Views on the Territorial Boundaries of Indonesia', *Australian Outlook*, 18, 1964, p. 31, footnote 4.

of power. This did not stop the American member of the Good Offices Commission, established during the first period of Dutch military action, designed to disarm and control the Indonesian paramilitary forces (who were behaving very largely as protectionist racketeers and terrorists against the Dutch estates, the Chinese and the Indo-European minorities), from talking of substituting 'ballots for bullets'. The absurdity of such a statement was amply demonstrated when the Dutch proceeded to establish a series of federal states, 'negaras', by travesties of plebiscites and the Republicans, seeing themselves outmanoeuvred, resumed guerilla warfare against the Dutch.

The central problem for the Dutch was that the Republican politicians, even though the so-called Indonesian Republic only covered a part of central Java, still disposed of armed forces more than adequate to destroy a federated United States of Indonesia once the Dutch troops were withdrawn. It was their hot-headed efforts to destroy these which stirred the United States by a note of 7 December 1948 to threaten an end to Marshall Aid to the Netherlands.[71] And when, despite this, the cabinet of the Netherlands proceeded to the second police action, American pressure forced the resignation of the democratically elected Dutch government, and Dirk Stikker, the Dutch Foreign Minister, a month before the American signature of the North Atlantic Treaty, was told outright by Averell Harriman, under instructions from the State Department, that no American military aid would be forthcoming to countries which had not solved their colonial problems.[72] At this moment the Berlin blockade was still in full swing. Had Stikker revealed the details of American pressure to the Dutch Parliament, the Netherlands would not have joined NATO. With aid from an outraged British Foreign Minister he was able effectively to get the threat withdrawn – but the way was made clear for the victory of the Republican leadership in Indonesia, the collapse of the separate federal governments under force or the threat of force, the execution of those political leaders who did not come over or escape, and the proclamation on 15 August 1950 of a unitary constitution. Armed opposition by the Darul Islam movement in West Java and Sumatra and by survivors of the east Indonesian federal forces in Celebes was to last until the end of the

[71] Dirk Stikker, *Men of Responsibility*, London, 1966, p. 139.
[72] Stikker, *Men of Responsibility*, p. 145.

1950s – so little did the Republican parties represent the Indonesian people.

The final example, the most surprising of all, also concerns Indonesia and the Netherlands. This is the case of the Indonesian claims on Dutch New Guinea or, as the Indonesians preferred to call it, West Irian. Here, under Netherlands rule, there developed a local Papuan nationalist movement. Its origins go back to a Messianic movement which sprang up in 1938, acquired nationalist overtones during the period of Japanese occupation, and took courage from the appearance of American negro troops in 1944. As part of Indonesian–Dutch fighting in the years 1946–9, a small Indonesian nationalist movement emerged among the Indonesian minorities living in Hollandia and Saroli – which provided a model for the first Papuans to be conscious of their own possibilities of power. A part of them reacted against Indonesian claims in West New Guinea, enough to set up a network of pro-Dutch committees, under the name Gerakan Persatuan Nieuw Guinea (GPNG).[73] In 1949 the Dutch refused to hand over western New Guinea to Indonesia. A police training school, a Papuan battalion 400 strong, a school of administration, a boarding continuation school and a secondary school, together with the decision on the part of the Dutch Protestant Church to reorganise themselves into a single organisation with Papuan ministers and to set up a labour organisation which had 3,000 members by 1960, provided the basis of a growing Papuan élite. In 1960 there were 32,000 pupils in primary schools, 3,000 in continuation schools, 600 in teacher-training and technical schools, 400 trainee nurses, 700 village lecturers, 200 missionary teachers, 300 nurses, 35 police patrol officers and small military corps. It was, however, not until the end of the 1950s that the Dutch allowed the formation of local political parties, and began an accelerated programme of political and economic progress. There followed a mushroom growth of local parties, some tribal in basis, but all sharing three points of view in common: hostility to Indonesian claims; a desire not to be rushed into premature independence, which sprang from a knowledge of how heavily dependent Papuan development was upon a subsidy from the Netherlands; and a hostility to racialism of any kind, but especially towards the

[73] Justus M. van der Kroef, 'Nationalism and Politics in New Guinea', *Pacific Affairs*, 34, 1961.

superiority complex of the Indonesian minority, symbolised in the name chosen by one of the larger political groupings, Sama Sama Manusai (we are all humans together).[74]

In April 1960 Indonesia began landing small groups of would-be guerillas in western New Guinea. In April 1961 elections both direct and indirect set up the New Guinea Council which immediately resolved that the Dutch were no longer free to make any change in the status of the territory without Council approval. Dutch, Australian, New Zealand, British and French representatives attended the opening sessions – American representatives were conspicuously absent.

American policy-makers were apparently anxious at the gradual Indonesian drift towards Moscow and fearful that a Dutch–Indonesian confrontation would accelerate the process. Robert Kennedy's own anti-colonialist sentiments on this occasion swung him against the Dutch, into the assumption that the Papuans were simply Dutch stooges. Over State Department protests, it was decided at the National Security Council to solve the western New Guinea issue before it became a major crisis.[75] The unfortunate Papuans were thus to be made the sacrificial goat on the altar of Indonesian independence from Moscow and good American–Indonesian relations. A telegram from thirty-three Papuan political figures to Kennedy protesting that they were not Indonesians was ignored.[76] And on American mediation, partly by Robert Kennedy and partly by Ambassador Ellsworth Bunker, over the opposition of the Dutch Parliament and despite their own protests, the Papuans found themselves sold to the Indonesians, a straightforward transfer of a colonial people from reasonably civilised Dutch rule to that of a corrupt, poverty-stricken tyrannical plebiscitary despotism, with one outstanding anti-colonialist virtue – it was not European.

President Sukarno was so encouraged by his success in playing on American illusions and anxieties that he swept on to play a similar game against the new union of Malaya with Singapore and the three Borneo territories of Sarawak, Brunei and North Borneo, to which

---

[74] Justus M. van der Kroef, 'Recent Developments in Western New Guinea', *Pacific Affairs*, 34, 1961.

[75] Arthur J. Schlesinger, *A Thousand Days*, Boston, 1965, pp. 646–65.

[76] Justus M. van der Kroef, 'The West New Guinea Settlement: Its Origins', *Orbis*, 3, 1963.

in 1961 he had allowed his Foreign Minister to declare he 'had no objections'. In the ensuing confrontation, however, the Malayan government and their British backers were to prove a very different 'kettle of fish'. The Kennedy government prepared for a personal intervention by the President; the assassination at Dallas intervened.[77] President Johnson was less thoroughly seized of the need to intervene; while the British government refused adamantly to give way. In the end the military coup and the removal of Sukarno from office ended Sukarno's expansionist and megalomaniacal career. The anti-colonialist card had temporarily lost its value. It was to return again, to plague and bedevil the American intervention in Vietnam, inspiring the interventionists in the initial phases of the war and blinding their opponents, as Ho had beguiled Major Thomas of the OSS in 1945, at the end.

To sum up: it has been argued that American policies towards the European colonial empires of Britain, France and the Netherlands were informed with a hostility to any system of colonial rule which in turn stemmed from a 'naïve populism'. In this concept the word 'naïve' is not used in any pejorative sense but as carrying the meaning of 'simple', 'unsophisticated', 'uninformed', 'insufficiently reasoned' or 'instinctive rather than thoroughly reasoned'. The word 'populism' is used not to imply that it is lineally descended from the views of the so-called American 'populists' of either the same or earlier periods, though there are elements common to all three views. It implies a belief in the existence of a recognisable political entity, 'the people' or 'peoples' of the colonially governed territories, with the consequential moral imperative that the exercise of sovereign powers in these territories should rest on, or stem from, the politically manifested 'consent' of all the members, or of a majority of the members, of that political entity.

It has further been argued that such a conceptualisation of the political problems of those colonial territories failed to correspond with the actual realities of the sociopolitical organisation of the inhabitants of those territories, was alien to their own approaches to politics, and was misleading to those who tried to use such concepts to guide the formulation of American policy. It led them to mistake what were the least representative elements in the native political

---

[77] Roger Hilsman, *To Move a Nation*, New York, 1967, pp. 382–409.

scene as the embodiment of 'the peoples', laid them open to manipulation by those elements who most understood how to use these concepts and made them mistake what were essentially manipulative or normative statements as though they were informative and verifiably true statements.

This 'populism', so it could continue to be argued, while anti-European in its manifestations (European colonial régimes and the social systems which supported them being seen as 'élitist', 'oligarchic', 'undemocratic', 'un-American', 'feudal', 'antiquated', 'exploitative' and 'tyrannous') derived two of its most important elements from Western European experience. In the first place it rested on the assumptions of a political geography which is of West European origin in that it assumes that the boundaries of sociopolitical organisations are coterminous with those of political geography; that if a geographical entity is endowed with a descriptive name that name can also be ascribed to the political entity which is assumed to correspond with the limits bounding the geographical entity; to take an example from British history, it is assumed that because there is an island called Ireland, the natural political organisation of its inhabitants would be a single political entity. The failure of existing political organisations to conform to this expectation becomes therefore an aberration from the norm, and the only right course is to support all efforts to correct that aberration.

It was equally assumed that there were, or ought to be, single political groupings such as the Indian, Indonesian or Vietnamese peoples; that in so far as such groupings could be shown not to exist, this was an aberration usually assumed to have been brought about and to be maintained by the colonial power so as better to preserve its rule, on the general principle, *divide et impera*.

The second assumption, one equally derived from West European political experience, was that the inhabitants of these colonially governed territories naturally identified themselves with one another by virtue of their common coinhabitation; that they felt loyalties to their common coinhabitation in the way that inhabitants of the states of Western Europe and their quondam settler and emigrant states in the Americas are expected to feel loyalty towards the states whose territories they inhabit. That this was a condition to which European countries only attained as a result of the secularisation of politics in the eighteenth century, following the establishment of dynastically defined states at the time of the European reformation, was entirely forgotten. That the inhabitants of the colonially ruled territories tended in most cases to define their loyalties by units no larger than the village, and beyond that by religion or language in multilinguistic states, was not recognised, or if recognised, was again made the responsibility of the colonial power. That the adoption of a secularised nationalism by certain groups indicated mainly their dissatisfaction with the inferior status accorded to them by their existing society, organised as it so often was on religious–hierarchical lines rather than their genuinely 'popular' and 'progressive' nature, defined as a desire and a willingness to approximate as closely as possible to the American system of politics and society, was rarely, if ever, recognised.

A third assumption, equally derived from the experience of the states of the North Atlantic littoral, was that a system of political processes which allowed for and encouraged the ready articulation of the views of individual members was so natural as to be readily understandable by, and acceptable to, the politically active and conscious among the inhabitants of these colonial territories.

The last point which was made was that a distinguishing mark of this American 'populist' approach was the willingness to use American political superiority in a manner untrammelled and uninhibited by any feelings of respect for, loyalty to, obligation to, or community with, the colonial powers. Where American policymakers did not succeed in forcing their views through it was not so much, as some 'revisionist' historians have argued, from their fear of Communism and consequent need for the friendship of the European powers, but simply that their power to act turned out in practice to be illusory. Behind all this lay not an economic imperialism *per se*, as sometimes argued by revisionists with Marxistic views, but a moral imperialism and an arrogance of power which has done much in its turn to induce the growth in Western Europe of a consciousness of separateness from, and lack of identity between, its own political systems and that of the United States.

Bibliographical note

As was explained in the first chapter, this book is based only partly on the author's own research. To a much greater extent it draws on the work of a great many historians, British, American and others who have worked in the fields of the history of British and American foreign policy, and that of Anglo-American relations in this century. The approach the author has adopted, that of looking at the subject matter through the attitudes and perceptions of the foreign-policy-making élites in both countries, confronts him, in compiling a bibliography, with a fundamental dilemma: whether to attempt a comprehensive bibliography which would list all the private papers, memoirs, diaries, letters and biographies of the members of the élite on each side of the Atlantic, and continue with all the relevant secondary works; or whether to provide the reader with a more limited bibliography, which would be confined to those secondary works which the author has actually used in writing the book. Since the author's own research into the private archives of both Britain and the United States is only partial, and his knowledge of the immense volume of histories of American foreign policy and diplomacy a good deal less than total, honesty dictated that the author followed the second of these two courses. The bibliography which follows is confined to those secondary works which the author has himself used; memoirs are only cited where the author feels that they might be unfamiliar to the orthodox historians of British or American foreign policy. Although various primary sources, both printed and archival, are cited in the footnotes, they are not listed in the bibliography. It is assumed that any competent historian who wishes to ascertain their location knows of the existence of the British National Register of Archives, and is familiar with the standard works which list American and British collections of private papers. As for the personal biographies of individual members of the élite, apart from the *Dictionary of National Biography*, both British and American, *Who's Who?* and *Who Was Who?*, and the *Foreign Office and Diplomatic Service Lists*, the only other works used were John E. Findling, *Dictionary of American Diplomatic History*, Westport, Conn., 1980, and

253

the biographical section of volume III of Alexander de Conde (ed.), *Encylopaedia of American Foreign Policy*, New York, 1978. The bibliography which follows is organised on a chapter-by-chapter basis; where a book or monograph is used in, or covers the span of, more than one chapter, it may be listed separately under the chapters in which it appears.

Select bibliography

Chapter 1

Books

Selig Adler, *The Isolationist Impulse. The Twentieth Century Reaction*, New York, 1961.

H. C. Allen, *Great Britain and the United States. A History of Anglo-American Relations, 1783–1952*, London, 1954.

H. C. Allen and Roger Thompson, *Contrast and Connection: Bicentennial Essays in American History*, London, 1976.

E. Digby Baltzell, *The Protestant Establishment: Aristocracy and Caste in America*, London, 1966.

Corelli Barnett, *The Collapse of British Power*, London, 1972.

Herbert Bass (ed.), *The State of American History*, Chicago, 1970.

K. Bourne, *Britain and the Balance of Power in North America, 1815–1908*, London, 1967.

David Calleo and Benjamin W. Rowland, *America and the World Political Economy. Atlantic Dreams and National Realities*, Bloomington, Indiana, 1973.

David Caute, *The Fellow-Travellers: A Postscript to the Enlightenment*, London, 1973.

Mark L. Chadwin, *The Warhawks; American Interventionists before Pearl Harbor*, New York, 1970.

David Dilks (ed.), *Retreat from Power. Studies in British Foreign Policy of the Twentieth Century*, vol. I, London, 1981.

Ian S. Drummond, *British Economic Policy and the Empire, 1919–1939*, London, 1972.

Imperial Economic Policy 1917–1939. Studies in Expansion and Protection, London, 1974.

John Ehrmann, *Cabinet Government and War, 1890–1940*, Cambridge, 1958.

W. B. Fowler, *British American Relations 1917–1918. The Role of Sir William Wiseman*, Princeton, NJ, 1969.

Ortega y Gasset, *The Modern Theme*, London, 1933.

Man and Crisis, London, 1933.

Norman Graebner (ed.), *An Uncertain Tradition, American Secretaries of State in the Twentieth Century*, New York, 1961.

Ideas and Diplomacy, Readings in the intellectual tradition of American Foreign Policy, New York, 1964.

Thomas S. Hachey (ed.), *Confidential Dispatches: Analyses of America by the British Ambassador, 1939–1945*, Evanston, Illinois, 1974.

M. T. Hogan, *Informal Entente: The Private Structure of Anglo-American Economic Diplomacy, 1918–1928*, Columbia, Missouri, 1977.

Warren F. Ilchmann, *Professional Diplomacy in the United States, 1779–1939*, Chicago, 1961.

Franklyn W. Johnson, *Defence by Committee. The British Committee of Imperial Defence, 1885–1939*, Oxford, 1960.

James Joll, *The Second International, 1889–1914*, London 1974, new edition.

Morton Keller, *Affairs of State. Public Life in Late Nineteenth Century America*, Cambridge, Mass., 1977.

Richard Koebner and Helmut D. Schmidt, *Imperialism: The Story and Significance of a Political Word, 1840–1960*, Cambridge, 1964.

S. D. Krasner, *Defending the National Interest*, Princeton, NJ, 1978.

Cleona Lewis, *America's Stake in International Investments*, Washington, DC, 1938.

F. S. Lyons, *Internationalism in Europe, 1815–1914*, Leiden, 1963.

Karl Mannheim (ed. Paul Kecskemeti), *Essays on the Sociology of Knowledge*, London, 1952.

Lucy Masterman, *C.F. Masterman. A Biography*, London, 1939.

H. C. G. Matthew, *The Liberal Imperialists: The Ideas and Politics of a Post-Gladstonian Elite*, Oxford, 1973.

François Mentré, *Les Générations Sociales*, Paris, 1920.

Allan Nevins (ed.), *America through British Eyes*, New York, 1948.

H. G. Nicholas, *Britain and the United States*, London, 1954.

H. G. Nicholas, *The United States and Britain*, Oxford, 1975.

H. G. Nicholas (ed.), *Washington Dispatches, 1941–1945; Weekly Political Reports from the British Embassy*, London, 1981.

Robert E. Osgood, *Idea and Self Interest in America's Foreign Relations*, Chicago, 1953.

Henry Pelling, *America and the British Left: From Bright to Bevan*, London, 1956.

Bradford Perkins, *The Great Rapprochement*, London, 1969.

Ernest H. Preeg, *Traders and Diplomats. An Analysis of the Kennedy Round of Negotiations under the General Agreement on Tariffs and Trade*, Washington, DC, 1970.

J. W. Rosenau, *The Domestic Sources of Foreign Policy*, New York, 1967.

Public Opinion and Foreign Policy, New York, 1961.

G. R. Searle, *The Quest for National Efficiency: A Study in Politics and in British Political Thought, 1899–1914*, Berkeley, 1971.

Bernard Semmel, *Imperialism and Social Reform: English Social–Imperial Thought, 1895–1914*, London, 1960.

E. Wilder Spaulding, *Ambassadors Ordinary and Extraordinary*, Washington DC, 1961.

J. D. Squires, *British Propaganda at Home and in the United States, 1914–1917*, Cambridge, Mass., 1935.

W. Stevenson, *A Man Called Intrepid*, London, 1976.

Cushing Strout, *The American Image of the Old World*, New York, 1963.

A. J. P. Taylor, *The Struggle for Mastery in Europe, 1848–1914*, Oxford, 1954.

The Trouble-Makers, Dissent over Foreign Policy, 1792–1939, Oxford, 1956.

Alice Teichova, *An Economic Background to Munich. International Business and Czechoslovakia, 1919–1938*, Cambridge, 1974.

Seth W. Tillman, *Anglo-American Relations at the Paris Peace Conference of 1919*, Princeton, NJ, 1962.

Ronald Tree, *When the Moon was High. Memoirs of War and Peace, 1897–1942*, London, 1975.

Kenneth A. Waltz, *Foreign Policy and Democratic Politics: The American and British Experience*, Boston, 1967.

D. C. Watt, *Personalities and Policies. Studies in the Formulation of British Foreign Policy in the Twentieth Century*, London and South Bend, Indiana, 1965.

Too Serious a Business: European Armed Forces and the Coming of the Second World War, London, 1974.

Gerald E. Wheeler, *Prelude to Pearl Harbor: the U.S. Navy and the Far East, 1921–1931*, Columbia, Missouri, 1963.

Robert Wiebe, *The Search for Order, 1877–1920*, London, 1967.

Mira Wilkins, *The Emergence of Multinational Enterprise. American Business Abroad from the Colonial Era to 1914*, Cambridge, Mass., 1970.

The Maturing of Multinational Enterprise. American Business Abroad from 1914 to 1970, Cambridge, Mass., 1974.

Robert Wohl, *The Generation of 1914*, London, 1980.

Articles

Max Beloff, 'The Myth of the Special Relationship', in Martin Gilbert (ed.), *A Century of Conflict. Essays in Honour of A. J. P. Taylor*, London, 1966.

Donald S. Birn, 'Open Diplomacy at the Washington Conference of 1921–1922. The British and French Experience', *Comparative Studies in Society and History*, 12, 1970.

A. E. Campbell, 'Open Diplomacy (Comment on Birn and Singer)', *Comparative Studies in Society and History*, 14, 1972.

David Carlton, 'Great Britain and the Coolidge Disarmament Conference of 1927', *Political Science Quarterly*, 14, 1972.

Alan K. Henrikson, 'The Geographical "Mental Maps" of American Foreign Policy-Makers', *International Political Science Review*, 1, 1980.

Walter LaFeber, ' "Ah, if we had studied it more carefully"; The Fortunes of American Diplomatic History', *Prologue*, 11, 1979.

John de Novo, 'The Movement for an Aggressive American Oil Policy Abroad, 1918–1920', *American Historical Review*, 61, 1956.

Marvin Rinntala, 'A Generation in Politics: A Definition', *Review of Politics*, 25, 1963.

'Political Generations', *International Encyclopaedia of the Social Sciences*, New York, 1968.

Alan Sharp, 'The Foreign Office in Eclipse, 1919–1922', *History*, 61, 1976.

David Singer, 'Popular Diplomacy and Policy Effectiveness', *Comparative Studies in Society and History*, 12, 1970.

Alan B. Spitzer, 'The Historical Problem of Generations', *American Historical Review*, 78, 1973.

Roberta Warman, 'The Erosion of Foreign Office Influence in the Making of Foreign Policy, 1916–1918', *Historical Journal*, 15, 1972.

Gerald Wheeler, 'Isolated Japan; Anglo-American Diplomatic Cooperation, 1927–1936', *Pacific Historical Review*, 30, 1961.

Chapter 2

Books

Max Beloff, *Imperial Sunset. Britain's Liberal Empire, 1897–1921*, London, 1969.

John W. Blum, *The Republican Roosevelt*, Cambridge, Mass., 1954.

K. Bourne, *Britain and the Balance of Power in North America, 1815–1908*, London, 1967.

W. R. Braisted, *The United States Navy in the Pacific, 1897–1908*, Austin, Texas and London, 1958.

The United States Navy in the Pacific, 1909–1922, Austin, Texas, and London, 1971.

Edward H. Buehrig, *Woodrow Wilson and the Balance of Power*, Bloomington, Indiana, 1955.

Peter Calvert, *The Mexican Revolution, 1910–1914: The Diplomacy of Anglo-American Conflict*, Cambridge, 1968.

A. E. Campbell, *Great Britain and the United States, 1895–1903*, Glasgow, 1960.

Charles S. Campbell Jr, *Anglo-American Understanding, 1898–1903*, Baltimore, Maryland, 1957.

Richard D. Challener, *Admirals, Generals and American Foreign Policy, 1898–1914*, Princeton, NJ, 1973.

George Dangerfield, *The Strange Death of Liberal England*, London, 1936.

Patrick Devlin, *Too Proud to Fight: Woodrow Wilson's Neutrality*, London, 1974.

Calvin Doens, *The United States and the First Hague Peace Conference*, Ithaca, New York, 1962.

Frances Donaldson, *The Marconi Scandal*, London, 1962.

Jost Dülffler, *Regeln gegen den Krieg. Die Haager Konferenzen 1899 und 1907 in der internationalen Beziehungen*, Berlin, 1981.

John H. Dunning, *American Investment in British Manufacturing Industry*, London, 1958.

Herbert Feis, *Europe the World's Banker, 1870–1914*, New Haven, Conn., 1930.

W. B. Fowler, *British–American Relations, 1917–1918: The Role of Sir William Wiseman*, Princeton, NJ, 1969.

Lawrence E. Gelfand, *The Enquiry: American Preparations for Peace, 1917–1919*, New Haven, Conn., 1963.

Donald C. Gordon, *The Dominions Partnership in Imperial Defence, 1870–1914*, Oxford, 1965.

Henry F. Grady, *British War Finance, 1914–1919*, New York, 1927.

Norman A. Graebner (ed.), *An Uncertain Tradition: American Secretaries of State in the Twentieth Century*, New York, 1961.

John A. S. Grenville, *Lord Salisbury and Foreign Policy. The Close of the Nineteenth Century*, London, 1964.

John A. S. Grenville and George B. Young (eds.), *Politics, Strategy and Diplomacy: Studies in Foreign Policy, 1873–1917*, New Haven, Conn., 1966.

Paul Guinn, *British Strategy and Politics, 1914–1918*, Oxford, 1965.

Elie Halévy, *A History of the English People in the Nineteenth Century*: vol. V, *Imperialism and the Rise of Labour*, London, 1949.

Lord Hankey, *The Supreme Command*, 2 vols. London, 1961.

The Supreme Control at the Paris Peace Conference, London, 1963.

Richard H. Heindel, *The American Impact on Great Britain, 1898–1914*, Philadelphia, 1940.

F. H. Hinsley (ed.), *British Foreign Policy under Sir Edward Grey*, Cambridge, 1977.

Richard Hofstaedter, *Social Darwinism in American Thought*, Boston, Mass., 1955.

W. Stull Holt, *Treaties Defeated by the Senate*, Baltimore, Maryland, 1933.

Edmund Ions, *James Bryce and American Democracy, 1870–1922*, London, 1968.

Burton K. Kaufmann, *Efficiency and Expansion. Foreign Trade Organisation in the Wilson Administration, 1913–1921*, Westport, Conn., 1974.

George Kennan, *American Diplomacy, 1900–1950*, Chicago, 1951.

Walter LaFeber, *The New Empire: An Interpretation of American Expansion, 1860–1898*, Princeton, NJ, 1963.

N. Gordon Levin, *Woodrow Wilson and World Politics*, New York, 1968.

Arthur L. Link, *Woodrow Wilson and the Progressive Era, 1910–1917*, New York, 1954.

Wilson the Diplomatist, Baltimore, Maryland, 1957.

Wilson. A Biography, Princeton, NJ, in progress.

Peter Lowe, *Great Britain and Japan, 1911–1915. A Study of British Far Eastern Policy*, London, 1968.

Arthur J. Marder, *The Anatomy of British Sea Power*, New York, 1940.

From the Dreadnought to Scapa Flow. The Royal Navy in the Fisher Era, 1904–1919, 5 vols., Oxford, 1960–70.

Lawrence W. Martin, *Peace Without Victory. Woodrow Wilson and the British Liberals*, New Haven, Conn., 1958.

H. C. G. Matthews, *The Liberal Imperialists: the Ideas and Politics of a Post-Gladstonian Elite*, Oxford, 1973.

Ernest R. May, *Imperial Democracy. The Emergence of America as a World Power*, New York, 1961.

World War and American Isolation, 1914–1917, Cambridge, Mass., 1959.

Arno J. Mayer, *The Political Origins of the New Diplomacy*, New Haven, Conn., 1959.

Politics and Diplomacy of Peace-Making. Containment and Counter-Revolution at Versailles, 1918–1919, New York, 1967.

George Monger, *The End of Isolation. British Foreign Policy, 1900–1907*, London, 1963.

E. Victor Morgan, *Studies in British Financial Policy, 1914–1925*, London, 1952.

George Mowry, *The Era of Theodore Roosevelt, 1900–1912*, New York, 1958.

R. G. Neale, *Great Britain and United States Expansion, 1898–1900*, East Lansing, Mich., 1966.

Ian H. Nish, *The Anglo-Japanese Alliance. The Diplomacy of Two Island Empires, 1894–1907*, London, 1966.

Carl Parrini, *Heir to Empire. United States Economic Diplomacy, 1916–1923*, Pittsburgh, Ohio, 1969.

Edward B. Parsons, *Wilsonian Diplomacy. Allied–American Rivalries in War and Peace*, St Louis, Missouri, 1978.

Bradford S. Perkins, *The Great Rapprochement. England and the United States, 1895–1914*, London, 1969.

Richard S. Preston, *Canada and 'Imperial Defence'. A Study in the Origins of the British Commonwealth's Defence Organisation, 1867–1919*, Durham, NC, 1967.

Victor Rothwell, *British War Aims and Diplomacy, 1914–1918*, Oxford, 1971.

Henry R. Rudin, *Armistice 1918*, New Haven, Conn., 1944.

Jeffrey J. Safford, *Wilsonian Maritime Diplomacy, 1913–1921*, New Brunswick, NJ, 1978.

Robert J. Scully, *The Origins of the Lloyd George Coalition: The Politics of Social Imperialism, 1900–1918*, Princeton, NJ 1975.

G. R. Searle, *The Quest for National Efficiency: A Study in British Politics and British Political Thought 1899–1914*, Berkeley, 1971.

Bernard Semmel, *Imperialism and Social Reform: English Social–Imperial Thought, 1895–1914*, London, 1960.

Daniel M. Smith, *The Great Departure, the United States and World War I, 1914–1920*, New York, 1965,
   Aftermath of War. Bainbridge Colby and Wilsonian Diplomacy 1920–1921, Philadelphia, 1970.

Harold and Margaret Sproat, *The Rise of American Naval Power, 1776–1918*, Princeton, NJ, 1939.
   Towards a New Order of Sea Power: American naval policy and the World Scene, 1918–1922, Princeton, NJ, 1943.

J. D. Squires, *British Propaganda at Home and in the United States, 1914–1917*, Cambridge, Mass., 1935.

Seth P. Tillman, *Anglo-American Relations at the Paris Peace Conference of 1919*, Princeton, NJ, 1961.

David F. Trask, *The United States in the Supreme War Council. American War Aims and Inter-Allied Strategy, 1917–1919*, Middletown, Conn., 1961.
   Captains and Cabinets: Anglo-American Naval Relations, 1917–1918, Columbia, Missouri, 1972.

Barbara W. Tuchmann, *The Proud Tower*, London, 1966.
   The Zimmermann Telegram, London, 1959.

Joseph S. Tulchin, *The Aftermath of War. World War I and United States Policy Towards Latin America*, New York, 1971.

Charles Vevier, *The United States and China 1906–1913. A Study in Finance and Diplomacy*, New Brunswick, NJ, 1955.

Alan J. Ward, *Ireland and Anglo-American Relations, 1899–1921*, London, 1969.

Arthur Willert, *The Road to Safety: A Study in Anglo-American Relations*, New York, 1958.

Samuel R. Williamson Jr, *The Politics of Grand Strategy. Britain and France prepare for War, 1906–1914*, Cambridge, Mass., 1969.

Henry R. Winkler, *The League of Nations Movement in Great Britain, 1914–1919*, New Brunswick, NJ, 1952.

Llewellyn Woodward, *Great Britain and the War of 1914–1918*, London, 1967.

Articles

Howard Allen, 'Republican Reformers and Foreign Policy', *Mid-America*, 44, 1962.

Barton J. Bernstein and Franklin A. Leib, 'Progressive Republican Senators and American Imperialism, 1898–1916: A Reappraisal', *Mid-America*, 50, 1968.

Nelson Manfred Blake, 'Ambassadors at the Court of Theodore Roosevelt', *Mississipi Valley Historical Review*, 41, 1954–5.

Leon E. Boothe, 'A Fettered Envoy: Lord Grey's Mission to the United States, 1919–1920', *Review of Politics*, 33, 1971.

Kathleen Burk, 'The Diplomacy of Finance: British Financial Missions to the United States, 1914–1918', *Historical Journal*, 22, 1979.

'Great Britain in the United States, 1917–1918: The Turning-Point', *International History Review*, 1, 1979.

David H. Burton, 'Theodore Roosevelt and his English Correspondents? The Intellectual Roots of the Anglo-American Alliance', *Mid-America*, 53, 1971.

P. R. Calvert, 'Great Britain and the New World, 1905–1914', in F. H. Hinsley (ed.), *British Foreign Policy under Sir Edward Grey*, Cambridge, 1977.

W. G. Carleton, 'Isolationism and the Middle West', *Mississipi Valley Historical Review*, 32, 1946.

John Milton Cooper, 'The Command of Gold Reversed: American Loans to Britain, 1915–1917', *Journal of American History*, 60, 1973.

Clarence B. Davis, 'The Limits of Effacement. Britain and the Problem of American Cooperation or Competition in China, 1915–1917', *Pacific Historical Review*, 48, 1979.

Roberta A. Dayer, 'Strange Bedfellows: J. P. Morgan and Co., Whitehall, and the Wilson Administration during World War I', *Business History*, 18, 1976.

George W. Egerton, 'Britain and the "Great Betrayal"; Anglo-American Relations and the Struggle for the Ratification of the Treaty of Versailles, 1919–1920', *Historical Journal*, 21, 1978.

J. A. S. Grenville, 'Diplomacy and War Plans in the United States, 1890–1917', *Transactions of the Royal Historical Society*, 5th Series, 1961.

Padraic C. Kennedy, 'La Follette's Foreign Policy: From Imperialism to Anti-Imperialism', *Wisconsin Magazine of History*, 46, 1963.

William E. Leuchtenberg, 'Progressivism and Imperialism: The Progressive Movement and American Foreign Policy, 1898–1916', *Mississipi Valley Historical Review*, 39, 1952–3.

J. Kenneth Macdonald, 'Lloyd George and the Search for a Post-War Naval Policy, 1919', in A. J. P. Taylor (ed.), *Lloyd George. Twelve Essays*, London, 1971.

Arthur Mann, 'British Social Thought and American Reformers of the Progressive Era', *Mississipi Valley Historical Review*, 41, 1954–5.

C. M. Mason, 'Anglo-American Relations: Mediation and Permanent Peace', in Hinsley (ed.), *British Foreign Policy under Sir Edward Grey*, Cambridge, 1977.

Roberta Mayer, 'The Origins of the American Banking Empire in Latin America: Frank Vanderlip and the National City Bank', *Journal of Inter-American Studies and World Affairs*, 15, 1973.

John de Novo, 'The Movement for an Aggressive Oil Policy Abroad, 1918–1920', *American Historical Review*, 61, 1956.

Edward B. Parsons, 'Why the British Reduced the Flow of American Troops to Europe in August–October 1918', *Canadian Journal of History*, 12, 1977–8.

Emily S. Rosenberg, 'Anglo-American Rivalry in Brazil During World War I', *Diplomatic History*, 2, 1978.

M. L. Sanders, 'Wellington House and British Propaganda during the First World War', *Historical Journal*, 18, 1975.

Harry N. Scheiber, 'World War I as Entrepreneurial Opportunity: Willard Straight and the American International Corporation', *Political Science Quarterly*, 84, 1969.

Warren Sutton, 'Progressive American Senators and the Submarine Crisis, 1915–1916', *Mid-America*, 47, 1965.

Philip M. Taylor, 'The Foreign Office and British Propaganda during the First World War', *Historical Journal*, 23, 1980.

Walter Trallner, 'Progressivism and World War I: A Reappraisal', *Mid-America*, 44, 1962.

Samuel P. Wells, 'British Strategic Withdrawal from the Western Hemisphere, 1904–1906', *Cambridge Historical Review*, 49, 1968.

'New Perspectives on Wilsonian Diplomacy: The Secular Evangelism of American Political Economy', *Perspectives in American History*, 6, 1974.

David R. Woodward, 'The Origins and Intent of David Lloyd George's January 5, 1918 War Aims Speech', *The Historian*, 34, 1971–2.

Theses

Stephen Hartley, 'The Irish Question as a Problem in British Foreign Policy, 1914–1918', London, Ph.D., 1980.

Peter Neary, 'The Embassy of James Bryce in the United States, 1907–1913', London Ph.D., 1967.

Nicholas Reeves, 'British Film Propaganda during the First World War', London Ph.D., 1981.

Warner R. Schilling, 'Admirals and Foreign Policy 1913–1919', Yale Ph.D. 1953.

Sherrill P. Wells, 'The Influence of Sir Cecil Spring-Rice and Sir Edward Grey on the Shaping of Anglo-American Relations, 1913–1916', London Ph.D., 1978.

Chapter 3

Books

Hans E. Bärtschli, *Die Entwicklung vom imperialistischen Reichsgedankes zur modernen Idee des Commonwealths im Lebenswerk Lord Balfour*, Berne, 1957.

E. Bennett, *Germany and the Diplomacy of the Financial Crisis of 1931*, Cambridge, Mass., 1962.

Wolf Heinrich Bickel, *Die Anglo-Amerikanische Beziehungen 1927–1930 im Licht der Flottenfrage*, Zurich, 1970.

Joseph Brandes, *Herbert Hoover and Economic Diplomacy: Department of Commerce Policy, 1918–1928*, Pittsburgh, Ohio, 1962.

David Carlton, *MacDonald versus Henderson: the Foreign Policy of the Second Labour Government*, London, 1970.

David S. Cheever and H. Field Havilland Jr, *Organising for Peace*, Boston, 1954.

Steven V. O. Clark, *Central Bank Co-operation, 1924–1931*, New York, 1967.

   The Reconstruction of the International Monetary System. The Attempts of 1922 and 1933, Princeton, NJ, 1973.

Maurice Cowling, *The Impact of Labour, 1920–1924: The Beginning of Modern British Politics*, Cambridge, 1971.

Roberta Allbert Dayer, *Bankers and Diplomats in China, 1917–1925: the Anglo-American Relationship*, London, 1982.

Byron Dexter, *The Years of Opportunity: the League of Nations 1920–1926*, New York, 1967.

L. Ethan Ellis, *Republican Foreign Policy, 1921–1933*, New Brunswick, NJ, 1969.

Herbert Feis, *The Diplomacy of the Dollar. First Era, 1919–1932*, Baltimore, 1950.

   1933. Characters in Crisis, Boston, Mass., 1966.

Robert W. Ferrell, *American Diplomacy in the Great Depression: Hoover–Stimson Foreign Policy, 1929–1933* New Haven, Conn., 1953.

   Peace in Their Time, The Origins of the Kellogg–Briand Pact, New Haven, Conn., 1952.

Michael G. Fry, *Illusions of Security: North Atlantic Diplomacy, 1918–1922*, Toronto, 1972.

Waldo Heinrichs Jr, *American Ambassador. Joseph C. Grew and the Development of the United States Diplomatic Tradition*, Boston, 1966.

Michael Hogan, *Informal Entente: The Private Structure of Cooperation in Anglo-American Economic Diplomacy, 1918–1928*, Columbia, Missouri, 1977.

R. F. Holland, *Britain and the Commonwealth Alliance, 1918–1939*, London, 1981.

Michael Howard, *The Continental Commitment*, London, 1971.

H. Montgomery Hyde, *British Air Policy Between the Wars, 1918–1939*, London, 1976.

Jon Jacobson, *Locarno Diplomacy: Germany and the West, 1925–1929*, Princeton, NJ, 1972.

Kenneth Paul Jones (ed.), *U.S. Diplomats: America's Search for Peace in Europe, 1919–1941*, Oxford, 1981.

Melvyn G. Leffler, *The Elusive Quest: America's Pursuit of European Stability and French Security*, Chapel Hill, NC, 1979.

W. R. Louis, *British Strategy in the Far East 1919–1939*, Oxford, 1971.

Nicholas Mansergh, *Survey of British Commonwealth Affairs: Problems of External Policy, 1931–1939*, Oxford, 1952.

D. E. Moggridge, *British Monetary Policy, 1924–1931: the Norman Conquest of $4.86*, Cambridge, 1972.

Harold G. Moulton and Leo Pasvolski, *War Debts and World Prospects*, Washington, DC, 1932.

Ian H. Nish, *Alliance in Decline: A Study in Anglo-Japanese Relations, 1908–1923*, London, 1972.

R. G. O'Connor, *Perilous Equilibrium. The U.S. and the London Naval Conference of 1930*, Lawrence, Kansas, 1962.

Carl C. Parrini, *Heir to Empire: U.S. Economic Diplomacy 1916–1923*, Pittsburgh, Ohio, 1969.

Sir John Pratt, *War and Politics in China*, London, 1943.

George H. Quester, *Deterrence Before Hiroshima*, New York, 1966.

Stephen W. Roskill, *British Naval Policy Between the Wars*, vol. I: *The Period of Anglo-American Antagonism, 1919–1929*, London, 1962.

Stephen A. Schuler, *The End of French Predominance in Europe. The Financial Crisis of 1924 and the Adoption of the Dawes Plan*, Chapel Hill, NC, 1976.

Benjamin Shwadran, *The Middle East, Oil and the Great Powers*, London, 1947.

Robert Skidelsky, *Politicians and the Slump. The Labour Government of 1929–1931*, London, 1967.

Michael B. Stoff, *Oil, War and American Security*, New Haven, Conn., 1980.

Christopher Thorne, *The Limits of Foreign Policy. The West, the League and the Far Eastern Crisis of 1931–1933*, London, 1972.

Seth P. Tillman, *Anglo-American Relations at the Paris Peace Conference of 1919*, Princeton, NJ, 1961.

Joseph S. Tulchin, *The Aftermath of War. World War I and United States Policy Towards Latin America*, New York, 1971.

J. Chal Vinson, *The Parchment Peace: the U.S. Senate and the Washington Conference, 1921–1922*, Athens, Ga, 1955.

Sir Charles Webster and Noble Frankland, *The Strategic Bombing Offensive Against Germany*, vols. I, IV, London, 1961.

Wythe Williams, *Dusk of Europe*, London, 1937.

Joan Hoff Wilson, *American Business and Foreign Policy, 1920–1933*, Lexington, Ky, 1971.

P. G. Wrigley, *Canada and the Transition to Commonwealth. British–Canadian Relations, 1917–1936*, Cambridge, 1977.

Articles

Paul P. Abrahams, 'American Bankers and the Economic Tactics of Peace, 1919', *Journal of American History*, 56, 1969.

Selig Adler, 'The War Guilt Question and American Disillusionment, 1918–1928', *Journal of Modern History*, 23, 1957.

Leon E. Boothe, 'A Fettered Envoy. Lord Grey's Mission to the United States, 1919–1920', *Review of Politics*, 33, 1971.

David H. Burks, 'The United States and the Geneva Protocol of 1924: a "New Holy Alliance"', *American Historical Review*, 66, 1959.

David Carlton, 'Great Britain and the Coolidge Disarmament Conference of 1927', *Political Science Quarterly*, 83, 1968.

'The Anglo-French Compromise over Arms Limitation, 1928', *Journal of British Studies*, 8, 1969.

Frank C. Costigliola, 'Anglo-American Financial Rivalry in the 1920s', *Journal of Economic History*, 37, 1977.

'The Other Side of Isolationism: The Establishment of the First World Bank', *Journal of American History*, 59, 1972.

R. N. Current, 'The Stimson Doctrine and the Hoover Doctrine', *American Historical Review*, 59, 1953–4.

Roberta Allbert Dayer, 'The British War Debts to the United States and the Anglo-Japanese Alliance, 1920–1923', *Pacific Historical Review*, 45, 1976.

Robert A. Divine, 'F.D.R. and Collective Security, 1933', *Mississipi Valley Historical Review*, 45, 1976.

George W. Egerton, 'Britain and the "Great Betrayal": Anglo-American Relations and the Struggle for United States Ratification of the Treaty of Versailles, 1919–1920', *Historical Journal*, 21, 1978.

M. G. Fry, 'The North Atlantic Triangle and the Abrogation of the Anglo-Japanese Alliance', *Journal of Modern History*, 39, 1967.

Fred Greene, 'The Military View of American National Policy, 1904–1940', *American Historical Review*, 65, 1960–1.

H. Duncan Hall, 'The British Commonwealth of Nations in War and Peace', in William Y. Elliot and H. Duncan Hall (eds.), *The British Commonwealth at War*, New York, 1943.

Ellis W. Hawley, 'Herbert Hoover, the Commerce Secretariat and the Vision of an "Associative State"', *Journal of American History*, 61, 1974.

R. A. Hecht, 'Great Britain and the Stimson Note of 7 January 1932', *Pacific Historical Review*, 38, 1969.

Norman Hillmer, 'The Foreign Office, the Dominions and the Diplomatic Unity of the Empire', in D. Dilks (ed.), *Retreat from Power. Studies in British Foreign Policy of the Twentieth Century*, vol. I, London, 1981.

'The Anglo-Dominions Alliance, 1919–1939' *15e Congrès International des Sciences Historiques, Rapports*, vol III, Bucharest, 1980.

P. Kaswak, 'American Foreign Policy Officials and Canada, 1927–1941: A Look Through Bureaucratic Glasses', *International Journal*, 32, 1977.

Paul C. Koistinen, 'The Industrial–Military Complex in Historical Perspective in the Inter-War Years', *Journal of American History*, 46, 1970.

Melvyn G. Leffler, 'The Origins of Republican War Debt Policy, 1921–1923: A Case Study in the Applicability of the Open Door Concept', *Journal of American History*, 59, 1972.

'Political Isolationism, Economic Expansionism or Diplomatic Realism:

American Policy towards Western Europe, 1921–1933', *Perspectives in American History*, 8, 1974.

M. Ruth Megaw, 'Undiplomatic Channels: Australian Representatives in the United States, 1918–1939', *Historical Studies* (Melbourne), 15, no. 60, 1973.

John de Novo, 'The Movement for an Aggressive American Oil Policy Abroad, 1918–1920', *American Historical Review*, 61, 1956.

Stephen G. Rabe, 'Anglo-American Rivalry for Venezuelan Oil, 1919–1920', *Mid-America*, 57, 1976.

Paul Mellish Read, 'Standard Oil in Indonesia, 1898–1928', *Business History Review*, 32, 1958.

Benjamin D. Rhodes, 'Herbert Hoover and the War Debts, 1919–1933', *Prologue*, 6, 1974.

Elliot A. Rosen, 'Intranationalism v. Internationalism: The Interregnum Struggle for the Sanctity of the New Deal', *Political Science Quarterly*, 81, 1966.

Arthur W. Schatz, 'The Anglo-American Trade Agreements and Cordell Hull's Search for Peace, 1936–1938', *Journal of American History*, 57, 1970.

C. Thorne, 'The Shanghai Crisis of 1932: The Bases of British Policy', *American Historical Review*, 75, 1970.

D. C. Watt, 'American Strategic Interests and Anxieties in the West Indies, 1912–1940', *Journal of the Royal United Services Institute*, 108, 1963.

'U.S. Isolationism in the 1920s. Is it a Useful Concept?', *Bulletin of the British Association of American Studies*, New Series, no. 6, 1962.

William Appleman Williams, 'The Legend of Isolationism in the 1920s', *Science and Society*, 1954.

Fred H. Winkler, 'The War Department and Disarmament, 1926–1935', *The Historian*, 28, 1966.

Theses

Adelphia Jan Bowen Jr, 'The Disarmament Movement, 1918–1935', Columbia University Ph.D., 1956.

T. McCulloch, 'Anglo-American Economic Diplomacy and the European Crisis, 1933–1939', Oxford D.Phil., 1978.

J. Kenneth Macdonald, 'British Naval Policy and the Pacific and Far East. From Paris to Washington, 1919–1922', Oxford D.Phil., 1975.

B. J. C. McKercher, 'The British Foreign-Policy-Making Elite and its Attitudes Towards the United States, November 1924–June 1929', London Ph.D., 1979.

Chapter 4

Books

F. Adams, *Economic Diplomacy. The American Export–Import Bank, 1934–1939*, Columbia, Missouri, 1976.

Irvine H. Anderson Jr, *The Standard Oil Vacuum Company and United States East Asian Policy, 1933–1941*, Princeton NJ, 1975.

Charles E. Beard, *American Foreign Policy in the Making, 1932–1940. A Study in Responsibilities*, Hamden, Conn., 1946.

John Morton Blum, *From the Morgenthau Diaries*, 3 vols., Boston, Mass., 1961–7.

Dorothy Borg, *The United States and the Far Eastern Crisis of 1933–1938*, Cambridge, Mass., 1964.

Dorothy Borg and Shumpei Okamoto (eds.), *Pearl Harbor as History. Japanese–American Relations, 1931–1941*, New York, 1973.

Thomas B. Buell, *Master of Sea-Power. A Biography of Fleet-Admiral Ernest J. King*, Boston, Mass., 1981.

Orville Bullitt, *For the President, Personal and Secret*, Boston, Mass., 1972.

Richard Dean Burns and Edward M. Bennett (eds.), *Diplomats in Crisis: United States–Chinese–Japanese Relations, 1919–1941*, Oxford, 1974.

Warren I. Cohen, *The American Revisionists: Lessons of Intervention in World War I*, Chicago, 1967.

Wayne S. Cole, *Senator Gerald P. Nye and American Foreign Relations*, Minneapolis, 1962.

James V. Compton, *The Swastika and the Eagle. Hitler, the United States and the Origins of the Second World War*, London, 1968.

Robert Dallek, *Franklin Roosevelt and American Foreign Policy, 1932–1945*, Oxford, 1979.

Alexander De Conde (ed.), *Isolation and Security*, Durham, NC, 1957.

Robert A. Divine, *The Illusion of Neutrality*, Chicago, 1962.

Max Domarus (ed.), *Hitler, Reden und Proklamationen, 1932–1945*, 2 vols., Munich, 1963–5.

Donald F. Drummond, *The Passing of American Neutrality, 1937–1941*, Ann Arbor, 1955.

Herbert Feis, *Seen from E.A.: Three International Episodes*, New York, 1947.

Henry M. Field, *M Project for FDR: Studies in Migration and Settlement*, Ann Arbor, 1962.

Lloyd C. Gardner, *Economic Aspects of New Deal Diplomacy*, Madison, Wis., 1964.

John McVickar Haight Jr, *American Aid to France, 1938–1940*, New York, 1970.

Stanley E. Hilton, *Brazil and the Great Powers, 1930–1939: The Politics of Trade Rivalry*, Austin, Texas, 1973.

Nancy Harrison Hooper (ed.), *The Moffat Papers: Selections from the Diplomatic Journals of Jay Pierrepont Moffat, 1919–1943*, Cambridge, Mass., 1956.

Manfred Jonas, *Isolationism in America, 1935–1941*, Ithaca, New York, 1966.

Detlef Junker, *Der unteilbare Weltmarkt: Das ökonomische Interesse in dem Aussenpolitik der USA, 1933–1941*, Stuttgart, 1975.

Charles P. Kindleberger, *The World in Depression 1929–1939*, London, 1973.

Richard N. Kottman, *Reciprocity and the North Atlantic Triangle, 1932–1938*, Ithaca, New York, 1968.

Bruce R. Kuniholm, *The Origins of the Cold War in the Near East*, Princeton, NJ, 1980.

James R. Leutze, *Bargaining for Supremacy: Anglo-American Naval Relations, 1937–1941*, Chapel Hill, NC, 1977.

Callum A. Macdonald, *The United States, Britain and Appeasement*, London, 1981.

Arnold A. Offner, *American Appeasement. United States Foreign Policy and Germany, 1933–1938*, Cambridge, Mass., 1969.

Ritchie Ovendale, *'Appeasement' and the English-Speaking World. Britain, the United States, the Dominions and the Policy of Appeasement, 1937–1939*, Cardiff 1975.

George Peden, *British Rearmament and the Treasury, 1932–1939*, Edinburgh, 1979.

Stephen Pelz, *Race to Pearl Harbor: The Failure of the Second London Naval Conference and the Onset of World War II*, Cambridge, Mass., 1974.

Julius Pratt, *Cordell Hull*, 2 vols., New York, 1964.

Laurence W. Pratt, *East of Malta, West of Suez: Britain and the Mediterranean Crisis, 1936–1939*, Cambridge, 1975.

David Reynolds, *The Creation of the Anglo-American Alliance, 1937–1941. A Study in Competitive Cooperation*, London, 1981.

Esmonde Robertson (ed.), *The Origins of the Second World War*, London, 1971.

Stephen Roskill, *Naval Policy Between the Wars*, vol. II, London, 1976.

Benjamin A. Rowland, *Balance of Power or Hegemony: The Inter-War Monetary System*, New York, 1976.

Robert P. Shay, *British Rearmament in the 1930s: Politics and Profits*, Princeton, NJ, 1977.

Ann Trotter, *Britain and East Asia 1933–1937*, Cambridge, 1975.

D. C. Watt, *Personalities and Policies. Studies in the Formulation of British Foreign Policy in the Twentieth Century*, London, and South Bend, Indiana, 1965.

John E. Wiltz, *In Search of Peace: The Senate Munitions Enquiry, 1934–1936*, Baton Rouge, La., 1963.

Randall Bennett Woods, *The Roosevelt Foreign Policy Establishment and the 'Good Neighbors'. The United States and Argentina, 1941–1945*, Lawrence, Kansas, 1979.

Articles

William R. Allen, 'Cordell Hull and the Defence of the Trade Agreements Programme, 1934–1940', in Alexander De Conde (ed.), *Isolation and Security*, Durham, NC, 1957.

Meredith William Berg, 'Admiral William H. Standley and the Second London Naval Treaty, 1934–1936', *The Historian*, 33, 1970–1.

Dorothy Borg, 'Notes on Roosevelt's "Quarantine" Speech', *Political Science Quarterly*, 52, 1957.

John C. Cairns, 'A Nation of Shopkeepers in Search of a Possible France, 1919–1940', *American Historical Review*, 79, 1974.

Wayne S. Cole, 'Senator Key Pittman and American Neutrality Policies, 1933–1940', *Mississipi Valley Historical Review*, 46, 1960.

F. Coughlan, 'Armaments, Economic Policy and Appeasement: Background to British Foreign Policy, 1931–1937, *History*, 54, 1972.

D. Dilks, 'Appeasement Revisited', *University of Leeds Review*, 15, 1972.

Foster Rhea Dulles, 'The Anti-Colonial Policies of Franklin D. Roosevelt', *Political Science Quarterly*, 70, 1955.

S. L. Endicott, 'British Financial Diplomacy in China: The Leith-Ross Missions, 1935–1937', *Pacific Affairs*, 46, 1973–4.

John McVickar Haight Jr, 'Franklin D. Roosevelt and a Naval Quarantine of Japan', *Pacific Historical Review*, 40, 1971.

'Roosevelt and the Aftermath of the Quarantine Speech', *Review of Politics*, 24, 1962.

Edward L. Henson, 'Britain, America and the Month of Munich', *International Relations*, 2, 1960–5 (April 1962).

Norman Hillmer, 'Defence and Ideology: The Anglo-American Military Alliance in the 1930s', *International Journal*, 33, 1977–8.

Stanley E. Hilton, 'The Welles Mission to Europe, February–March 1940: Illusion or Realism?', *Journal of American History*, 58, 1971.

Warren F. Kimball, 'Beggar my Neighbour: America and the British Interim Finance Crisis, 1940–1941', *Journal of Economic History*, 29, 1969.

Richard N. Kottman, 'The Canadian–American Trade Agreement of 1935', *Journal of American History*, 52, 1965.

Donald Lammers, 'From Whitehall to Munich: The Foreign Office and the Future Course of British Policy', *Historical Journal*, 16, 1973.

Francis L. Loewenheim, 'An Illusion that Shaped History. New Light on the History and Historiography of American Peace Efforts before Munich', in Daniel R. Beaver (ed.), *Some Pathways in American History*, Detroit, 1969.

Peter Ludlow, 'Papst Pius XII, die britische Regierung und die deutsche Opposition in Winter 1939/40', *Vierteljahresheft für Zeitgeschichte*, 20, 1974.

'The Unwinding of Appeasement', in Lothar Ketternacker (ed.), *The 'Other Germany' in the Second World War: Emigration and Resistance in International Perspective*, London/Stuttgart, 1977.

Callum A. Macdonald, 'Britain, France and the April Crisis of 1939', *European Studies Review*, 2, 1972.

'Economic Appeasement and the German "Moderates" 1937–1939. An Introductory Essay', *Past and Present*, 56, 1972.

Elizabeth Kimball Maclean, 'Joseph E. Davies and Soviet–American Relations, 1941–1943', *Diplomatic History*, 3, 1979.

Arthur Marwick, 'Middle Opinion in the 'Thirties: Planning, Progress and Political Agreement', *English Historical Review*, 79, 1964.

M. Ruth Megaw, 'Australia and the Anglo-American Trade Agreement, 1938', *Journal of Imperial and Commonwealth History*, 3, 1975.

'The Scramble for the Pacific: Anglo-United States Rivalry in the Pacific in the 1930s', *Historical Studies* (Melbourne), 15, 1973.

Gunther Moltmann, 'Franklin D. Roosevelt's Friedensappel von 14 April 1939', *Jahrbuch für Amerikastudien*, 1964.

James R. Moore, 'Sources of New Deal Economic Policy: The International Dimension', *Journal of American History*, 61, 1974.

Arnold Ofner, 'Appeasement Revisited: the United States, Great Britain and Germany, 1933–1940', *Journal of American History*, 64, 1977.

O. S. Ogbi, 'The Foreign Office and Yoshida's Bid for Rapprochement with Britain in 1936–1937', *Historical Journal*, 21, 1978.

R. A. C. Parker, 'Economics, Rearmament and Foreign Policy: The United Kingdom before 1939. A Preliminary Study', *Journal of Contemporary History*, 10, 1975.

R. H. Pear, 'The Impact of the New Deal on British Economic and Political Ideas', *Bulletin of the British Association of American Studies*, New Series, no.4, 1962.

Lawrence W. Pratt, 'The Anglo-American Naval Conversations on the Far East in January 1938', *International Affairs*, 47, 1971.

Benjamin D. Rhodes, 'The British Royal Visit of 1939 and the "Psychological Approach" to the United States', *Diplomatic History*, 2, 1978.

V. H. Rothwell, 'The Mission of Sir Frederick Leith-Ross to the Far East, 1935–1936', *Historical Journal*, 18, 1975.

Arthur W. Schatz, 'The Anglo-American Trade Agreement and Cordell Hull's Search for Peace, 1935–1938', *Journal of American History*, 57, 1970.

Hans Jurgen Schroeder, 'Die Vereinigte Staaten von Amerika und die britische Appeasementpolitik'. Paper presented to German Historical Institute, London, Conference on 'Appeasement', June 1980.

Ann Trotter, 'Tentative Steps for an Anglo-Japanese Rapprochement in 1934', *Modern Asian Studies*, 8, 1974.

Richard H. Ullman, 'The Davies Mission and United States–Soviet Relations, 1937–1941', *World Politics*, 9, 1957.

William V. Wallace, 'Roosevelt and British Appeasement', *Bulletin of the British Association of American Studies*, New Series, no. 5, 1962.

D. C. Watt, 'Appeasement. The Rise of a Revisionist School?', *Political Quarterly*, 1975.

'The Historiography of Appeasement', in Alan Sked and Chris Cook (eds.), *Crisis and Controversy. Essays in Honour of A.J.P. Taylor*, London, 1976.

'Roosevelt and Chamberlain, Two Appeasers', *International Journal*, 28, 1973.

'Les Alliés et la résistance allemande (1939–1944), *Revue d'Histoire de la Deuxième Guerre Mondiale*, 36, 1959.

'*The Week* That was', *Encounter*, 38, May 1972.

Lowell T. Young, 'Franklin D. Roosevelt and America's Islets; Acquisition of Territory in the Caribbean and the Pacific', *The Historian*, 35, 1972–3.

Theses and Dissertations

Charles C. Bright, 'Britain's Search for Security, 1930–1936. The Diplomacy of Naval Disarmament and Imperial Defence', Yale Ph.D., 1970.

Roger W. Buckley, 'The American Press Corps' View of Nazi Germany. Memoirs of Selected Correspondents', London M.A. Dissertation, 1965.

Ernest Gilman, 'Economic Aspects of Anglo-American Relations in the Era of Chamberlain and Roosevelt, 1937–1940', London Ph.D., 1976.

T. McCulloch, 'Anglo-American Economic Diplomacy and the European Crisis, 1933–1939', Oxford D.Phil., 1978.

O. S. Ogbi, 'British Imperial Defence and Foreign Policy in Asia and the Pacific and the Impact of Anglo-Japanese Relations', Birmingham Ph.D., 1975.

R. J. Pritchard, 'Far Eastern Influences upon British Strategy towards the Great Powers, 1937–1939', London Ph.D., 1979.

James W. Weinberger, 'The Attitude of the British Embassy, Washington D.C. and the Foreign Office towards Senator William E. Borah, 1935–1940', London M.A. Dissertation, 1979.

Chapter 5

Books

Paul Addison, *The Road to 1945: British Politics and the Second World War*, London, 1975.

Terry H. Anderson, *The United States, Great Britain and the Cold War, 1944–47*, Columbia, Missouri, 1981.

Philip Bailey, *America Lost and Found*, London, 1981.

Thomas Bailey, *The Marshall Plan Summer: An Eye-Witness Report on Europe and the Russians in 1947*, Stanford, Cal., 1977.

Elizabeth Barker, *Churchill and Eden at War*, London, 1978.

Robert Beitzell, *The Uneasy Alliance: America, Britain and Russia, 1941–1943*, New York, 1972.

John Morton Blum, *V Was for Victory: Politics and American Culture During World War II*, New York, 1976.

Alan Bullock, *The Life and Times of Ernest Bevin* 2 vols., London, 1960, 1967.

Angus Calder, *The People's War. Britain 1939–1945*, London, 1971.

David P. Calleo and Benjamin M. Rowland, *America and the World Political Economy: Atlantic Dreams and National Realities*, Bloomington, Indiana, 1973.

Thomas M. Campbell, *Masquerade Peace: America's U.N. Policy, 1944–45*, Tallahassee, Fla, 1973.

Mark L. Chadwin, *The Warhawks: American Interventionists before Pearl Harbor*, New York, 1970.

Diane Shaver Clemens, *Yalta*, New York, 1970.

Wayne S. Cole, *America First: The Battle Against Intervention, 1940–1941*, New York, 1970.

Senator Gerald P. Nye and American Foreign Relations, Minneapolis, 1962.

Charles A. Lindbergh and the Battle against American Intervention in World War II, New York, 1974.

Lynn E. Davis, *The Cold War Begins: Soviet-American Cooperation over Eastern Europe*, Princeton, NJ, 1974.

Hugh de Santis, *The Diplomacy of Silence: The American Foreign Service, the Soviet Union and the Cold War, 1933–1947*, Chicago, 1981.

Robert A. Divine, *The Reluctant Belligerent: American Entry into World War II*, New York, 1965.

Roosevelt and World War II, Baltimore, 1970.

Armand van Dormael, *Bretton Woods: Birth of a Monetary System*, London, 1978.

Saul Friedlaender, *Prelude to Downfall. Hitler and the United States, 1939–1941*, London, 1967.

John L. Gaddis, *The United States and the Origins of the Cold War, 1941–1947*, New York, 1972.

Richard N. Gardner, *Sterling–Dollar Diplomacy: The Origins and Prospects of our International Economic Order*, New York, revised edition, 1969.

John Gimbel, *The Origins of the Marshall Plan*, Stanford, Cal., 1976.

Philip Goodhart, *Fifty Ships that Saved the World: The Foundation of the Anglo-American Alliance*, London, 1965.

Margaret Gowing, *Britain and Atomic Energy, 1939–1945*, London, 1964.

Independence and Deterrence; Britain and Atomic Energy, 1945–1952, 2 vols. London, 1974.

H. Duncan Hall, *North American Supply*, London, 1958.

Robert M. Hathaway, *Ambiguous Partnership: Britain and America, 1944–1947*, Columbia, Missouri, 1981.

H. Montgomery Hyde, *The Quiet Canadian: the Secret Service Story of Sir William Stephenson*, London, 1962.

Frank L. Israel, *Nevada's Key Pittman*, Lincoln, Nebr., 1963.

Manfred Jonas, *Isolationism in America, 1935–1941*, Ithaca, New York, 1966.

Warren F. Kimball, *The Most Unsordid Act: Lend-Lease, 1939–1941*, Baltimore, 1969.

William L. Langer, *Our Victory Gamble*, New York, 1947.

William L. Langer and S. Everett Gleason, *The Challenge to Isolation 1937–1940*, New York, 1952.

The Undeclared War, 1940–1941, New York, 1952.

Joseph P. Lash, *Roosevelt and Churchill, 1939–1941: The Partnership that Saved the West*, New York, 1976.

Norman Longmate, *The GIs: The Americans in Britain, 1942–1945*, London, 1975.

W. Roger Louis, *Imperialism at Bay: The United States and the Decolonisation of the British Empire 1941–1945*, Oxford, 1977.

Peter Lowe, *Great Britain and the Origins of the Pacific War: A Study of British Policy in East Asia, 1937–1941*, Oxford, 1977.

John Lukacs, *The Last European War: September 1939/December 1941*, London, 1977.

Robert J. Maddox, *William E. Borah and American Foreign Policy*, Baton Rouge, La., 1969.

René Massigli, *Une Comédie des Erreurs, 1943–1966*, Paris, 1978.

Maurice Matloff and Edwin M. Snell, *Strategic Planning for Coalition Warfare 1941–1942*, Washington, 1953.

W. N. Medlicott, *The Economic Blockade*, 2 vols., London, 1952–9.

Aaron David Miller, *Search for Security: Saudi Arabian Oil and American Foreign Policy: 1939–1949*, Chapel Hill, NC, 1980.

Harley A. Notter, *Post-War Foreign Policy Preparation, 1939–1945*, Washington, 1949.

Henry Pelling, *Britain and the Second World War*, London, 1970.

E. F. Penrose, *Economic Planning for the Peace*, Princeton, NJ, 1953.

Forrest C. Pogue, *George C. Marshall*, 2 vols., New York, 1966.

Willard Range, *Franklin D. Roosevelt's World Order*, Athens, Ga., 1959.

David Rees, *Harry Dexter White: A Study in Paradox*, London and New York, 1973.

Victor Rothwell, *Britain and the Cold War, 1941–1947*, London, 1982.

Bruce M. Russell, *No Clear and Present Danger: A Sceptical view of the U.S. Entry into World War II*, New York, 1972.

Tony Sharp, *The Wartime Alliance and the Zonal Division of Germany*, Oxford, 1975.

Michael S. Sherry, *Preparing for the Next War: American Plans for Post-War Defence, 1941–1945*, New Haven, Conn., 1977.

Martin J. Sherwin, *A World Destroyed: The Atomic Bomb and the Grand Alliance*, New York, 1975.

Michael B. Stoff, *Oil, War and American Security. The Search for a National Policy on Foreign Oil, 1941–1949*, New Haven, Conn., 1980.

Mark A. Stoler, *The Politics of the Second Front: American Military Planning and Diplomacy in Coalition Warfare, 1941–1943*, Westport, Conn., 1977.

Christopher Thorne, *Allies of a Kind: The United States, Great Britain and the War against Japan, 1941–1945*, London, 1978.

Patricia Dawson Ward, *The Threat of Peace. James F. Byrnes and the Council of Foreign Ministers, 1945–1946*, Kent, Ohio, 1979.

Mark S. Watson, *Chief of Staff: Pre-war Plans and Preparations*, Washington, 1980.

Sir John Wheeler-Bennett (ed.), *Action This Day: Working with Churchill*, London, 1968.
Special Relationships: America in War and Peace, London, 1975.
Sir John Wheeler-Bennett and A. J. Nichols, *The Semblance of Peace: The Political Settlement after the Second World War*, London, 1972.
Theodore A. Wilson, *The First Summit: Roosevelt and Churchill at Placentia Bay, 1941*, London, 1970.
John E. Wiltz, *From Isolation to War, 1931–1941*, London, 1969.
Randall Bennett Woods, *The Roosevelt Foreign Policy Establishment and the 'Good Neighbors'. The United States and Argentina, 1941–1945*, Lawrence, Kansas, 1979.
Sir Llewellyn Woodward, *British Foreign Policy in the Second World War*, 5 vols., London, 1970–6.
Daniel Yergin, *Shattered Peace: the Origins of the Cold War and the National Security State*, London, 1978.

Articles

Barton J. Berstein, 'The Quest for Security: American Foreign Policy and the International Control of Atomic Energy, 1942–1946', *Journal of American History*, 60, 1973–4.
Robert Bothwell and J. L. Granatstein, 'Canada and the War-time Negotiations over Civil Aviation', *International History Review*, 2, 1980.
Peter Boyle, 'The British Foreign Office View of Soviet–American Relations, 1945–46', *Diplomatic History*, 3, 1979.
John L. Chase, 'The Development of the Morgenthau Plan', *Journal of Politics*, 1954.
Alfred E. Eckes, 'Open Door Expansionism Reconsidered: the World War II Experience', *Journal of American History*, 59, 1972–3.
Raymond A. Esthus, 'President Roosevelt's Commitments to Britain to Intervene in a Pacific War', *Mississipi Valley Historical Review*, 50, 1963.
William Franklin, 'Zonal Boundaries and Access to Berlin', *World Politics*, 16, 1963–4.
Martin Gilbert, 'Churchill and Roosevelt, the Background of the Relationship and its Testing Times'. Paper presented to the British and United States National Committee for the History of the Second World War, London, July 1980.
Margaret Gowing, 'Anglo-American Scientific Cooperation in the Second World War'. Paper presented to the British and United States National Committee for the History of the Second World War, London, July 1980.
Richard J. Grace, 'Whitehall and the Ghost of Appeasement, November 1941', *Diplomatic History*, 3, 1979.
Fred Greene, 'The Military View of American National Policy, 1904–1940', *American Historical Review*, 66, 1960–1
David C. Haglund, 'George C. Marshall and the Question of Military Aid to

England, May–June 1940', *Journal of Contemporary History*, 15, 1980.

George C. Herring Jr, 'Lend-Lease to Russia and the Origins of the Cold War, 1944–45', *Journal of American History*, 56, 1969–70.

'The United States and British Bankruptcy, 1944–45: Responsibilities Deferred', *Political Science Quarterly*, 81, 1971.

Douglas J. Hudson, 'Vandenberg Reconsidered; Senate Resolution 239 and American Foreign Policy,' *Diplomatic History*, 1, 1977.

E. J. Hughes, 'Winston Churchill and the Formation of the United Nations Organization', *Journal of Contemporary History*, 9, 1974.

Scott Jackson, 'Prologue to the Marshall Plan: the Origins of the American Commitment to a European Recovery Program', *Journal of American History*, 65, 1978–9.

Warren F. Kimball, 'Beggar My Neighbour: America and the British Interim Financial Crisis, 1940–1941', *Journal of Economic History*, 29, 1969.

'Churchill and Roosevelt: The Personal Equation', *Prologue*, 6, 1974.

' "Gabble": Churchill and Roosevelt Talk'. Paper presented to the British and United States National Committee for the History of the Second World War, London, July 1980.

'Lend-Lease and the Open Door: The Temptation of British Opulence, 1937–1942', *Political Science Quarterly*, 86, 1971.

Jonathan Knight, 'American Statecraft and the 1946 Black Sea Straits Controversy', *Political Science Quarterly* 90, 1975.

James R. Leutze, 'The Secret of the Churchill–Roosevelt Correspondence, 1939–1940', *Journal of Contemporary History*, 10, 1975.

Callum A. Macdonald, 'The Politics of Intervention: The United States and the Argentine, 1941–1946', *Journal of Latin American Studies*, 12, 1980.

Elizabeth Kimball Maclean, 'Joseph E. Davies and Soviet–American Relations, 1941–1943', *Diplomatic History*, 3, 1979.

Robert G. MacMahon, 'Anglo-American Diplomacy and the Reoccupation of the Netherlands East Indies', *Diplomatic History*, 2, 1978.

Barbara C. Malament, 'British Labour and Roosevelt's New Deal: The Response of the Left and the Unions', *Journal of British Studies*, 17, 1978.

Eduard Mark, 'American Policy towards Eastern Europe and the Origins of the Cold War, 1941–1946: An Alternative Explanation', *Journal of American History*, 68, 1981.

Robert L. Messer, 'Paths not Taken: The US Department of State and Alternatives to Containment', *Diplomatic History*, 1, 1977.

Wilson D. Miscamble, 'Anthony Eden and the Truman–Molotov Conversations, April 1945', *Diplomatic History*, 2, 1978.

Louis Morton, 'Germany First: The Basic Concept of Allied Strategy in World War II', in Kent Greenfield (ed.), *Command Decisions*, Washington, DC, 1960.

Thomas G. Paterson, 'The Abortive American Loan to Russia and the

Origins of the Cold War, 1943–46', *Journal of American History*, 56, 1969–70.

Richard Pfau, 'Containment in Iran, 1946: The Shift to an Active Policy', *Diplomatic History*, 1, 1977.

Martin J. Sherwin, 'The Atomic Bomb and the Origins of the Cold War', *American Historical Review*, 78, 1973.

Mark A. Stoler, 'The "Pacific First" Alternative in American World War II Strategy', *International History Review*, 2, 1980.

Frank Straker, 'The Multinational Corporation. The New Imperialism?', *Columbia Journal of World Business*, 5, 1980.

Christopher Thorne, 'Britain and the Black GIs', *New Community*, 3, 1974.

William M. Tuttle Jr, 'Aid to the Allies Short of War Versus American Intervention, 1940', *Journal of American History*, 56, 1969–70.

D. C. Watt, 'Every War Must End: War-Time Planning for Post-War Security in Britain and America in the Wars of 1914–1918 and 1939–1945. The Roles of Professional Historians', *Transactions of the Royal Historical Society*, Fifth Series, 28, 1978.

'Hauptprobleme der britischen Deutschlandpolitik, 1945–1949', in Claus Scharf and Hans-Jurgen Schroeder (eds.), *Die Deutschlandpolitik Grossbritanniens und die britische Zone, 1945–1949*, Wiesbaden, 1979.

Theses

Sean Greenwood, 'Anglo-French Relations and the Origins of the Treaty of Dunkirk', London Ph.D., 1982.

Julian Lewis, 'British Military Planning for Post-War Strategic Defence, 1942–1947', Oxford D.Phil., 1981.

Chapter 6

Books

Hervé Alphand, *L'Etonnement d'être*, Paris, 1978.

George Ball, *The Discipline of Power. Essentials of a Modern World Structure*, London, 1968.

G. Barraclough (ed.), *Survey of International Affairs, 1958–1960*, Oxford, 1962.

John Biggs-Davidson, *The Uncertain Ally*, London, 1957.

David Carlton, *Anthony Eden, A Biography*, London, 1981.

Honoré M. Catudal, *Kennedy and the Berlin Wall Crisis. A Case Study in US Decision-Making*, Berlin, 1981.

Sir John Colville, *The Churchillians*, London, 1981.

Footprints in Time, London, 1976.

François Crozier, *Le Conflit de Chypre, 1946–1959*, Brussels, 1973.

Robert Divine, *Eisenhower and the Cold War*, Oxford, 1981.

Christopher P. Driver, *The Disarmers: A Study in Protest*, London, 1964.

bibliography

Leon D. Epstein, *Britain. Uneasy Ally*, London, 1954.

M. A. Fitzsimons, *The Foreign Policy of the British Labour Government, 1945–1951*, Notre Dame, 1953.

Edward Fursdon, *The European Defence Community. A History*, London, 1980.

Waldemar J. Gallman, *Iraq Under General Nuri. My Recollections of Nuri es-Said*, Baltimore, 1964.

Wilhelm G. Grewe, *Rückblenden, 1976–1951; Auszeichnungen eines Augenzeuges deutscher Aussenpolitik von Adenauer bis Schmidt*, Frankfurt, 1979.

A. J. R. Groom, *British Thinking about Nuclear Weapons*, London, 1974.

Donald Hawley, *The Trucial States*, London, 1970.

Louis Heren, *Growing up on 'The Times'*, London, 1978.

George C. Herring Jr, *America's Longest War*, New York, 1979.

Timothy Ireland, *Creating the Entangling Alliance: The Origins of the North Atlantic Treaty Organization*, Westport, Conn. and London, 1981.

Baron Ismay, *NATO: The First Five Years, 1949–1954*, London, 1955.

H. K. Jacobson and Eric Stein, *Diplomats, Scientists and Politicians*, Ann Arbor, 1966.

Herman Kahn, *On Escalation. Metaphors and Scenarios*, London, 1965.

Lawrence W. Kaplan, *A Community of Interests: NATO and the Military Assistance Programme, 1948–1951*, Washington, DC, 1980.

J. B. Kelly, *East Arabian Frontiers*, London, 1964.
Arabia, the Gulf and the West, London, 1980.

John F. Kennedy, *Why Britain Slept*, London, 1940.

Walter Lipgens, *Die Anfänge der europäischen Einigungspolitik, 1945–1950: Erster Teil: 1945–1947*, Stuttgart, 1977: for an enlarged English translation by P. S. Falla and A. J. Ryder, see Walter Lipgens, *A History of European Integration, 1945–1947: The Formation of the European Unity Movement*, Oxford, 1982.

Iverach Macdonald, *Man of the Times*, London, 1976.

David S. McLellan, *Dean Acheson: The State Department Years*, New York, 1976.

Eugene J. Meehan, *The British Left Wing and Foreign Policy*, New Brunswick, NJ, 1960.

D. J. Morgan, *The Official History of Colonial Development*, 5 vols., London, 1980.

Yonosuke Nagai and Akira Iriye (eds.), *The Origins of the Cold War in the Far East*, Tokyo and Chicago, 1977.

Richard Neustadt, *Alliance Politics*, New York, 1970.

David Nunnerley, *President Kennedy and Britain*, London, 1972.

Richard Pearce, *Three Years in the Levant*, London, 1949.

Henry Pelling, *America and the British Left, from Bright to Bevan*, London, 1956.

Robert J. Randle, *Geneva 1954. The Settlement of the Indo-China War*, Princeton, NJ, 1972.

Escott Reid, *Time of Fear and Hope: The Making of the North Atlantic Treaty, 1947–1949*, Toronto, 1977.

Arthur Schlesinger Jr, *A Thousand Days. John F. Kennedy in the White House*, Boston, 1965.

Anthony Short, *The Communist Insurrection in Malaya, 1948–1960*, London, 1975.

Jean Edward Smith (ed.), *The Papers of General Lucius D. Clay*, 2 vols., Bloomington, Indiana, 1974.

Robert W. Stookey, *America and the Arab States: An Uneasy Encounter*, New York, 1975.

Charles Thayer, *Diplomat*, London, 1960.

Hugh Thomas, *The Suez Affair*, London, 1967.

D. C. Watt, *Britain Looks to Germany. British Opinion and Policy Towards Germany Since 1945*, London, 1965.

D. C. Watt (ed.), *Survey of International Affairs, 1961*, Oxford, 1965.
Survey of International Affairs, 1962, Oxford, 1970.
Survey of International Affairs, 1963, Oxford, 1972.

Gerhard Wettig, *Entmilitarisierung und Wiederbewaffnung in Deutschland 1943–1955*, Munich, 1957.

John Wheeler-Bennett (ed.), *Action This Day. Working with Churchill*, London, 1968.

Mira Wilkins, *The Maturing of Multinational Enterprise: American Business Abroad from 1914 to 1970*, Cambridge, Mass., 1974.

Michael R. Wright, *Disarm and Verify*, London, 1964.

Articles

Roy Alan, 'Arab Voices, British Accents and the Pitfalls of Propaganda', *The Reporter*, 19 September 1957.

Winthrop Aldrich, 'The Suez Crisis: A Footnote to History', *Foreign Affairs*, 45, 1967.

Clement Attlee, 'Britain and America. Common Sense, Different Opinions', *Foreign Affairs*, 32, 1954.

Aneurin Bevan, 'Britain and America at Loggerheads', *Foreign Affairs*, 35, 1957.

Denis W. Brogan, 'Politics and US Foreign Policy', *International Affairs*, 33, 1957.

Alastair Buchan, 'The Campaign Seen from Europe', *The Reporter*, 23, no. 7, 27 October 1961.

Russell D. Buhite, '"Major Intent". American Policy Towards China, Taiwan and Korea, 1945–1950', *Pacific Historical Review*, 47, 1978.

Lord Coleraine, 'Britain and America. The Need for Compromise', *Foreign Affairs*, 32, 1954.

Richard Crossman, 'The Rift in Anglo-American Relations', *Foreign Affairs*, 35, 1957.

Geoffrey Crowther, 'Reconstruction of an Alliance', *Foreign Affairs*, 35, 1957.

Francis Dawson, 'Atomic Energy and Anglo-American Relations, 1964–1954', *Orbis*, 9, 1969.

Raymond Dawson and Richard Rosecrance, 'Theory and Reality in the Anglo-American Alliance', *World Politics*, 19, 1966–7.

Vincent P. De Santis, 'Eisenhower Revisionism', *Review of Politics*, 38, 1976.

Leon D. Epstein, 'The British Labour Left and US Foreign Policy', *American Political Science Review*, 14, 1957.

James Fetzer, 'Senator Vandenberg and the American Commitment to China, 1945–1950', *Historian*, 36, 1974.

M. A. Fitzsimons, 'British Labour in Search of a Socialist Foreign Policy', *Review of Politics*, 12, 1950.

John Gaddis, 'Containment. A Reassessment', *Foreign Affairs*, 55, 1977.

Margaret Gowing, 'Britain, America and the Bomb', in David Dilks (ed.), *Retreat from Power: Studies in British Foreign Policy of the Twentieth Century*, vol. II, London, 1981.

Fred I. Greenstern, 'Eisenhower as an Activist President: A New Look at the Evidence', *Political Science Quarterly*, 94, 1979–80.

Lord Harlech, 'Suez SNAFU, Skybolt SABU', *Foreign Policy*, 2, 1971.

Daniel Harrington, 'Kennan, Bohlen and the Riga Axioms', *Diplomatic History*, 1, 1977.

Roy Harrod, 'Hands and Fists Across the Ocean', *Foreign Affairs*, 29, 1951.

Alan K. Henrikson, 'The Creation of the North Atlantic Alliance, 1948–1952', *Naval War College Review*, 32, 1980.

Baron Ismay, 'Report to the Ministerial Meeting of the North Atlantic Council at Bonn, May 1957', *NATO Letter*, 5, 1957.

Scott Jackson, 'Prologue to the Marshall Plan', *Journal of American History*, 65, 1978–9.

Lawrence Kaplan, 'Towards the Brussels Pact', *Prologue*, 12, 1980.
  'The United States and the Origins of NATO, 1946–1949', *Review of Politics*, 31, 1969.

David McLellan, 'Who Fathered Containment?', *International Studies Quarterly*, 17, 1973.

K. van Meurt, 'Les Etats-Unis et les Communautés Européennes (1955–1963)', *Chronique de Politique Etrangère*, 1973.

William D. Miscamble, 'The Origins of the North Atlantic Treaty: Policy Formulation in the Department of State'. Paper delivered to the Australian and New Zealand American Studies Associations, Sydney, Australia, August 1980.

Scott Newton, 'The Schuman Plan in Post-War British–American Relations'. Paper delivered to the Association of Contemporary Historians, London, July 1981.

Thomas G. Paterson, 'If Europe, Why Not China? The Containment Doctrine, 1947–1949', *Prologue*, 13, 1981.

Alexander Rendel, 'On the Eve of the Truman Doctrine', *NATO Review*, no. 5, October 1978.

Arthur J. Schlesinger Jr, 'Origins of the Cold War', *Foreign Affairs*, 65, 1977.

Clifton Uttley, 'The Rift in Anglo-American Relations', *The Listener*, 21 May 1953.

Geoffrey Warner, ' "Collusion" and the Suez Crisis of 1956', *International Affairs*, 55, 1979.

D. C. Watt, 'Britain and the Cold War in the Far East, 1945–1951', in Yonosuke Nagai and Akira Iriye (eds.), *The Origins of the Cold War in the Far East*, Tokyo and Chicago, 1977.

'British Intervention in East Africa: An Essay in Strategic Mobility', *Revue Militaire Générale*, 5 May 1966.

'Churchill und die kalte Krieg. Löste er ihn aus? Was unternehm er ihn zu be-enden?', *Schweizer Monatsheft, Sonderbeilage*, November 1981.

'Grossbritannien und Europa, 1951–1959; die Jahre Konservative Regierung', *Vierteljahresheft für Zeitgeschichte*, 26, 1980.

'The High Dam at Aswan and the Politics of Control', in W. N. Warren and N. Rubin (eds.), *Dams in Africa: An Inter-disciplinary Study of Man-made Lakes in Africa*, London, 1968.

'The Possibility of a Multilateral Arms Race: A Note', *International Relations*, II, no. 6, 1962.

Samuel F. Wells Jr, 'Sounding the Tocsin: NSC 68 and the Soviet Threat', *International Security*, 4, 1979.

C. Ben Wright, 'Mr "X" and Containment', *Slavic Review*, 35, 1976.

X, 'The Sources of Soviet Conduct', *Foreign Affairs*, 25, 1947.

Gretha Yarnd, 'The Atlantic Alliance and European Integration, 1948–1949', *NATO Review*, no. 2, April 1978.

Theses

Manfred Michel, 'German Rearmament as a Factor in Anglo-German Relations, 1949–55', London Ph.D., 1963.

Chapter 7

Books

Coral Bell, *The Diplomacy of Detente*, London, 1977.

Henry Brandon, *In the Red: The Struggle for Sterling, 1964–1966*, London, 1966.

Honoré M. Catudal, *The Diplomacy of the Quadripartite Agreement on Berlin. A New Era in East–West Politics*, Berlin, 1978.

Chester L. Cooper, *The Last Crusade*, London, 1970.

John Lewis Gaddis, *Strategies of Containment. A Critical Appraisal of Post-War American National Security Policy*, Oxford, 1982.

Doris Kearns, *Lyndon Johnson and the American Dream*, London, 1976.

J. B. Kelly, *Arabia, the Gulf and the West*, London, 1980.

James Mayall and Cornelia Navari, *The End of the Post-War Era: Documents on Great Power Relations 1968–1975*, Cambridge, 1980.

Christopher Mayhew, *Britain's Role Tomorrow*, London, 1967.

Bruce Mazlish, *Kissinger: The European Mind in American Policy*, New York, 1976.

R. Morris, *Uncertain Greatness: Henry Kissinger and American Foreign Policy*, New York, 1977.

David Owen, *The Politics of Defence*, London, 1972.

Michael Palmer, *The Prospects for a European Security Conference*, London, 1971.

J. G. Stoessinger, *Henry Kissinger: The Anguish of Power*, New York, 1976.

Elaine Windrich, *Britain and the Politics of Rhodesian Independence*, London, 1978.

Articles

H. C. Allen, 'The Anglo-American Relationship in the Sixties', *International Affairs*, 39, 1963.

Alastair Buchan, 'Anglo-American Discords', *Ditchley Journal*, 1975.
'Mothers and Daughters (or Greeks and Romans)', *Foreign Affairs*, 54, 1976.

Leslie H. Gelb, 'New US Establishment is called the Community', *Herald Tribune*, 22 December 1976.

Norman Gelb, 'Anglo-US Relations: A Conundrum Neither Side is in a Hurry to Solve', *Round Table*, April 1980.

Carl Gershmann, 'The Rise and Fall of the New Foreign Policy Establishment', *Commentary*, 70, 1980.

D. C. Watt, 'The Decision to Withdraw from the Gulf: A Study in Political Irrelevance', *Political Quarterly*, 39, 1969.
'Henry Kissinger: 'An Interim Judgment', *Political Quarterly*, 48, 1977.

Chapter 9

Books

David M. Baldwin, *Economic Development and American Foreign Policy 1945–1962*, Chicago, 1966.

George Ball, *The Discipline of Power*, London, 1968.

Arnulf Baring, *Aussenpolitik in Adenauer's Kanzlerdemokratie*, Munich, 1969.

Arnold Beichman, *The 'Other' State Department. The United States Mission to the United Nations – Its Roles in the Making of Foreign Policy*, New York, 1968.

Max Beloff, *The Soviet Union and the Far Eastern Crisis*, Cambridge, Mass., 1964.
The Intellectual in Politics, London, 1970.

Michael Beschloss, *Kennedy and Roosevelt: The Uneasy Alliance*, New York, 1981.

Dorothy Borg, *The United States and the Far Eastern Crisis*, Cambridge, Mass., 1964.

Raymond Carr, *Spain, 1808–1939*, Oxford, 1966.

Robert A. Divine, *The Illusion of Neutrality*, Chicago, 1962.

Dennis Duncanson, *Government and Revolution in Vietnam*, Oxford, 1968.

Robert Ellsworth Elder, *The Foreign Leader Program Operations in United States*, Washington DC, 1961.

Robert H. Ferrell and Jerry N. Hess (eds.), *Conference of Scholars on the Marshall Plan, 1964*, Independence, Missouri, 1964.

W. B. Fowler, *British–American Relations, 1917–1918. The Role of Sir William Wiseman*, Princeton, NJ, 1969.

David Hopgood and Meridian Bennett, *Agents of Change. A New Look at the Peace Corps*, Boston, Mass., 1964.

Irving Louis Horowitz, *The Rise and Fall of Project Camelot: Studies in the Relationship between Social Science and Practical Politics*, Cambridge, Mass., 1967.

J. E. Howard, *Parliament and Foreign Policy in France*, London, 1948.

Michael Howard, *Studies in War and Peace*, London, 1970.

H. Montgomery Hyde, *The Quiet Canadian*, London, 1962.

Joseph Jones, *The Fifteen Weeks*, New York, 1955.

William W. Kaufmann, *The McNamara Strategy*, New York, 1964.

Jere Clemens King, *Foch versus Clemenceau: France and German Dismemberment, 1918–1919*, Cambridge, Mass., 1960.

Hubert Lagardelle, *Ma Mission à Rome*, Paris, 1955.

Folke Lindberg, *Scandinavia in Great Power Politics, 1905–1908*, Stockholm, 1958.

Arthur Marder, *Fear God and Dreadnought*, 5 vols., London, 1916.

Lawrence W. Martin, *Peace Without Victory. Woodrow Wilson and the British Radicals*, New Haven, Conn., 1958.

Arno J. Mayer, *The Political Origins of the New Diplomacy, 1917–1918*, New Haven, Conn., 1959.

Conor Cruise O'Brien, *To Katanga and Back*, London, 1962.

Raymond Gish O'Connor, *Perilous Equilibrium. The United States and the London Naval Conference of 1930*, Lawrence, Kansas, 1962.

Nils Ørvik, *Sikkerheitspolitikken, 1920–1939*, 2 vols., Oslo, 1961.

Julius Pratt, *Cordell Hull*, 2 vols., New York, 1964.

Walt W. Rostow, *The Stages of Economic Growth: A Non-Communist Manifesto*, Cambridge, Mass., 1960.

James T. Shotwell, *At the Paris Peace Conference*, London, 1957.

Maurice Waters, *The Ad Hoc Diplomat*, The Hague, 1963.

D. C. Watt, *Personalities and Policies. Studies in the Formulation of British Foreign Policy in the Twentieth Century*, London and South Bend, Indiana, 1965.

D. C. Watt (ed.), *Survey of International Affairs, 1961*, Oxford, 1966.

Survey of International Affairs, 1962, Oxford, 1970.
Richard Whalen, *The Founding Father*, New York, 1965.
Sir Arthur Willert, *The Road to Safety*, London, 1952.
Group Captain F. W. Winterbotham, *Secret and Personal*, London, 1970.

Articles

Paul Baudouin, 'Un voyage à Rome', *La Revue des Deux Mondes*, 1 May 1962.
Walter C. Clemens Jr, 'The Soviet World Faces West', *International Affairs*, 46, no. 3, 1970.
John McVickar Haight Jr, 'Roosevelt as Friend of France', *Foreign Affairs*, 44, 1966.
William W. Kaufmann, 'Two American Ambassadors: Bullitt and Kennedy', in Felix Gilbert and Gordon Craig (eds.), *The Diplomats, 1919–1939*, Princeton, NJ, 1953.
Francis L. Loewenheim, 'An Illusion that Shaped History', in Daniel R. Beaver (ed.), *Some Pathways in the Twentieth Century*, Detroit, 1969.
Lord Murray of Elibank, 'Franklin Roosevelt, the Friend of Britain', *Contemporary Review*, 138, 1955.
Nils Ørvik, 'From Collective Security to Neutrality: The Nordic Powers, the League of Nations, Britain and the Approach of War, 1935–1939', in K. Bourne and D. C. Watt (eds.), *Studies in International History*, London, 1967.
Lawrence W. Pratt, 'The Anglo-American Naval Conversations on the Far East in January 1938', *International Affairs*, 47, 1971.

Theses

Adelphia Jan Bowen Jr, 'The Disarmament Movement, 1918–1935', Columbia University Ph.D., 1956.

Chapter 10

Books

Allan W. Cameron, *The Vietnam Crisis: A Documentary History*, 2 vols., Ithaca, New York, 1971.
Claire L. Chennault, *The Way of a Fighter*, New York, 1949.
Pierre Courou, *L'Utilisation du sol en Indo-Chine française*, Bordeaux, 1936.
Edward R. Drachman, *United States Policy Towards Vietnam, 1940–1945*, Rutherford, NJ, 1970.
Dennis J. Duncanson, *Government and Revolution in Vietnam*, Oxford, 1968.
Henry Field, *M Project for FDR. Studies on Migration and Settlement*, Ann Arbor, 1962.

Lloyd C. Gardner, *Economic Aspects of New Deal Diplomacy*, Madison, Wis., 1964.

Charles de Gaulle, *War Memoirs*, vol. III, London, 1960.

Charles Robequin, *L'Evolution économique de l'Indo-Chine française*, Paris, 1939.

Charles F. Romanus and Riley Sutherland, *Time Runs Out in CBI*, Washington, DC, 1959.

Elliott Roosevelt, *As He Saw It*, New York, 1946.

Articles

George Herring, 'The Truman Administration and the Restoration of French Sovereignty in Indo-China', *Diplomatic History*, 1, 1977.

Gary Hess, 'The First American Commitment in Indo-China: The Acceptance of the "Bao Dai" Solution', *Diplomatic History*, 2, 1978.

Walter LaFeber, 'Roosevelt, Churchill and Indo-China, 1942–1945', *American Historical Review*, 80, 1975.

Christopher Thorne, 'Indo-China and Anglo-American Relations, 1941–1945', *Pacific Historical Review*, 45, 1976.

Chapter 11

Books

Clair L. Chennault, *The Way of a Fighter*, New York, 1949.

Edward R. Drachman, *United States Policy Towards Vietnam, 1940–1945*, Rutherford, NJ, 1970.

Dennis J. Duncanson, *Government and Revolution in Vietnam*, Oxford, 1968.

W. H. Elsbree, *Japan's Role in South-East Asian Nationalist Movements, 1940–1945*, Cambridge, Mass., 1953.

Bernard Fall, *The Two Vietnams, a Political and Military Analysis*, London, 1963.

Lloyd C. Gardner, *Economic Aspects of New Deal Diplomacy*, Madison, Wis., 1964.

Gerald N. Grob (ed.), *Statesmen and Statecraft of the Modern West*, Barre, Mass., 1967.

Roger Hilsman, *To Move a Nation*, New York, 1967.

A. N. J. den Hollaender (ed.), *Contagious Conflict. The Impact of American Dissent on European Life*, Leiden, 1973.

J. Laniel, *Le Drame indochinois*, Paris, 1957.

Samuel Eliot Morison, *History of US Naval Operations in World War II*, vol. III, Boston, 1968.

R. J. Randle, *Geneva 1954: The Settlement of the Indo-China War*, Princeton, NJ, 1971

Charles F. Romanus and Riley Sutherland, *Time Runs Out in CBI*, Washington, DC, 1959.

Arthur J. Schlesinger, *A Thousand Days*, Boston, 1965.
Dirk Stikker, *Men of Responsibility*, London, 1966.
Robert Strausz-Hupé and Harry Hazard (eds.), *The Idea of Colonialism*, New York, 1958.

Articles

H. J. Benda, 'The Beginnings of the Japanese Occupation of Java', *Far Eastern Quarterly*, 15, 1956.
Gareth Jones, 'Sukarno's Early Views on the Territorial Boundaries of Indonesia', *Australian Outlook*, 18, 1964.
Carey Joynte, 'John Foster Dulles and the Suez Crisis', in Gerald N. Grob (ed.), *Statesmen and Statecraft of the Modern West*, Barre, Mass., 1967.
Justus M. van der Kroef, 'Nationalism and Politics in New Guinea', *Pacific Affairs*, 34, 1961.
 'Recent Developments in Western New Guinea', *Pacific Affairs*, 34, 1961.
 'The West New Guinea Settlement: Its Origins', *Orbis*, 3, 1963.
Julius W. Pratt, 'Anti-Colonialism in United States Policy', in Robert Strausz-Hupé and Harry Hazard (eds.), *The Idea of Colonialism*, New York, 1958.

Index

Abrahams, Paul P., 44n, 51n
Acheson, Dean, 103, 122, 129, 180, 185
  and Far East, 124
  and Kennedy, 139, 142
  and Marshall Plan, 188
  and Truman, 127, 171
  Present at the Creation, 188n
  resignation, 67
Action Group for Europe, 167
Adenauer, Konrad, 111, 128, 134, 143, 175
Africa, decolonisation of, 135
agriculture, American, 65, 72
AIOC, *see* Anglo-Iranian Oil Company
Alan, Roy, 126n
Albion, R.G., 74n
Aldrich, Winthrop, 133
Algeria, 134
Allen, H.C., 21n
Allen, Howard, 25n
Allen, William R., 75n
Alphand, Hervé, 141n
ambassadors, British, 176
America, *see* United States
Amery, Leo, 46, 48, 49, 234
Anderson, Chandler P., 44n
Anglo-American historians, 20–3
Anglo-Iranian Oil Company (AIOC), 126, 127
Anglo-Japanese alliance, 52, 72
Annapolis, USS, 67
anti-colonialism, American, 108, 126, 141, 220–52
Arab–American Oil Company (ARAMCO), 126, 127

Arab nationalist movement, 107–8
ARAMCO, *see* Arab–American Oil Company
Argentia Conference, 93
Argentina, 80, 101, 115
Army, British, 94–5
Army, US, 91–4
Ataturk, Mustafa Kemal, 169
Atlantic Charter, 222, 234
Atlantic Declaration, 167
atomic power, 97, 130
Attlee, Clement R., 71, 91, 105, 106n, 107, 123
Auden, W.H., 162
Australia, 56

Baghdad Pact, 131
Bailey, Philip, 98n
Baldwin, David M., 189n
Baldwin, Stanley, 46, 53, 68n, 85n
  anti-American views, 60, 63n, 161
  government of, 54–60, 81, 83–4
Balfour, Arthur James, 10, 27n, 33, 36, 48, 49
Ball, George, 140n, 146, 173
Ballantyne, Joseph, 221
Baltzell, E. Digby, 9n
Bandung Conference, 115
Bangladesh, 228
Bank of England, 11, 50, 56
  and Wall Street Crash, 62
Bank of International Settlements, 3
bankers, American, 37–8, 41, 43–4, 51, 53, 56
Baring, Arnulf, 175n

287